THE
GOODYEAR
STORY

THE
GOODYEAR
STORY

AN INVENTOR'S OBSESSION
AND THE STRUGGLE FOR
A RUBBER MONOPOLY

Richard Korman

ENCOUNTER BOOKS
SAN FRANCISCO, CALIFORNIA

First edition published in 2002 by Encounter Books, an activity of Encounter for Culture and Education, Inc., a nonprofit tax exempt corporation.

Encounter Books website address: www.encounterbooks.com

Manufactured in the United States and printed on acid-free paper.

The paper used in this publication meets the minimum requirements of ANSI/NISO Z39.48-1992 (R 1997) *(Permanence of Paper)*.

FIRST EDITION

Library of Congress Cataloging-in-Publication Data

Korman, Richard.
    The Goodyear story : an inventor's obsession and the struggle for a rubber monopoly / Richard Korman.
    p. cm.
    ISBN 1-893554-37-6 (alk. paper)
    1. Goodyear, Charles, 1800-1860.   2. Rubber.   I. Goodyear Tire and Rubber Company.   II. Title.
TS1885.U6K67 2002
678'.2'092
[B]
                                                            2001055635

10   9   8   7   6   5   4   3   2   1

For Elaine

"Yes: does that leave hope for me?"

"Hope of what, sir?"

"Of my final re-transformation from India-rubber back to flesh?"

—Edward Rochester asking a question of Jane Eyre
in Charlotte Brontë's 1847 novel, *Jane Eyre*

CONTENTS

PROLOGUE

Upstart Americans

he Great Exhibition of 1851 triggered a wave of tourism, talk, worry, wonder, jealousy and exultation. Its London opening on May 1 drew twenty-five thousand guests to the great greenhouse-like exhibition hall. Women in bell-shaped dresses of silk and satin, shoulders covered by shawls, lined the edges of the warm orange-red carpet surrounding the small platform prepared for Queen Victoria and Prince Albert. Men in waistcoats stood behind the women. Thousands looked down from galleries hung from the sides of the long hall, and more waited outside in London's Hyde Park, hoping to get in. It was the beginning of the most splendid summer ever known in the world's most powerful nation.

The sun broke through the overcast as a procession of nine carriages from Buckingham Palace pulled up on Rotten Row. The vast, translucent enclosure of the hall—a great old elm and other trees had been left inside—easily swallowed the gathered audience and reduced the statues, potted palms and glass fountain at ground level to props on a spacious stage. Cheers and a flourish of trumpets erupted at the sight of the royal couple entering through the huge bronzed iron gates. A youthful-looking Queen Victoria felt "much-moved" by what she later called "a sensation I shall never forget." The sight was magical—so vast, so glorious, so touching, the Queen said, that she felt "filled with devotion."

"God bless my dearest Albert," the Queen wrote of her husband, who had conceived the event, "and my dear country, which has shown itself so great today."

The unusual building, dubbed the Crystal Palace, and the large number of visitors converging on London produced anxiety as well as wonderment. The King of Prussia had written Prince Albert to find out if it would be safe to visit. Albert conveyed with sarcasm all the doomsday predictions: powerful gusts could conceivably shake the Crystal Palace's galleries from its walls; a scarcity of food might starve the overcrowded city; the various races of people coming into contact with each other could bring back the Black Death.

Royalty might fret, but the public had no qualms. In May, 735,000 people arrived; in June, 1.13 million. The peak came in July, with 1.31 million. The Royal Commission gradually lowered the price of a ticket from a pound to pennies, and in August the gate was 1.02 million; in September, 1.15 million; finally, with the end of the exhibit in sight, 841,000 people jammed into the Crystal Palace during the first eleven days of October. Only a few years earlier such "popular movements" would have "been pronounced on the highest authority most dangerous to the safety of the state," said one writer. But the novelist Charlotte Brontë found the 30,000 people on hand one day so restrained they seemed like a "living tide" that "rolls on quietly, with a deep hum like the sea heard from the distance." During the entire exhibition police charged only twenty-five people with crimes, all for pickpocketing or petty larceny in the exhibit stalls.

Bumpkins from English provinces rode the new steam railroads to London and were amazed by what they saw. "When I entered at the door of the south transept I beheld a sight which absolutely bewildered me," said a man from Nottingham. "I gazed with astonishment. I knew not what direction to take." A more sophisticated writer said the view down the hall's long transept seemed "more like the fabled palace of Vathek than a structure reared in a few months by mortal hands." And an English clergyman echoed the theme of man's mastery of the world around him: "That majestic palace of iron and glass! Awhile ago, its pillars were coarse rude particles, clodded together in some deep recess of the earth, and its transparent plates were sandy masses, without beauty or coherence. How a little fire and a little art have changed them!"

Conceived by Prince Albert in 1849 as an expression of international amity, the Great Exhibition of the Industry of All Nations would in his mind be the "true test of the point of development at which the whole of mankind had arrived." In Albert's view, a turning point in history had been reached in which friendly economic rivalry among nations would replace warfare. But the exhibition was also conceived as a contest in which juries would rate products and award prizes, and the English fully expected to triumph in many categories. England's artwork was cluttered in the style of the time with curlicues, cherubs and historic motifs. Its industrial exhibits thrummed and clattered in their display stalls, powered by a steam generator just outside the hall. England was especially proud of its textile machinery, including a self-acting spinning mule and a huge Jacquard loom.

Decades earlier machines like these would had been concealed almost as closely as state secrets, and with good cause. The breakaway colonies in America had successfully stolen the designs of England's early innovative textile machinery, Treasury Secretary Alexander Hamilton actually having promoted industrial pilfering to build up his country's industry. U.S. manufacturers also copied most of their early machine tools, except for milling machines, from British prototypes. Not content merely to steal English ideas, the United States germinated its own energetic culture of industrial creativity. Spurred by a revised patent law, Americans had filed 2,193 patent applications in 1850, triple the number of a decade earlier. This burst of ingenuity helped propel the backward colonies from a society of farmers into a modern industrial power in fifty short years—an economic transformation unequaled until the advent of post–World War II Japan. In the next fifty years Americans would create the greatest industrial nation the earth had known. Evidence of this future greatness could be seen in the Crystal Palace, and the English took jealous and admiring note of what their cousins from across the ocean had brought to London.

As the five hundred U.S. displays were arriving, the false teeth, ice-making machine, hand-cranked dishwasher, cornhusk mattress, artificial eyes and limbs, printing press and cast-iron stove revealed a pragmatic frame of mind. Some ingenuity was also evident in ideas like the metal coffin equipped with a pump for removing the air inside. A human body, it was said, could be preserved for ages without decay. Other inventions made more lasting impressions. A salesman named Alfred C. Hobbs flabbergasted the makers of locks that had guarded the vaults of the Bank of England by picking them in less than half an hour, which led the bank to order a set of locks from Hobbs' company. A showman named Samuel Colt urged visitors to test-fire his six-shooter and convinced the *London Times* that his "revolvers even threaten to revolutionize military tactics as completely as the original discovery of gunpowder." A Virginia farmboy named Cyrus Hall McCormick displayed a contraption that the English press at first mocked as a cross between a flimsy chariot, a treadmill and something resembling a "flying machine." But when it had been tested in a wet field and the English saw that it could cut and bundle more wheat than any other contrivance in existence, the *Times* reversed itself and declared the reaper worth the cost of the entire exhibition.

One of the most celebrated American exhibitors—notorious was the word his competitors would have used—bent on outdoing the English was a former Philadelphia hardware store owner named Charles Goodyear. He epitomized the spirit of the upstart American technologists, but was also, as some of his American colleagues saw, "a different breed." Little more than five feet tall, he had a complexion the color of buckskin and slightly out-turned ears. Behind his square jaw a thin line of whiskers fringed his neck. That he intended to stand apart from his countrymen could be seen in the fact that he installed his main exhibit of his vulcanized rubber on the second level of the Northeast Gallery, well away from them. It was immediately noticeable as "costly in character, but very pure in taste," said one writer, an elaborate display that would draw interest to that part of the hall. Clearly Charles Goodyear was using his presence at the Great Exhibition to establish himself once and for all as one of the century's leading "men of progress," an identity he had been chasing much of his life.

Many of the other Americans and a few of the English "technologists" displaying their innovations in the Crystal Palace were aware of Goodyear and regarded his story with awe and censure. The precocious first child of a hard-working Connecticut farmer-blacksmith and button maker, Goodyear was groomed for a career in business almost from birth. At seventeen he entered a hardware store apprenticeship and eventually, in partnership with his father and brother, set up a shop in Philadelphia that seemed to flourish. Then suddenly the business plunged into financial ruin and his family returned to the blacksmith's trade, but with Goodyear burdened by a huge debt.

When Charles Goodyear was just a boy, there were few signs in the United States of the manufacturing might that was developing in England. Industry consisted largely of water-powered mills and crafts pursued in barns and sheds. Americans were dependent on Europe for most of their manufactured goods. But some heard distant rumblings as the revolutionary improvements in steam engines and steam-powered boats and trains began to transform the country. American mechanics became obsessed with "ingenuity" as much as the "rugged individualism" that was also part of the emerging national identity. The virtue of industriousness, technology and prosperity became for many Americans almost "providentially linked," in the words of historian Gordon Wood. Goodyear made a conscious decision to become a full-time inventor at a time when the New England tinkerer still had an exalted place in the American imagination.

As he searched for the technological handhold that would give him a place in the world of invention, Goodyear discovered what he quickly convinced himself could be a miracle substance. It was rubber, and he believed that if he could unlock its potential it would change his fortunes and change the world as well. With no background in the developing science of chemistry, he was poorly prepared for the task. Although Goodyear understood that carbon in coal united with iron to become steel, he knew nothing of molecular science. He never fully understood that what he eventually accomplished by adding chemicals and heat to the pasty raw rubber—the creation of a thermoset material through the cross-linking of rubber's long, chain-like molecules—was one of the auspicious early milestones of the new age of synthetics. Over the next century technologists would make the journey from manipulating natural chain molecules called polymers to custom-designing synthetic ones, including some that serve as "scaffolds" inside the human body on which doctors can build artificial tissue. All Charles Goodyear knew was that he had a versatile miracle material that he at first called Heated Metallic Gum Composition and another time lightheartedly described as the Mighty Elastic Substance. Using his process, boot and shoe makers set a new standard for quality that an English paper proclaimed would "do away with the risk of corns and bunions, the cure of which has sprung into an actual profession." Rubber tents and capes kept thousands of Civil War soldiers dry. Still another product line, made quietly but prolifically, consisted of condoms and diaphragms.

In the 1830s and '40s, as he struggled to find the way to change rubber, Goodyear became obsessed with his miracle substance. He dressed in rubber and extolled its virtues to anyone who would listen. He had the mentality of the wildcatters who would soon populate the Pennsylvania oil fields. His spendthrift borrowing and spending and his unwillingness to return to safer means of earning a living exposed his family to terrible hardship and set events in motion that cost some of them their lives. To justify his family's suffering, he rationalized his economic plight—his "embarrassments," as people of the time called such misfortune—as a test of his Christian faith. Yet in his suffering and perseverance, his compulsive pursuit of his dream, he made himself a living embodiment of the age of invention. The Goodyear story, told and retold, held tremendous appeal for Americans who feared his brush with debtors' prison but admired his self-made success. The story inspired inventor Gail Borden, an American who was also at the Great Exhibition displaying his dried meat biscuit. "I should have given up in despair if I had not read a sketch of your father's life," he told one of Goodyear's sons.

Goodyear's obsession seemed justified by the Great Exhibition. In Horace Greeley's words, "India Rubber was everywhere" in the Crystal Palace, with perhaps ten English, French and American companies showing their wares. The Macintosh exhibit held special significance for Goodyear and set up a drama of competition within the show. Well known for its water-repellent coats, or "macks," the company had dominated English rubber making for twenty years thanks to partner Thomas Hancock's secret rubber-grinding machine. When Goodyear was still struggling to feed his family, he sent samples of his heated gum to Macintosh & Company, hoping it would pay to use it. Instead, Hancock made Goodyear the victim of a transatlantic intellectual property theft and claimed credit for the innovation. But if Goodyear looked like a victim in this situation, he looked like the victimizer almost at the same time. Another rival with an exhibit in London, Massachusetts-born Horace Day, sought to discredit the inventor in his own country. Day was challenging the validity of Goodyear's U.S. rubber patent and considered him the original "confidence man."

Goodyear had come to London to show once and for all that whatever his rivals might claim, he was the true inventor of the miracle material. Arriving that spring, he rented a suite of rooms, borrowed or bought a horse and carriage and hired a driver. Sparing no expense, Goodyear hired architect Stannard Warne to design his exhibit.

Sometime after the May 1 opening, Goodyear bought tickets for his wife, Clarissa, and four of their five children, and instructed them to meet him outside. Waiting until the last minute, as was his habit, Goodyear came out to meet them near a large statue of a mounted Richard the Lion-Hearted. Thousands of visitors clustered near the entrance. Clarissa, wearing a yellow silk dress with a blue shawl, reached up to take her husband's arm. The Goodyears fed themselves into the currents of humanity and entered.

Charles Goodyear stepped unevenly—his gout was acting up—and used a walking stick with a sculpted hard rubber handle. He directed the family to look down the long transept. Sculptured figures (his teenage daughter Cynthia squelched a giggle at the naked forms) stood in many places in the hall. Charles turned his head to the right to show Clarissa the east end of the nave and the United States of America department, where mannequins of Native Americans stood in front of a teepee. Looking left, Clarissa saw the display from England and her còlonies. The family proceeded through the exhibition hall, through the Medieval Court, with its imposing neo-Gothic furniture, past the Turkish department, with its kafeyah-capped attendants. Then they stopped awhile at a refreshment stand for iced syrups. Still, they had not set eyes on Charles' exhibit. Finally, Goodyear led his family up a staircase to a gallery on the second floor. There was a canopied suite with the word "Goodyear" above it.

Unlike the Macintosh exhibit, Goodyear didn't just display a handful of rubber objects, but created a vision of a rubber-made world. An entire facade of hard rubber had been constructed across the face of his exhibit. On stepping inside, visitors found they were looking at walls and ceilings covered with rubber veneer and furniture cast in or coated with rubber. Hydrogen-filled rubber balloons of all colors, some as big as six feet in diameter, floated in the air, and portraits painted on rubber sheet hung on the walls. Arrayed in display cases were rubber plates, trays, boxes (some with inlaid pearl), bracelets, brooches, rings, fans, picture frames, eyeglasses, ink stands, paper folders, pencil cases, cups and buttons. In other cases Goodyear placed medical instruments, canes, umbrellas, combs and brushes. Rubber curtains and fabrics hung from the walls. Potted rubber plants sat on pedestals on either side of the entrance.

Goodyear had spent about $30,000 on his creation. It was an astonishing amount, but it paid off. He was one of only three Americans, along with McCormick and Borden, to take home the top award, a Council Medal. The once-desperate man shambling around in the blistered rubber jacket had placed himself among the great inventors of his time. Soon, his licensees would become one of the most powerful monopolies of antebellum America. His legend would outlive the monopoly that bore his name and his own fluctuating personal fortune. In the end his name would become synonymous with the heroic, solitary inventor who risked everything for his ideas. The name became so valuable that a new generation of rubber entrepreneurs would steal it to create an air of legitimacy for their rubber company, just in time for the age of the automobile. But while almost everyone knew his name and miraculous discovery, few knew the rest of the Goodyear story.

CHAPTER ONE

Yankee Notions

*I*n many accounts of post-revolutionary America, New England is pictured as a landscape of frugal farmer-mechanics, barnyard technicians who helped transform the United States from agricultural *naif* to economic juggernaut. What's missing from the conventional "drama of industrialization" is an entire cast of secondary characters who belong more to Dickens than de Tocqueville: farmers who combed rocky soil with ungainly iron plows; tradesmen starved for hard-to-find paper money or minted hard currency; laborers who became sick and fell behind on payments to shop owners and were dragged off to prison. It was a time when hardworking businessmen of humble birth could vault into the class of the newly wealthy, but could also take breathtaking falls.

For most, unending toil won only subsistence, and a good many New Englanders simply left the land. Between 1790 and 1820, about 800,000 people emigrated from Rhode Island, Massachusetts and Connecticut. The population of Boston stagnated as New York, Philadelphia and Baltimore flourished.

One bright spot following the Revolution was the return of ship-carried trade to the New England coast. With protection furnished by the tariff act of 1789, U.S. vessels regained control of the foreign goods entering American ports, especially spices from Asia. In New Haven, shipping entrepreneurs tried to reopen the contentious West Indian trade routes guarded by the French and English. But even here the human dramas often had ambiguous outcomes, as was shown by the locally famous experiences of one Olney Burr. He had saved $800 and in 1801 became the master of a cargo sloop bound for the West Indies. On the voyage down he was captured by the French, who stole the cargo and condemned the ship. Burr lost all but $50. Back in New Haven, he sailed as master of another sloop; it arrived safely and netted him $1,800, which he used to buy the schooner *Venus*. But on the way back from the West Indies the *Venus* was cast away, and when the shipping company involved in the trip also failed, Burr's loss rose to $1,000. After that, Burr says he worked only as a common ship hand and sometimes a tanner and was "barely" able to support his wife and four small children. Creditors were "constantly threatening him with suits" and he was "daily liable to be confined in a prison." He petitioned the Connecticut General Assembly for bankruptcy as an insolvent debtor, saying he had "struggled with adversity" and done all he could to "satisfy his creditors and free himself from embarrassment." He listed debts of $1,284 owed to local merchants and investors. The largest was $500, the smallest $3. One debt of $64 was listed to Amasa Goodyear.

A fifth-generation descendant of Stephen Goodyear, one of the founders of the New Haven colony and for a time its deputy governor, Amasa was a typical combination of farmer-artisan-storeowner, neither rich nor poor, shifting restlessly from venture to venture, seeking any advantage in a fast-changing regional economy. He spent an inordinate amount of time in his workshop, a boxy structure from whose walls hung serrated hay knives, adzes and hammers with black iron heads. Saws, scythes, planes and chisels dangled from the joists like sausages in a butcher shop. In winters Amasa shaped spiky nails over a fire nurtured with an accordion-like bellows. The shop was primitive by today's standards, but it was the place of the most sublime activity in Amasa's life. He honed scythes with graceful handles and hung the balance and weights of a crude twenty-four-hour clock. Making things silenced the murmurings of discontent caused by the exhausting repetitions of farm life. And "making things" was a regional fixation. Not far away, New Haven neighbor Eli Whitney had set up a system for assembling thousands of rifles for the federal government using a system of interchangeable parts. Rebounding from near-ruin from his stolen invention, the cotton gin, Whitney narrowed his focus and ignored his own wasting health to make his operations a success.* As a result of examples like his, entrepreneurs all around New England reinvented the farmer's tool shop as a site for rapid production rather than handcrafted perfection. Fortunes were made and lost. More than most, the Goodyears would repeatedly climb into and fall out of the armchair of success.

---

*Whitney's cotton gin was widely infringed, pushing him near financial ruin.

Amasa's wife, Cynthia, gave birth to a first child, Charles, on December 31, 1800, and two years later she had another boy, Robert. The family's early years revolved around the family farm on Oyster Point, a small peninsula jutting into Long Island Sound just southwest of New Haven. In 1805, Amasa bought an interest in a button-making patent from some brass-manufacturing entrepreneurs, and the Goodyears relocated twenty miles north to Salem, later called Naugatuck (just outside present-day Waterbury) to a farm along a tributary of the Naugatuck River. There Amasa could set up a shop and drive his machinery with water power.

The town of Salem sat in a hill-framed valley cut by a shallow, rock-strewn riverbed. Farms had been cleared on the hillsides. A single dirt toll road running through the valley connected Salem with New Haven to the south; a tollgate and inn overlooked the river. A handful of prim buildings, widely spaced, made up the town center.

In Salem, even more than New Haven, making things was a way of life. By the time the Goodyears had arrived, a fortune had already been secured by a foul-tempered individual by the name of Jared Byington, Salem's first manufacturer and the second Connecticut resident to receive a U.S. patent. Byington hired local boys at low rates to do his farm work, and used his nail-cutting and nail-heading machines and a staff of six, large for the time, to churn out nails by the hundreds. By 1801 he had done well enough to sell his blacksmith shop to new owners who used it for making buttons, the trade Amasa Goodyear took up.

Salem's increasingly freewheeling economic life reflected the resourcefulness of the people. After the Revolution, when the colonies were cut off from English trading privileges and lacked the cash to buy manufactured goods, Salemites would rely on a reservoir of mechanical skill that originated with the town's early blacksmiths and the saw, grist and corn mill operators on the river. And Salem's mechanically minded farmers, often more focused on their shops than their fields, turned out the needles, pins, buckles, combs, eyelets, pen knives, shears, mousetraps, forks, spoons, pans, kettles and clocks—"Yankee notions"—carried by peddlers to faraway consumers in every backwoods settlement.

Versatile Amasa Goodyear made scythes and spoons and hoes and, for a period, clocks. He also understood the potential value of what a later time would call intellectual property, a right embedded in the U.S. Constitution since the 1790s in federal patent and copyright law. The first patent he took out was for his method of tempering round-tined table forks. Later, he patented an enclosed oil-burning lantern and, in 1810, a special spring steel hay fork.

For a time, local farmers stubbornly scorned lightweight steel forks, believing the metal heads fixed to wooden stems would not hold up under heavy duty and sticking with the iron models even though these traditional forks were hefty and the brittle points were easily bent and battered. Eventually they had to admit that the steel fork was not only lighter, but its "spring" effect, the elastic ability of the forged steel prongs to give under the weight of a load of manure and hay without permanently deforming, made it more long-lasting. After initial resistance was overcome, the countryside around Salem seemed filled with Goodyear forks. "So completely has the article formerly used been superseded by this improvement, that the rising generation of farmers do not know what article their fathers were obliged to make use of," Charles Goodyear wrote later of his father's invention. The fork became part of a family foundation myth. In Charles' view, his father had emancipated the farm tool business from the "country blacksmiths" who exemplified the outworn past.

When he became a button maker, Amasa invested in an existing patent filed by Henry Grilley of Waterbury, who in 1790 had coaxed the secret formula for casting and finishing pewter buttons from an English workman. Grilley eventually set up his button works on Fulling Mill Brook's south branch and proceeded to make buttons using the stolen method. Others took notice. In the shop on the Fulling Mill Brook, where his house and farm were located, Amasa made the first pearl buttons, and later, worked with a partner to produce bright metal buttons. These were a mixture of copper, tin and other material poured into molds. A lathe was used to polish the buttons to the bright finish required by tailors for swallowtail coats.

The Goodyear children, now including a daughter, Harriet, born in 1805, and a son, Henry, born in 1807, attended local grade schools, which were in essence parochial schools of the Congregational Church. They learned to read and write, and they learned the basics of geography, math and economics. As part of their arithmetic lessons, they probably calculated payments for socks and horses and wagon wheels. Above all, they studied Scripture and submitted their thoughts on it to the stern interpretation favored by their elders.

The Salem Congregationalists had authority over every aspect of members' lives and to a large extent over the civil affairs of the town. Salem clung to a comparatively strict Calvinism that was already fading in other Congregational churches. Quarrels were meant to be settled by the brethren, not the courts. Marital discord and adulterous fornication also fell within church jurisdiction. The church's moral sanctimony required the brethren to form a committee to combat the "unchristian walk" followed by some women in town. Even contact with members of other churches was limited until the brethren had ascertained their impeccable Christian character. According to the church's 1783 Confessions of Faith, the congregation agreed to prohibit "occasional Communion with Persons recommended from other Churches for a longer Term than twelve Months if they do not within this Term give us satisfaction with regard to their soundness in the faith." Although a faithful member of the congregation, Amasa Goodyear was not as strict as some of his fellow parishioners, causing some comment later on when he showed little sympathy for the violent attacks made on Roman Catholics.

His eldest child, Charles, was like any other boy thirsting for fun and new experiences in the small, well-ordered world of Salem. And like his friends he was intrigued by glimpses of other worlds with which he had no firsthand contact. Strangers came and went from the Collins Tavern and Hotel in Straitsville, about a mile from the center of Salem. It had a taproom and four big ovens, and the proprietor, Ahira Collins, showing a taste for the grandiose, put up a sign that said Collins Hotel, rather than inn or tavern. Across the street was a bowling alley and later a store. After school was over for the day, Charles and his brothers and schoolmates hurried down the hill from the schoolhouse to Chauncey Lewis's tavern and stage waystop, and if they were lucky, they would get there in time to see the stagecoach pull up to the tavern and discharge its passengers. After the horses had been watered, the driver would return the way he had come, splashing through the river shallows to get back to the dirt turnpike.

When it came time to cultivate their son's intellectual and spiritual development, the Goodyears sent twelve-year-old Charles off to Ellsworth, in Litchfield County, to attend a school run by the Reverend Daniel Parker, a Congregationalist minister whose pedagogy drew children from as far away as Buffalo and Boston. At one time enrollment in the school numbered two hundred. Parker's energetic preaching won acclaim, and it energized Charles. For the first time he read and discussed the Book of Job, a story of torment and faith that would fascinate him later on as his own life became a chronicle of tribulations.

Since his arrival in 1802, Parker believed the congregation and townspeople had exploited him. He complained that the congregation paid him inadequately and forced him to pay for school construction, make loans at below-market interest rates to needy congregants and pay the tuition of an orphaned boy. Adding to Parker's burdens, the Holy Spirit suddenly arrived in Litchfield County and a great many new congregants crowded the benches. "This shower of divine grace spread over the parish, and its effects were deep and pungent," Parker wrote. "It was evidently the still small voice which caused multitudes to exclaim with deep solicitude, 'What shall we do to be saved?'"

This great awakening led a congregant with a background in education to open a competing school, a treachery that stunned and enraged Parker. The tangled relationship between town and minister grew even more complex when a local woman who became drunk at Parker's home was excommunicated for her sin. And finally, some leading congregants complained that an orphaned boy whose tuition Parker had paid was seen around town behaving a bit too gaily and dressed in clothes with an inappropriate amount of color and dash. By now, Parker's joint business ventures with the locals were going sour, too. He asked to be dismissed and was granted his wish. The brethren included a phrase in Parker's letter of dismissal that said he was too much involved in "worldly matters." The comment stung Parker so deeply he sued for slander.

Charles returned home from this drama of overwork, debt and betrayal just as the Goodyear family's button business began to decline. So far none of Amasa's product lines, except for the spring steel hay and manure fork, had achieved more than temporary successes. The high point of Amasa's button business seems to have been the War of 1812, which hurt the New England economy generally but brought him a military contract for uniform buttons. It isn't clear when or why his button works shut down, but when it did he opened a store at the town center. Eventually he shut down operations at this location, too, and set up a small shop in the village center where he made forks, buttons and molasses gates, a device for regulating the flow of the slow-moving syrup. By now, he and Cynthia had new children to care for with the birth of Nelson in 1813 and Amasa Jr. soon after.

As the oldest, Charles became accustomed to serving as a surrogate parent for his brothers and sister. He also asserted himself confidently in dealings with his father, who lacked some of the worldly knowledge and the never-ending stream of new ideas his son seemed to possess. In many ways, Amasa remained a simple farmer and blacksmith who patiently sought and followed the boy's suggestions. In the Goodyear role reversal, the teenage son offered as much guidance as his father about the future of the family business.

Still, Charles needed a mentor who would not yield to him as easily as his father did. He resumed his studies at home with the occasional help of a tutor named William C. DeForest. A tall, broad young man, red-faced and energetic, DeForest took a special interest in his short, slim protégé. DeForest found Goodyear ridiculous, boastful and unrealistic, but he also was delighted in the boy's precocity and the way he easily mastered his lessons and had so much to say about the world around him. Of the two, Goodyear had a far more active imagination and the ability to articulate his ideas with passion and humor and wordplay. But in one respect he saw DeForest as a role model. Although just twenty, his tutor was already a partner in a textile business in Naugatuck.

Charles' own ambitions drew him to merchandising and trade and to the larger world of the metropolis. On his seventeenth birthday, Amasa and Cynthia enrolled him in a five-year apprenticeship at Rogers & Brothers, an importer of English hardware and tableware, at 52 High Street in Philadelphia, an area dominated by wholesalers. Living in a boarding house or with friends of Amasa's, Charles probably worked ten to twelve hours a day, six days a week, learning the basics of retailing and importing in a way he never could have in Naugatuck and probably not anywhere else in New England. The hard work wore him down, and he became so sick that by the time he completed his obligation to Rogers & Brothers, at age twenty-one, he had to return home to Connecticut. He would have preferred to remain in Philadelphia to start his own business (Amasa journeyed to the city twice a year to sell goods there), and Charles wrote that he was "greatly disappointed by being obliged to abandon the idea" of establishing himself "in the business he had designed to pursue."

His frailty always seemed to draw people who wanted to protect or save Charles. While recuperating from his malaise at home and working with his father, Charles began to court Clarissa Beecher, the daughter of an innkeeper whom he had known since childhood. Clarissa had a plain face with high cheekbones, dark thick eyebrows and a strong chin. She found in the young Goodyear someone endearing in his infirmity and noble in the way he pressed forward with his work while still not at full health. They married on August 25, 1824, and by the following July they had a baby girl, Ellen.

Clarissa began to serve as a sounding board for Charles' business ideas. He had already assumed the intellectual leadership of his own family's fortunes and was always figuring out new implements—although he had no special affinity for mechanical devices or machines—and how they could be sold. Life may have revolved nominally around family and faith, but business was the deeper framework in which everything functioned. It was an obsession that enveloped all Goodyears but possessed Charles in particular. Clarissa learned that loving Charles meant loving to hear his ideas, which he discussed obsessively.

Charles and his father formalized the equality that had always characterized their relationship when they set up A. Goodyear & Sons, which mainly sold agricultural hardware produced in Amasa's shop, along with clocks. Amasa concentrated on producing the hardware and devising new products while Charles focused on sales. The spring steel hay and manure forks continued to sell well, according to Charles, "to the great benefit of the farming interest, throughout the United States."

The next year the Goodyear family decided that Charles and his brother Robert should move to Philadelphia to open a store that sold only Goodyear and other domestically produced hardware. It was an idea that built on the Goodyears' existing customer base in Philadelphia and was also consistent with the shift of the nation's agricultural focal point southward as the Northeast became the center of industry.

The idea of a domestic-only hardware store had a patriotic flavor. The War of 1812 had battered the U.S. economy and as soon as hostilities were over the English manufacturers poured their goods into the United States. The precarious new American industries were vulnerable. Although its soldiers had been defeated twice on U.S. soil, England could still dominate on the economic battlefield, and English manufacturers from time to time deliberately engaged in price wars to injure the long-term health of their U.S. competitors. Heavy-spending Americans borrowed to buy the imports and soon prices for domestic-made goods collapsed and many of the new plants built in New England shut down. *Niles' Weekly* estimated the excess of imports over exports for the years 1816 to 1819 at over $100 million. The U.S. economy was a lurching, sputtering contraption, such as Amasa Goodyear or another of the farmer-mechanics might have made, one minute promising to make untold thousands rich and comfortable, and another smashing those dreams.

Congress adopted a new tariff in 1816, expanding the protection first afforded under prior tariffs adopted during the Washington administration. The new tariff levied duties of 25 percent on imported cotton goods and also protected other industries. By the middle 1820s, U.S. cotton makers had fought off the English onslaught—and the tariff became mainly a policy of the industrial North. By pitting northern manufacturers who favored it against southern planters whose purchases of imports and domestic goods were made more costly, the tariff soon would become a flash point in the evolving dispute over states' rights.

The Goodyears' "Made in the USA" shop promised to defuse tariff tension. They certainly hoped to cash in on Charles' and Amasa's Philadelphia connections when in 1826 they opened A. Goodyear & Sons at 40 Church Alley, a byway running from 20 North Second Street to 11 Third Street, within a block of Rogers & Brothers, where Charles had served his apprenticeship. For the first time the Goodyears may have obtained loans from bankers rather than financing their work from cash on hand. They also for the first time began to sell hardware made by others on a commission basis. The hoes and scythes and forks probably all came from the Goodyears' shop in Connecticut, with Amasa in charge, while Charles, with his brothers' assistance, sold their wares and managed the business.

The store's domestic-made approach, while scoffed at by some, soon proved "visionary," Charles later wrote. The store occupied a narrow building and probably stretched forty to sixty feet deep, for an annual rent of less than $1,000. Shelves running backward to the rear were probably stocked with shells and buttons and other items that would soon no longer be defined as hardware. But shoppers could also send Charles Goodyear back into the store to find leather faucets, cast bits and screws, wooden awl handles, homemade spinning-wheel heads, carpenters' planes and, of course, hay forks, shovels and scythes. Some merchandise was known by its maker's name, such as Goodyear's own patented molasses gate, or Fenn's patented cockstop, or nail, shoe and side-strap hammers made by Charles Hammond of Philadelphia.

Charles soon expanded operations into several states and extended credit to southern farmers, who shared some of his disdain for the seamier side of big-city life. According to Goodyear, his family earned "a handsome fortune" and, like the dry goods business, domestic hardware sales soon became a constantly increasing department of trade. "It will be remembered by many hardware men of the present day," Charles wrote two decades later, "that from 1826 to 1830, the inventor was known in our commercial cities to be the pioneer in domestic hardware," and "occupied a position in business every way desirable."

Clarissa gave birth to another daughter, Cynthia, in 1827, and some time afterward the Goodyears enrolled Ellen in a Quaker kindergarten and grade school. The family had every chance to feel prosperous and well rewarded. They often passed time together at home reading and discussing the Bible. Ellen would sit in her parents' bedroom watching them point to pictures in the family Bible that illustrated the Ten Commandments. The fullness of Goodyear's late twenties as an innovative, wealthy merchant, and a happy husband and father, was captured by an unknown artist hired to paint the father and his two daughters. In the picture, the slender boy has given way to a radiant young man, dark locks tucked behind his ears, beard obscuring his bowtie. The artist featured Goodyear's prominent brow, deep-set, patient eyes and arched eyebrows. Nesting in Goodyear's lap is baby Cynthia, now about two years old, and standing before father's right leg is Ellen, now approaching six. Both girls have their father's eyes, and both are wearing formal, off-the-shoulder dresses. Ellen is smiling at the viewer but Cynthia's mouth is tight and her eyebrows are drawn down in a look of worry.

While relishing his apparent success, Charles still sought a purity that prayer and Bible study alone could not provide. Compared with Salem, the commercial centers of the Northeast were full of vice. So Charles dedicated himself to abstinence and drew a circle of piety around his family. "I have quit smoking, chewing and drinking all in one day," he wrote Clarissa from New York during a business trip. "You cannot form an idea of the extent of this last evil in this city among young men. By way of setting our faces against the world at large, I invite you to forbid in our house any thing stronger than wines and cordial except in cases of illness."

Charles' enterprising nature was fully engaged. He had returned to the city of his apprenticeship and found success within a few short years. He was now sending hardware to warehouses in other states. He probably invested in real estate—speculation was rampant—and he became a partner in two new inventions patented by other inventors, a cutting device called a stella rota and a self-winding clock. Each new idea and each new opportunity cried out to be exploited. He was, like other Americans of the time, grateful for what he had but also vexed whenever he saw a new opportunity slipping away. This effort to seize the main chance, in fact, was to prove the undoing of his first business career.

By expanding, granting credit to the southern farmers and investing in real estate and inventions, Goodyear tied up the cash generated by his hardware store. When trouble struck, there was no cushion. And the stella rota and self-winding clock both bombed commercially. "They were unsuccessful at the time," he later wrote in his third-person chronicle of his career. "They are alluded to here as deserving of notice, first, because they were among the principal causes [of his failure] not so much in consequence of the amount of money lost by them, as on account of the affect the speculation had on his credit as a merchant." In other words, Goodyear's risky stake in these inventions injected doubt about his reliability in the minds of his lenders.

Some time in 1828, southern planters who had been buying Goodyear's farm implements and making him feel rich stopped paying their bills. That was the year Congress adopted what the southerners called the Tariff of Abominations, which sent the cost of imported merchandise to new highs and launched John C. Calhoun into deep thought about the right of a state, his South Carolina in particular, to suspend a repugnant federal law. Goodyear's southern customers may in fact have used the tariff as an excuse to suspend payment to Goodyear for the hardware they had purchased on credit. Thousands of dollars of billed sales revenue vanished.

In 1829, just as Goodyear's liquidity was drying up, the U.S. economy shivered and coughed and sank into a full-blown illness. The "Good Feelings" of the early part of the 1820s had by now dissolved into an ugly tumult with an unpredictable new president, Andrew Jackson, preparing to go to war with an institution not far from Goodyear's shop, the Second National Bank of the United States. The bank was becoming the focus of dissatisfaction of the increasingly frustrated majority that had voted Jackson into office. Everywhere people agonized over debt and paper money and the role of the banks. A group of working men met in Philadelphia to oppose "the chartering of any more new banks" and blamed the trouble on "too great an extension of paper credit." According to historian Arthur Schlesinger Jr., westerners opposed the bank because they wanted their home states to issue and control the paper money that some believed had been handed out too freely. A deeply felt suspicion that banking was a game rigged for the rich took hold among the East's working people and poor, and these people "fought the whole banking swindle, as it seemed to them, root and branch."

Perhaps in part because of these developments, Charles began to experience severe stomach pains. Doctors of the day referred to the sickness as dyspepsia, a term that could cover everything from mild indigestion and heartburn to bleeding ulcers. The cramps and fever were so debilitating that Charles was confined to his bed. His agony was so great that he had delusions, talked nonsense and seemed disconnected from the world around him. Some believed the illness had affected his mind, but in several weeks he was back at work again.

Yet despite his best efforts, A. Goodyear & Sons was unraveling. It was unable to repay its loans as a result of defaults by its customers. In 1830, the creditors induced the Goodyears to "continue their business with extension of payments" which went to retiring as much of their prior debt as possible. The result was protracted misery. The Goodyears were back to practicing the blacksmith's trade, living on a subsistence income and working to pay off their debt by developing products for which patents had been granted or were pending. Charles moved his business to smaller quarters at numbers 2 and 15 Church Alley, cutting the rent.

The original creditors sold the uncollected portion of the debt to strangers, and the Goodyears had to post bonds. This meant they had to pledge to pay debt-holders in several states in order to avoid arrest and imprisonment. Gradually, the creditors began to strip the Goodyears of the rest of their property, a good portion of which consisted of patents of unknown value, for products not yet finished or for sale. It was a double bind. Goodyear said he could not make an assignment of the value of the invention to a creditor without divesting himself of "the titles to the unfinished inventions, in which state they would have been of no value to himself or his creditors."

The Goodyears turned to Charles' old tutor William DeForest, who was now prospering in the textile business in Salem. On February 3, 1830, they signed a note for $500 to DeForest, due in six months with interest. In April the struggling merchants took another note, for $575, and then in December one for $800. The next year, the Goodyears needed more money to finance their hardware business and also probably to pay debts and living expenses. Charles visited DeForest's office at his fabric and textile works in Salem. The bustling complex provided a sad contrast to his own ruined venture. DeForest had been a partner of Leverett Candee, who made wool cloth in a small shop on the brook. Candee's half-interest was transferred several times between 1822 and 1825, after which the company's name was changed to William DeForest & Company. DeForest gradually built up the operation, bought additional land, erected new buildings and powered a finish shop at the lower end of the brook with water diverted from the Naugatuck River. Later he would branch into making satinet, a cheap fabric created by pressing wool fibers into cotton cloth. To provide needed labor, DeForest built a boarding house where young women from the surrounding countryside could reside. In this respect DeForest copied Francis Lowell of the Waltham, Massachusetts, cotton spinners. The approximate pay in these mills: $1.25 a week. In any event DeForest's accomplishments were resplendent compared with the Goodyears' plight.

DeForest was the first to learn how expensive it was to be the best friend of Charles Goodyear. In 1831, Goodyear said to his friend, "William, we want to realize more money than we can conveniently raise just at this time, but with your assistance we think we can raise it through D. Holt & Company or James DeForest. Will you assist us?" DeForest agreed, and Goodyear either wrote or took from his pocketbook a guarantee written in the name of W. DeForest & Company for $2,000 and handed it to him for his signature. In 1832 and 1833, DeForest signed still more notes.

The loan failed to save the Goodyears. Step by step, creditors dismantled all signs of their earlier prosperity. With their backs to the wall, Charles and Amasa Sr., who had had the fork manufacturing business for twenty years, surrendered a piece of the fork sales to Curtis & Hand, hardware merchants who had taken over their Philadelphia shop. Goodyear later wrote ruefully of the loss of the fork factory and patent, citing his "real regret" at parting "with the last pecuniary advantage of a business" from which he had "anticipated an independence for life." At this time, the Goodyears lost their last remaining stake in the Connecticut shop, and still they had huge debts and worries over being forced into prison. Finally, the last piece of the fork business, which was to have been an annuity to pay for his and his parents' retirements, had to be surrendered. Amasa and Cynthia lost the house and farm and had to move to Philadelphia to live with Charles and his family.

The Goodyears had followed their oldest son into a robust new business, hardware retailing, that promised to provide, along with their patents, a measure of comfort and security that the family to this point had never known. When the new venture and Charles' related investments crashed, the Goodyears, their individual businesses unshielded by separate corporate identities, tumbled into ruin together. All savings, all equity, and a good deal of their reputation crumbled, too. For Amasa and Cynthia's eldest son, the man who considered his business "visionary," the fall may have been hardest of all. Charles had led his family to disaster and rightfully assumed the remaining unpaid debt of about $12,000. It was like starting life at age thirty owing a fortune it would take a lifetime to repay.

No ordinary trade or profession could overcome so heavy a debt, so Charles decided he would "make a profession of invention." Striking it rich by inventing was as wild a form of speculation as any that existed at the time. Success had little to do with merit. An invention had to be matched with a market and promoted; it had to strike a hot iron. As often as not, Goodyear wrote later, con artists promoted worthless gadgets. "Things of little or no value catch the public favor, and, by being prosecuted by shrewd and discerning individuals, large fortunes are made by them. The wonders of the day explode, and are never heard of afterwards."

The problems Goodyear observed were partly the fault of a patent system first set up by Thomas Jefferson in 1790 that had been outgrown by the mid-1830s. Originally, patent examinations took an excruciatingly long time under Secretary of State Jefferson. Then the U.S. Patent Office dispensed with the careful examinations and allowed inventors simply to register their inventions. Patent speculators abounded and legitimate inventors needed to engage in costly lawsuits to protect their rights. Almost forty years later, the Jackson administration reformed the patent system, reinstituting examinations, and an 1836 patent law required public access to the patent-covered innovations. With the link between individual reward and public benefit restored, American inventors focused on areas such as steam power or machine tools and patented devices that drove industrialization onward. Metal products replaced wooden ones. Small shops were organized into factories. As marketplace values swept aside the old craft system, manufacturing entrepreneurs striving for cheaper, more efficient methods devised many of the early mechanical inventions of the nineteenth century. And new American mechanics began knocking at the doors of a pantheon of successful inventors that included Benjamin Franklin and Robert Fulton.

Goodyear was aware of the potential for both glory and abject failure in his newly adopted profession. He took this fateful step because he would never be able to "shake off the epithets of inventor, mechanical genius, or visionary, which terms are generally considered as ... diametrically opposed to money-getting—all things considered." Nevertheless, Goodyear set to work as an inventor, first working with materials he knew well. In 1831, he patented a method for making "the safe-eye button" and a new spring steel fork; in 1832, a spring-lever faucet and a new way of making spoons. In 1834 came faucets and more molasses gates; in 1835, an air pump. Except for the innovations he produced and patented, there was very little difference between him and the primitive blacksmiths from whom he at one time hoped to distinguish himself through the hardware business. Meanwhile, Goodyear watched as the two immediate successors of his own firm, Curtis & Hand and Heaton & Denckla, evolved into "two of the most respectable and wealthy" of the "numerous domestic hardware houses that have since been established in all our large cities."

Through their hardships and financial emergencies the Goodyears had tried to hold on to a normal existence. Clarissa gave birth to two more children in the space of two years: a girl, Sarah Beecher, in 1830, and then their first son, Charles Jr., in 1831. But the respectable life they had known was fraying. They had to move to cheaper quarters in Germantown, outside Philadelphia. Ellen remembered awakening mornings to find her father gone. Clarissa explained gently to the seven-year-old that Charles was in jail because of debt. There was little hope of shielding the children from the cascading effects of the family plight. Ellen was left to care for tiny Sarah Beecher while Clarissa went to jail every day to try to arrange Charles' release. They had another daughter, Clarissa, late in the year, but the infant died. Then, in the next year, three-year-old Sarah Beecher became sick and died. Grieving, Clarissa focused on caring for the diminished family while Charles buried himself in business, managing the huge debt and salvaging some money to live on.

Jail seemed to complete the ruin into which the Goodyears had fallen. Creditors forced Goodyear into Philadelphia's Arch Street prison, an aged building constructed of massive stones and crammed in the early 1830s with a cross-section of the city's unfortunate: hardened criminals, down-on-their-luck laborers, drunks, the sick and handicapped, madmen, prostitutes and a small number of fallen entrepreneurs. The debtors had the run of the grounds and could obtain passes to leave for a day, reporting back at nightfall. Prisoners in the debtors' apartments were allowed one five-cent loaf of bread, two blankets and a fire. Beds weren't provided, and illness was the biggest threat to survival. In August 1832, during a citywide epidemic, forty-nine inmates died of cholera in an eight-day period, and, the Prison Discipline Society reported, "on examination after the cholera, were found, in the basement story, some fetid sheep-skins, and hair in small amount."

Goodyear made the most of his time under lock and key, doing any work that he could and talking to the guards and inmates. But his jail days filled him with a sense of unjust persecution. "If any one is desirous to learn more of human nature than he can learn in any other way, or wishes for a moment to look upon the darkest side of life's fleeting shade," Goodyear later wrote, "let him, for such a cause as debt and misfortune, be placed within the bars of a prison door, without a dollar in his pocket, and in conscious innocence look out upon the world, and reflect upon the wide contrast in his condition with that of those who are enjoying liberty without; while within he finds his fellow sufferers all upon the same level, whether incarcerated for the sum of one hundred pence or of one hundred thousand pounds."

His father and his brothers arranged for his release, but Goodyear's Philadelphia creditors continued to dog him. The Goodyears packed up their belongings in Germantown and rented a cottage in New Haven in 1834, close to their old hometown. It was not so much a move as an escape.

CHAPTER TWO

Salvation through Rubber

Charles Goodyear's search for salvation through invention had begun while he still lived in Philadelphia. Strapped with debt and responsibility, Goodyear trolled restlessly for winning ideas and opportunities. He was looking for a miracle, and it was not going to come from the petty hardware items he had invented to this point in his career. To have a miracle he needed a miracle substance.

In the summer of 1834, when the Goodyears still lived outside Philadelphia, he visited New York City and stopped into the lower Manhattan store of the Roxbury India Rubber Company, the best capitalized of the dozen or so rubber companies that had sprung to life in Massachusetts and New York in the early 1830s. About a million dollars worth of stock had been sold. By the time Charles Goodyear arrived, the rubber investment boom had already burst because of the stubborn intractability of the miracle substance, and the initial investors had been wiped out. Rubber making seemed destined to become one of North America's great follies.

The native peoples of South and Central America seemed to understand rubber better and had used it creatively since pre-Columbian times. Archaeologists have found evidence that Mayan Indians in South America used rubber as early as the eleventh century and that Central and South American Indians used rubber at least five hundred years ago to make bottles, boots and waterproof garments. Natives also found religious uses for the substance by making figurines and burning it as a foul-smelling incense. Some used it to make puffers to inject narcotics into their nostrils.

Peruvians referred to the material as "koo-chook," a variation of the Indian word meaning "weeping tree." The best sources were the tall, slim-trunked trees with thick tufted foliage that grow in the Amazon River basin. Later called *Hevea brasiliensis,* these trees stretch as high as sixty feet. The milky ooze just behind the bark is actually an emulsion of rubber in a solution sometimes referred to as latex.

Brazilian Indians were among the most skilled in drawing the latex from the trees. A team of two would hack a looping trail linking eighty to one hundred trees and after it was done would set out into the jungle early in the morning and stop at each tree to slash an oblique incision in the bark with a hatchet. As many as six slashes were made in large trees. Clay cups were strapped to the lower end of each incision and a few ounces of the latex would trickle in. The rubber collectors would gather as much as two gallons of the latex in a hollowed-out gourd or bucket. Then the women often took over, pouring the sap in layers over clay forms in the shape of jugs or pouches or over wooden lasts in the shape of shoes. They would smoke the articles they had made over burning wassou palm-nuts and hang them up to dry for four or five days. When the articles were dry, the women removed them to hang on poles. In this way they were carried to markets.

When Europeans arrived they liked what they saw of the strange stuff. In 1511 a Spanish writer conveyed a description of an Aztec game witnessed by Cortez' secretary in which Indians played with balls that when struck on the ground would rebound "incredibly into the air." Spanish Conquistadors waterproofed their cloaks with rubber, and rubber shoes and toys made their way back to Europe. It was only a "remarkable national ineptitude," according to two technology historians, that the job of formally reporting on the substance's intriguing qualities was left to scientists from other countries in the mid-eighteenth century. In 1736, Charles Marie de La Condamine published in Paris the observations of his friend François Fresneau, who described rubber collecting in detail for the first time. Fresneau recommended using the substance for hose, diving suits and airtight bags. In 1770, English scientist Joseph Priestley noted that what La Condamine and Fresneau referred to as *caoutchouc* was "excellently adapted to the purpose of wiping from paper the unwanted marks of a black lead pencil." He called the material "India rubber," because it was known to come from "The Indies."

Portuguese merchants brought the Brazilian rubber craftwork to Europe, but the substance found only sporadic uses through the eighteenth century because of the trouble of importing crude rubber for more precise manufacturing in European factories. Rubber's usefulness was limited by the need to dissolve the imported rubber "biscuits," or blocks, and rework the material into a new shape. Turpentine dissolved rubber, but it was hard to work with.

It took an industrious Scot and an Englishman to build Europe's first significant rubber company. In 1819, a fifty-three-year-old Glasgow dye maker named Charles Macintosh discovered that naphtha, an oily waste product from coal processing, dissolved rubber. It allowed Macintosh to coat fabrics with the rubber and make them waterproof, replicating an idea that originated in the jungles of the New World. He patented the process in 1823 and called the product in which the sticky rubber was sandwiched between layers of fabric Waterproof Double Textures. Later the garments made in this way were known simply as "macks."

Thomas Hancock, a London businessman whose brother would run steam-powered coaches on English roads, had been using rubber as elastic in gloves and boots in place of lacing. This left a lot of scraps, which he re-used with the help of a machine he invented, the "masticator." When Hancock built his first masticator he was looking for a way to reduce the rubber back to liquid form without using solvents like turpentine or camphene, which cost money and seemed to compromise the quality of the finished rubber fabric. Inside the grinding central chamber of Hancock's machine, a cylinder studded with sharp teeth and turned by a man hour after hour gnawed and macerated the rubber scraps. But destruction begot creation. "It soon became evident that some action was going on inside that I had not reckoned upon, as much greater power became necessary to turn the winch," Hancock wrote. When he opened the chamber, he found to his great surprise that the masticated rubber had re-collected into a round solid ball.

He put the ball back in and subjected it to another round of punishment. This time the ball emerged very hot from friction and amalgamated into a solid homogeneous mass. The heat had converted the rubber. Hancock kept this up until his experimental wooden masticator disintegrated; then he hurried to find engineers to make a sturdier one. For twelve years Hancock, who had become a partner with Macintosh in 1826, had a monopoly on the use of the masticator, never bothering to file for a patent but instead making his staff take an oath not to talk about it. To disguise the nature of the machine, Hancock and his colleagues referred to it as a "pickle." In 1832 a former worker finally broke his vow of silence and competitors went into action. But by this time, Hancock and Macintosh's venture made rubber a solid business and gave England the lead in rubber technology. They stayed ahead of the competition by enforcing the patents they had taken out on rainwear and other products.

Rubber had also caught the eye of American entrepreneurs. In 1823, Thomas Wales of Boston began importing large quantities of shoes from South America crudely crafted by indigenous people. Despite their primitive execution, 43,000 pairs of native-made shoes were imported from the Amazon area alone in 1837 and double that the next year. Not much rubber manufacturing was going on in the United States. Only 17,000 pounds of raw or almost raw rubber entered the country in 1837 and even less the next year. But then American shoemakers recognized the potential of the rubber shoes, particularly if they could be made to be more stylish and longer lasting. The Roxbury India Rubber Company's co-founder, mechanic Edwin M. Chaffee, had been the foreman of a patent leather factory when he began sifting for methods of curing rubber and providing it with a smooth, shiny finish. In 1832, he invented a small machine that would coat ten yards of cloth with rubber in a single application. He kept the machine's existence a secret and then carefully rounded up investors, letting in influential local residents one at a time. Eventually, the company produced shoes, life preservers, wagon covers, coats, caps and carriage traces. Its total capitalization reached $300,000. With raw rubber selling by the pound and each pair of rubber shoes priced at a few dollars, the possible profits were enticing.

Too enticing for the average rubber worker, as it turned out. Tempted by bribes, Roxbury workers broke their pledges of secrecy and supplied information about company operations to competitors. Five new manufacturers raised capital and opened shop in the Boston area in 1835, displaying "the impetuosity and daring so characteristic of American enterprise," Goodyear later wrote. Rubber seemed to be all anyone talked about.

One detail, one very big detail, had been left unattended amid all the stock selling and speculation: the companies were unable to deliver a durable product that would last in the North American summers. The shoes and clothing that the rubber makers produced were in some cases poorly designed, but the biggest problem was that the rubber hardened in winter and softened in summer, the surface becoming sticky and generally unpleasant to touch. Sun playing on the surface began to break down the outermost layer after an hour or so. And it also began to smell. Even Charles Macintosh, who sandwiched a layer of sticky rubber between two plies of cloth, sold his products in England with a proviso: keep them away from stoves and fires. But while the English avoided over-promising on performance, U.S. rubber makers, eager to sell stock, pressed their rubber products on a credulous public, claiming the material would withstand anything short of a thunder-bolt thrown down from the heavens.

At first consumers stampeded to buy articles made of this miracle substance. But then they began listening to what their noses told them and the returns came pouring back. In the summer of 1832 the owners of the Roxbury Company secretly buried, in a giant grave dug on their own property, hundreds of pairs of decomposing shoes and other rubber wares whose Limburger aroma oppressed all who came near. The value of what was put in the ground in one night came to more than $20,000, and with the burial the Roxbury's investors laid their hopes to rest, too.

The rubber business had pretty much ruined anyone who had hitched his hopes to it, but Charles Goodyear knew little of this when he stumbled upon his new fixation; years later he would consider himself blessed by his ignorance. When he called at the Roxbury India Rubber Company shop in New York, he examined a life preserver, decided the tube or valve through which it was inflated could be better designed and bought it. Several months later he returned with an improved valve. The agent in the store told Goodyear that he should try to improve the rubber itself, and that all the rubber companies that had sprung up in the Boston area were doomed to failure soon. Goodyear was surprised that this wonder substance "had baffled all the efforts of chemists and manufacturers."

When he returned home to Germantown, near Philadelphia, he brought with him some raw rubber. Although he did not know it, he had discovered his life's work—the substance that would give him triumph and cause his tragedy. He immediately began to experiment, applying other substances to the rubber, searching for a way to cure it and make it "insensible" to climatic extremes. He even worked on his experiments, it is said, during the time he spent in a debtors' prison.

The cottage the Goodyears rented in New Haven in 1834 was their third home in five years. It was a plain, three-room saltbox with an attic and a steep, shingled roof, in the Sodom Hill section of the city. Charles converted the kitchen to a laboratory. "It was at this time," his daughter Ellen recalled later on, "that I remember beginning to see and hear about India rubber. It began to appear in little patches upon the windowpanes and on the dinner plates. These patches were peeled off when dry. Pieces of printed muslin were covered with transparent gum. Father took possession of our kitchen for a workshop. He would sit hour after hour, working the gum with his hands." Ellen said the first rubber article she remembered was a purse with a steel clasp that she took with her to school.

In New Haven, Goodyear could draw on the goodwill of old acquaintances and return his family to a more normal life. Clarissa enjoyed being able to gather the family for meals around her own table. She resumed the prolific childbearing that had kept her pregnant or caring for very small children through most of her married life, and a new son, William Henry, was born. There was hardly ever a moment of rest. Clarissa from time to time would serve as the brake on Charles' rapid and clamorous thoughts: "Do not make up your mind too hastily," she would tell him. "Hadn't you not better wait until tomorrow?" But she couldn't slow her husband down. Clarissa remained a willing, though sometimes hesitant, believer in Charles' vision.

He didn't immediately give up on his metal inventions. For most of 1834, Goodyear tried to build his design for a tin boat of tubular construction, attempting to join two silver humidors in a single lightweight craft. His concept, based on the idea that the overall density of a tubular craft would be less than water, was meant to imitate the buoyancy of hollow cylindrical animal and bird bones. Goodyear, working with two assistants, struggled to unite the fabricated halves and tubes in a watertight unit. Little came of the effort and expense.

As the boat project died, Goodyear funneled his attention to rubber. Against a high board fence separating his cottage from another on the next lot, Goodyear erected a shed for his rubber work. Dressed in an apron or smock tied at the back, he immersed the gray or brown blocks of stiff rubber in a tub of turpentine, the best-known solvent for the substance (but one suspected of contributing to the irritating stickiness of the finished product). When the rubber had softened, he placed it on a stone slab and worked it with his hands, kneading like a chef and rolling it flat with a pin. With the rubber spread into a pad or sheet, Goodyear tried to find a substance that would cure its stickiness and provide long-lasting resistance to heat and cold. Powders and chemicals, applied to the surface, were worked manually into the pad or sheet until Goodyear believed the substances were mingled completely, and until his hands ached. One goal was to work the rubber into a state where it could be pressed together with a conventional fabric, making a composite with the potential to improve upon the Macintosh double textures.

Goodyear's first breakthrough seemed to come with powdered magnesia. When one-half to one pound of powder was mixed with a pound of rubber, the rubber dried and the powder communicated a desirable white color to the surface of the material. He bound a book with rubber prepared in this way, but over time the cover softened and fermented and later hardened until it was as tough as shell, the combination of magnesia and turpentine having apparently reacted to calcify the rubber.

Goodyear pressed on, using money advanced to him by a thirty-four-year-old New Haven coppersmith and stove dealer, Ralph B. Steele, whose stoves Goodyear had sold in his Philadelphia hardware store. Steele knew of Goodyear's failure in Philadelphia when Goodyear first started borrowing money from him in 1832. But Goodyear didn't tell Steele that he was also deeply indebted to DeForest and others. Or Steele didn't ask. For the time it didn't matter because Goodyear seemed to be on to something big.

Figuring out a way to roll the rubber into light plies, Goodyear glazed the fabric and embossed the surface in preparation for making shoes. This time, instead of shaping his products from rubber bricks, Goodyear got hold of about fifty casks of India rubber sap, including several in which the rubber had not yet coagulated and separated from the natural watery solution in which it seeps from a cut rubber tree. Working with pure rubber, not previously dissolved, would eliminate another variable.

On the morning Goodyear was to begin to work with the pure rubber, an Irish immigrant he employed prepared a surprise for his boss. On his arrival at the rubber shop, Goodyear found that his worker was wearing a pair of rubber trousers. The laborer had opened one of the sap casks the night before and simply dipped his trousers in. In the morning the pants were dry enough to wear. "The job was so completely done," Goodyear later wrote, that it looked as if "experiments with gum-elastic were nearly at an end." Not long after the worker sat down to work that morning, mixing the rubber sap before a fire, trouble struck. His pants had melted into the chair, fixing him to his seat. He had to be pulled from his pants, "to the merriment of the bystanders."

Goodyear concluded that the gum was adhesive by nature, not simply because it had been treated with solvents.

The experiments went on. Steele regularly endorsed Goodyear's notes and allowed him to draft funds against his account in amounts as high as $1,000. Working from his home shop, Goodyear, together with family members and three or four young female laborers, stitched together several hundred pairs of shoes and, before putting them on the market, stored them where they would be exposed to cold and heat. Goodyear believed the glazed

ENCOUNTER BOOKS

665 Third Street

Suite 330

San Francisco, CA 94107-1951

Please put me on your mailing list for future announcements.

Name

Company

Address

City, State, Zip

E-mail

rubber footwear with embossed decorative designs would last and he reported his expectations to neighbors and creditors. "Even now," he wrote twenty years later, the shoes "would be considered beautiful."

But his predictions backfired. The shoes melted and the patience of his creditors wore thin. Neighbors and friends refused to offer what Goodyear termed "further assistance for such purposes." Grocers stopped supplying the Goodyears on credit. With bills accumulating, Goodyear sold off his furniture and paid some debts owed to the backers of his rubber business. He managed to repay a few thousand dollars to Steele, but several thousand more remained outstanding. By now Goodyear had to think hard to remember all his debts, for he kept scant financial records. Two thousand dollars remained outstanding mostly to business associates in Philadelphia, but while living in New Haven he had also drawn liberally on funds from acquaintances in Waterbury, including Abijah Osborn ($3,000), Milo and P. B. Hine ($800) and Jesse Worcester ($300).

In January 1835, the owner of the Goodyears' cottage obtained an eviction notice to force the family out. Goodyear apparently hadn't paid rent nor had he endeared himself to neighbors with his rubber work in the yard. And once again, the Goodyears seemed to pay for Charles' miscalculations with the life of one of their children. One-year-old William Henry died, breaking their hearts again. The Goodyears bore their grief submissively, bewildered by the coupling of financial emergency and the loss of a child. They packed what they had and moved again, to "a retired place in the country," near Salem (soon to be known as Naugatuck). This time they needed to hand over as security some linen spun by Clarissa years earlier. After moving his family into their new home, Goodyear headed for New York City. It was one of many times when he left Clarissa behind with little money and small children to care for while he tried to make the fortune he always believed was just around the corner.

And there were always others who found Goodyear's vision contagious. One friend in New York City, John W. Sexton, put him up in a room in his Gold Street house, and another, pharmacist Silas Carle, provided him with chemicals with which to treat rubber. Again Goodyear attacked the substance, first trying to neutralize the effect of the turpentine, which he believed made the rubber decompose. So he boiled his rubber, turpentine and magnesia in quicklime and water, apparently tanning the goods and drying them. Out of this method he fabricated sheets of rubber fabric. Again, Goodyear declared victory and applied for a patent for his rubber fabric.

Within a few weeks, however, he rinsed his rubber fabric with a weak acid solution and found it returned to its sticky condition.

About this time Goodyear also visited the General Society for Mechanics and Tradesmen, meeting on Crosby Street in New York City, where he found other people with similar fixations. Goodyear submitted his quick-lime-and-water-boiled sheets to the society's fair and won a medal based largely on the finish of the surface before it reverted to its sticky state. While the society's members included engineers and architects and some business-minded entrepreneurs, the majority consisted of bookbinders, sash makers, varnish makers and plumbers—in other words, people who would identify more closely with the "country blacksmiths" than with the more cosmopolitan company of "inventors." The society's records don't show that Goodyear ever joined, but the awards he won at their fairs over the next year or so conferred respectability on the entrepreneur, now somewhat frayed in the cuffs.

During one visit to the General Society for Mechanics and Tradesmen, Goodyear met a machinist and knife manufacturer named William Ballard who lived in lower Manhattan. After describing his work with rubber, Goodyear invited Ballard to finance the work in return for an unspecified portion of the profits. Ballard later said that all he knew was that Goodyear had been in Philadelphia manufacturing pitchforks and hoes and that he had lost money. "It was at his suggestion that I advanced him money to go into the rubber business; in representing his circumstances to me, he said in substance, that his goods were new, and if he had the means to manufacture them it would be a good thing; he wanted money from me to assist him to start the manufacture; from his appearance and conversation I supposed he had no money or property of his own." Without making any arrangement about dividing profits, other than that Goodyear would remunerate him "very liberally for the monies I had advanced," Ballard began financing his work. Goodyear moved to better quarters downtown in a former rubber factory near Washington Square. Ballard himself opened a store near Broadway to sell the rubber fabric that Goodyear was to make.

But Goodyear still hadn't figured out how to tame the rubber. One idea was to mix in quicklime to dry the rubber, but the mix "was too powerfully caustic to be worked by hand." He rented access to a mill operated by a man named Pike in Greenwich Village, who was fabricating rubber using horse-powered equipment. Goodyear later said that he frequently carried a gallon jug of slacked lime mix from his room on Gold Street the three miles to the Greenwich Village mill.

He was now nearly thirty-six and had aged dramatically from his days of success in Philadelphia. He had taken to wearing a rubber coat he had made as a way of demonstrating the versatility of his treated rubber, but the coat probably put off as many people as it impressed. William DeForest, the tall, fleshy textile captain who had tutored Goodyear as a teenager, came to see his friend at his apartment on Gold Street and was surprised at Goodyear's worn appearance and shabby clothing. Goodyear indirectly acknowledged his addiction, pointing to black and brown streaks of rubber on his hands. He proclaimed to his old friend that he "did not know how to rub India rubber off," and added, as an indication that he knew he was dealing in metaphor, that "there was only one way, by rubbing more on." On reaching the third-floor room where Goodyear lived and worked, DeForest found a space littered with kettles, gum shellac and rubber.

Goodyear chirped optimistically, "William, here is something that will pay all my debts and make us comfortable."

"The India rubber business is below par," answered DeForest.

"And I am the man to bring it back again," replied Goodyear.

Goodyear missed Clarissa and the children, and he also felt he could use another pair of hands. Soon his daughter Ellen, now ten years old, rode down to New York to stay with him. Father and daughter moved to Holt's Hotel, where they occupied two attic bedrooms. At work one day at either Gold Street or Pike's Mill, Goodyear stumbled into his first lucky break. He had boiled lime with metal bronze to decorate the rubber, but when it didn't work he applied nitric acid to remove the bronze. The acid discolored the rubber so Goodyear threw it away. But he retrieved the acid-treated rubber from the refuse and after examining it believed he had finally found the method of curing rubber that would last. Satisfied that he had achieved his long-sought goal, Goodyear returned to his attic rooms at Holt's Hotel and met Ellen in the attic hall. He asked her if she could keep a secret. When she said yes, he told her he had made a great discovery and had learned how to cure India rubber and overcome its stickiness. Ellen feigned great happiness. Like all Charles' children she understood that loving and being loved by her father meant sharing his obsessions.

To bolster his image for potential customers and investors, Goodyear presented his findings to Professor Leonard D. Gale of New York University, a man who would later become a partner of Samuel F. B. Morse in the communications business. The nitric acid, Gale wrote in a testimonial for which Goodyear very probably paid a small fee, removes the rubber's stickiness. Gale believed a chemical change had been made in the rubber and that as a result "there seems to be no obstacle to its practical application." Goodyear printed maps and engravings and handbills on his acid-treated rubber fabric, trying every way he could to stimulate interest in the substance.

Under the process Goodyear developed, gas vapors acting on the surface of the rubber were believed to provide a significant part of the curing effect. So the room in which the rubber was treated had to be small to confine the vapors. One day, while preparing rubber fabric in a vapor-filled room, Goodyear lost consciousness. After being revived, he developed a fever that took weeks to subside. Dr. Thomas Bradshaw, Goodyear's doctor, not only resuscitated his patient but also became interested in his experiments. Bradshaw offered to take samples of acid-treated rubber to London to interest manufacturers there in Goodyear's method. With rubber in disrepute in the United States, Europe seemed like a more promising outlet. Goodyear provided Bradshaw with samples of rubber drapery before he set sail.

While Bradshaw carried Goodyear's samples to England, hoping to interest Thomas Hancock and the Macintosh Company, Goodyear continued to push his acid-gas treatment. After his medals and write-ups in newspapers, Goodyear needed to gear up for producing more than the specimens on hand. Ballard rented an abandoned factory on Staten Island and a big warehouse on Broadway in Manhattan. He sent Charles $500 for advance payment of the rent on Staten Island, for which Goodyear professed everlasting friendship. Ballard borrowed $2,000 more under his own name and gave it to Goodyear.

Having only Ellen with him in New York, Charles had few comforts other than prayer. Two attic rooms at a New York hotel offered few chances for the domestic joys Goodyear relished: Bible reading and tricks and jokes that amused the children. He belonged to no church congregation. After a few months Goodyear vacated his Washington Square offices and, after sending for Clarissa and the other children, moved the family into a cottage next to the Staten Island factory. Once settled, the family and a staff of laborers (who probably boarded in other buildings on the premises) began to churn out rubber aprons and piano covers with decorative embellishments. The factory, which had belonged to the New York Rubber Cloth Company, had machinery, engines, drying rooms and other things ready for making rubber. But the cottage and the remote location, a long ferry ride from New

York City on lower Manhattan Island, always signified isolation to Goodyear.

Ballard continued to pay into the business, handing Goodyear cash and settling invoices for goods purchased by his partner. Ballard realized only later on that he was Goodyear's primary source of money not only for business but for family living expenses. Soon the amount Ballard had given Goodyear or invested in their venture was over $5,000.

Just as the little business was getting on its feet in 1836, another panic and financial depression, deeper and longer-lasting than its predecessors, once again brought the U.S. economy to its knees. President Jackson had abolished the Second National Bank of the United States, but his actions in transferring assets to state banks and requiring that public lands be paid for in specie undermined confidence in the national currency. After a New Orleans cotton brokerage firm, Herman Briggs & Company, failed in March 1837, the national economy unraveled and 618 banks failed. Over 39,000 people became insolvent debtors or bankrupts and hunger was rampant. Ballard sustained significant losses and not only withdrew further funding for Goodyear but also asked him to pay back some of the money already advanced to him. Unable to tap Ballard for living expenses, Goodyear now was dependent on selling. He employed about five hands to help make the rubber materials on Staten Island, but fell behind on both his rent and his payment to his workers.

The Goodyears once again lapsed into a wretched subsistence. Charles would make the ferry trip to Manhattan with cups or spoons or other family possessions in his pockets, hoping to pawn them in the city. Tradition has it that he once traded his umbrella as ferry fare. Brother Robert and Robert's wife and four children moved in so that both families could share Robert's furniture. Goodyear's parents also joined them, crowding the little saltbox cottage near the factory. Robert fished to provide food, and Clarissa made bonnets of pasteboard and built decorative rubber globes to sell. Ellen helped make rubber piano covers.

Clarissa reminded the children to be grateful for what they had and to trust the future would be better. The discipline the family was suffering, she told them, was probably because they may have been uncharitable toward the poor. Now they knew what poverty was like.

Amasa Sr. seemed dumbfounded with despair. They were once rich, he told some people he met. To help keep the family warm he hunted for stray briquettes of coal that had fallen from delivery wagons into the streets. Charles' heart broke to see his aging parents "stripped of every comfort."

Through the haze of hardship, Clarissa conceived and carried to term still another child, a boy they named William Henry after their dead son. Six-year-old Charles Jr., who resembled his mother more and more each day, and his two older sisters treated the newly arrived sibling as a temporary guest, preferring to wait to become deeply connected emotionally until he had proved his durability.

All the borders between work and family had now been erased by Charles' obsession. He had partially indoctrinated Clarissa into his vision, but he knew she wished he would return to work as a blacksmith. So Charles let her think he might give up on rubber soon and that he was attending to other kinds of business during his long absences in the city. Although he never admitted it even to himself, Charles was now unable to break his addiction and take up another line of work.

He also concealed from Ballard the truth about where he was going and what he did with the small amount of money he made from selling rubber goods. This caused great bitterness: "Mr. Goodyear frequently told me he had sold such and such pieces of goods; I consider that all the money he received was squandered for his own living; Goodyear got it all; I got none of it; not a penny."

Charles hid his guilt under a resolve to make everything right again. If he had a little more time, and a little more money, he would prove the value of his acid process. He told himself he intended to repay Ballard along with the workers he employed and everyone in Philadelphia, but at the moment he had to show people his rubber goods were the best ever made. And to do this he needed to raise more money.

Goodyear tried to get the owners from whom he rented the abandoned rubber factory to invest in his new process, but no one was interested. He continued to pawn his few possessions. Even the ferry fare became a burden.

Coming to New York to look for new investors, moreover, was dangerous because there was always a chance of running into someone to whom he owed money. On one trip to the pawnshop in lower Manhattan, Goodyear met a creditor. He expected a sharp rebuke but instead the creditor asked him what he could do for him. Goodyear, who was searching for food, was incredulous and said $15 would oblige him, and the man handed it to him. While he was able to keep the object he intended to pawn until another day, he remained "at the mercy of the pawnbroker, however, and every article that could be made available was pledged." At one point the family is said to have counted its only asset as a set of teacups worth fifty cents.

As he walked New York's streets, Goodyear's rubber clothing became his trademark. ("If you meet a man who has on an India rubber cap, stock, coat, vest, and shoes, with an India rubber money purse, without a cent of money in it, that is he," said one acquaintance.) Goodyear's shabby appearance troubled his friends. DeForest, who was still in the textile business up in Naugatuck, met him in front of his former residence, the Holt Hotel. "Give me ten dollars, brother," Goodyear said. "I have pawned my last silver spoon to pay my fare to the city." DeForest, towering over his friend, said: "You must not go on so; you cannot live in this way." But like any gambler, Goodyear could not stop from rolling the dice again.

On one of his visits to Manhattan, Goodyear stopped in again at the Roxbury India Rubber Company store and met John Haskins, who had been one of the original stockholders in the company. Goodyear showed Haskins his rubber goods treated with nitric acid gas. Haskins was encouraging and invited him to Roxbury.

It was in Roxbury that the rubber boom had begun and ended. The crash had consumed all the invested capital, thrown hundreds of people out of work in Massachusetts and sent the business into such a tailspin that thousands of tons of rubber were either given away or sold at ruinous prices. Bonfires proved the best solution to the stench of decomposing rubber in the summer of 1835. As a local historian wrote, "Hilltops blazed with its ignited masses, and the illuminations of the Fourth of July succeeding the failure were made unusually brilliant by the aid of the India-rubber panic."

Only the Roxbury Company managed to survive. In 1836 its managers mounted one last desperate effort to succeed. They gave mechanic and founding stockholder Chaffee the go-ahead to build a $30,000 coating machine nicknamed "The Monster." It was an evolutionary descendant of prior coating machines that used steam-heated iron rolls rotating at different speeds to tear and soften rubber until it obediently flattened into smooth sheets. Until this time all rubber-coated fabric had been made by applying dissolved rubber onto a textile. Now, Chaffee hoped his sheets of rubber could be affixed directly to the textile without being dissolved and liquefied first.

It worked. The Monster saved the company thirty-six barrels of 80-cents-a-gallon turpentine every week, or about $50,000 a year. The machine's four rollers, each six feet long, seemed finally to have the power to bring rubber to heel, to force it to do as commanded. Goodyear later wrote, "The invention of this machine resuscitated the Roxbury Company, and caused the stock to advance to par, after nearly the whole capital of the company had been sunk in fruitless attempts to manufacture the goods with solvents." Without the solvents and the stickiness with which they encumbered the finished products, along with the problems of decomposition, all troubles would be surmounted and "the gum would be at least as good as in its native state."

Charles Goodyear, now regarded as rubber's Don Quixote, was intrigued with the idea of visiting the Roxbury Company. He wanted to learn what he could about its Monster and to demonstrate the value of his own acid-gas process. An idea germinated, a fantasy in which Goodyear, financed by new backers, breathed life into the rotting corpse of the Roxbury Company, and Goodyear and his family became its new owners. With Haskins' help it might just be possible. The whole visit would be ripe with opportunity and smoothed by friendly familiar faces. Roxbury was the last redoubt of the American rubber business; the Monster was its iron savior; Goodyear himself could become the resident genius of the renaissance.

Charles couldn't tell Clarissa the full scope of his plan; she would despair. He couldn't write to DeForest; his friend would think him mad.

CHAPTER THREE

The Scent of Brimstone

*A*t the time they met in New York, William F. Ely, who eventually became the mystery man in Charles Goodyear's life, was in his mid-twenties, had served in the Army and had inherited a substantial sum of money, probably around $10,000. He was very likely engaged in the clothing or textile manufacturing business and probably ran into Goodyear at the Mechanics Society. Although neither was a member, they were able to rub elbows and trade stories with other like-minded craftsmen and entrepreneurs. The exhibitions and competitions held by the society also provided information about business and a chance to make useful contacts. Ely was subjected to what by now was Goodyear's familiar routine: a stirring evocation of the vast potential of rubber, a recitation of Goodyear's own experiments leading to his acid breakthrough, a request for the one last investment that would bring the dream of a rubber empire to fruition, and his honor-clad intention to pay back all he owed with interest. In the first draft of a memoir he wrote later on, Goodyear delivers homage in the most sentimental terms to the "good hearts" that helped him in times of need: William DeForest, James DeForest, Ralph Steele, Silas Carle and John Sexton. Even people who later turned against Goodyear are thanked. All except for William F. Ely, who for many years was Goodyear's dearest and most intimate friend.

Soon after they met, Goodyear convinced Ely that he had reached the edge of success and Ely became his partner. The business relationship between the two started out as an amorphous verbal agreement with Ely giving money to Goodyear to patent the acid process and drum up sales. In late February, with Ely paying Goodyear's legal fees and travel expenses to Washington, D.C., everything looked sunny for the budding enterprise. "Whether I shall come off with all the patronage I expect, remains to be proved; but that I shall lay the foundation for heavy operations—put that down certain," Goodyear reported. Although Goodyear's virtual penury during the previous several years had not altered his perception of himself as the most important man in the rubber business, when he set off to patent his acid-gas process in early 1837 after joining forces with Ely, his thirst for publicity surged. He delivered a printed rubber fabric and some rubber bandages to President Andrew Jackson. To Senators Henry Clay of Kentucky and John C. Calhoun of South Carolina he sent samples of rubber and rubber-coated fabrics, which they returned with notes of gratitude.

For a poor man who was chronically dependent on other people's money, Goodyear did not seem to be fazed by the public's obvious skepticism about rubber. With everything in order for the patent filing, Goodyear wrote Ely saying that he was in no hurry to arrange sales prematurely but hinting that there were plenty of potential customers. "It's hard work to keep buyers off," he wrote. But Goodyear also nourished secret dreams of wealth, fueled by stories of riches from deals with a wealthy European royal. "I have become well acquainted with the young man Cochran, who took $50,000 from the hands of the Grand Turk for a single pistol, and expects some millions more," he wrote of another investor. The idea that he could make a fortune in Europe was one that Goodyear had communicated to Ely and one he would cling to.

After Goodyear had returned from Washington, he and Ely formalized their working relationship, framing a contract in which they would share equally in the proceeds of the acid-gas process and Ely would pay all the legal costs incurred by their patent agent, Thomas P. Jones. In June, Goodyear and Ely signed another contract under which Ely agreed to finance the production of rubber goods made by Goodyear on Staten Island, with Goodyear acting as Ely's agent, in exchange for 50 percent of the proceeds. Goodyear agreed to superintend the manufacturing operation and "to devote his time and attention to carry on the said business profitably." On the same day, Goodyear and Ely executed still another agreement under which Ely promised within a year to pay off $6,000 of notes signed by Goodyear and held by Ballard, or, if that wasn't possible, after a year to pay Goodyear $6,000 in cash. In exchange, Goodyear promised to convey to Ely a 25 percent interest in a patent right "for an improvement in the manufacture of the substance commonly called India rubber." It isn't clear what the improvement was or how it was related to the acid-gas patent, but any breach of the agreement triggered a $10,000 penalty.

By late summer 1837 everything was in place for Goodyear's planned visit to the Roxbury Company to see the Monster in action and to show off his acid-gas process. He decided to take his father with him on the three-to-five-day trip. Amasa had hardly ever left Staten Island since the family had moved there; Charles thought that accompanying him might help lift his father's spirits. But the departure from Staten Island pained Charles deeply because of the dismal state of his extended family. His mother, brothers Henry and Robert, Robert's family, Clarissa and their children all remained behind. He told them that he very much wanted to take them with him and begin a new life in the Boston area, but that wasn't yet possible. Clarissa had only fifty cents on hand when Charles left; otherwise she was dependent on selling rubber goods or household possessions to pay for food.

Once he was traveling, Goodyear's mood improved. The three-day journey even triggered his buried sense of playfulness. He had thought that Roxbury was miles away from Boston rather than part of the city: "I conclude India Rubber destroys the memory; truth is, I haven't had any."

Goodyear arrived in Boston not as a supplicant but as a self-promoted captain of the industry. Already he considered his acid process, and possibly the Roxbury Company's Monster machine, as the twin pillars of a future rubber empire. That was saying a lot for a process from which hardly a dime had been made and for a costly machine that hadn't even started paying for itself. But the new financing from and partnership with earnest young Ely— most of the young man's $10,000 inheritance was now pledged to Goodyear— buoyed his spirits.

The reality was that the Roxbury Company, which occupied a three-story building, was winding down its operations when Goodyear arrived. Parts of the building were already advertised as being for rent. The Monster, housed in a separate building, had arrived too late to save the company, which had run out of cash and credit and was preparing to shut its doors. A skeleton staff remained to fill the last of the company's orders for sheet rubber, and after that the banks and other creditors would oversee the sale of the equipment. So what had been in Goodyear's mind a revived and still-promising rubber business was instead a dejected staff awaiting the end. No one rolled out the red carpet for him. The Roxbury staff and managers, most of whom had suffered financial disaster, were not happy to allow Goodyear use of the facilities, which is what he had expected after his conversation with Haskins in New York about the new acid-gas process. The company's manager, Samuel Armstrong, and chief mechanic and inventor of the Monster, Edwin Chaffee, greeted him coolly.

Goodyear had hoped to be given sheet rubber on credit and then to treat it using his acid-gas process. He had never had access to large quantities of well-prepared sheet rubber like that the Monster could produce. In Goodyear's view the possibility that his revolutionary new process would reignite the industry should have been enough to convince Armstrong and Chaffee to let him have the rubber on credit. "I have come here to avail myself of the facilities offered by yourself. Mr. Armstrong, you have apparently changed your mind. I shall not leave until I know the cause. Who are the Roxbury Company? I find them, or I transact my business with their agent."

Later in the same day, Armstrong and Chaffee were more receptive. "Mr. Goodyear," he recalled being told. "We are ready to do anything to serve you." Instead of offering him sheet rubber on credit, however, they offered to trade the right to use Goodyear's process for stock in the company, which was worthless, and offered him a sample spread of rubber fabric rolled out of the Monster.

Goodyear didn't want to decide on the trade; he wanted his sheet rubber. "I will answer you that question another day," Goodyear told them. "First fill this order, be reasonable."

Goodyear requested that the Roxbury Company provide him with 2,000 yards of umbrella cloth, 2,000 yards of carpeting cloth and 1,000 yards of sheet gum, all in specified weights. But the Roxbury Company expected to be paid $370 up front. Goodyear anticipated that Ely would be upset by such a large and unexpected expense. He appealed to Ely to stay calm. "Keep cool," he said.

Before Ely's money arrived, Goodyear, hot with excitement, hatched an even more costly plan. He believed he could buy out the Roxbury Company's factory and equipment at bargain prices. Goodyear wrote Ely that the Roxbury Company would have sold the Monster and the building housing it for $30,000 and maybe for half as much had they not learned of Goodyear's acid-gas process. The company's present owners "have not the shadow of a prospect, and the agents in possession are ready to live upon and then abandon the ranch (this to ourselves)." Through Haskins' kind offices Chaffee had already begun helping and working for Goodyear, who toured the factory and made some trial patches of rubber. Goodyear pronounced his own samples "the best silk melted; my favorite sheet bears the baking, and proves the fact that we can make patent cloth and leather to his entire satisfaction—mine, of course."

Since Ely had not yet sent the $370 needed to start the work on the sheet rubber, he should consider the great opportunity at hand, Goodyear said, encouraging his partner to send the funds. But Ely had already signed a contract to pay $6,000 for a completely different rubber business venture, on Staten Island, not in Boston. And now Goodyear was asking for $370 more and talking about buying out the Roxbury plant. Where was this heading?

Goodyear impatiently suggested that they would be able to buy out the Roxbury Company's equipment and then, once his breakthrough acid-gas process was publicized and old prejudices against rubber were overcome, they could hold a new stock offering to raise funds from outside investors. Ely wasn't so confident that the Roxbury owners would do as Goodyear wanted. Goodyear assured him, "If your ideas of gum are not high enough, come—they know what rubber is—and hear them give in." He added that he believed shares in Goodyear and Ely's new rubber venture, despite Boston area investors' recent rubber-stock wipeout, nonetheless had a greater chance of selling in Boston. "I am not sure but a stock would be taken up sooner here than in New York."

Just send the money, Goodyear wrote, and good fortune would rain down on them: "Nothing is wanting but the cloth and a few funds to fill this order." As soon as the rubber material was in hand, a wave of successful sales would carry Goodyear and Ely across the Atlantic: "We only want a stock of goods from this machinery; we can then arrange things in this country, quick time. Then for old England, France, Emp. of Austria, and the Autocrat."

By October 5, Ely had sent more money to Goodyear, who then attempted to provide an accounting of a sort. The $100 spent so far "enabled me to leave with decency, has renewed the age of my father (between coal and gum at least one hundred years)." Goodyear was referring to his father's gathering of coal to keep the family warm and the stressful effects of Charles' rubber work. In other words, broken Amasa had been refreshed by the experience of living with Charles (and off Ely) in Boston. The money provided by Ely also permitted Goodyear to conduct business and present himself as a respectable inventor and businessman rather than a scuffed and impoverished eccentric. In Goodyear's words, the money helped him to "form an independent acquaintance of the first stamp."

The unrequested accounting to Ely was "intended for an apology for fingers which are not sticky enough to hold cash, all of which, I know, you do not require." But Goodyear offered the accounting, apparently, because Ely was short of cash and had debts, too.

As he nervously played his hand in Roxbury, and confided in and manipulated Ely, Goodyear's heart suddenly flooded with remorse over his family. Near the end of one letter he asked Ely not to tell Clarissa he had received Charles' letter. "Don't tell Mrs. G. I write you first," he said, but not because "I love her, she knows it." The purpose of the fib would be to prevent Clarissa from being hurt or misperceiving her husband's priorities. He realized he must remain in Boston indefinitely although he had told his family he was on a limited trip. And he owed so much money on Staten Island and in New York that he feared another stint in debtor's prison if he returned.

Finally, after a month Goodyear could stand it no more. He had been deceiving Clarissa for weeks by not telling her that he did not intend to return to New York or Staten Island and that he was more deeply committed to the rubber business than ever. Goodyear asked Ely to pay to bring his family to Boston, cannily offering to send back some of the money he had already received from Ely for his business trip so that Ely could use it to pay for their transportation:

> Your favor with $140, is at hand, which makes me quite comfortable. I am not at all certain that I shall not return a part of it with a request that you will accompany my wife and children to Roxbury. I can't say which of you I want to see most. I fear I carry the joke too far with Mrs. G. Physical evils she can endure like a heroine, and they do not harm; but, unlike ourselves, if she encounters other trials, she is in no way qualified to endure them.
>
> Excuse me for perplexing you with private matters, as I may in my next. But Mrs. G. must leave Staten Island, and who can shield me from the charge of an absconded debtor? It is impossible for me to think on returning until I have accomplished my object, and she cannot remain there until then.

Goodyear was preoccupied with getting the Roxbury Company assets again. Buying low involved a delicate manipulation, including paying journalists to place stories in a local Boston newspaper. He had arranged an interview with a Mr. Simmonds, who held a quarter of the Roxbury Company's stock and whose favor would be needed if a deal was to be struck. "I do not know that you yet understand what I would be after," Goodyear wrote Ely. "I have so far aimed to secure Chaffee's influence, and so much of the public's as to gain their attention in the right way, at the same time not raise so much steam as to induce them to fix big prices." He noted that the company's agents had kept the stockholders "in a fog" and Haskins, Simmonds and other stockholders remained unaware that he wanted to buy the company to put his patented process into production: "I am astonished at their ignorance of my doings and the manner in which they stare at my [rubber] patches."

Goodyear never explained how his ambition to buy the Roxbury assets squared with his attempt to mythologize himself as a "pure" inventor. Or exactly how he planned to finance his acquisition of those assets. He and Ely could barely scrape together enough money to buy supplies and to live, but reality was no hindrance. When Ely sent the $370, Goodyear paid in advance for cloth and sheet rubber from the Roxbury Company and then assured Ely he would soon start shipping him product to sell in New York. Ely's resources were dwindling and Goodyear was destitute: "I shall pledge myself that by this aid of a kind Providence I shall be able to satisfy the reasonable or unreasonable expectations of the world as to gum." Meanwhile, Goodyear worked hard to keep Ely enthused. Chief mechanic Chaffee had lately displayed a friendlier attitude toward Goodyear, who repeated the compliments to Ely, adding: "We may be flattered when such authority comes out on our side."

Meanwhile, Goodyear sent a letter to Clarissa with $10 enclosed from the money Ely had given him. He continued to charge his room and board in Boston in the expectation that Ely would pay the bills later. And he kept pressing his partner and benefactor to bring his family to Boston. "When may I expect you with them; I am so conscience smitten on this score that I shall keep a fund in reserve for this purpose in preference to anything else, else how can I prosper any way." Four days later, he told Ely that if he couldn't escort the family personally he could simply put them on a steamer to Providence where Goodyear would come to meet them. Ely should just give Clarissa $12 and send them in the charge of the ship's captain or some other man. "Mrs. G. is ill provided for the cold weather," he said. Within a few days Ely agreed to bring the Goodyears to Providence or as far as Boston.

Clarissa had dressed the children for the trip in clothes made from fabric she traded for at a Staten Island grocery store. Ellen, as the oldest, and Cynthia, second oldest, helped look after Charles Jr. and little William

Henry during the steamboat trip to New England. Her mother-in-law, Cynthia, also helped with the children and the luggage. Charles' younger brothers Nelson and Amasa Jr. also arrived. When the family reached Boston, they found that Charles had arranged for them to live in a boarding house in Roxbury, called Norfolk House. The spare apartments, which had beds and simple furniture, were a far cry from the home they had once known in Philadelphia, but it was an improvement over the ramshackle factory grounds saltbox on Staten Island. Curtains and other small touches made a difference. The family, which had all been sharing the same bedroom, now had one additional room. But lest anyone forget what controlled their lives, when they arrived they found the tables loaded with rubber fabrics Charles had prepared for exhibit. Already he was using the modest apartment as a workshop and warehouse, and people involved in the rubber trade began to drop by looking for Charles even as the family unpacked. Charles was preoccupied as usual but noticed that his father, now over sixty, looked much older than he had remembered when the two had left for Boston.

The Goodyears settled into a new routine. Clarissa involved herself in a congregation to which the Goodyears had been admitted, attending meetings of the church benevolent societies with better-dressed and socially more substantial women. She had only plain calico to wear until an old gentleman the Goodyears met made her a gift of a black bombazine dress. She remained resourceful, taking brown silk whose pattern Charles had used to emboss rubber in the shop and making a dress out of it for one of the girls.

The family resumed their Bible reading and Charles was rewarded with the simple domestic intimacy that he craved. Clarissa, the children and his parents all still were expected to pitch in with work, making rubber wares at home. But there were moments of repose, too, especially on Sunday. He often brought home little surprise gifts for the children, all of whom were healthy. When he played with them, he could be silly and self-mocking. His sense of the ridiculous even let him laugh at their poverty. Willie, as they called William Henry, was two years old and once tried to put on his shoe by crowding a fat foot through a big hole in the toe. Charles, who with his family made many hundreds of pairs of rubber shoes, was especially amused by this incident and retold it often in years ahead.

Financed by Ely, the extended Goodyear family regained its ballast. The Philadelphia hardware store disaster had stripped the family of one business identity and now, years later, Charles had provided another. At home the Goodyears ate from the same pot and sat by the same fire. At work, Nelson and Amasa Jr. considered themselves rubber men, like their older brother.

Armstrong and Chaffee finally made two thousand yards of sheet rubber for Goodyear, but until he could make things to sell he needed more money. Goodyear joked his way into yet another request of Ely. "I know of nothing in the way now to be genteel—good morning your majesties—unless it be the pocket money, say $100, $50, $25, $000,000,000,000,000,000, will do in a pinch, until the goods are done, then we will find ways enough to settle the Roxbury bill."

Ely and Goodyear decided Ely should come to Boston so they could all work together more closely. They rented a warehouse/store at 12 Water Street in Boston, planning to sell the rubber products there instead of in New York. The idea of buying the Roxbury Company faded as Goodyear concentrated on refining his methods of treating the rubber with acid.

Goodyear rented one of the rooms at the Roxbury building, put his freshly rolled sheet rubber there and filled tubs with acid. He put some of the company's under-occupied staff to work making coats, carpets, and piano and table covers. He decorated the products by stamping them with carved wooden blocks, leaving an impression in the surface. Goodyear also made rubber capes, laying thread across the rubber fabric in diamond patterns to strengthen the composite and give it a more pleasing texture and appearance.

At this point he saw his sheet rubber primarily as a textile, considering its weight and texture by holding plies between his thumb and forefinger and tracing his fingertips over its surface. But soon other uses for rubber began to spring into his mind. Most rubber produced at the time was naturally gray or gray-brown. To blacken it, rubber makers added lampblack. Goodyear believed rubber had to be brightened and made more interesting if it was going to regain favor with consumers. He brought packages of red, white and green paint to the Roxbury Company and tried to find ways to color his rubber. He also saw the rubber surface as an inviting blank sheet waiting to be engraved with drawings or words. He took some sheet rubber to a printer and had maps printed on it.

Still picturing himself as a rubber mogul in the making, Goodyear made himself the hub of much activity at the Roxbury plant and a source of irritation to those around him. In the rubber factory, he often was more of an apprentice than a journeyman, watching carefully the craftsmanship of his resourceful workers and claiming ownership of new techniques that they devised. Other business owners had been known to patent new processes in the names of their workers rather than claiming corporate ownership. Not Goodyear. Not even in someone else's house. Goodyear told L. S. Maring that he needed all the help he could find with his rubber experiments and he "was poor, but meant to be rich, and when he was would do what was right by those who worked for him, but was too poor to pay them then." After he had made a rubber shoe that Goodyear admired and then strengthened it by laying in a mesh-like cloth between two thicknesses of rubber, Maring said, "Mr. Goodyear agreed with me for a certain salary for a certain number of years, to say nothing and allow him to get a patent for it." The patent was granted July 24, 1838, and Maring would spend years trying to claim the pay he had been promised from Goodyear.

As Goodyear tried different ways of treating the rubber, the flaws of his patented acid-gas process and of curing rubber with acids became clearer. He had been immersing his rubber in baths of cold acid, but the process took a long time and the acid did not penetrate deeply beyond the surface of the rubber or change equally all areas of the surface. Some areas of the rubber came out ruined, and too much acid was needed. Placing rubber in cold acid was too passive. To treat the rubber more effectively with the acid gasses, Goodyear's workers devised a system of delivering the gas from a boiling kettle of acids through pipes into a closed room. The toxic vapors helped cure the rubber surface but the effect still wasn't perfect.

John Nash, another Roxbury worker employed on a pay-you-later basis, tried to solve the problem. He brewed a mix so potent it might have been the devil's own digestive juices. Combining equal parts of nitric and hydrochloric acid (a small splash would eat right through a shirt) and adding a dash of antimony, Nash brought the mixture to a boil. Then he immersed the rubber in it. Within a minute, the liquor effected a far-reaching change, smoothing and drying the surface. Nash claimed to have discovered an important new process, but Goodyear insisted the discovery belonged to him on the grounds that he employed Nash. The two men took their dispute to Armstrong. "They came into the office and referred the matter to me to settle the differences between them; I declined doing anything about it, and told them they had better arrange their own matters," Armstrong later recalled. Goodyear and Nash agreed the method would be considered Goodyear's property and that Goodyear would pay Nash later.

Meanwhile, Ely was holding the fort at 12 Water Street, the store he and Goodyear had rented. Sales of rubber aprons and piano covers remained slow. Goodyear came around sometimes, but for the most part he stayed focused on the workshop.

Consumers previously suspicious of anything rubber gradually began to come around, and sales at Goodyear and Ely's Fancy Rubber Establishment picked up. In addition to the rubber-coated fabric goods, such as coats, carpets and capes, Goodyear and Ely sold rubber or rubber-coated bathing tubs, portmanteaus, life preservers and mailbags. "The prejudices of the public gave way," Goodyear later wrote, and he described his fortunes at this time as "altogether in the ascendant." A tireless marketer and promoter, he asked the editor of the *Boston Courier* to print "a few copies of your paper upon the gum elastic fabric I herewith send you." To convince the man to take the risk, he let it be known that the newspaper would be sent to "courts in Europe" with other samples. "As I have prepared some specimens to forward to several courts in Europe, with your aid, I will add to them a newspaper." And then another boast about his new process: "The change wrought in the gum by this improvement, makes it in reality a new material.... I am now prepared to satisfy the public that there is a wide field opened."

Apparently, he had already been softening up the editors of the *Courier* with gifts. On June 19, in an article headlined "Another New Thing under the Sun," the writer noted that a rubber map of New York City "hangs in our counting room" and is "particularly worthy of notice." The story went on: "Mr. Goodyear has a new way of preparing the article which deprives it of the adhesive quality which in most other preparations has been an objection and he also has deprived it of all those obnoxious smells which have prevailed in some articles we have purchased some year or two ago."

But patent licenses still paid more bills in the Goodyear home than did retail sales. The acid-gas process's shortcoming was obvious—it only treated surfaces—but it was all Goodyear had and it worked well enough with thin rubber sheet and lighter-gauge rubber-coated fabric. Combining his acid process with Maring's method of shoe construction, Goodyear obtained a patent (No. 849) on July 24, 1838, and licensed it to two businessmen in Providence. He also sold an acid-gas license to Luther Clark of Northampton for making carriage cloths.

Goodyear had by now worn out his welcome at the Roxbury India Rubber Company. He and Ely had burned through two or three thousand dollars of credit for sheets of rubber and use of the premises. In early 1838, Armstrong told Goodyear he had to leave. No amount of goodwill from Haskins, the optimist charmed by Goodyear's monomaniacal ardor, could prevent it. Years later Armstrong remembered Goodyear and Ely's unpaid debts and said that the pair never sold much of anything at their store and that Ely only pretended to be Goodyear's partner. But the comment by Armstrong that was most often quoted was his assertion that "Goodyear would get tired of building castles in the air after a while." He couldn't have been more wrong. The castles were built of rubber.

Without a workshop or a source of rubber sheet, Goodyear turned to a man he had met either at his downtown Boston store or at the Roxbury factory. Fat-necked Nathaniel Hayward was a former stable operator from Easton, Massachusetts, who had actually been doing what Goodyear was attempting to do, breathe new life into the rubber business and in the process create a future for himself. His similarities to Goodyear—one writer called them "kindred spirits"—began and ended with their rubber-making masochism. Despite his single-mindedness, Goodyear was literate and worldly; Hayward didn't learn to read until late in life. Hayward was respected by tradesmen in his field; Goodyear was a fringe figure. To Hayward, who was plainspoken and trusting, Goodyear was Mephistophelean, guileful and unworthy of trust. And Goodyear, who once decried Hayward's "treachery," brought out the worst in Hayward: timidity, gullibility, resentment, deceit and, eventually, jealousy over their respective claims on a place in industrial history. Even after Goodyear was dead and he himself was a wealthy rubber industry potentate, Hayward continued to catalogue and publish the injuries he had suffered at Goodyear's hands.

Hayward was in many ways the quintessential ruffian industrialist. Born in 1808, he went to Boston while still a youth and operated a livery stable, living in a building attached to the stable. Ambitious and mechanically inclined, he was aroused by the talk of fortunes to be made in rubber during the miracle substance's first boom. "By considerable excitement about the Roxbury Company, they were making a great deal of money, and being sick of my own business, set me thinking about this rubber business," he wrote later in life. Hayward sold his stable and went back home to Easton with the same goal that obsessed Goodyear: finding a way to keep the rubber from decomposing and becoming sticky in summer. With $500 and a horse and buggy, he shut himself up in a mill and experimented for two months. After spending time trying to make a waterproof shoe blacking with India rubber, he started to work with India rubber fabric. People in the rubber business who saw Hayward's samples told him he "could depend on being well rewarded." Nothing of immediate consequence resulted, but his wish for success in the rubber business penetrated his deepest thoughts. One night in August 1834, Hayward had a dream that rubber, sulfur and lamp-black were "all that were necessary to make India Rubber." Still he made no progress. He decided to make one final attempt by mixing all the chemicals he had in a nauseating blend—white vitriol, blue vitriol, sugar of lead, sulfur, and miscellaneous other chemicals—and dissolving his rubber in it. The fiendish brew yielded promising results. He showed the rubber cloth he had made to the Eagle India Rubber Company in Woburn, a leather-making and shoemaking town about fifteen miles north of Boston. The Eagle Company immediately offered him a job. After going back to prove he could repeat what he had made before, Hayward accepted the job at an annual salary of $1,000 and moved into a clapboard house a short walk from the factory.

Its proximity to the forests of New Hampshire, and the tree bark needed for tanning acids, favored Woburn's leather-making operations. The fast-flowing Aberjona River, a mile or so outside the town center, and the flat, silty land stretching out from its banks attracted New England's usual complement of mill operators and manufacturers. Woburn, sometimes called Woburn Plains, also knew the importance of transportation, for like the Naugatuck River, the Aberjona could not support commercial navigation. The Middlesex Canal ran down the town's center and connected Woburn to Boston and the textile center in Lowell. Small shops and factories with as many as fifty employees abounded and the town's sense of its place in the industrial-technological future was such that for a while, in the early 1800s, it called itself Fultonville after the steamship innovator.

The area's economy was still sputtering from the recession of 1829 when several leading area businessmen, in March 1830, formed the Woburn Agricultural and Manufacturing Association. Its industrial development program would pump funds into two spectacular flops: silk and rubber.

The silk venture can best be described as a voyage into the theoretical. Silk worms had not been known to spin their cocoons on mulberry trees very prolifically outside of Asian climates. Nonetheless, the Woburn Association set aside hundreds of silty acres on the banks of the Aberjona and bought and planted ten thousand mulberries. When the silkworms, apparently immobilized by the bitter New England cold, refused to do their work, the trees were sold off for pennies apiece. What possessed the sensible industrialists of Woburn to flush their money away on silk farming puzzled generations that followed. It proved that usually prudent farmers and shoemakers could "occasionally lay down their common sense," in the words of local historian Tom Smith: "This was a sheltering environment for the lunatic fringe."

The Eagle India Rubber Company was also toting up its losses when Hayward arrived. Yet rubber was more tractable than silk. In his spare time, Hayward again played chemical mix-and-match. After trying to whiten some rubber aprons with sulfur fumes, he found that the aprons endured heat much better after the exposure. He also found that sprinkling rubber fabric with sulfur and exposing it to the sun prevented melting. That process was later dubbed "solarization," but it had more to do with the sulfur than with the sun. Sulfur, or brimstone, as it was called in the Bible, was a plentiful element known to be a useful drying agent. Neither Hayward nor anyone else in the rubber business knew it, but sulfur combines readily with many other elements and is second only to carbon in its ability to bond to itself. That self-bonding ability allows sulfur to form ring systems and chain structures that exist in many common useful compounds. At the time, knowledge of molecular structure was still in a primitive stage of development.

In the fall of 1837, the Eagle Company was at the end of its line. Hayward and a partner bought out the factory and equipment and worked together for ten months. The assets consisted mainly of factory and storage space, vats and some rolling machines. Hayward dipped and dusted rubber with all kinds of things, making rubber covers and garments, doing anything he could to generate income while fiddling with the stuff to see if he could improve it. Then Hayward sold his interest and worked as an employee for a while until he again bought out the owners, probably for back wages owed, and forged ahead by himself in the spring of 1838. During this period, Hayward and his brother Martin sold rubber-working machinery to the Roxbury Company. The Haywards had a large tub with churning blades for mixing turpentine and rubber, stills for distilling spirits of turpentine and another vessel with holes for straining turpentine. One of the machines, a spreading or knife machine, may in fact have been the inspiration for Chaffee's Monster. It had three internally heated rollers. Rubber was fed between two of the hot, spinning rollers to complete the grinding and tearing to produce a consistent dough. This dough was then pushed into contact with a flat-edged spreader and forced between two of the rollers to create a thin sheet. Both Haskins and Chaffee were acquainted with the Haywards and their machines.

On March 27, 1838, Jacob Richardson, one of the former directors of the Eagle Company, wrote Hayward that "Mr. Goodyear, of the fancy rubber establishment" wanted two or three hundred yards of cloth coated with white rubber. Ely was going to come see Hayward about it, Richardson wrote, "but I thought you had better come to the city and make a bargain with them yourself; your cloth is whiter than any they make, and I think than they can make."

Goodyear was more than willing to travel up to Woburn to the Eagle factory, not far from the railroad station. "They would undoubtedly like to find out your method of doing it, and see your machinery," said Richardson. "I am not yet convinced that they possess a vast superiority in their knowledge of rubber, over what you do. I think you can make a grand job, in taking their cloth to spread, and should like to see you this week, if convenient."

Goodyear needed to show "the Roxbury folks" that he was not dependent on them, Richardson said. Showing some pride over who had the stuff when it came to rubber, he declared: "We shall have the credit of whatever is done at our place," and then as an afterthought added: "I mean the credit to the reputation of the Eagle Company, not in interest."

In April, Charles and his father, Amasa, once again set off on a business trip, driving a chaise to Woburn to find Hayward at the Eagle Company's premises. They intended to offer to buy the plant—the financing would obviously have to be creative—but soon learned that Hayward was a hard bargainer. No immediate deal was struck.

A few weeks later, Hayward called on Goodyear at his Boston store. According to one account, Hayward praised Goodyear and told him he had advanced the state of rubber making ahead of all others, especially when it came to color and finish quality. But whatever compliments he offered, Hayward didn't admire the short shelf life of some samples of Goodyear's rubber fabric. As he later said: "His samples were white, brown, some transparent, and some bronze or gilt on pure gum. I nailed them up beside some of my own black fabric in the sun and weather. Goodyear's did not last more than three or four weeks; they melted and became sticky, and wasted away with the weather." Goodyear's samples lacked the curing and drying that sulfur provided.

Hayward went to bed that night knowing he was still the leader in the quest to manufacture long-lasting rubber. In July 1838, Goodyear sent him an order for thirty yards of yard-wide sheet rubber. Hayward didn't want

Goodyear to get wind of his sulfur method so he filled the order without using the sulfuring process. The quality was poor. Hayward needed to make the sale and wanted to give a good account of his prowess. So he then made another sheet of rubber using sulfur, and Goodyear, he wrote, pronounced it "very nice, just what he wanted." They completed the sale on August 11.

While handling Hayward's rubber cloth, Goodyear picked up the scent of the brimstone and traveled to Woburn several times to see the plant. But Hayward didn't let him in, although he continued to sell Goodyear rubber cloth. "At one of his visits to my factory, after snuffling at my cloth, he asked me if I used sulphur in the manufacture of my goods," he reported. But Hayward brushed the question away by indicating that if he used sulfur the "smell would be offensive."

Goodyear would not be put off. "Hayward," he demanded. "I want you to tell me if you use sulfur or not; if you have not used it, I want you to say so." Pressing hard for a confession, Goodyear threatened to take the idea of using sulfur for himself. Hayward later noted, "He said if I did not use sulphur he intended to get a patent for using it, as he had found out it worked well with rubber."

Hayward then gave in and told Goodyear his whole story, saying that he, who could not write, intended to get a patent for it as soon as he was able. Then the two men began talking about ways to do business together. One of them involved Goodyear taking over the Eagle Company from Hayward. On September 17, 1838, Hayward sold the remnants of the Eagle India Rubber Company to Goodyear and agreed to work for him for one year at a salary of $800—provided they could generate the money through the sale of rubber goods.

The two men also discussed ways to speed up patenting Hayward's sulfur method. Hayward had no experience with patents, and they agreed that Goodyear, a patent veteran with an agent in Washington, D.C., who handled the legal procedures, would step in to help. Goodyear would do all the work in getting Hayward's sulfur and sulfur-solarization process patented for him, and then Hayward would assign his interest in the patent to Goodyear. Goodyear's part of the bargain was to pay the costs of getting Hayward's patent, pay Hayward $100 down and give him a note for $900, due in six months. The arrangement would allow Hayward to make and sell three hundred yards of rubber cloth a day until Goodyear came across with another $2,000. When that payment was made, Goodyear was to own the sulfur patent completely.

But then Goodyear suddenly changed the plan. He said that his patent agent, Thomas Jones, had told him that legal complications required that Goodyear take out the patent under his own name. After some hesitation, Hayward consented, provided such a course would not invalidate any part of their previous agreement. Goodyear said the deal would be the same and on November 23, the patent became his.

The two men began doing business together, but threads of mistrust ran all through their dealings. Goodyear always owed Hayward money for something, but he also enjoyed a certain power over Hayward. Although he was theoretically Hayward's employer, Goodyear treated him more like a partner working in exchange for equity.

In the shop, Hayward upped the amount of sulfur he used to dry his rubber cloth. He had used a total of only four ounces of sulfur in the previous eighteen months, but now he and Goodyear started packing pounds of it into their rubber. They also exposed their sulfur-treated rubber fabric and products to the sun, which dried and toughened the surface somewhat. Sun-exposed, sulfur-fumigated fabrics would "stand firm," in Hayward's words, while others would "melt and become sticky."

Combining Goodyear's acid-gas process with Hayward's sulfur and solarization methods, they churned out life preservers, cushions, beds, tents, shoes and mailbags. The two men won an order that seemed to confer all the respectability they craved: a contract from the U.S. Postal Service for 150 mailbags. Goodyear quickly trumpeted the news to the *Boston Post*, which ran a short story praising the postmaster general for availing himself of "every economical improvement" by giving Goodyear "a liberal order" for "impervious mail bags, upon trial."

The *Post* described the wonderful qualities of Goodyear's rubber and said that "should it be successfully applied as a substitute for leather and to canvas for ships, it is destined to produce important effects in trade and commerce." Goodyear had done a good job on the writer.

CHAPTER FOUR

The Remarkable Providence

With the mailbag contract, Goodyear thought he had finally begun "a successful career for the future." The reputation of his acid-gas process was established; with the addition of Nathaniel Hayward's sulfuring techniques, he believed that he could now transform rubber into the miracle substance he had always known it could be. So confident was Goodyear when the mailbag order arrived that his artistic side sprang to life. He focused on the beauty of the bags, intended to protect mail from moisture, and he indiscriminately mixed in coloring ingredients to produce a leather-like hue.

When the bags were finished, he displayed them from hooks in a room at the Woburn factory and welcomed any visitors to take a look. He also sought publicity from local newspapers. Then, when he left town for two weeks, the bags "were discovered to be decomposing," as he later admitted. The handles could not even support the weight of the pouch, which dropped off. After all the boasting he had done, the federal mailbag order went unfilled. Even that setback didn't stop Goodyear and Hayward from trying to make other rubber products. They sold several thousand life preservers, treated with the acid-gas process and fumigated with sulfur. Again, beautification backfired. The coloring agents sped the collapse of the rubber. Both the pouches and the preservers were too thick for the acid process to penetrate below the surface of the rubber and the pouches degenerated from within.

So what had been represented to the public as a revolutionary discovery was actually a continuation of a previous failure. Goodyear stopped paying Hayward a salary, in violation of their agreement, and began to wind up his rubber work and shut down the Woburn factory. He tried to get money from his acid-gas process licensees, but they were disgusted by his failed mailbags and felt that they had already licensed a useless process.

THE REMARKABLE PROVIDENCE   57

Friends implored Goodyear to give up and told him he "could no longer expect the countenance or sympathy" he had become accustomed to. Durable rubber, they said, was a thing no more to be realized than perpetual motion. There was no reason to believe he would ever succeed.

His renewed income now cut off, Goodyear once again pawned his belongings and watched in dismay as those close to him suffered from their connection to his obsessive quest. Soon his family would have to vacate the Roxbury apartments at Norfolk House that had provided such a welcome respite after Staten Island. All the indignities of poverty were about to return to the Goodyears' day-to-day lives.

Clarissa, Charles' father and Amasa Jr. rose up in rebellion, demanding that Charles stop spending money on rubber and return to hardware and the blacksmith's trade. They had had enough of the privations and humiliations that rubber had brought them. Charles' quest seemed less like the God-given mission he implied it was, than an ungodly elevation of self, a vainglorious striving swaddled in halfhearted promises about the responsibility to take care of family and pay debts. By returning to the blacksmith and hardware trade, or hiring himself out as a laborer, Charles could at least restore some predictability to his family life. Amasa Sr. and Amasa Jr. had continued to work as blacksmiths, repairing and making tools and doing anything else to bring in cash. They hadn't gotten rich. But they had helped the Goodyears survive.

There was another troubling, unmentionable aspect to Charles' quest. The Goodyears had four wonderful children and their youngest, little William Henry, was fat and full of life. But Charles and Clarissa had already lost one beloved infant and two sweet toddlers since he began to work with rubber. Was God testing Charles' faith because he had made an idol of his ambition?

These questions swirled around the family's complex, intergenerational decision making. But Charles seemed curiously uninterested in the answers. Rationalizing that the costs of continuing to experiment were minimal ("a few sixpences at a time"), he continued to seek the cause of the recent failures. "As had happened on former occasions," he wrote later on, he "hardly had time enough to realize the extent of his embarrassment, before he became intently engaged with another experiment." While his wife and parents worried, he was again "buoyant with new hopes and expectations." He set out to find the cause of the mailbag fiasco so he could eventually fill the order, and he began to heat sulfur-treated rubber samples to find out what had gone wrong.

At 12 Water Street in Boston, meanwhile, his partner William Ely, momentarily obscured by Hayward, heat and sulfur, pondered his own chastened future from a more sober perspective. Still a young man, he began to think of rescue through a rich widow. Winter was coming. Chill had crept into the air and Ely kept just enough coal in a flat-topped stove standing in the middle of the store to keep from shivering. One day Samuel Armstrong, the crusty manager of the Roxbury Company, dropped in on his way to the company's own store on Washington Street a few blocks away. As usual, he wanted to know if Ely and Goodyear could come up with any more money to pay down some of their debt. As they talked, Ely clasped one of his partner's sulfur-saturated patches made in Woburn and absent-mindedly tore off a piece and tossed it toward the flat-topped stove. The two men finished their chat. When Armstrong returned an hour or so later, Ely pointed out that the patch had undergone a strange transformation. Blackened, it seemed more like a piece of cured and weathered leather than rubber fabric. "Ely appeared to be a good deal excited at the time, and thought it was a new feature in India rubber," Armstrong later said.

This new durability they observed was caused by something still unknown to the great European chemists of the time, who were stuck behind some major conceptual roadblocks. England's John Dalton had already figured out that because chemicals combined in specific ratios, matter was made of indivisible atoms. Other scientists of the nineteenth century also figured out that it was possible to piece together inorganic chemicals to make some of the many organic compounds found in living things. But they weren't sure how to classify and organize in their minds the large number of organic compounds that were being discovered. Was it best to look at what glued together atoms of carbon and hydrogen and other elements, or how the atoms arranged themselves? The answer would help tell scientists why substances with identical chemical profiles, the same number of atoms of hydrogen or carbon or oxygen, often exhibited differing properties that showed they were clearly not the same stuff.

The answers wouldn't come until two decades after Ely's accident with the stove, and like Hayward's idea to combine sulfur with rubber, the inspiration would be dreams. German chemist Friedrich August Kekulé said he was riding a bus in London one evening in the summer of 1854 when he daydreamed that a carbon atom could form chemical bonds with up to four other atoms and the carbon atoms could join to create long chains. The cry of the conductor awakened him from his reverie. A decade later, when Kekulé dozed off while warming himself beside a fireplace in Ghent, the atoms this time "gamboled" before his eyes and he saw long rows, all twining and twisting in a snake-like motion. One of the snakes had seized hold of its own tail, and the form "whirled mockingly before my eyes." With this inspiration Kekulé visualized a benzene molecule as six atoms of carbon arranged in a hexagon, with one atom of hydrogen latched on to each carbon node. It was an efficient geometry made possible partly by the amiability of carbon in attaching to another carbon atom. And it suggested to Kekulé that molecules could arrange themselves in three-dimensional structures, like tinker toys.

The rubber in rubber latex, the jungle milk that drained from slashes made in rubber trees, was chiefly hydrogen and carbon strung together in long, heavy molecular chains. In their natural state, these chains are two-dimensional and can be likened to spaghetti strands, which stir very easily when hot but stiffen and stick when cold. If the spaghetti is reheated, it can again be easily stirred. If you heat rubber, its chain molecules will start slipping and sliding away from one another, like the spaghetti strands, making it soft and gooey.

Modern chemists refer to the molecule chains as polymers and call the naturally occurring polymeric material that is rubber a thermoplastic, meaning that the material can be reshaped through heating.

The introduction of sulfur and heat into the quest for usable rubber changed everything. Sulfur is one of the most social elements on the periodic table, hardly existing except in combination with another substance. And, like carbon, one sulfur atom bonds with another. In all condensed forms of elemental sulfur, each atom is connected to two other sulfur atoms and the atoms tend to aggregate into rings.

When the sulfur-saturated patch of rubber was thrown onto the stove by Ely, the sulfur rings fell apart and their fragments joined with the long carbon and hydrogen chain molecules, the spaghetti strands, and locked onto them through a tight bond, actually sharing electrons with the atoms on the chain in what is called a covalent bond. Once locked in, the cured structure is a network of strong three-dimensional covalent bonds, a well-connected tinker toy, and it can't be reshaped by heating it up again. It is actually now one big molecule. It holds together no matter what you do to it by stretching or applying more heat or cold or solvents.

Goodyear, Ely, Hayward, Haskins and Chaffee were not completely in the dark about chemistry, but neither they nor anyone else had worked

out the theories of three-dimensional molecular structure. Their experimentation was intuitive and episodic—taking whatever promising substance
was available, and putting it on or mixing it with rubber and hoping for the
best. They worked inside the box of tradition and craft. They watched what
other people did. But they were always aware that there was a world they
could not penetrate which held the key that would unlock the mystery of
mysterious substances like rubber. What the invisible world of molecular
structure hid, Goodyear endeavored to learn by patching together the iso-
lated best practices of the rubber technicians, and by outdoing them all in
terms of the acquisition of data, rumor and informed speculation. By 1839,
it appeared to him that acid and sulfur worked just the right way would
finally give him indestructible rubber. But he had not yet pondered or ver-
ified the implications of Ely's accident in which the sulfur on the scalded
patch, stimulated by high heat, had looped around the long twisting rubber
molecules of carbon and hydrogen. Once that happened, the rubber at any
temperature was much less likely to slump and deform and grow sticky
because the chains no longer pulled away from one another. The sulfur cross-
linked with the rubber molecules to create a new unitary structure, resilient
and elastic.

A day or two after the "providential accident" with the stove, Armstrong
returned to 12 Water Street and Goodyear entered not long afterward. Ely
presented the now transformed patch of rubber cloth to Goodyear, who
examined it and said with some surprise that he thought it was a great discovery, but couldn't be sure. Neither Ely nor Armstrong gave it much thought
subsequently.

Soon, while continuing the search for the cause of the mailbag melt-
down, Goodyear began to heat his own patches of sulfur-impregnated rubber on stovetops and in hearths in Boston and Woburn. He cooked his
patches wherever he had access to heat or fire, including a boardinghouse
operated by the Woburn Agricultural and Manufacturing Association. The
long two-story building, a short walk from the Eagle Company, had rooms
available since the silk and rubber businesses had gone bust. Each time
Goodyear cooked the sulfur-treated patches, a slightly different result
obtained. He lifted the charred patches to his face to examine them closely,
caressed them with sooty fingertips and sniffed them like a wine taster inhal-
ing bouquet. Rubber had always melted when heated. What if he could stop

the charring at just the right point? Maybe the gum could be made less sticky that way. After cooking it on an open fire, Goodyear saw a line that wasn't charred but was "perfectly cured."

Gradually, he realized that what he had seen in Ely's little patch and now his own patches could indeed be a breakthrough. His first thought was that they had discovered a way to fireproof the gum. How well it would stand up to future atmospheric temperature changes over many weeks he couldn't be certain and dared not yet say.

Later, Goodyear gave his own version of his discovery. He recalled stopping at a home where he occasionally stayed overnight while working in Woburn—the Agricultural and Manufacturing Association boarding-house. There he made some experiments to ascertain the effect of heat upon the same compound that had decomposed in the mailbags and other articles he had manufactured. As Goodyear told the story, after he carelessly touched a sample to the hot stove, it charred like leather. He said he tried to convey the importance of what he had learned to others who were present, including his skeptical younger brother Amasa Jr., but they paid no attention. He wanted to show them this strange response since previously the gum had always melted when heated. In his account of these events, Goodyear never mentioned Ely.

Things were changing fast now. Before the stove accident, Goodyear felt he had sufficiently pinned down the process to start promoting again. He recruited Dr. Benjamin Silliman of Yale, the pre-eminent American science educator of the time, to observe his experiments, and Silliman provided encouragement that Goodyear lacked from other quarters. He sold another acid license for treating rubber to Haskins and his partner. The unfilled postal mailbag order he now believed could be completed, and on October 5 he wrote his patent agent, Thomas Jones, in Washington, D.C.: "I have now brought the material to a state that is nearly indestructible." The riches of Europe were in his thoughts again and he asked Jones to pass along rubber fabric samples to suitable individuals in London and Paris: "Allow me to say [the samples] will meet a welcome reception anywhere." And then he added one final thought that betrayed his hunger for quick release from his financial worries: "Will you please inform me what society in Paris offered 30,000 francs" for the discovery of a paper from which no impression could be taken?

After the stove accident and his initial attempts to duplicate it, Goodyear wrote Jones again to add high heat to a patent application Jones was drafting. But he didn't completely discard his acid or Hayward's solarization method. In fact, he was confused. On December 21 he wrote to Jones increasing the amount of sulfur in the patent application and stating that heating at 300 degrees Fahrenheit was now an alternative to exposing the rubber to a clear sun for two days. "These are secrets not yet known, except to my friends; but there is now no time to be lost," he said.

Goodyear was in no position to capitalize immediately on the high-heat discovery. At first he could not consistently reproduce the result. At one point he heated a yard of rubber cloth in the family's fireplace and had the cloth made into a hat and vest that he wore. From the moment he believed the breakthrough that had eluded him so long was now a real probability, he brought the whole power of his mind to bear on it. He talked of little but heated rubber. He was still penniless and borrowing from friends, but more than ever he felt rich in prospect.

Haunting shops and factories in the Boston area, roaming from hearth to oven to boiler, Goodyear searched for heat. He needed more substantial sources that would allow him to raise the temperature in controlled increments. The Goodyear family's worst fears came true in the spring of 1840 as Charles started shuttling Clarissa, the children and Charles' parents wherever his rubber experiments took him. Their first stop was Lynn, Massachusetts, a town outside of Boston. Goodyear wrote to Haskins, the optimistic Roxbury Company founder, who now had a steam engine factory in Lynn, saying he wanted to come by to use some of the heat generated by the plant's boilers. When Goodyear visited he saw that getting the heat into the rubber wasn't such a simple matter. He first gingerly tied some of his rubber cloth to a dangerously hot exhaust pipe for the furnace heating the boiler, but that was a very awkward way to heat the rubber. Then he tried to place some rubber fabric inside the boiler itself by opening the hatch that allowed a man to clean the boiler out. Then he tried to thrust a shovelful of rubber cloth into the furnace mouth. "It interfered with my work considerably at the time, which I thought was more important than his, by letting the fire down," said James M'Cracken, who as fireman was in charge of stoking the boiler furnace. Parking himself in a corner of the factory, Goodyear also built a heater in which to make his own fire, a range over which he could hold a roll with rubber cloth wrapped around it, watching intently as it scorched and darkened over the flame.

The factory workers mocked him. "We used to laugh and think it was a trifling thing," said M'Cracken. During one instance when Goodyear rejoiced over a successful specimen, he was heard remarking that he meant to have a dress made of it sent to Queen Victoria, which elicited smirks. Haskins' partner, Luke Baldwin, pronounced Goodyear's heater and experiments good for nothing. Irritated, Goodyear returned to Woburn, leaving his family in Lynn, to "pursue his inquiries and experiments for some months quite alone."

The Goodyear family needed something more permanent than the rooms they had rented in Lynn, so around May 1 Charles brought them to a much better residence in Woburn, a two-story colonial-style house at 280 Montvale Avenue, a short walk from the Eagle Company factory. The house had a front porch and two big bay windows at one end. Charles and Clarissa took one bedroom, Little Willie sleeping with them; Charles' parents took another; and Ellen, Cynthia and Charles Jr. shared a bed in the third bedroom. Ellen, almost fourteen, was old enough to remember a better house in Philadelphia; Cynthia didn't care as long as they never went back to Staten Island; and Charles Jr. was thrilled by the structure's twenty-four separate windows, a luxury that allowed the ten-year-old to keep close track of events outside. One bedroom was reserved for two feeble old men who made rubber goods for the family in exchange for a bed and meager meals of milk and potatoes.

Goodyear borrowed money from the people at Haskins' factory while he stayed in Lynn trying to heat his rubber. One of the factory helpers he borrowed from, John McDermott, said Goodyear "used to be fussing about with those samples, and I thought it was silly and boy's play like, and I used to laugh at it. I used to be sorry for him, for I thought he was spending money to no use, and I thought the man could not afford it, and he owed me a trifle of money, and I couldn't get it out of him, and I kind of pitied the man and thought he could not pay me."

The house at 280 Montvale did double duty as a workshop. Not a day passed in which Goodyear didn't heat a rubber sample somewhere, including his own kitchen. "As I was passing in and out of the room, I casually observed the little piece of gum, which he was holding near the fire, and I noticed also that he was unusually animated by some discovery which he had made," daughter Ellen recalled later, believing herself to have witnessed a singular event but probably having only seen one of dozens of similar experiments. "He nailed the piece of gum outside the kitchen door in intense cold. In the morning he brought it in, holding it up exultantly. He had found it perfectly flexible, as it was when he put it out. This was proof enough of the value of the discovery."

Later, when he had done more work, Goodyear showed brother Amasa Jr. a new version of the process. The heated patch changed from white to a darker shade and finally to a slate tone. Amasa Jr., doubting his older brother, visited Hayward, now laboring alone in the shuttered Eagle factory, to get another opinion about what Charles had told him. Amasa Jr. told Hayward to get a bit of rubber cloth so that he could show him "how it is done." Not long after that demonstration, Goodyear told Hayward that he himself had made the discovery by putting a piece of rubber cloth on a hot stove.

To get a more reliable source of heat, Goodyear enlisted the aid of his Woburn neighbors. On a morning in May 1840, a party of five men equipped with pickaxes, bars and shovels appeared in the yard in back of Hayward's rubber factory in Woburn. Hayward now believed he was better off rid of Goodyear and could make a go of things himself. He watched the construction crew's arrival with bemusement and annoyance. Bricks had been stacked in the yard. For the construction Goodyear had recruited carpenter Alden Moore, ironworker Isaiah Wadleigh, and a mason named Daniel Burbank. Because of their skill with tools, Amasa Sr. was there with Amasa Jr., though his patience was stretched thin. The team set to work. The two Amasas dug a pit while Burbank layered courses of brick to form a box about six feet square. He lathed and plastered the inside walls. Wadleigh, working under Goodyear's direction, set a cast-iron stove in the wall that could be fired from the outside. A flue shot up one corner of the furnace and through the roof. A zinc-covered wooden door was built to hold the heat.

As they worked, a Woburn shoemaker, H. M. Beers, stitched together the last of a few dozen rubber shoes, made of quarter-inch-thick sulfur-treated sheet rubber that had been shaped around a wooden form. When he finished several days later, Goodyear brought the shoes to the oven. Hayward helped him stoke the fire and watched tendrils of smoke laze their way skyward. The stench of Goodyear's backyard rubber barbecue stung neighbors' nostrils and made stomachs quiver. The shoes melted or burned, and the wind carried tendrils of acrid smoke out beyond the yard, a spectral message that the effort had ended in failure. Hayward had had enough. "I gave it up myself; thought it was of no use. Goodyear continued experiments after that ... with his brothers; I paid little attention to it myself."

Three more weeks were needed to complete another batch of footwear, and this time, with a more gradual application of heat, the rubber shoes made it midway across a theoretical zone of transformation—half-changed, not entirely ruined but no better than uncured rubber. Beers went back to his shop and sewed together another batch of shoes. These Goodyear placed inside on iron slates, filled with sand instead of wooden lasts. It produced the best result. But another test-firing accidentally set the furnace door ablaze, destroying the contents again. Goodyear abandoned the homemade furnace built with his neighbors. For pay, he offered mason Burbank $4.59 worth of rubber goods.

At home Goodyear continued to tinker, thrusting rubber patches into the oven after a meal had been cooked and roasting rubber in the ashes of the fire. Each heating condition differed substantially and so did the outcome of each test. Goodyear monomaniacally set up heaters and gained access to boilers and stoves around the Boston area. He boarded temporarily near his heat sources, running up bills he could not pay. He constantly badgered employees of the saw factory of Richardson & Company to heat his rubberized cloth over their furnaces. At one point he challenged an impudent Woburn neighbor who had asked why he spoiled so much rubber to come up with a sound method himself. "By your talk I should think that you thought it was an easy matter to cure them," he told the man while offering him a dollar for every day he tried. As warm weather returned in late spring and early summer, the original test patches of sulfur-treated heated rubber stood up well, confirming his hopes and driving him on. As he worked he tried to keep fears at bay that if he should die before proving the value of his discovery, the future of rubber would die with him.

William Ely, Goodyear's young partner and source of support, was beginning to feel neglected. He had returned to New York hoping to run a rubber shop there and was eager to get started selling wares made by Goodyear in Boston. Goodyear believed it was premature to begin while the new process remained in development. Nevertheless, he promised to honor their pact and deliver products for Ely to sell, including "syringes" (funnels used by doctors and later by women as douches) and clothing made with rubber cloth. Goodyear promised that he now had a way of "giving a good surface upon anything" and making it "hold" beyond anything Ely had seen. He enthusiastically reported that a Parisian businessman had asked him if he needed money as "they could not do such things in Paris." Despondently, the lonely Ely wrote Goodyear and mentioned his thoughts about rich widows. Goodyear wrote back that he was sure Ely would become a rich man from the profits of India rubber and then he "might command a Virgin of the first order in Europe instead of talking about rich widows."

After the holidays, Goodyear's manic optimism evaporated. All the money from old friend DeForest and stove dealer Steele in New Haven had gone into experiments. That meant the adults and children in his family had to scrounge for food and fuel again, gathering wood wherever they could. Goodyear himself hunted the local streams for turtles and bullfrogs for Clarissa to cook, and he borrowed small amounts anywhere he could. "How he subsisted at this period," he later wrote of himself in the third person, "charity alone can tell, for it is as well to call things by their right names, and it is little else than charity, when the lender looks upon what he parts with as a gift."

The days grew cold and short and no one in the family could earn any money. Goodyear collected his children's schoolbooks and pawned them all for five dollars.

Feeding the family became a constant challenge for Clarissa. Although they now lived closer to the pond, a source of protein, the family subsisted mainly on potatoes, some dug half-grown. With help from her in-laws, Clarissa pondered each day how to repackage the potatoes in ways that would add interest to the meal. She pan-fried, breaded, and boiled. She made shapes and figures the way Charles always did with rubber, to amuse her children. Charles Jr., then nine years old, said his family should be grateful for the potatoes because they did not know what they should do without them. He himself had become an expert potato digger.

Groceries had to be bought on credit from wary local merchants, all feeling the effects of the depression. Eggs and meat were a rare delicacy and the Goodyears planted more potatoes on patches of soil around the house. Goodyear wrote Ely letters noting that "my potatoes are not nearly enough for little boys." Amasa Sr. continued his scavenging, looking for fuel and trying to get hired to repair or make tools. Sympathetic neighbors donated clothes and flour but sometimes expressed disgust with Charles and his airy promises of big things to come. Unable to conduct business face to face with distrustful merchants, Goodyear got village teamster William Beers, who owned the house where the family lived, to buy and borrow wheelbarrows of wood or quarts of meal and pints of milk and messes of potatoes and cups of sugar and tea. Beers remembers seeing tears in the eyes of Amasa Sr. when the old man explained that the Goodyears had once been rich.

With losses on Eagle Company stock still fresh in their minds, the Woburners regarded Charles Goodyear as a daffy, self-destructive dreamer, noble but dangerously egocentric. Once the steam trains made Boston only a twenty-two-minute ride from the Woburn station, Goodyear became a familiar figure there garbed in a drab rubber coat spotted black and gray where he had held the tails over a fire to demonstrate its heat resistance. "Many thought him almost insane," said Haskins. The quest for the rubber recipe, in the midst of a deepening national depression, seemed irrational.

Goodyear was oblivious to the impression he made and rejected advice to be more thrifty and use less expensive methods in his experiments. In fact, extravagance was part of his fundraising strategy. Buy loaf sugar when credit isn't good enough for brown, Goodyear told Roxbury co-founder Edwin Chaffee, and silk goods when credit isn't good enough for cotton. Five hundred dollars worth of silks can be gained on trust when you can't get trusted for a yard of cotton cloth.

"How do you think I manage to get on?" he wrote Ely. "Why, merry as a cricket."

Later that year, an almost farcical tone enters Goodyear's letters as he continues to draw money from DeForest. "I suspect I am quite as able to pay you the $100 as you are to lie out of it but as my own money is not zackly my own, but India Rubbers, I will feel obliged to you for your Indulgence in that, and request you to make all your charges of damage to that Mighty Elastic Substance."

Goodyear's hope of riches from Europe, fanciful as they might have seemed to some of his critics, appeared about to come true. He had used William B. Draper, a New Yorker who had resided in Paris, to market the old acid-gas process, and Draper received an offer for rights to use it from Messrs. Rattier & Guibal, Paris manufacturers, believed to be worth more than $30,000. Suddenly a big payday was at hand, and those who had grubstaked Goodyear over the years became attentive. Hayward and Haskins both wondered what share of his Parisian profits Goodyear would assign to them to repay loans. Goodyear resented the suggestion that he make the deal to pay back his creditors. "I sometimes think they intend to force me to it by starvation," he wrote on New Year's Day of 1840. Instead, Goodyear informed Draper, Hayward and Haskins that the new heating process he had been developing "would probably supersede" the acid-gas process. Rather than departing for Paris to seal the deal on the acid-gas process, Goodyear stayed in Woburn. Some later on seized on this decision as evidence of Goodyear's honesty, but it was probably his only prudent course, especially given the importance he put on future European sales and his knowledge that the acid process was flawed, treating only the rubber's surface.

Early in 1840, a supplier who badly needed the money Goodyear owed him but wouldn't pay won a court order forcing Goodyear into debtors' prison once again. A local sheriff came to arrest him and take him away. Once behind lock and key, he joked in a letter to Ely, "It is true, that I am on Staten Island, but all that does not break bones, but only give a good appetite when you do get a breakfast." Clarissa and his father arranged his release, and he went back to his heating tests, using additional money sent by Ely, until he was forced to his bed for a few days by fever. He continued to make small orders of rubber pouches for Ely but begged him to be patient. In the postscript to one letter Goodyear asked if the stoves in the upstairs of the store at 12 Water Street were borrowed or belonged to the landlord; he clearly intended to sell them or move them to a place where he could use them to heat samples.

One day, as a snowstorm buried the Boston area and the wind shaped snowdrifts on Woburn streets, the Goodyears ran out of food and fuel. The "face of nature was a fit emblem" of his condition, Goodyear later wrote of the situation. Then he remembered a kind greeting he had received from a stranger, neighbor O. B. Coolidge. Coolidge had done a little of everything in Woburn—serving as the railroad station ticket master, state legislator, justice of the peace and president of the defunct Woburn Silk Farm and of the Eagle Rubber Company. Off Goodyear went into the storm, weakened by illness but grasping at the straw of the greeting and the idea of wresting a few cents from the stranger. Arriving exhausted by the several-mile walk, he briefed Coolidge about his financial condition and hopes of success. Coolidge not only came across "with a sum adequate to his immediate wants, but also furnished him with facilities for continuing his experiments on a small scale." Like DeForest, Coolidge protected Goodyear from the harsher realities of his plight, squaring accounts with storekeepers on his behalf, paying for his rubber and turpentine and machinery. As a gesture, Goodyear gave Coolidge mortgages for the supplies, but Coolidge said "I did not consider them a great deal of security."

No amount of help was ever enough. With little cash, rising debts, and other, less patient creditors, Goodyear couldn't seem to get Ely the few things he needed to scratch out a living from the New York store. He promised to get down to see Ely, but couldn't say when.

Although Coolidge's loans had brought another respite and allowed the Goodyears to survive the hard winter, Charles anxiously tightroped his way past numerous "pecuniary embarrassments" each month. Over the year, his small debts had been sold off at a discount by merchants and business-men who needed the cash immediately, and keeping track of all his credi-tors was becoming increasingly difficult. New debt holders could demand that a sheriff haul him into court without his even knowing who they were. "After the current sets that way," Goodyear wrote Ely, "a man need not be disappointed or surprised to find himself imprisoned by his own wife."

The joke was more revealing than Goodyear intended. Clarissa was pregnant again and had a particularly trying few weeks as the due date approached. At night, Charles lay awake watching her swollen abdomen rise and fall in the moonlight like a great gumdrop. Her size seemed to indi-cate that twins were on the way. With help only from Charles' mother, Clarissa struggled to clothe and feed the family. Ellen as usual took the lead in helping Clarissa with housework. She also helped her father by making pouches of the charred and raw rubber pieces left everywhere in and around the house. She even learned how to shape a rubber shoe.

Now Clarissa insisted that Charles bring home some fabric for the infant suits that would have to be sewn for the new babies. When he picked up the fabric, he also bought a roll of broadcloth for a new suit he would need for his long-planned trip to New York to see Ely. At present he was stuck because Clarissa could no longer move around to care for the children or cook or clean. For the first time in her life, she spent days at a time in bed. Charles pitched in with the housework. Rubber would have to wait.

Importunate creditors continued to dog him. And some of Goodyear's customers in the Boston area began to prove unreliable, rejecting shipments made months earlier and refusing to pay what they owed. In mid-April, a Connecticut businessman who had lent $2,000 to A. Goodyear & Sons in Philadelphia sued William DeForest, who had guaranteed the loan. The world seemed to be closing in. Later in the month, while on a trip to Boston with Hayward, Goodyear was arrested and again taken to jail by a debt holder who had bought out the unpaid portion of a Goodyear IOU for a $75 ship-ment of acid. After being taken to the House of Corrections in South Boston, he was excused long enough to pawn for $6 the broadcloth he had bought for the suit. He returned and stayed until his family and friends could arrange to pay the balance of what was owed.

Luckily, the House of Corrections in South Boston had been trans-formed during the previous decade into a model short-term jail. There was much hymn singing and Bible study and the only punishment used was a cold shower. "We think the God of Love smiles upon this institution," declared the Prison Discipline Society, a reform organization.

Hayward visited him the next day and brought a rubber bed, a number of "fireproof" rubber samples and $2 cash. While waiting for release, Goodyear wrote Haskins and his partner: "Gentlemen: I have the pleasure to invite you to call and see me at my lodgings on matters of business, and to communicate with my family, and possibly to establish an India rubber factory for myself on the spot. Do not fail to call on the receipt of this, as I feel some anxiety on account of my family. My father will probably arrange my affairs in relation to this hotel, which, after all, is perhaps as good a resting-place as any this side of the grave."

When Goodyear wrote to Ely on the same day, his words were bitter and devoid of irony. "I have fallen into the hands of the harpies, and I do not suppose they will now let me alone, Here I am, and here I stay until my affairs are arranged for my family, until I have consulted my friends."

This time, Goodyear languished in prison longer than usual, heightening his anxiety, especially with Clarissa barely able to function and approaching her due date. Paying the debt to get himself released turned out to be complicated. He owed $25 to a gentleman named Mr. Munroe, who had obtained the arrest order against him, but Munroe had sold the debt to a James Barker, and Goodyear could not find Barker to pay him off. Meanwhile, a customer of Goodyear's, trying to avoid becoming involved in his debt problems, refused to take a delivery of rubber goods and pay for them until Goodyear had gotten out of jail and settled his account with Munroe.

During his wait Goodyear stewed over Hayward's "treachery." Hayward filled the orders slowly and then often not to Goodyear's specification. And every delay wasted the money granted to Goodyear by Coolidge. "I have found so much treachery in what was done for me by Hayward, that I have lost at least three-fourths of the aid afforded me by Coolidge for a week past," he wrote Ely. Yet Goodyear was more confident than ever in his sample products, made of the "nearly indestructible" and "everlastingly elastic" heated rubber. By April 29, he was out again, his lawyer having "discharged me from my shame, but that's a trifle compared with a thousand difficulties I have to contend with for the want of charge." He saw good fortune in the fact that Clarissa finally gave birth to one child, not two as expected. After a month of house "arrest," as Goodyear put it, he was let "off with a fine daughter," named Clara.

A few days later, the sheriff came for Goodyear again and took him to the Cambridge jail in connection with another debt for $40. Unlike the South Boston facility, Cambridge had not been touched by the Lord's reforming hand. Here, ordinary debtors were held with little freedom of movement in the same area as lunatics and criminals. Goodyear wrote to Ely: "Close confinement. No fun in this."

Once released, Goodyear spent much of his time throughout that spring foraging for money. He wrote to a friend in Boston who had once worked for him and the friend agreed to give him $50 next time he saw him. Goodyear quickly traveled to Boston, but the friend reneged on the promise, stranding Goodyear at his hotel from Monday to Saturday. Goodyear hoped to get money from someone else during his stay, but he was repeatedly turned down. The hotel presented him with a bill, which he couldn't pay. Mortified and saddened, he walked around Boston, meditating on his condition. He crossed the bridge over the Charles River, its banks cluttered with rickety docks, and strayed into the lonely side streets of East Cambridge, wandering among the row houses whose steps spilled out onto the sidewalks. Perhaps he remembered when he had owned a fine house in Philadelphia. He knocked on the door of a friend "who received him kindly and made him comfortable for the night."

The next day Goodyear walked ten miles to his house at 280 Montvale Avenue in Woburn. Clarissa, who had her hands full with the newborn girl, came to the door looking as though she hadn't slept in days. She told Charles that three-year-old William Henry was running a fever. The other children, who had come forward crowding around Father, fell back as he walked to the sick boy. The child was turned onto his side, staring straight ahead and hardly moving, drawing quick, tight breaths. Charles immediately took over the vigil Clarissa had been keeping, telling Ellen to bring in a new pot of water. He laid a moist rag over the boy's head, held it there a few minutes and dabbed at the pale flesh at the back of the toddler's neck. As William Henry slipped deeper into delirium, Charles pulled a small rubber horse from his pocket and danced it across his Little Willie's field of vision. The boy murmured "Papa." That night, William Henry again called out "Papa, Papa," then drew five or six more tight breaths and sighed and stopped breathing. Tears burst from Charles' eyes and ran down into his collar. Clarissa, craning her neck as she rocked Clara in a cradle on the other side of the room, understood what had just happened but was unwilling to stop rocking the baby until she had fallen asleep. When her mother-in-law took over the cradle Clarissa walked toward Willie and lifted his body to hers one last time. Charles went into the next room to tell the other children. Ellen and Cynthia cried but Charles Jr. was indifferent and wanted to get back outside to dig more potatoes.

Charles notified the graveyard manager and arranged to borrow a wagon. The next morning the Goodyears pulled on their best clothes. Charles fastened on a fresh collar. Then he carried Willie, bundled in a sheet, down to the wagon, and the family, too poor to hire carriages, walked alongside with the children straggling absentmindedly for the entire mile-long journey. Some of the neighbors said it was the saddest thing they had ever seen.

Immediately after the funeral, Goodyear summoned Ellen, Cynthia and Charles Jr. to their work, telling them that they needed to earn their daily bread even though they felt sad. Ellen went to find a rubber pouch to sew and Charles Jr. headed out on potato duty.

The Goodyears seemed to be coming to the end of their tether in Woburn. The relative luxury of 280 Montvale lasted only until August 14, when the family packed up their meager belongings into a wagon and moved to a smaller house belonging to another local resident. In a few months the family had to move again, becoming boarders with the Emersons, who had a farm nearby. The charge was $1.50 a week for each adult and $1 for each child. Eight family members crowded into the spare rented rooms. Goodyear asked everyone he knew for help. Haskins' partner advanced him $75 for rubber samples. Goodyear wrote to Ely again, this time addressing him as "Friend Ely," and speculating about where his next sales or subsidy would come from. "I do not say this expecting you can send me money but help will come and there is no knowing where it will come from for yesterday some firm in Boston sent me a barrel of flour that I don't know from Adam." In June, Goodyear had written to a friend in Boston asking for money, and the friend sent $7. At the place where the letter was read, another gentleman was so moved that he shipped the family a barrel of flour. Goodyear told Ely, "At least write me at Woburn directly all about matters and things." In July he wrote Ely that he had perfected his system for making rubber fabric and had "made such desperate efforts to accomplish this that I can't tell what more to make to obtain $10–$25 would get me to N. York and leave my family comfortable."

Goodyear's perseverance in the face of disaster had a mesmerizing effect on those around him. While some laughed at or pitied him, others clearly were drawn to his vision of riches from rubber and his dead certainty that he would triumph. He demanded to be listened to and, in an age when face-to-face communication remained the most electrifying source of ideas and feelings, won enough confidence to convince his neighbors to work for him for free or for very uncertain deferred wages. From ten to twenty family members and neighbors, including Goodyear's landlords and some young girls who worked as laborers, wound up involved in his schemes, often against their better judgment. They never were paid. Goodyear relied on his persuasive powers as a minister preaching to the unconverted. "You know me," he observed to Ely. "Little Health — a large family — no change — in the hottest of the Battle — sure of Victory."

Goodyear, meanwhile, continued to spend on his research as if he were already the rich man he never stopped envisioning himself to be. In the fall of 1840, he solicited $50 from DeForest to pay for a trip to New York City, bringing sample aprons, maps, globes and other things for Ely to sell. During the trip, Goodyear met William Rider, a manufacturer, who with his brother Emory agreed to finance both Goodyear's professional and house hold expenses. Now Goodyear had more breathing room than he had enjoyed in years. Ely kept up sales of rubber goods made in Massachusetts, including, during the year of a presidential election, Harrison Heads or Van Buren Labels. In a letter to Ely about making the electoral items, Goodyear's manic optimism was on full view now that he was momentarily free from immediate financial trouble and therefore from the persecution and siege that colored his thoughts earlier in the year. He wrote of being in "prime condition."

Despite the previous broken contract, Goodyear hired Hayward again, on April 3, 1841, for one year at $50 a month. He made Hayward sign a statement clarifying that Goodyear was the "true and original inventor of fireproof India rubber, and of other improvements caused by the use of large quantities of sulphur and lead, and of heating the same, and by that and other methods of removing the offensive smell." Hayward also agreed to the statement: "I am certain that the same has been accomplished by him at a great expense of time and money."

Although Hayward and Goodyear still concentrated on rubber as a textile, they occasionally went off on tangents related to Goodyear's interests in marine design. With a river, a canal and two sizable ponds within easy walking distance, the temptation was great. Goodyear directed the workers at the Eagle factory in the construction of three small rubber vessels. One of them had its perimeter encircled with a buoyant rubber bumper to prevent sinking. Three workers navigated the boat in the canal, but the boat capsized. Goodyear and Hayward had better luck with a submersible mine that they tested at Mill Pond, a few hundred yards from the factory and the flatlands where the ill-fated mulberry trees had been planted. The mine consisted of a large jug with gunpowder that Goodyear and Hayward sunk in ten feet of water. From the shore they ignited a fuse run through a long rubber tube, and waited. In a minute or so the jug burst with a muffled boom, sending sheets of water several yards over the surface. The two inventors congratulated each other and hoped to sell their invention to the U.S. Navy.

The search for the perfect rubber recipe went on. At some point, Goodyear found that lead, or lead salts and oxides, litharge in particular, hastened the transformation of rubber and sulfur. Lead had been mined and smelted for at least eight thousand years, and a first-century-B.C. Roman architect and engineer observed the sickly demeanor of the workers in lead factories and warned that contact with lead destroys the "vigour of the blood." He was right. Nineteenth-century laborers knew lead was bad—even if they didn't know why—and the work of mixing lead into other substances was left to the most desperate among them. Goodyear mixed his gum with lots of substances, including lead, working the material hard until the powders lodged under his nails and frosted his hair. He didn't care about the possible consequences.

Just as things seemed to be improving, a rift now split the Goodyear family. Amasa and Amasa Jr. had decided to strike off in a new direction and leave Charles and his rubber behind. In doing so, Amasa Sr. would reclaim some of the leadership he had ceded to his precocious oldest child years earlier. Amasa Jr., the second youngest, would free his own nuclear family from the madness he believed infected Charles. His younger brother, Nelson, might still be enthralled by Charles, and his older brothers, Robert and Henry, may have believed there was a future in retailing rubber goods made by Charles' formulas. But he and his father were leaving the destructive fantasy. Not ashamed to be merely country blacksmiths, they had decided to use money squirreled away from toolmaking and repair to invest in a produce-shipping venture. With their partners, they chartered a steam packet that was to sail to Florida to buy pineapples and carry them back north. A single successful trip, they believed, could restore the Goodyears' financial and social stature. It was a bold plan for anyone, especially for Amasa, who was sixty-nine, and Amasa Jr., who brought his wife, Melinda, and their three-year-old daughter.

Florida was a frontier where the Seminole Indians had recently risen up in rebellion, destroying whole towns, including the Dade County seat,

Indian Key. In swampy south Florida, yellow fever, a virus carried by mosquitoes, had been raging on and off for years. Within a short while of arriving for the pineapple harvest, in fact, each of the four Goodyears fell victim to the virus. Thousands of miles from home and the comfort of his wife and children, Amasa Sr. watched his son, then his daughter-in-law and then finally his granddaughter sicken and die. Then he died, too.

When news of the disaster in Florida reached him, Charles took to his bed for several weeks. His mother, Cynthia, now sixty-seven years old and shattered by the loss of her husband, her second son and his family, decided it was time to leave her eldest son's house. She moved to Newtown, Connecticut, to live with son Robert and his family. Robert was scratching out a living making and selling rubber goods with Josiah Tomlinson, his sister Harriet's husband. His brother Henry Bateman Goodyear sailed to Florida to bring back the dead for burial. Why had this tragedy happened? Maybe if Charles had left rubber alone, the family could have had a normal life rather than becoming desperate enough to undertake the doomed Florida venture. Maybe now that his father and brother were gone, Clarissa hoped, Charles would come to his senses. But when he recovered from his grief, instead of taking the Florida tragedy as a sign that he should stop, Charles saw it as a signal to press on.

The rubber bake-off continued. In a yard in Roxbury, where Haskins and his partner had returned to set up business yet again, Goodyear had brick-mason Samuel Felton construct a 4-foot-deep, 10-inch-wide box, open at the front. A coal fire was built up and then Goodyear held up a broomstick wrapped with a roll of rubber cloth. Over the course of two hours he unraveled the cloth at the narrow opening to the furnace, burning it in places, blistering it in others and curing it well in still other places. This furnace was never used again because Goodyear couldn't risk wasting more material in it. He had better luck passing rolled rubber through a heated cast-iron trough. As master chef, Goodyear also immersed rubber in a kettle containing boiling water, potash solution or melted lead and sulfur. Rubber boots went into the boiling potash and came out in wearable condition, although this method of immersion curing didn't catch on at first.

With his new financing from Rider, Goodyear set up a factory in Springfield, Massachusetts. Hayward, who had left Goodyear's employment and returned to the role of subcontractor, supplied several hundred pounds of fireproof sheet rubber that Goodyear cut up into thread for suspenders. The furnace and machines Hayward had developed for this were now very efficient, and, the wiser for his prior experience with Goodyear, he kept them secret.

At Springfield, Henry and Nelson Goodyear and at least a dozen neighbors and friends all pitched in. There, Charles constructed another heater of cast-iron plates, slotted on one side. A belt of rubber fabric was wrapped around a roller inside the steel box and fed into the heat and out through slots in the sides. In this manner several dozen feet of cloth were well cured.

Charles began to spend more and more time in Springfield, at various points boarding with John and Eliza Haskins and using their kitchen stove to supplement the experiments at Haskins' factory. His brother Henry, who was working with a relative at a rubber business in Naugatuck, stopped in Springfield during the winter of 1841 and was told of "an improvement in baking and manufacturing India Rubber, which was very valuable." Charles wanted his brother to stay but Henry declined, commenting later on that he had not much confidence in the improvements from what little he saw of them. But a year later, finding that Charles' experiments were more successful than he had anticipated, Henry returned to Springfield and agreed to take over the factory as manager of its operations. Still, they struggled to produce even small sections of perfectly prepared rubber and were unable to sell anything directly. "Most of the goods were either ruined by being blistered or burnt in the heater and were not considered fit for market," said Henry. Charles dictated that nothing was to be sold before they got it right, but Haskins and his partner, still operating the factory at Roxbury on a reduced basis, advertised coats, capes, caps, cushions, life preservers, air beds, pillows, trouting boats and cloths prepared "with Goodyear's improvements."

In addition to the mystery of how much heat to apply, in what manner and in what increment, the slightest impurities in the rubber or other ingredients ruined the samples. For example, rubber that had been left standing too long would begin to "ferment" and become useless. Turpentine, which was still being used as a solvent to prepare and shape the rubber brick shipped from South America and other locations, also introduced impurities that would block the transformation wrought by sulfur and heat. Hayward and Goodyear tried to purify the turpentine. In the fall of 1841 Nelson substituted camphene, with good results.

As the heating process evolved, so did the methods of marrying rubber with fabric. Up until this point, either textile fibers were mixed in with rubber and heated with it, or sheets of rubber were spread on fabric and then cooked. Neither process was ideal. Goodyear started to weave rubber thread, stretched into tension, with cotton fabric. When the woven fabric was set free the rubber threads contracted, puckering the fabric. Suspenders made of this hybrid textile, called shirred fabric, began to catch on. They had just the right amount of tension, and the puckered look soon became popular. It was a small sunburst of commercial promise.

Goodyear was edging closer to the El Dorado he had conscripted his family into seeking with him. His recipe for rubber now contained two critical elements, in addition to the gum itself. One was a ballooning proportion of sulfur: one-quarter to one-half pound for every pound of rubber. The other was white lead, which accelerated the changes in the rubber, in similar amounts. These hefty proportions lacked engineering elegance, but the triple compound worked. As 1842 drew to an end, Goodyear had patent agent Thomas Jones draw up a specification for a patent for heated gum elastic fabric based on this formula. In it Goodyear said the rubber is dissolved in turpentine and the white lead and sulfur are ground and dissolved in spirits of turpentine. When the rubber is joined with fabric or fibrous substances or pre-made cloth, Goodyear said, it is best to spread the dissolved rubber on the fabric or fiber and then expose them to 270 degrees of heat by running the fabrics between heated calenders, or before or through a furnace or oven, or a heated metal plate; still another way would be to immerse the rubber in any article that is melted or fluid, at about the degree of heat herein specified. Once processed, the fabric no longer can be injured by heat, oils or turpentine.

With the drawing of the patent specification, Goodyear took a step closer to protecting the processes he had developed. He had yet to prove that he could produce fireproof rubber products on an economical and consistent basis, but at least for now the triple compound—rubber, sulfur and lead—had been enshrined as his innovation, even if more refinement was still needed. In the future, his experiments would focus on methods for using the recipe in production.

Just as this new phase was beginning, Goodyear became sickly. His joints ached; he felt weak and couldn't move. He was not immobilized by fever, but he was enfeebled by a general "lameness which resembles rheumatism, or gout, and in the joints of his hands," as Haskins described the malaise.

For a man who never drank or smoked, the symptoms were mystifying. Goodyear first thought his symptoms came from handling India rubber dissolved in camphene or spirits of turpentine. John Haskins suspected it was too much kneading of the rubber with his hands. No one knew for sure nor suspected that the large amounts of lead Goodyear was handling could be causing his illness.

Meanwhile, even as distrust simmered between them, Hayward and Goodyear continued to do business. Working on his own at Woburn, Hayward made several hundred pounds of fireproof sheet rubber, which he cut up into suspender threads that would be sent to Goodyear's factory at Springfield to be prepared as suspenders. As usual, Goodyear fell behind in his payments to Hayward, who complained that his associate was "owing me considerable sums of money on back arrearages, which he was either unable or unwilling to pay." To pay taxes Hayward was forced to sell off personal property. In this weakened financial state he found himself vulnerable to Goodyear's talent for extracting information. "While thus embarrassed, Goodyear told me if I would inform him how I compounded my articles, and the exact proportions, he could then get all the money he wanted, and would pay up all he owed me—a promise which he never fully performed." Hayward caved in again and told how he combined the rubber and sulfur and other ingredients, and as a result Goodyear's operations at Springfield were, in Hayward's opinion, "greatly improved."

Privately, Hayward seethed. Goodyear had again used his indebtedness as a way of prying out proprietary information. At one point Goodyear employee Benjamin Coburn pointed out to a group that included Goodyear licensee Leverett Candee and friend and lender Ralph Steele that several samples of heated rubber cloth that Goodyear was showing them had actually been produced by Hayward at the old Eagle plant in Woburn. Hayward "knew more about rubber in half an hour, than Goodyear in all his life," Coburn told them. Candee and Steele were surprised, "as they did not suppose anybody knew anything about rubber except Charles Goodyear." The proclamation by Coburn gave Hayward some satisfaction and cooled his smoldering resentment for the time being.

Goodyear continued to make hoses and tents and other rubber products on a modest scale. And he continued to send a trickle of goods to Ely, who had lent him $6,000 with little return except effusively sentimental expressions of gratitude. Ely, meanwhile, gradually gave up any hope of running a rubber goods shop in New York City with Goodyear as his supplier.

He told Goodyear that he had decided to travel south to seek his fortune. A renewed tour of service with the Army might be his best career prospect. Ely told Goodyear that he had been insensitive about his difficulties and needs during this period of frustration. Nevertheless, he did not hold it against Goodyear and wished him well.

Goodyear was all wounded innocence at the suggestion that he had neglected his friend. "I assure you that I place a high value upon your feelings," he wrote Ely on January 16, 1841. "I beg of you to accept from me the like good wishes for your welfare."

Ely had trusted and believed in Goodyear even more than DeForest or Goodyear's own brothers. His devotion had made him Goodyear's most intimate confidante during a period of deepening personal tragedy. Cares and worries Goodyear concealed from other men came spilling out when he talked to young Ely. And Ely had been a favorite of Clarissa's ever since he had escorted her and the Goodyear children out of Staten Island. He had been kind and courteous and had never carped about the more than $10,000 he had pumped into the venture with only a meager and unpredictable flow of income in return. He had to be content with only lasting affection from his partner.

"I part with you as with a brother, a tried friend, and you can depend upon meeting me again as such. (God grant we may meet)," Goodyear told Ely. "In this respect, you are on precisely the same footing with my wife, and in all that relates to me, you, I think, have been equally true. May God bless you always, William. Adieu, my dear boy."

Democratic opponents of Whig William Henry Harrison, who won the presidential election of 1840, suspected that the margin of victory had been provided by insolvent debtors in the northeastern states. It is a telling example of how sectional differences were aggravated by the issue of whether the federal government should provide order to the patchwork of state bankruptcy laws. Northern manufacturing states generally supported debtor relief through bankruptcy, but the southern farming states and westerners in general saw bankruptcy as a license to all the Northeast's speculators, promoters and plungers to get out from under their obligations or as a way for fast-talking businessmen to rig the system in their favor. Among the opponents of the 1841 federal bankruptcy law passed after Harrison's election was Charles Goodyear, whose personal grandiosity and conservative political views provided him the perspective of a Georgia plantation owner rather than someone who had become deeply indebted in his obsessive pursuit of the perfect formula for rubber. Goodyear termed the 1841 bankruptcy law "odious" and was pleased when, within about a year, a congressional majority was secured to repeal it.

Ten days before the law expired, however, Goodyear grabbed hold of the protections it provided and filed for relief in federal court in Springfield. He had recently been forced into prison once more by an unknown creditor in that town. In defending his turnaround, Goodyear wrote that although he "had always opposed and firmly resolved not to accept of any of the advantages" of the controversial federal law, "the provocation, in this instance, was such that his resolution gave way."

Goodyear could not have been a more prolific borrower if he had picked his lenders up by their legs, turned them upside down and shaken all the money out of their pockets and purses. His avalanche of debt had grown to $59,629, many times the average laborer's lifetime earning capacity. From 1830 until 1843, years when a laborer's salary was below $500 per annum, Goodyear had siphoned cash and credit from anyone he could infect with his own vision of rubber riches. It was a time when most local information stopped at the town line, when private borrowings could easily be concealed and when disclosure of past debt was up to the conscience of the needy borrower. Each new lender believed that only he or she kept Goodyear from being swept off to jail.

Earlier in their bizarre financial journey, the Goodyears had apparently paid back most of what they owed after the bottom fell out of the hardware business, except for a few straggling loans. They still owed $200 to their old warehouseman, David W. Prescott, and there was the $3,000 that had been guaranteed by William DeForest. But then, in the mid-1830s, when Goodyear began his rubber quest, his borrowing from business acquaintances accelerated. From J. W. Sexton in New York, $100; from druggist Silas Carle & Nephew, $500. From businessman William Draper, $650; and from the Riders in New York, $2,400 or so. To Nathaniel Hayward he owed $1,000, and to the Chicopee Bank of Springfield, Massachusetts, $1,700. Woburn women responded to his appeals—Jane Brown, Rebecca Emerson, Isabel Beers, Elvira Richardson, Fidelia Richardson and Mary Anne Lathe were each hit for $20 to $25. Not everyone who dealt with him came away empty-handed. Isabella Read, for example, provided Goodyear transportation in June 1841 on a journey that took the two of them from Woburn to Boston to New York and back, and collected $17.62. On the never-paid side of the ledger, the longer side, stood those benefactors whose resources Goodyear mined until all productive veins gave out. Ralph Steele let Goodyear get into him for $6,000. From all-forgiving boyhood friend William DeForest, Goodyear wrested $10,053. And trusting mechanic-manufacturer William Ballard was out $3,000.

Goodyear specifically excluded from his filing the $10,053 he owed to William DeForest, most of it borrowed in the aftermath of the hardware bankruptcy. Their fond, brotherly relationship stretched back over decades. But what about the others? Just how Goodyear convinced so many laborers and tradesmen and merchants to turn over so much money to him is a matter of some puzzlement. Goodyear's earnest zeal about rubber and his evangelical pitch about why he was the one to harness its potential certainly played a part in his amazing ability to raise money. Perhaps the innocent optimism of his vision was the key element in his pitch. As years went by, unpaid creditors for the most part spoke without asperity of his desperation and difficulty in perfecting rubber and held no grudges.

On Goodyear's part, when benefactors such as Ballard and the Riders were themselves wiped out by financial panic, his chief reaction was only irritation to have been deprived of their philanthropy. He never re-evaluated his sense of entitlement by its negative affect on others. All that mattered was his rubber. He wrote later on that he "never had cause to regret" his decision to file for bankruptcy protection because soon his "invention began to be appreciated."

CHAPTER FIVE

Patent No. 3633

The oil lamps burned past midnight in the attic of Marlborough Cottage, in the town of Stoke Newington, north of London. Mutton-chop-sideburned Thomas Hancock, partner in England's Charles Macintosh & Company, stared through a magnifying glass at the stamp-sized gray patches of rubber that had been packed in ice. After a while, he put the patches down, stoked his hearth and started to cook more patches, working long into the night. When he went to bed he snuffed the fire and closed the attic door behind him. The attic was off-limits even to his servant. That spring of 1843, Hancock had begun the most exciting months of his career. What he was doing now topped the invention of the masticator almost twenty years before. And it was more interesting than the fifteen years of success he enjoyed as the licensee and then partner of Charles Macintosh, with whom he had built the company into England's pre-eminent rubber goods manufacturer.

Their success with the "waterproof double textures," the sandwich of a layer of rubber between layers of fabric, had not come easily. Their "macintoshes" had to overcome the objections of tailors, who wanted nothing to do with rubber fabric that would leak through stray or carelessly made needle holes, or stubborn shop owners, who spurned the unusual coats. So they opened their own shops. They found a way to keep the rubber's odor to a minimum. They even overcame objections from doctors claiming that tight-fitting rubber garments, and the perspiration they trapped against the skin, were as much a threat to health as the cold rain these coats were designed to repel. Hancock noted later with irritation that before rubber garments existed doctors mainly blamed illness on chills from cold and moisture, from which Macintosh raincoats provided the best protection yet known. Loose-fitting styles allowed the raincoat trade to regain some momentum and the Macintosh Company used legal action to fight back against patent infringers.

But railroads posed a bigger threat to their raincoat trade than industrial renegades. Stagecoach travel, which exposed riders to weather and road muck tossed up by the wheels and made their rubberized coats a veritable necessity, was fast dying out under competition from trains. In cities, horse-drawn omnibuses were chasing away the short-distance stages, and light open carriages were becoming a thing of the past. People were better protected against the elements.

The drop-off in raincoat demand stimulated Hancock to try to improve rubber and use it in new ways. Sales of rubber hose and rubber cement grew, but he saw—as Charles Goodyear had—that rubber's full potential could never be exploited while its sensitivity to cold and heat remained, and while its sticky surface needed to be shielded by conventional fabric. So he set out to produce single-texture garments with a smooth, clean, nonstick surface, to free the rubber fabric from the confines of the textile sandwich in which Macintosh had always hidden it. In this effort he was about to receive a great gift from unknown sources in America who would help Hancock reach his breakthrough.

The first sign of new life that Hancock noticed in the U.S. rubber industry, in the late 1830s, hardly suggested the stirrings of a slumbering giant. William R. Draper, formerly of Paris, had shown him samples of Goodyear's rubber-lined cambric (Hancock later recalled that it had a dingy yellow color) with the print of "a female" on it. Draper also gave Hancock a printed rubber map "which would expand by the elasticity of the material." Neither item made much of an impression on him.

The next set of samples sent from the United States was more interesting. Goodyear had filed his preliminary specifications of patent in the United States and, still hoping to strike it big in Europe, had provided samples of his rubber products—improved by heat and sulfur—to young Stephen Moulton, an Englishman visiting the States. Told that Goodyear wanted £50,000 for the license to use the secret method, Moulton brought the samples to Manchester, where he met with Charles Macintosh and other members of the firm. Moulton told them Goodyear's samples would not stiffen in cold and were not much affected by solvents, heat or oils.

Macintosh and his colleagues in Manchester responded to these new samples with a certain skepticism. It was one thing to come up with small samples of a miracle material, quite another to manufacture it economically for profit. Take out a patent for it, they advised Moulton, and then the matter can be discussed. They also asked that the inventor himself come to England to talk it over. As he prepared to leave, Moulton, who knew nothing about rubber making, told Hugh Birley, one of the Macintosh partners, in the presence of one of his sons, that the samples would be left in confidence and were not to be used "to the prejudice of Mr. Goodyear."

"Suppose we find the secret without the use of the samples?" Birley asked.

"I will leave that to your own honor," Moulton answered.

In the fall of 1842, a Macintosh employee named William Brockedon brought the samples left in Manchester to London. From one of them he cut two pieces, little bigger than postage stamps, which he gave to Hancock, noting "that the mode of manufacturing this rubber was a secret and that the agent that had shown them to him, declared himself totally ignorant of it; all he knew was, that it had been done by some new solvent which was very cheap in America."

Hancock found the sample he first examined was "of a dirty yellowish grey colour, and a little dusty powder upon it; when cut across, the cut edge appeared of a dark colour: the other bit was of a dark reddish brown colour throughout, with a clean surface without any dusty appearance." As he later wrote, "The little bits given me by Mr. Brockedon certainly showed me for the first time that the desirable change in the condition of rubber of not stiffening by cold had been attained, but they afforded no clue to the mode by which it had been brought about."

An unusual odor floated up from the samples; Hancock smelled the scent of brimstone as Goodyear had when examining Nathaniel Hayward's samples. The scent clung to Hancock's fingers after he touched the patches. He believed it was a diversion: "I thought that a little sulphurous powder had been rubbed on to mislead." The samples intrigued him, though. Stretched out, they were opaque. Cold didn't stiffen them.

It was these samples that caused Hancock to retreat into the secrecy of his attic at night and begin to compound his own rubber with sulfur, as he had done earlier in his career, but he never believed sulfur or any other chemical could make the rubber cold-resistant. Hancock tested thousands of small scraps of rubber treated with different substances at different temperatures, working long hours after complicated days in London or Manchester, where the company had a factory. His servant purchased ice from a cart that passed his gate every morning. At night Hancock packed his treated rubber patches in the ice and then waited until the next day to see if they had become brittle.

Hancock was, in every respect, better prepared than Goodyear to find the secret recipe. He had years of rubber manufacturing experience and the security of knowing where his next meal would come from. The biggest uncertainty he faced was whether or not to charge the ice he began using to cool the patches to the Macintosh Company as a business expense. (He ended up paying for it himself.)

On Moulton's return to the United States in December of 1842, Goodyear gave him the rough outlines of how the gum was combined with sulfur and lead and then heated, but didn't give him the proportions or temperatures. Moulton crossed the Atlantic again to discuss the matter in Manchester with Hancock's associates in April 1843. They told Moulton that they had tested the samples, which had successfully withstood the cold. Had Goodyear heard more about these tests he probably would have recognized how vulnerable he was, but Moulton did not report the conversation. In August he returned to the United States and got more samples from Goodyear, which he forwarded to Macintosh. And that fall he finally received an order for Goodyear from Leaf & Company, an agent for Macintosh, for some of the heated rubber. Things looked promising.

Goodyear's new attorney, William Judson, sailed for England with the authority to negotiate a deal. Judson was a thirty-year-old native of Stratford, Connecticut, educated at Yale with a legal practice based in lower Manhattan. He had wide experience in patents and trade and showed great skill in crafting intricate clauses about the obligations of parties to a contract. But his interests in law often took a back seat to his desire to get in on good business opportunities that came to his attention from his legal work. His interest in Goodyear, who made it clear he had not a penny to pay him, was purely speculative. Goodyear was flattered by Judson's fascination with his rubber methods and believed he would prove to be a capable representative for this most important business prospect, the Macintosh Company. Most importantly, Judson was willing to pay his own way to England.

In Manchester, Judson called on Hancock's associates, sipping tea and smoking pipes with them and hoping to talk about terms. Lulled into complacency by English manners, Judson wasted weeks while Hancock hurried to discover how to unlock Goodyear's ability to make cold-resistant rubber.

Hurrying to his attic after normal business hours, Hancock at first tried combining the rubber with silicate of magnesia, but it didn't help.

Breaking rubber down with solvents always caused lots of problems and extra work—in this case, the need to dry the rubber. To expedite drying, Hancock sometimes laid his 1-inch-by-2-inch rubber scraps on a small metal plate heated over a chamber lamp, or a larger plate heated by the fire, and at other times he put them in the oven just as Goodyear had done in Woburn and New Haven and other cities. There were several near-successes, when Hancock heated some rubber compounded with sulfur. But he always took it out before it had cooked long enough. So discouraging were these failures, Hancock admitted, that "for a time [he] relinquished the use of sulphur in most of the compounds as useless, and pushed on with other matters."

Hancock worked through thousands of trial scraps, throwing aside most and holding on to a few that aroused his interest. He noticed that in some of the scraps containing sulfur there were variations he could not account for. He wasn't sure when he "struck out the first spark of the 'change,'" because there were so many samples all around; he still wasn't clear what exactly produced the effect or how important the degree of heat was in effecting the change. But he was gradually closing in on the combination of heat and sulfur. With Judson now in London trying to move Macintosh & Company into a deal, Hancock took out a provisional patent on November 21, 1843, although he had not yet successfully heated any rubber or made it cold-resistant. Without lead or litharge, which is essential for the change to occur in the presence of air, he had no way to do it by conventional heating methods.

Ten weeks later, tiring of Macintosh's temporizing, Judson directed patent lawyers to submit Goodyear's application for an English patent involving his triple compound of sulfur, rubber and lead heated to 270 degrees. Goodyear, of course, had successfully heated many pounds of rubber in this fashion, although he still hadn't figured out how to do it in large volumes. But his move came too late.

Hancock was still grappling with how hot and how long to cook his rubber and sulfur compounds when it occurred to him that since sulfur melts at 240 degrees he would immerse a slip of sheet rubber in sulfur and give the rubber a good hot sulfur bath. The first time he tried this he noticed the rubber's surface had assumed a yellowish tan color. He tried again and found the tan color had penetrated below the surface, and when he tried it yet again he found that the entire strip had changed color. But when he subjected them to the cold test they failed.

Next he let the rubber cook in the sulfur almost an hour, hitting temperatures approaching 275 degrees Fahrenheit. That much heat profoundly changed the molecules. Below the surface of the sulfur bath, the sulfur molecules had journeyed down among the long, tangled rubber molecules and formed a friendly bond with them. As long as the rubber was heated to 265 or 270 degrees for about an hour, depending on thickness, the change occurred. In the patent that resulted from these experiments Hancock described a variety of heating methods—immersing rubber in melted sulfur, and vice versa, or combining the substances mechanically, and then heating them until they were very hot. When immersed in melted sulfur at more than 300 degrees Fahrenheit and for more than two hours, the rubber turned coal-black and hard like horn. As much as soft rubber, the hard version heralded the coming of the synthetic age.

Years later Hancock would write that some chemists of his day speculated that the sulfur and rubber didn't combine at all, that the changes took place "simply by contact of the two substances" in the right conditions. Other chemists theorized "that some new molecular arrangement takes place." To Hancock, the changes he had brought in the rubber were the lucky and surprising result of trial and error. "No analogy or reasoning on the relative nature of the two substances would ever have suggested or anticipated the possibility of such a result." But unlike these chemists, Hancock had samples of rubber made by Goodyear using the process.

While Goodyear was being outmaneuvered in England, his U.S. operations rattled on like a soot-stained, turpentine-drenched industrial circus, always in rehearsal and never quite ready for opening night. Other than the samples sent down to Ely, and some hoses and other waterproof materials made for military or outdoor use, the problems of reliably making things of rubber were proving nearly insurmountable. Goodyear had spread himself among four or five furnaces or heating operations. The main one was in Springfield, Massachusetts, but he also had mixing and heating operations in Newtown, Connecticut, and New Haven. He found a place to live wherever he most needed to be, heating and mixing and directing the work of others with what Haskins later described as "superhuman perseverance." The only way Goodyear could survive was by selling licenses to his imperfect, partly patented method of making "fire-proof gum." But what he lacked in scientific

know-how he more than made up for in public relations. Goodyear prose-
lytized ceaselessly about his improvements and rubber in general and others took notice. Even though no one, not even Goodyear, had consistently
used his method with success, the value of his heating secret ripened in people's minds.

Around this time, Goodyear's licensees were beginning to sell more
of the shirred fabric, the cotton or wool that had been woven with some rubber threads, creating a corrugated look. Sales of the shirred rubber suspenders,
made with threads of Goodyear's patented heated rubber, took off as men
saw the benefit of the elastic material's versatility and stylishness. Goodyear
sold several new licenses based on the growing demand.

Manufacturing entrepreneur Horace H. Day—who, along with the
Englishman Hancock, would become Goodyear's nemesis—was one of
those who took notice of the progress Goodyear had made. Like other entrepreneurs of his time, Day had started his business career while still a teenager,
first going to live and work with his uncle, shoe manufacturer Samuel H.
Day, in New Brunswick, New Jersey, and later striking out on his own, opening a small factory in New Brunswick while running other businesses in his
hometown of Great Barrington, Massachusetts. In his twenties, Day had
already accumulated a fortune—perhaps a million dollars—and after he
married in 1838 he became active in Great Barrington politics. He was short
and powerfully built, with a full white beard and thatches of white hair that
flew up from the sides of his head. Fascinated by spiritualism, Day became
one of the movement's most important financial supporters, renting space
in a building he owned in New York City to spiritualist groups and a spiritualist publication. He regularly attended séances and believed he communicated with the dead. Arrogant and brusque in his dealing with others, Day
spoke out often on subjects such as labor and monetary policy. He often told
others he was "a born leader of men," although he didn't say if this applied
to lost souls looking for direction in the hereafter as well as those needing
leadership while still alive.

As the manufacturer of leather shoes at his small factory in New
Brunswick, Day was aware that rubber was a potentially revolutionary agent
in the footwear business and that craftsmen who had worked to waterproof
shoes and other articles were trying to adapt rubber and rid the material of
its maddening imperfections. Day used both rubber and sulfur from 1828
onward, often drying sulfur-treated rubber shoes and other products by placing them out in the sun. The odor sometimes went home with pieceworkers

employed by Day. Lydia Ann Mitchell, wife of John Mitchell, one of the workers, worried about the sulfur odors from trimmings that fell to the floor of their house. Lydia Ann's sister-in-law advised her to take the trimmings back to the factory shop, otherwise "people would think we had the itch," meaning lice.

Day had visited the Roxbury Rubber Company in 1837 and 1838 to try to pick up some cheap equipment during the company's liquidation. He struck up a friendship with manager Samuel Armstrong, and they both watched as Charles Goodyear, whom they regarded as an itinerant nuisance with an overblown sense of self-importance, bustled about the premises in a series of what appeared to be pointless experiments. Both Day and Armstrong agreed that Goodyear's alleged improvements in India rubber using nitric acid and its gas would come to nothing. But Day's disregard for Goodyear in the next few years escalated into a bitter antagonism after he had spent time talking to Goodyear's associate Nathaniel Hayward. Hayward had watched Goodyear's fortunes rise with the sale of shirred or corrugated fabric, which suspender makers had found useful. Impressed by Hayward's accounts of Goodyear's treachery in using his techniques and never paying him wages he owed, Day sought to re-balance the scales of injustice by learning Goodyear's secret for making heated gum and then using it to make the popular shirred goods himself.

Day's idea was to buy the secrets from Horace Cutler, a rubber goods maker with a small factory not far from Goodyear's place in Springfield, who had paid Goodyear $250 for the right to use the heated gum method. The terms of their agreement required Cutler to mark everything he made with the words "Goodyear's Patent." A small, sandy-haired man with grand whiskers and a Roman nose, Cutler later made a loan of some kind to Goodyear that Goodyear could not pay back. Realizing he had paid $250 for a process whose owner was in dire financial straits, Cutler concluded that the license and process were worthless. Someone else might be able to make money from a Goodyear license, but Cutler saw no evidence that he would be able to. To recoup his loss he wrote to Day, promising to work for low wages and give Day information about heating the gum. On December 3, 1842, Day invited Cutler to visit him at his Manhattan store at 45 Maiden Lane and suggested that he bring samples: "I wish to know if you can cut the rubber thread which G. uses for suspenders. He says it is spun." Two weeks later, when Cutler was in Day's store, the two men agreed that Cutler would go to Day's factory in New Brunswick, New Jersey, to teach

Goodyear's methods to Day's employees for a fee of $30 per month. Day told Cutler that when he arrived he should say he was from Massachusetts but not mention the town.

After a week at Day's New Brunswick factory, Cutler said he wished to leave because he didn't like the place. Then Day asked how much it would cost for Cutler to tell him outright Goodyear's method of compounding and heating. After thinking about it, Cutler said $75, but Day balked and told Cutler if he didn't give him the information he "could find out some other way." The two then agreed on $50 plus expenses for the trip to and from Springfield.

Cutler had brought some "green samples" of unheated rubber that had been prepared with sulfur at Goodyear's factory. Together, the two men went to Day's boilers, used to create steam power. Cutler took out the gray-brown wad, pierced it with a stick and began to barbecue it over the hot coals inside the furnace. As the heat engulfed the men Day said, "It's so hot Cutler, let me toast awhile." So he took the stick and turned it to allow the rubber wad to heat. After a while he said, "That will do, won't it?" Day then asked Cutler to go into the finishing room to tell him how Goodyear's shirred fabric was made with India rubber thread, and to tell him whether the threads were cut or spun. Day also asked Cutler to describe the mixing of the sulfur and lead compound, whether Goodyear used white lead that painters used and whether the sulfur was pure.

The biggest problem Day faced was the same one confronting Goodyear: how to raise the temperature high enough, gradually enough and keep it there long enough to change the rubber without blistering or burning it. So he and Cutler walked out to a small brick box Day used to dry rubber garments. There Cutler described Goodyear's oven: the five-foot-square box of cast-iron plates, set on a brick foundation with a furnace underneath and pipes rising from the furnace to convey the heat into the iron plate box. He also described the way the India rubber sheet goods were wound through the heating chamber on a reel, and how a belt slowly turned the reel. He told Day that Goodyear hung a thermometer inside the heater to govern the degree of heat "but much depended on the judgment and skill of the person who heated the articles of sheet rubber, in knowing when they were fully cured." And then Day asked Cutler to write it all down for him in a memo.

Cutler hesitated and told Day about Goodyear's pending patent and said that if Day started making things "under Goodyear's inventions, he must take responsibility."

Day answered, "Never mind that, I will manage that thing."

After Cutler had written his memo, Day gave him a note for $66 and some cents. Over the weeks and months that followed, Cutler worked at his shop in Springfield and fed Day other information about Goodyear. Day remained curious. "What is being made most new?" he asked in a typical letter dated January 27, 1843. On that same day George Eldridge, a former partner of Day's, finished an iron plate oven at Day's factory. That spring Eldridge built a drum or reel for the oven around which sheet rubber could be moved.

Cutler let Day know that Goodyear had had a machine made for cutting rubber threads to be used in suspenders, and that when Goodyear couldn't pay Amaziah Warner, the craftsman who made it, Warner had taken the machine back. On Day's instruction, Cutler bought the machine for $40 and sent it to the New Brunswick shop.

Even with all his purloined knowledge Day couldn't produce perfect rubber goods any more predictably than Goodyear could. Day wrote to Cutler in spring or summer of 1843 to ask him about problems with blistering on the surface of the heated rubber. In response Cutler again tried to explain the subtleties of the rubber toasting to Day, returning Day's letter to him, a security measure Day had requested. Soon afterward Day hired Joseph W. Harman, who had worked for Goodyear in Springfield, to learn everything he knew, too. But it was slow going.

Frustration finally forced Day out into the open. That summer he rode up to Springfield and appeared unannounced at the door of the Goodyear factory, where he met Charles' brother Henry. Day asked for the privilege of looking at the works inside, but Henry told him it was against the house rules. "He said he was well-acquainted with my brother Charles, and he knew if he was there, that he would let him go through and examine the works," Henry later recalled. Day's bluff failed. Henry told Day that Charles was upstairs and that he would get him. Goodyear came down and spoke with Day for a while but never let him inside.

Around this time Goodyear decided the moment had arrived to pen a final specification of patent. He drafted it in the form of another letter to his Washington, D.C., patent agent, Thomas Jones. Rather than being the result of an epiphany of material science, Patent No. 3633 amounted to a collage of what Goodyear thought worked best at the time. Untested by systematic scientific inquiry, it was no more than a pencil sketch of a process no one else and possibly not even Goodyear himself could reliably repeat. But these shortcomings in his patent did not strike him as odd, for, as with others of his time, he understood that patents, like ideas, were a species of speculation rather than the culmination of a proven design. A patent was just another milestone in a sharp-elbowed marathon heading toward the ultimate goal: the creation of a salable process. Once a process was discovered, the idea was to build as high a legal barbed-wire fence around it as the government would allow.

The opening section of his patent application repeated the triple compound of the last application in 1841—the combination of rubber, white lead and sulfur. But this time the proportions of lead and sulfur were reduced: 25 parts rubber, 5 parts sulfur and 7 parts white lead. Another change: in this version, Goodyear suggested that spirits of turpentine, as opposed to raw turpentine, was better in order to avoid impurities that marked the final product with blisters.

In the next section, Goodyear dealt with the grinding and compounding of the rubber and the sulfur. As an alternative to grinding, he wrote, these materials could be integrated using heated cylinders or calender rollers, like the Monster's, to create sheets of varying thicknesses. Goodyear also wrote about his method of laying a coat of compounded gum on a fabric, covering it with a bat of cotton wool and then layering on another coat of gum to produce "a very thin and strong fabric." In this regard Goodyear seemed to envision his rubber only as a fabric, or a sort of synthetic leather or animal hide.

The heating process, Goodyear's ultimate secret, was the key element in the application. He wrote that the heating could not begin until the compounded rubber and sulfur and lead had been dried in a heated room or in the sun. To heat the rubber, the fabrics could be run over a heated cylinder, but Goodyear preferred to "expose them to an atmosphere" of the proper temperature, which could best be done by the aid of an oven with openings in its side through which the sheets of rubber would pass. The mysterious change in the rubber would occur between 212 degrees and 350 degrees, Goodyear wrote, but for best effect the temperature should be kept as close as possible to 270 degrees Fahrenheit. He did not say how long the heat should be applied.

Up until the last moment Goodyear was still changing his mind about what represented his best patentable ideas about rubber making. In the final version of the patent, he said there was some leeway in the proportions of the triple compound "within such limits as will produce a like result." Such vagueness embodied a legal strategy because it prevented someone else from varying the proportions slightly as a way of circumventing the patent. But it also reflected just how uncertain Goodyear was about the best way to use his breakthrough to produce perfect rubber. His limited grasp of the prize he had sought so long meant that Goodyear's reign as America's rubber monopolist, which began with the granting of the patent on June 15, 1844, was based on a shaky claim.

Unaware of the legal traps his enemies at home and abroad were laying for him, Goodyear felt some relief that Patent No. 3633 was now safely in hand. He named the new substance Metallic Gum Elastic Composition and touted its durability.

At the time the patent was granted, the federal government was gearing up for the new waves of potential technological breakthroughs beginning to flood Washington, D.C. Following a fire that burned down the U.S. Patent Office in 1836, destroying most of the original patent models, Congress beefed up its operations in 1836 and 1837. As the portents of an unfolding industrial revolution spread among the states, applications poured in—from 765 proposed new patents in 1840 to 1,274 in 1845—and the Patent Office added staff to meet the demand for its services. The number of patents approved did not grow as dramatically—435 patents granted in 1837 grew to only 502 by 1845—but the upward trend was a measure of the young country's industrial progress.

If the future belonged to the patent-rich, Horace Day wasn't going to be left behind. Within a few weeks after Goodyear submitted his final, flawed application, Day, at last satisfied that he understood the secret of heating sulfur-compounded rubber, sent in his own patent application. Not surprisingly, it closely resembled Goodyear's. On the same day it granted Goodyear's Patent No. 3633,s the Patent Office rejected Day's heated-rubber patent for want of novelty.

CHAPTER SIX

"Do you think you are a scoundrel?"

The Lewis family of Salem, Connecticut, had a golden touch that produced fortunes over the course of several generations. The first to come to the area, weaver Joseph Lewis arrived about 1700, and during the next thirty years he parlayed his small holding of land into seven hundred acres, becoming the town's richest man. He added to his properties by lending money and caring for a widow, and was repaid with land. He also made money growing rye and exporting it to the West Indies. Joseph's great-grandson, Milo Lewis, proved equally prescient about trends. A small, wiry man with a thatch of red-brown hair, Milo was regarded as the first shrewd businessman of Salem because he organized the town's most ambitious industrial operation of its day. In a two-story, red-painted building at the mouth of the Beacon Hill brook, Lewis operated a cotton mill that spun fabric from dawn until dusk six days a week, with a bell in a tower ringing out the beginning of the workday each morning at 6 A.M. Despite their considerable wealth, Milo and his sons William, Samuel and Thomas elevated family ties above those of business. They even formalized their arrangement in a written agreement stating that although each had distinct responsibilities—one handled the farm, the other the cotton factory, etc.—all their property except for the clothes on their back was held in common.

Charles Goodyear invited red-headed Milo Lewis and his slim, sleepy-eyed son Samuel, along with William DeForest and a New Haven businessman named Thomas Elliott, to join him for a demonstration of rubber in DeForest's textile finishing shop. Starring in the demonstration would be Ellen Goodyear, now seventeen years old, a prim, plain auburn-haired teenager who was already something of a rubber-making prodigy. She had a high-school-level education, but her childhood had been cut short by family emergencies.

She had become her father's aide and assistant, and she was seated at a work table with a scarred butcher-block top. With her gray skirts touching the floor and her white blouse buttoned high up her neck, Ellen looked up at her father and Samuel Lewis on the other side of the table and raised her thick, arching eyebrows to acknowledge the men. Odd-shaped cutout patterns of unheated, sulfur-laced rubber, a spool of heavy black thread and a knife with a four-inch straight blade were arrayed in front of her. A chocolate-brown wooden form carved in the shape of a foot also sat on the table.

With the five men gathered around, DeForest towering above the others, Goodyear asked his audience if they were ready, then pulled a watch up from a chain in his vest pocket and told Ellen she could begin. Her sinuous fingers quickly stitched together the patches on top of the wooden last and, when finished, turned the unit inside out, concealing the seams. Goodyear looked down at the watch. The entire task of making a shoe had taken only eight minutes. Lewis's eyes met DeForest's as they both mentally calculated the fraction of a penny it would cost to pay a girl to repeat Ellen's exercise. She had proven her father's expectation that a skilled laborer could turn out many pairs of rubber shoes in a day of work. The shoe was carefully heated and shown to the Lewises; it was so impressive that they agreed to invest in Goodyear's venture. In September, Goodyear licensed Samuel J. Lewis & Company to make rubber footwear and twenty-nine men and women in their employ started turning out the new product.

Asking the neighbors from his old hometown to become his licensees proved to be fortuitous both for Goodyear and for the town itself. In 1843, Salem had not yet been renamed Naugatuck and set aside as a separate town from Salem Bridge, and the community was still very much as it was in Goodyear's childhood: sober, insulated, self-involved. The rugged hills and valley that held the rock-strewn riverbed had not yet been penetrated by the railroad line that would arrive in 1848, and dangerous rapids in the river meant that most of the manufactured goods had to be hauled by horse and wagon over the turnpike connecting the town to New Haven. Within the town's limits, rutted roads separated well-spaced farms and businesses. But change was coming. Western emigration was draining the population of New England: almost a hundred families left Naugatuck in the decades leading up to 1843. Membership in the Congregational Church had slipped badly, to about thirty-five. With an Episcopal Church now solidly established, the Congregationalists no longer had exclusive domain over town life and the threat of excommunication no longer meant total ostracism. To stay competitive, the Congregationalists adopted a milder Covenant that allowed for ascension to Heaven not only of the "Elect" but of any person coming to God. In 1842 the town's first Catholic family moved in. Between 1839 and 1844 a lyceum discussion group flourished in which male participants weighed in on subjects such as "Is the possession of a bad Wife a greater misfortune than the loss of a good one?" and "Is Infidelity more to be deprecated than religious fanaticism?"

For all the clocks and knives and Yankee notions produced in Naugatuck's small shops, textiles had turned out to be the town's industrial staple. The largest concentration of mills and factories still was located on the banks of the Fulling Mill Brook, where the Goodyears had once toiled. But the longest-operating manufacturer, on the Long Meadow Brook, belonged to DeForest. He had found success in the sale of satinet, the inexpensive fabric made of wool fibers pressed into cotton cloth. He had a house, a family and property, and for now, his loan of tens of thousands of dollars to Charles Goodyear had not caused him any discomfort.

Rubber, properly made, promised to be the next important textile. But first it had to be made with some predictability. The first licensed shop, the Samuel J. Lewis Company, was reincorporated as Goodyear's Metallic Rubber Shoe Company in 1845, and the same men, with new investors, also formed the Naugatuck India Rubber Company (later renamed the Union India Rubber Company and merged with the shoe company). It similarly made rubber clothing, with Charles' brother Henry as its superintendent and Thomas Lewis as its president. The initial stock of the shoe company was valued at $30,000, and of the clothing company at $40,000, enough capital to start a dozen other types of small business in the town. While the sales of the companies hit $120,000 a year in 1845, a huge volume, profitability remained elusive because of the trouble in making the process work reliably. Products routinely spoiled in the manufacture, and piles of burnt shoes and rubber sheet accumulated, the cash losses mounting along with the spoliation. The factories still needed to be resupplied regularly, with lead, sulfur, oxides of zinc, potash, coal for the engines, whale oil for the rolls and the machinery, lampblack, a potash vat, a new heater, a bleachery and cloths.

The best chemists in the country were stumped when called in for advice on how to limit the losses from spoiled product. They "were unable to throw any light upon the subject of difficulties or give any information of means of obviating them," recalled Benjamin Cooke, the Naugatuck Company's clerk. Making products of rubber was harder than "making the invention," he said.

The Naugatuck India Rubber Company's first factory, situated on what would later be called Rubber Avenue, centered on a three-story brick structure, the main building in a complex of smaller structures set at the foot of a lightly wooded hummock. From a smaller building behind the main structure rose a masonry smokestack.

The workday began early, before the sunlight had bled through the factory windows, brightening the dim bronze cast of the lamplight. Aproned men, shaking off their early morning languor, picked up the dun-colored bricks of raw rubber, set them on a worn wooden work table with a heavily scarred block top and chopped the rubber with axes and knives, like butchers working over new sides of beef. The cutters then deposited the rubber shreds in a 12-foot-by-4-foot vat, 2 feet deep, and poured water in to produce a dishwatery soup. Running through the vat was a knife- or blade-studded shaft or drum, which the workers then turned by hand, shredding the rubber in the gumbo. If the rubber had been well bought, the shredded virgin gum contained no vegetable acids to compromise the final product and the slashing and washing would prepare a clean charge for the next step in the process. However, any variable in age, origin and method of harvesting and transporting could foul the final product. Rubber kept for more than a few warm days soured and fermented—the odor of curdled milk or rotted vegetation was a warning sign. If used in finished products, this contaminated rubber was a time bomb whose defects could appear days or weeks later. Said Cooke: "I've known articles that appeared well when complete and had all the evidence of being properly [changed] but would decompose and become sticky a number of months after they were manufactured and in use."

Then the workers drained the vat and carried the cut and chopped gum up to the factory loft, where it was left to dry. In another area of the main factory floor, other aproned crewmen were already feeding scraps of dried and washed rubber into a long line of grinding machines. The machine consisted of rotating hollow steel rollers, heated by steam like a home-heating radiator. Through pressure and slipping and tearing and heat the rubber was reduced to a plastic, doughy mass. Five to ten pounds of rubber could be prepared in half an hour. An educated worker knew when to stop. If the heat was too intense or the grinding too long, the gum would change and partly decompose.

The next step for the rubber crews, compounding the doughy rubber with sulfur and other substances, was equally critical. For some products, the workers added the sulfur when the rubber was being fed through another grinding and crushing machine, this time with bigger rollers. The workers spooned in a half-ounce of sulfur for each pound of rubber. Where fabric was being made, they ladled the sulfur powder onto the surface of the dough, like a baker flouring his bread. Inattention or confusion could be costly at this point. If the lead and sulfur weren't fully and evenly distributed throughout the mass, one part would heat differently from another. The aproned rubber workers, knowing that lead was a poison, turned the process over to less-skilled laborers when it came to adding lead powders. "None but the poorest kind of operatives can be procured" for that labor, Cooke said.

Heating frustrated all efforts at quality control, with the worst problems caused by blistering, the result of gases escaping and exploding from the rubber. The gases made their way into the rubber via the solvents, such as turpentine, in which the rubber had been dissolved; so solvents were eliminated from the process. But sulfur sometimes came with acid in it, which produced gases when heated, and impurities crept into other aspects of the process if the workers weren't scrupulous.

The firemen or furnace and oven operators were the chefs of rubber making, but sometimes their tools failed them. The first heater built in Naugatuck would not distribute heat uniformly, and once that problem was solved, new ones appeared. Although fans were used to distribute the heat, parts at the top of the heater were well cooked while other parts were not. Banding and hose wouldn't heat where they were in contact with the wood over which they were hung. "We then tried iron funnel pipe to suspend belt and hose, but that overheated the part in contact with the iron," said Cooke.

Controlling the heat itself involved more intuition than anything else. Easing the heat up from 230 degrees to 260 degrees Fahrenheit, where the sulfur molecules would be coaxed into bonding with the rubber's isoprene molecules, required a craftsman's feel for the mingling of rubber, fire and sulfur. The only means of adjusting the temperature was to add or subtract coal or wood, but it was like steering a ship at sea. Once the thermometer was on its way up, cutting down the size of the fire almost never immediately reversed a fast-climbing temperature. Then, once the heat reached 260 degrees, it had to be sustained there and after a while eased up further to 280 and sometimes 300 degrees. The temperature and atmospheric conditions threw another devilish intangible into the mix. "It was impossible to fix scales of degrees of heat that would answer all kinds of weather," said Cooke. In the early days of rubber baking, the firemen and furnace operators, as the sun began to set, felt they had accomplished a fair day's labor if just half the goods they had started out with turned out well.

Providence seemed finally to be smiling again on the Goodyear family. With the money from the licensing fee from the Lewises, the family was freed from its long years of almost Dickensian penury. They moved into a modest house on the edge of New Haven (currently West Haven) in 1845, putting an end to their days of going-and-coming in Massachusetts. They applied for membership in the Congregationalist Church of Christ in New Haven. Clarissa and Ellen obtained a recommendation from the Eliot Church in Roxbury. Cynthia, the second-oldest daughter and the child most prone to worrying about what would happen to them all, had been attending a church school in Maine far from the hubbub of Goodyear family life and now returned to the family. Charles had traveled so much he had to go back to a Presbyterian church in Philadelphia for a recommendation for membership with the Congregationalists. "Mr. Goodyear has for several years been absent from this city, and from the circumstances that his personal residences in any place has been short and uncertain, he has refrained from connecting himself with any other Church," wrote the Philadelphia church's moderator on February 14, 1846. "Still I am happy to believe and state that his walk and conversation have been exemplary, and that he has uniformly enjoyed the worship and ordinances of God with the Church with which, for the time being, his lot has been cast."

Goodyear still traveled often around New England and New York, but no longer did he have to cadge a meal or a lodging or worry that the footstep behind him was the sheriff about to arrest him for debt. He hired a local minister as his personal secretary. The Sabbath was never breached. Sundays were reserved for the Bible, religious services and religious poetry. Not even during trips to New York did Goodyear let business come between himself and God. His secretary, A. S. Hunt, said that Goodyear was often at his hotel in New York, overwhelmed with business, "callers pouring in upon him every day," but never did he listen to a subject of a worldly character on the Sabbath. At home, he presided in his yellow smoking jacket while Clarissa and the children and nieces and nephews sat reading together. During worship in his own house Goodyear prayed in a loud, fervent whisper. In church during hymns his voice often soared over the voices of the other congregants. He was thankful that God had finally rescued him from his tribulations.

Clarissa was also grateful but still found their new life a bit unsettling. True, her two oldest girls, Ellen and Cynthia, were being spared the embarrassment of poverty during their sensitive teenage years. Charles Jr., still in school, was a hardworking boy eager to help his father in business. But Charles still made frequent and prolonged trips and often was preoccupied and distracted by work. Although their personal financial emergency had abated, he still played only a walk-on role in the family's daily drama, arriving for meals and worship and Bible reading but otherwise occupied with rubber. For the first time in her life, instead of being eager always to discuss business with Charles, Clarissa found herself feeling oddly jealous of his trips to New York and Boston. Much as he loved them all, her husband only slept at home about a dozen days a month. When the children asked her when Father would be home and why Father always had to work and travel, Clarissa defended her husband. But in her heart she felt rubber was a mistress with whom she was now in competition. The only way to get Charles' attention, it sometimes seemed, was to bear him more children. In 1846 she had a little boy, the third in a row they would name William Henry. This kept Charles in New Haven for an uninterrupted month.

Still, Clarissa couldn't help but feel as if she was on the outside looking in at Charles' manic strivings. He would ramble on endlessly about his business cares and ideas. He talked about the God-given mission he had to make rubber things, including life preservers that would prevent needless drowning. When Clarissa's turn came to talk about her friends, goings-on in town or what little Clara or the new baby had done, Charles' attention wandered. He would come alive again around his daughters—spontaneously hooking Ellen and Cynthia around the waist and dancing them across the parlor, shrieking with joy—but Clarissa felt unheard and self-conscious about her graying hair and thickening waist.

A stab of jealousy ran through her when Charles lavished kindness and attention on other friends and relatives. And Goodyear found it easier now that he had income to show his love and appreciation to them, constantly making gifts of rubber jewelry and other trinkets. To his young cousin Ellen Marie Goodyear, for instance, who lived in New Haven until the 1930s, he gave a rubber-framed watch after a breakfast get-together.

Goodyear's generosity knew few limits. "He could not look upon want or suffering unmoved, but acted instantly," wrote the Reverend Bradford K. Peirce. "His gifts were constant, and scattered in the quietest and most unostentatious manner, and often without thought." Goodyear's personal secretary,

Reverend A. S. Hunt, recalled a time when Goodyear heard that a friend's daughter was sick. Believing she would be made more comfortable by a rubber waterbed, Goodyear sent a messenger "at his own expense" to a rubber factory in Naugatuck with orders to make a bed immediately if none was available. Within a few hours the bed was delivered to New Haven. Another time, Goodyear and Reverend Hunt were riding to the train station, only minutes before the train was due "for he only allowed himself the shortest possible time after leaving his house to reach the station." On their way they met a "lame man, hobbling along upon his crutches." Goodyear drew up the reins, bringing the carriage to a stop, and handed the reins to Hunt. Bending down to the man, Goodyear asked, "What is the trouble with you, my poor fellow?" and without pause handed him $5 and then drove on.

But even his new prosperity couldn't keep the tragedy that had haunted his larger family for two decades at bay. His mother, Cynthia, had never fully recovered from the loss of her husband, son, daughter-in-law and grand child in the ill-fated Florida trip of 1841. As a survivor, she now was forced to watch as her second-oldest son, Robert, and another daughter-in-law died within a short span of months. As she and Robert's children were packed up to move to New Haven where they would live with Charles and Clarissa, Cynthia's heart gave out and she died. With the arrival of Robert's children in 1845, Charles now became responsible for four more school-age children. He felt a heavy burden to work harder to take care of them all.

Licensing agreements still constituted Goodyear's most lucrative form of currency and, on paper at least, the signing bonuses and tariffs made him a wealthy man. But so far, little of the full value of the licenses ended up in his pockets because he used them to chip away at some of the tens of thousands of dollars owed to Steele and all the other creditors. Now Goodyear also set about paying back the businesses and individuals in New Haven and New England that had supported him over the years. To D. Smith & Son and F. T. Jarman & Company, from which he had bought supplies, Goodyear returned $200 each. To Woburn neighbors who had lent a hand to his experiments, such as Fidelia Richardson and Rebecca Emerson, Goodyear gave $30 each. Years later the inventor would say that all $33,126 of his Massachusetts bankruptcy debt had been repaid, to the penny. Although this was unlikely, Goodyear did earnestly steer a substantial amount of his income toward those he was no longer legally obliged to repay because of his bankruptcy discharge.

Freed from the reputation of deadbeat that had shadowed him for years, Goodyear began to reinvent himself as a local industrial leader, a sort

of Prometheus who had produced from fire and brimstone a miracle material. Gone was the rubber-clad vagabond of Woburn Plains and Sodom Hill
in New Haven. And the itinerant nuisance that Horace Day had believed
he could easily "manage" had proven himself to be something other than a
gadfly. Guided by a coldly effective attorney, William Judson, and surrounded
by a constellation of affluent licensees, some linked by family ties, Charles
Goodyear had finally emerged as an apostle of industry.

He was often seen in Naugatuck and New Haven with his old friend
and supporter William DeForest. To Emmett A. Saunders, who managed
one of Naugatuck's rubber factories, the two men made an unusual pair. Big
DeForest often wore a buff-colored waistcoat with brass buttons and a furry
brown hat with a glistening nap. While DeForest could not hold forth the
way a college-educated man could, he still made, according to Saunders, a
beau idéal of a fine gentleman who had thrived mostly on his faculty for commerce. His fondness for Goodyear was evident: "He always spoke of Goodyear
with a wholly loving but half contemptuous accent, as if he were a dearly
beloved *enfant terrible,* that should not be held responsible for anything
except to be his own blessed self."

Saunders also recalled Goodyear as "a dreamer, reaching for the moon,
careless about such small and entirely material things as food, shelter and
clothing for himself and family." For these Goodyear depended on his friends.
"He would give anyone anything he had if they wanted it just then, and he
would take from anyone, borrow from anyone. Not because he was a men-
dicant or deadbeat, but because these things were of little importance and
sometime when his ship came in he would fix it all."

When his family was fed and housed by DeForest, Goodyear accepted
this charity as his due. For his part DeForest never kept account, wrote Saunders, but when Goodyear had anything that could be sold or traded, DeForest would competently take hold and help. But perhaps he supported
Goodyear to his own detriment. In 1846, DeForest's textile businesses sank
into bankruptcy after the market for satinet collapsed. DeForest's debt at
the time of his bankruptcy were reportedly the highest of any business in
New Haven County's history.

In the past, Goodyear had considered rubber a textile and had spoken of it
in the language of fabric and clothing. Like a haberdasher expounding on
derbies and bowlers, he fantasized about silks and silesias, double and single

textures, only occasionally daydreaming about other uses for rubber. His rubber was strong. Goodyear said his Metallic Gum Elastic Composition was resistant to cold and heat, to powerful chemical reagents such as sulfuric acid, and to pests such as rats and moths. The composition "can be washed in boiling water with lime or lye, without injury," and can be woven or braided, he wrote.

Now that he no longer had to scramble just to feed his family, Goodyear allowed his imagination to wander and began thinking systematically about how his miracle material could be used for other objects improved by elasticity or water resistance. The new composition, he wrote, could be adapted for belts and banding of machinery, for bags, rope and tarpaulin and as a substitute for paper and parchment. It could be used for maps and charts. One use that Goodyear had not yet envisioned for his heated rubber was a pneumatic tire. An Englishman named Robert W. Thompson had patented that idea in his own country the previous year. Thompson's idea was to encase a rubber tube in leather, so he was as ignorant as Goodyear about the potential durability of rubber on wheels. The notion was so premature, so far ahead of its possible application, that the pneumatic tire had to be reinvented nearly forty-five years later in Belfast, Ireland, by John B. Dunlop, at the onset of the age of the bicycle and the automobile.

In an October 1844 circular, Goodyear claimed that the federal government would find extensive uses for his metallic gum in mailbags for the Post Office and in artificial buffalo robes "cheaper and better than any blanket" for the Indian Department. "In now presenting it to the public," he asserted, "the subscriber invites the most searching investigation, and the most severe trial."

Goodyear took it on himself to demonstrate the viability of some of his ideas, such as rubber ship sails. He reasoned that the impervious rubber fabric would provide more air-resistant surface and therefore allow ships to go to sea with smaller sails, and that rubber's toughness would make it longer-lasting than canvas. Spending his own money, he first coated a sail with rubber in 1844 for the packet ship *Patrick Henry*. But the canvas was too light and the sail was stored in a warehouse. Unbeknownst to Goodyear, the clerks, "in a frolicksome mood, and not knowing why the sail had not been tried," had it raised on the Liverpool packet ship *Stephen Whitney* and then invited Goodyear "to go to sea under an India rubber sail."

First Goodyear felt annoyed at the clerks, but soon, "with feelings mingled with regret, hope, and fear for the result of the first experiment of so important an application," saw the sail set and fill with a stiff breeze outside the bay. The performance of this sail impressed Captain Popham, who ran the ship *Stephen Whitney* and crossed the Atlantic with it six times in winter and summer. It remained pliable and clear of ice "when other sails are frozen and stiff," Popham wrote on January 9, 1846. And he seemed to have been right when in the next year many of the New York and Liverpool Line ships were fitted out with rubber-coated sails rather than the best Russian duck.

This promising trial was enough for Goodyear to start planning to manufacture more sails for use in trials, at considerable personal expense. "He felt that halfway measures were inefficient, and that time was more than money," Charles Jr. said years later of his father. "He often found that an experiment tried on a very limited scale, though attended with apparent success, would be impracticable when attempted on a large scale; while the reverse might be equally true."

The other area in which Goodyear spared no expense was in his ceaseless priming of the publicity machine. It was beginning to bear fruit, especially the stories of how the inventor had suffered for his invention. In 1847, the *New Orleans Courier* reported on the remarkable advances that had been made in adapting heated rubber, transformed by Goodyear's patented secret process, into a material that could take the place of iron, leather, wood, linen, cotton, silk and wool. "The housewives of New England are beginning even to use it for culinary purposes, instead of tin ware and pot metal," the *Courier* reported, in words that bore Goodyear's distinctive signature. The story might have been paid for, but if so, it was worth the money. Goodyear sent the *Courier*'s correspondent a memento of their collaboration, a rubber map of Connecticut. And he couldn't keep from rhapsodizing about its construction: "Printed on the preparation, which is a kind of felt composed of a raw cotton and the gum adhered to it somewhat after the fashion in which hatters prepare bodies of hats. It is made much thinner than this specimen — so thin as to be very little heavier than the common silk for dresses, and, as thus prepared is now used for covering umbrellas, &c. There are nearly fifty factories at work on it already, and in time it is destined to be one of our most valuable branches of manufacturing industry."

In the first few years after winning his patent, Goodyear sold licenses as prodigally as he signed IOUs, often without close attention to legality. For example, one of his earliest licenses, for shirred rubber to be used in suspenders, went to Leverett Candee, a New Haven manufacturer, and his partner, stove-maker Steele, whose $6,000 in loans Goodyear had included in his bankruptcy filing. The license was part of Goodyear's attempt to make good some of that debt. But after about a year Candee and Steele's license was transferred to David Suydam, who paid Goodyear $15,000 for the right to make rubber products, including shirred fabric, under Goodyear's four rubber-related patents. Suydam also was supposed to pay Goodyear a tariff of a few pennies per product, which came to about $2,000 in the first year he held it. Goodyear sold a license for shoemaking to Milo Lewis and Samuel J. Lewis in Naugatuck. He also licensed the use of his patent to make rubber clothing to brother-in-law Josiah Tomlinson (married to Charles' sister Harriet) and for shoemaking to Nathaniel Hayward and his partner Henry Burr. Altogether, nine companies had licenses by 1845.

Although Goodyear took in considerable sums of money, he spent heavily on experiments and on servicing existing debts. His wealth was theoretical; his debt was real.

Patent No. 3633 had put him into a new field of operation. Now he was not only able to license a technology protected by his patent, but he also could tap another potential source of income by pursuing infringers. With so many rubber workers and small shop manufacturers churning out rubber shoes, turning up infringers was not difficult. Attorney Judson stepped in to fill the need for legal services that Goodyear now required on an ongoing basis. Still living on and spending borrowed money, Goodyear had no immediate way to pay for Judson's services. So he did what he had become accustomed to doing, stripping off a layer of the equity in his invention and patent and using it as a payment. Thus Goodyear executed the first of a series of agreements with Judson making the attorney a 5 percent partner in Patent No. 3633 and "any and all" rubber inventions and a 10 percent partner in any future inventions. The agreement was conditioned on winning or successfully settling lawsuits against Horace Day, the New Jersey–based businessman who tried so unscrupulously to find out Goodyear's process and patent it first. This stocky man, full of energy and confidence, now loomed as the biggest threat to the Goodyear group's control of the rubber business.

Day had started making shirred rubber, the combination of rubber and elastic thread that created a puckered fabric, on his own. Goodyear accused him of selling hundreds of thousands of dollars worth of shirred goods in violation of his patent. Day's supporters said that Goodyear and Judson sold Goodyear licenses to companies as a reward for infringing Day's several rubber-related patents. The lawsuits set in motion two trials in federal court in

New York, but they resulted in hung juries. The Goodyear licensees then unleashed another barrage of lawsuits, targeting Day's agents and customers in Massachusetts, Pennsylvania, New Jersey, Maryland and New York. Goodyear and Judson hoped the lawsuits would show that buying rubber from Day was dangerous. Goodyear's principal lawsuit against Day was filed in federal court in Boston. In that lawsuit Goodyear succeeded in winning a court order against Day that prevented him from shipping the rubber products his company had made.

A less determined—or malicious—opponent might have thrown in the towel at this time and realized that he was facing a deep-pocketed opponent willing to wear him down. But Day was single-mindedly bent on Goodyear's destruction. Moreover, he had discovered a valuable ally in Hayward, who in many ways was more skilled in rubber making than Goodyear. When Leverett Candee, an early Goodyear shoe licensee, saw that Hayward could heat thirty pairs of rubber shoes at one time with good results, he bought out Hayward and hired him for a year to work at his factory in Hamden, Connecticut. "I worked for this company through the year, and made perfect shoes," said Hayward. He had stamped goods he sold with the inscription "N. Hayward, Inventor of the Improved Gum," and printed business cards saying "N. Hayward, Original Inventor of Spring-Tempered Rubber." This left open the question of what improved the gum or made it spring-tempered: the sulfur, which was Hayward's contribution, or the heating, which was Goodyear's. But it scarcely mattered any longer. Hayward had sold the patent for his sulfur process to Goodyear. His only remaining goal was getting recognition for his contribution.

As Goodyear's prospects grew more promising, Hayward's generalized resentments crystallized. On September 24, 1844, he had a writing service send this message to Day: "I understand that Mr. Charles Goodyear has commenced a lawsuit against you for an infringement. If so, please write me, for I am the inventor of the heated gum, and the improved gum, which I can give any information you may want on your case."

When they met, the nominal topic of discussion was how Day would obtain a settlement of the suit against him by Goodyear. Day said his strategy would be to question the validity of Goodyear's patent until Goodyear agreed to a settlement. The strategy was not far-fetched given the number of people who had used sulfur and heat in some form before Goodyear applied high heat. Another reason it made sense was that Goodyear's methods weren't working well in the field, raising a question as to the usefulness of the patent—an important element in its legitimacy. Day knew that some Goodyear licensees were exploring the use of steam heat originated by Thomas Hancock in London. Nowhere in his patent did Goodyear mention steam. Day promised never to settle with Goodyear until Hayward had obtained justice, although what form that would take wasn't clear.

Hayward soon after started visiting witnesses with Day and advising Day's clerk about whom to ask for damaging testimony. Hayward's reputation among the rubber workers was enough to convince many of them to testify for Day. With Hayward's help, Day fended off the Goodyear group's battery of lawsuits. Some of the evidence collected was so convincing that Goodyear refused to go to trial on lawsuits in which he was the plaintiff, leading to charges being dismissed. And who wanted to waste time in court when there was money to be made? The market for shirred suspenders by now had reached about $1 million a year. Four or five factories run by companies controlled or allied with Day and Hayward baked rubber for the shirred fabric.

No matter how much satisfaction Hayward may have felt about lining up witnesses hostile to Goodyear, he still found it hard to break free of Goodyear's gravity. Goodyear still owed him money, the two knew much about each other's operations and Goodyear had a patent built on a technological advance created by Hayward. Although Hayward had proved his staying power in the rubber business by setting up a factory at Lisbon, Connecticut, where he made shoes stamped "Hayward's Spring Tempered Rubber," and he made a good living, he feared what would happen if Goodyear discovered that he was working with Day. "You must keep still, and not have Goodyear find out that I am assisting you about evidence," he wrote to Day on October 28, 1844.

As the months of litigation dragged on, Day felt Hayward slipping away from him. Hayward and his partner Henry Burr had begun negotiating for a license under Goodyear's patent. But this time Hayward was dealing with Goodyear from a position of strength he never before had enjoyed. In the presence of Halsey Brower, Day's former chief clerk in New York and a man whom Judson had hired away at a bigger salary, Hayward, Goodyear and Judson talked tough to each other over the terms of their arrangement. In Hayward's hand was the sulfur patent he had sold to Goodyear and which was bound up with Goodyear's patent as a vital step in the patented process. Hayward's testimony on the validity of the sulfur patent—say, a word or two against its novelty or usefulness, two critical elements needed for a legitimate patent—could pull the legal rug out from under Goodyear's successor patent in any future hearing or litigation. "Gentlemen," Hayward said, threatening to destroy the sulfur patent, "come up to scratch and do what I say, or I'll blow it all to the devil. The sulfur patent is worthless, and I can expose it." Judson agreed that as a stand-alone patent sulfur-treated rubber "was good for nothing."

Goodyear retaliated with his own threat: "Your patents are good for nothing; and if you don't pay me the sum of $3,000, I'll blow you all up."

Day tried to capitalize on the ill will. "Goodyear had the impudence to intimate that I had bribed you; pretty bold, was it not?" Day wrote Hayward on November 21. "He must think you, who have by your inventions, and his taking advantage of them, are a pretty considerable of a scoundrel."

Day pressed on. "Do you think you are a scoundrel? Do you think a man who deliberately patents an invention of another, an honest man? . . . Goodyear has done that thing exactly; and therefore, what he has said of you will not lessen my confidence in you in the least."

Nonetheless, Hayward broke off support for Day by December 12, when Day wrote of his disappointment: "From what I saw and have heard of Hayward's operations, I infer he has made all the benefit he could to Goodyear; and I would simply ask Nathaniel Hayward, how he feels in the inward man. Life has a long road to some, affording abundant time for reflection now, and memory to mark the place that knew us in flesh and blood; but I suppose you fancy yourselves better off. Mark what I write; you are cheated by your profess friends [sic], but your aid to Goodyear shall not save him."

Day did inflict pain on Goodyear. When his lawsuit didn't settle quickly, the licensees stopped paying Goodyear the pennies-per-product tariff portion he was owed under his agreement. And much of the money Goodyear took in went straight to settle his many debts. So by late 1845, he once again had to scrape along to survive.

When Goodyear's old friend William F. Ely returned from New Orleans earlier that year and got in touch, it wasn't clear exactly what he had in mind. Ely had not found his rich widow; he was still looking for a career and a business and some sign that the $10,000 he had provided Goodyear had purchased more than undying appreciation. And for a while it looked promising because Goodyear told Ely that his lawsuits "and other affairs are getting on finely, most of the pirates have quit." Without raising the possibility of how he might help Ely, Goodyear decided that there was a service Ely could render. "It would give me a great deal of pleasure to see you; in fact, you might be of great advantage to me in your testimony." Goodyear instructed Ely to write down what he could remember of the heating process, when Goodyear started it and the troubles he had in building the oven.

Goodyear didn't tell Ely that he had signed new licensing agreements worth tens of thousands of dollars during his absence, but Ely suspected that's what had happened. Nor did Goodyear suggest a way to compensate Ely. As in the past, he just appealed for help. "My care and perplexities are more than you ever knew them," he wrote to Ely. Goodyear wrote that until recently he had believed he was "beyond the reach of misfortune" and were it not for the lawsuits his income from his licensees would be $200 a day. But "the attack made upon my patents by H. Day is so daring and desperate, and the effect upon the minds of these establishments [Goodyear's own licensees] is such, that I am compelled to wait the result of the suits with him to know whether I am a rich man or a beggar."

Ely rode to Naugatuck for a reunion with Goodyear. The ex-soldier had agreed to contribute testimony to help in Goodyear's legal struggle, but Goodyear also sensed a cooler, distant and disdainful feeling from his old partner and confidante. So he pampered Ely on his return, lest he, like Hayward, end up talking business in the parlor of Horace Day. "Ely has rendered me great assistance, and is a very ingenious man, and he would be a dangerous enemy to me and my business," Goodyear told Charles Gilbert, the new majority stockholder in the Naugatuck Company, who had bought out most of the Lewis family's interests. Ask no questions, take good care of Ely, keep his friendship, for he is the most important man in sustaining me as an inventor, Gilbert was told. As a result, he allowed Ely to occupy the factory along with Goodyear, performing tests and experiments on new rubber-making techniques.

Ely, the one figure who knew the truth of Goodyear's "discovery," came up with a new rubber-making method involving shoes and fabric. He applied for a patent, through the company, and Goodyear advised the Naugatuck Company's owners and managers to buy him out for $10,000 (the amount owed under Goodyear's factory contract with Ely ten years earlier in Staten Island). Then Ely headed down to Brooklyn to market rubber goods made at a factory co-owned by Charles' brother Henry. When there was a delay in the government's granting the patent, Ely's resentments boiled over.

Goodyear was playing him false, and if he wanted to he could break down Goodyear's claim to patent. Goodyear would find he was a dangerous man to trifle with, Ely said ominously, and the world would find out who was the true inventor of heated India rubber. Goodyear did his best to placate his old friend.

Goodyear's licensees gathered together and decided to put up another $10,000 to drive the Boston infringement lawsuit against Day to conclusion. The money was raised and given to James Bishop, another Goodyear lawyer. Judson had been negotiating with Day but finally gave up. Goodyear and Judson set their final terms: in exchange for the right to all shirred products, Day would make a one-time $10,000 payment to Goodyear. Day insisted he would only pay $5,000. Negotiations between Day and Judson broke off, and Bishop stepped in to try to clinch the deal.

Day wrote to Goodyear to bargain with him directly, assuming that it was in Goodyear's interest not to go to trial. "I think if you was in New York a settlement could be made yet," he said. After reviewing the $5,000 difference in their positions, Day indicated he was glad to let Goodyear continue suing him while he continued to enjoy a monopoly. Strong feelings on both sides might be overcome if Goodyear would come to New York. "I cannot but fear that we never shall again get as near a compromise as now, and tis my most deliberate advice to you to save while you may, or Judson will damn it beyond retrieve."

The settlement agreement was drawn up and initialed by Day with the terms unchanged and still requiring Day to pay Goodyear $10,000. Day found Judson so disagreeably hard-nosed, so confident in his willingness to grind him down with legal costs, that he left New York to see if he would fare better dealing one-on-one with Goodyear in New Haven. Goodyear's lawyers, Judson and Bishop, hurried up to New Haven when they realized Day had gone to see Goodyear. There was no telling what Goodyear would do or sign without them. Day told Goodyear, and Bishop when he joined them, that the agreement drawn up in New York was too hard on him. Judson joined them in New Haven, and the four men talked a great deal but nothing was settled.

After returning to the New York City area, Day still believed he could turn Goodyear against Judson. Come to New Jersey "with Mrs. G." today, "make a visit at my house and enable me to have undisturbed intercourse with you for mutual advantage," Day continued. "Your old opponents must save you from your friends, come to New York at once and stay here, or at Jersey City." Without revealing specifics, Day said he had still more information that Judson was conspiring with others to wrest control of Goodyear's patent from him. "If you want my best help henceforth you shall have it, but do not be heedless of my warning, the worst part of this battle is yet to come I fear, and the danger you are in is greater than you are all aware."

Instead of dumping Judson, Goodyear deepened his business relationship with the lawyer by selling him a bigger slice of Goodyear patents. In August, Goodyear and Judson executed a new pact entitling Judson to a 12.5 percent interest in Goodyear's existing patents, to be collected after a court decision or settlement.

The Boston lawsuit was due to start just after Christmas. Day sent Goodyear one last note urging him to compromise, and Judson and Goodyear finally relented. The two sides agreed to the terms previously negotiated but with the lower payment Day had sought. In exchange for a one-time $5,000 payment, Goodyear granted Day the exclusive right to make all rubber for shirred suspenders, garters and such, but he could not touch any other part of the heated-rubber goods market, such as fabric or shoes. Day also promised Goodyear three cents for every yard of shirred goods he made and pledged to mark the rubber with the name Goodyear as patentee. In exchange, Goodyear was to wage a legal campaign to run everyone else out of the shirred goods market, giving Day an effective monopoly.

With that pact Day became a Goodyear licensee, and the very next order of business was for Goodyear and Day to begin besieging the other shirred goods manufacturers in New Jersey, New York and New England with lawsuits, based on infringement of Goodyear's heated gum patent. In January 1847, Day published an ad in the *Fredonian* offering a $50 reward for information leading to the conviction of anyone "who may be found after this date, engaged in the piratical use of any of his patents," or those granted to Goodyear, used in the manufacture of shirred goods. Three weeks later, under Goodyear and Day's names, another ad ran in the *Fredonian* informing the public that all the lawsuits between Day and Goodyear had been settled and that violations of Goodyear's patents would be immediately prosecuted.

The settlement brought Day inside the circle of licensees led by Judson. That summer, they gathered at a hall on the east side of Broadway, below Liberty Street in Manhattan, to smooth relationships among them and secure prompt and regular payment of the pennies-per-product tariffs due to Goodyear. Assembled for the meeting were William H. Elliot, Goodyear attorneys James Dorr and James Bishop and William Judson, and licensees such as Nathaniel Hayward and Horace Day, the dramatis personae of Goodyear's business life. Goodyear also hoped to inspire confidence among the licensees and tell them that trustees had been appointed to hold his patents who would create a fund to prosecute infringements, collect the revenue and disburse it. To get the fund going to prosecute infringers, all the licensees agreed to make a contribution of $50,000 against future settlements won against infringers, secured by a note with a very long term. Unity temporarily relieved Goodyear's licensees of their domestic competitors. But the struggle to control rubber was far from over.

CHAPTER SEVEN

A Capacious Monopoly

Goodyear remained in New Haven and Naugatuck factory workshops testing new applications for rubber. In the mornings and evenings, his joints ached—doctors told him he had gout, but more likely he suffered from lead poisoning. His feet and toes hurt so much that he often used a cane or crutches to move around, giving him the appearance of being older than his fifty-two years. His face had a yellowed, unhealthy color. His hair had receded at his temples but a proud pompadour still topped his widow's peak, an unruly lock sometimes falling boyishly across his forehead. His eyes seemed to have retreated into his head.

The inventor's career, Goodyear had learned, was a melancholy pursuit. On paper he was quite wealthy, having earned tens of thousands of dollars in licensing fees. Yet after paying William Judson his percentage, retiring some loans and financing his experiments, Goodyear had just enough for his family's living expenses. To be sure, his standard of living had improved and his children attended good schools. But the recently completed legal battle had cut into the pennies-per-product fees he was owed on sales—some licensees didn't pay him at all until the lawsuits were settled—and his borrowing, particularly from Ralph Steele, had accelerated again by 1850.

"A volume might be written in explanation of the peculiar difficulties and embarrassments to which [inventors] are subject—as a general rule their labors begin, continue, and end in 'necessity,'" Goodyear wrote. The very first inventor he mentioned in his catalogue of woe, John Fitch, was an early developer of steamships who, failing to get support from the federal government for his steamship company or patent protection from rivals, despondently abandoned his effort and committed suicide. Goodyear felt impelled to do the opposite and give the world his gift no matter what the personal cost. Yet he knew that no matter how much compassion the public expressed for inventors, "there are too many ever ready to encroach upon their inventions, without their knowledge or consent. However valuable and important an improvement may be, it seldom happens that the rightful owners are benefited by it."

Goodyear resolved to carry on. He wrote that "on the whole I am satisfied with the past and the present on account of the great success of the art, although at the present time of writing I am hardly benefited in a pecuniary sense, in requiring as large an expenditure to complete the system" of rubber applications while receiving comparatively paltry payments from his licensees. He still hoped to score a decisive financial coup by selling new military applications he had dreamed up to the U.S. Army and Navy, after which "I should have no reason to complain of my lot in a pecuniary sense."

Under Goodyear's original license agreement with the Lewises, he was provided space at the Naugatuck factory to continue his experiments and the company was supposed to make and sell new products he invented. The arrangement apparently survived a transfer of a major portion of the company stock to Charles Gilbert, a man with little patience and fewer long-term ties to Goodyear than the Lewises. Gilbert reluctantly furnished Goodyear with rooms, machinery, workers, raw India rubber and other stock in an arrangement reminiscent of Goodyear's stay at the Roxbury Company in 1837, when for a number of months he helped himself to whatever he needed and had it all charged to his account, to be paid at some indefinite time in the future. Goodyear ran the tab at the Naugatuck Company to $2,300, but as far as anyone could tell he never paid any of it.

The Naugatuck Company wanted Goodyear to concentrate on the rubber business's standard products: suspenders, shoes, clothing and elastics. But his vision now embraced all kinds of eclectic applications. Gilbert and others concluded that Goodyear had "an inveterate propensity for inventing, and a fondness for new things." They mentioned this as a criticism, but this was exactly how he saw himself. Rubber, not profit, was his *raison d'être*. He had once feared dying before the secret heating method had been perfected and proven. Now he worried that people would be deprived of all the important applications he wanted to chaperone into the world. And he linked his need for new licensees, the only way he could make financial progress, to rubber's limitless potential. Goodyear's famous patented and improved metallic rubber—that was how it was described on dozens of products— was now established in the popular mind as what he had always thought it to be: a miracle material. "It was a cloth impervious to water. It was a paper that would not tear. It was a parchment that would not crease. It was leather which neither rain nor sun would injure. It was ebony that could be run into a mould. It was ivory that could be worked like wax. It was wood that never cracked, shrunk, nor decayed," enthused one writer. It was elastic metal and through "trifling variations" in its preparation could be "pliable as kid, tougher than ox-hide, as elastic as whalebone, or as rigid as flint." Rubber would defend from dampness speculators who packed off to California to pan for gold. It would speed ships across the sea. Whatever Americans needed, rubber could provide.

All the licensees urged Goodyear to put some money in his pocket while he could by sticking to line extensions of existing products. As he later wrote in the third person, "With kind intentions, no doubt, they, together with his other friends, earnestly deprecated his devoting more time or money to experiments, and constantly urged him to turn his attention to obtaining a pecuniary compensation from the branches already established." Instead, he imagined a world of rubber bag clasps, rubber sword and pistol covers, rubber pontoons and pontoon boats, rubber breast pumps and urine bags. This world was taking shape in an 8-inch-by-6-inch hardcover journal on whose gold-edged pages he sketched, in delicate, sure-handed pencil lines, his visions: rubber inflatable invalid cushions, baby jumpers and swings, fetlock fenders for horses and footbath tubs.

Goodyear kept his journal and pencils at his bedside, and he rose frequently during the night to record his latest epiphany. His experience had "put him in possession," he believed, of much "information that would otherwise be lost in the event of my death." If he died anytime soon, hospital patients and invalids might never lie down to rest in a rubber air or water bed. The hard of hearing could never benefit from a rubber ear trumpet and hernia sufferers would never be soothed by the abdominal supporters and trusses he had designed. He worked to record his vision so that these benefits would outlive him.

Most of all, he was haunted by the shipwrecks and steamboat disasters that claimed so many lives in the early years of steam navigation. Often, there were too few lifeboats and life preservers on board ships, and the ones that were provided were leaky and unreliable. Goodyear felt certain his suite of flotation devices and life preservers could end the tragedies. "What! Must men continue to be drowned because their fathers were! Must treasures continue to go to the bottom of the deep because there are offices where they can be insured! The loss to the world on that account is none the less, and such a state of things in the present age need not, and ought not, to exist."

Occasionally Goodyear had to return to the real world, especially when his legal troubles interrupted his fantasies. Horace Day was once again a problem. The precarious relationship had shattered over shoes.

With the discovery of gold at Captain Sutter's land in California, a new customer base had opened up. Rubber merchandisers promoted their products to the California-bound, hawking them in flyers and newspaper ads. Daniel Hodgman, a Goodyear licensee with a store at 27 Maiden Lane in Manhattan, sold rubber hats and shoes explicitly marketed for gold mining. Patented overshoes, "manufactured from Goodyear's metallic rubber," would "retain their brilliancy of gloss, will not stiffen in cold weather, and are extremely light and durable." Horace Day tried to sell into the gold fever, too, advertising a rubber boat at his store at 23 Cortland Street in Manhattan. He lauded his product as a "Patent India Rubber Boat which can be converted in a few minutes (as now made) into a most convenient Tent (more like a house with windows than an India Rubber Tent.)" The boat could carry up to six passengers and Day claimed that "With this boat Colonel Fremont crossed rivers, navigating their rapids." He didn't mention that Fremont had spoken of the boat's bad odor and of how its seams came apart on the Great Salt Lake and it had to be bailed.

Footwear was more promising. High rubber boots with springs or gussets in the soles or heels were inexpensive favorites. Sweat was still a problem, so the shoe manufacturers built an inner sole of fabric or leather or another porous material, or cemented a stay around the edge of the upper and stitched a leather sole to it. Rubber was also used to make popular Buffalo-skin shoes more water-resistant, and to provide elasticity to the upper part of the shoe that circled the ankle as an alternative to laces or clasps or other means of fastening. By 1850, Leverett Candee's factory in Hamden and William DeForest's in Naugatuck were baking fifteen thousand shoes and boots a day.

Horace Day had no right under his settlement pact with Goodyear and Judson to make or sell any rubber footwear, but with sales booming he decided to make rubber footwear anyway. He rationalized breaking the agreement with the thought that the Goodyear group had used the armistice as a ploy to smother him. In the words of one lawyer involved with the matter, Day felt that if he had been welcomed into the Goodyear family, it was in the way the python welcomes the lamb, embracing it and squeezing out its life.

In Day's revisionist account, the Goodyear licensees ran their factories around the clock in order to dump as much shirred rubber as possible onto the market before January 1, 1847, when he was to begin his monopoly. This flood of inferior suspenders and garters struck Day as a consummate act of bad faith. He took no legal action and wrote no letter of complaint but collected evidence—and grievances—for later use.

He was not appeased by the fact that he was turning a profit, churning out shirred rubber fabric at a cost of between $1 and $2 a yard and selling it in strands of thread that put the retail value at $4 a yard. Day's opponents put his total sales as high as $90,000, but his friends said the total market had fallen to $20,000. From then on, however, shirred rubber sales would retract. A new type of suspender made in France began to win favor among American men—not of rubber thread combined with ordinary fabric to create a puckered look, but completely made of rubber. The reign of the shirred suspender was over, and Day's monopoly in that market category became less profitable as the total sales fell. Horace Day was left high and dry.

In 1848, he repudiated all his contracts with Goodyear and jumped back into the shoe business, as did others who infringed Goodyear's patent. Day also began the manufacture of all kinds of fabrics, and he bought the right to make rubber railroad-car springs from a patent holder, despite the fact that he knew other investors had already bought from Goodyear a right to them under his patent. Day refused to become a subcontractor to Goodyear's intellectual property, and he set himself on a collision course.

Judson and his legal team filed new lawsuits against Day and his agents, in different states, with the help of the railroad-car spring and packing manufacturing companies. Attempts to negotiate settlements went nowhere, and Judson and the other plaintiffs tried to get court injunctions shutting down Day's operations. His goods were attached, a court officer was placed in his factory and his creditors or the courts required Day to post security. "The whole litigation," according to *Hunt's Merchants' Magazine*, which supported Day against Goodyear, "was renewed with more virulence than ever, with new interests involved, and a fresh corps of litigants."

Another challenge faced Goodyear and his licensees in England. Thomas Hancock, aided by his long experience in chopping and heating rubber, now heated much of his rubber in steam boilers. It put him and his licensees far ahead of the Americans in developing and bringing to market new applications. Among his new ideas were ship sheets, giant rubber patches that could be applied to the gashed hulls or leaky pressure vessels of the new steam ships, allowing them to be repaired at sea without costly journeys back to dry dock. Hancock's licensees also were using his heated rubber to make machine belting (December 1844) and washers and packing for steam-pipe joints (December 1844). Soon he or his licensees were producing rubber engine valves (May 1845), and then selling billiard cushions, spongy rubber for musical instruments, hose-pipe, tubing and surgical bottles (June 1845). As another year ended, Hancock found markets for blankets, gig and carriage springs, buffer springs for railcars, artificial leather, pump-buckets and buoys.

In 1845, Hancock's crew also lined the perimeter of a carriage wheel with solid rubber about one and a quarter inches thick and an inch and a half wide. Hancock noted that "wheels shod with them make no noise and they greatly relieve concussion on pavements and rough roads." Later that year, Hancock also made for the first time an inflatable wheel-tire. While Goodyear licensees in the United States still searched for ways to make similar processes economical, Hancock was putting steam-heated rubber tires on the Queen's carriage.

Sometimes new uses were imagined for rubber that it was unable to fulfill. Hancock had experimented during the Crimean War with a combination of metal and rubber to serve as protection from bullets and cannon balls for infantry and riflemen in the trenches. (In a doomed demonstration, Hancock fired a shot through a wall-mounted breast of mutton shielded by a pad of rubber: the bullet easily pierced both.)

Up until now, Hancock had referred to the transformation wrought in the heated gum only as "the change," but now he felt a new term was needed. While discussing the subject with William Brockedon, the resourceful friend who had first shown Macintosh some sample patches of heated rubber made by Goodyear, Brockedon suggested "vulcanization," a reference to Vulcan, the Roman god of fire and craftsmanship. Hancock liked it.

Hancock had understood the issue of heat in the rubber manufacturing process. He wrote that heating in an oven worked all right with sheet goods, especially when the sheeting could be kept in motion by rollers or conveyors, much the way Goodyear first had heated sheet rubber in Massachusetts. But steam heating under pressure in a boiler was the only way to

Goodyear, with daughters Ellen and Cynthia, around 1830.
Courtesy of Goodyear Tire & Rubber Company.

Clarissa Goodyear, year unknown. Courtesy of Goodyear Tire & Rubber Company.

Goodyear, age 45 or 50, about the time or shortly before the Great India Rubber Trial in Trenton. Daguerreotype by Southworth and Hawes. Courtesy of the Society for the Preservation of New England Antiquities.

Goodyear, age 58 or 59, not long before he died. Photo by Alexander Gardner/National Portrait Gallery, Smithsonian Institution.

Nathaniel Hayward, year unknown

Horace H. Day, year unknown.

Thomas Hancock, 1850.

Daniel Webster. Courtesy of the New York Public Library Picture Collection.

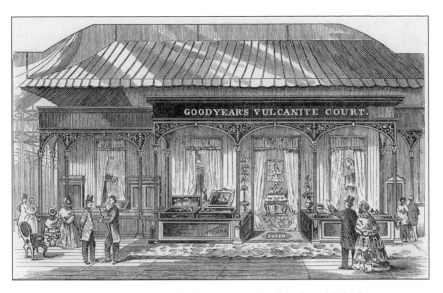

Goodyear's London exhibit (at the second site of the Crystal Palace).

"HE WAS CONSTANTLY RIDICULED AND CALLED CRAZY"

Illustration of Goodyear accompanying story of his life published 10 years after his death.

Opening ceremonies of the Great Exhibition in London.
Courtesy of the New York Public Library Picture Collection.

Christian Schussele's Men of Progress, painted in 1862, shows Goodyear (seated at left with cane leaning against his leg) looking toward Samual F. B. Morse at imaginary gathering of other prominent 19th century inventors. National Portrait Gallery, Smithsonian Institution.

Statue of Goodyear at the doorway to the Goodyear Tire & Rubber Company exhibit in Akron.

heat more massive shapes. Steam heat was always uniform in every part of a boiler. It's one thing to oven-heat a pair or dozens of pairs of shoes; it's quite another to do the trick with a railcar bumper. If rubber was going to make its way off of the sweaty feet and arms of Englishmen and Americans and into the fuller service of mankind, it would have to take many shapes, some of them quite bulky. And heating with steam, under pressure, proved the far better style.

There were other advantages. Sulfur, which never smelled good, had a way of migrating to the surface during oven heating, producing a sulfur bloom or efflorescence. With steam heating, the sulfur and its aroma stayed put inside the rubber. "I believe it to be utterly impossible to do this by any other mode, certainly not by dry heat," Hancock wrote.

When Goodyear heard about the advances in England, he denied that steam heating without lead could catalyze the transformation of rubber. Making rubber without lead and sulfur together was impracticable, he believed, and so far all the steam-heating tests he had performed or observed had been inconclusive. But after Charles Gilbert invested in the Naugatuck Company in June 1846, he and Goodyear discussed Hancock's steam method and Goodyear began to take the subject more seriously. Other rubber makers operating in the Northeast could license steam heating from Hancock or adapt their own system and compete with Goodyear's licensees. Even William Rider, who had helped Goodyear in the 1830s, was now using a steamed steel cylinder for curing India rubber.

Meanwhile, Day was continuing to attack the validity of the patent from his own battleground. When Goodyear's process of heating triple-compound rubber in an oven was dissected in court, Day would be able to show that Goodyear's method was based on a process that couldn't deliver perfect fireproof gum. Worse yet, Day could argue that Hancock's processes had already superceded Goodyear's method.

Gilbert advised Goodyear to "take some energetic steps to protect his monopoly and defend his patents." The licensees inventoried their options and decided they needed to bolster the intellectual property "to cover and embrace all other processes for making vulcanized rubber," said Gilbert.

The general plan was to form a strong combination and a large fund that would sustain Goodyear at all hazards, right or wrong, and deter all other parties from manufacturing vulcanized rubber unless they paid tribute under Goodyear's patent. With "plenty of money, and combined effort, and the most effective patent lawyer," said Gilbert, an amendment could be written to the patent of 1844 "for re-issue as to cover everything that had been discovered in England and this country up to that time." It had to be written so that it appeared that Goodyear did not intend, in his specification and claim, to confine himself to the curing of a triple compound specifically by a heated atmosphere alone.

When the sulfur-bath and steam-heating methods Hancock had patented first appeared in scientific journals, they were speedily adopted in France and extensively in America. Even though Goodyear himself had never successfully used them, much less invented them, he soon enough linked his name to the process as if it had been his idea all along. He wrote that "doubts of the success of the manufacture were not wholly removed until the gum came to be ground and worked with steam heat, instead of being dissolved with turpentine."

Judson and the licensees regrouped, with six boot and shoe companies aligned in a separate association. So it was that on July 1, 1848, the Goodyear Associates and Licensees (or, the Shoe Associates) was born. In addition to one of the original Naugatuck companies, its members consisted of L. Candee Company, New Haven; the Hayward Rubber Company, Colchester, Connecticut; the Newark India Rubber Manufacturing Company, Newark; Ford and Company, Milltown, New Jersey; and Onderdonk & Letson, of New Brunswick. Their first order of business was to pay Charles Goodyear $10,000 and promise him a tariff of a half-cent per pair for exclusive rights to manufacture shoes, far below the three and a half cents per pair that the original licensees had agreed to pay. The association immediately sold rights to make shoes to the Goodyear Metallic Rubber Shoe Company and Hartshorn & Company, in Providence, for a tariff of three and a half cents per pair, providing the association a significant source of income over time and guaranteeing it license revenue from the beginning of its existence. Like the original group of Goodyear licensees, each member was subject to penalties for violating the terms of its agreements to control prices and styles.

But higher on the agenda was crushing anyone making rubber shoes who was not a member of the group, particularly Horace Day. For this purpose the licensees assessed themselves a three-cents-per-pair royalty to fund a legal war chest.

By mid-1849, Goodyear and his Washington, D.C.-based patent agent, Thomas Jones, were ready to submit the revised specification to the U.S.

Patent Office. It was, as far as patent writing went, an unusual composition. For one thing, its preamble was an essay on rubber that went on to describe Goodyear's exploits and exertions. Finally the patent got down to describing in detail what was to be patented. This time, however, Goodyear and his lawyers phrased things a bit more universally:

> The leading feature of my invention, and that which chiefly constitutes the substance or essence of its usefulness, is the discovery of the effects produced on India rubber, by the action of artificial heat, at a temperature above that to which the fabric would be exposed in ordinary or common use.... Although I have above only described the mode of preparing and curing sheets of India rubber [which, along with shoes, was the only form of rubber Goodyear's process could transform], it will be obvious that my method of curing is applicable to articles of any desired form.... What I claim for my invention, and desire to secure by letters patent, is the curing of caoutchouc, or India rubber, by subjecting it to the action of a high degree of artificial heat, and substantially as herein described, and for the purpose specified.... And I also claim the preparing and curing the compound of India rubber, sulphur, and a carbonate or other salt or oxide of lead, by subjecting the same to the action of artificial heat, substantially as herein described.

So the fire mattered more than the brimstone. And Goodyear had intended his patent all along to mean any kind of rubber cooking, with any ingredients, not just with sulfur and lead, the elements that comprised two-thirds of the triple compound in the previous version of the patent. It was the counterintuitive combination of rubber, which seemed to melt when heated, with very high temperatures that Goodyear now made out to be his innovation, even if he had no idea of what it was when he discovered it. As far as Judson and the licensees were concerned, woe to any who crossed onto the sacred ground now staked by the 1849 replacement patent.

In attacking the Goodyear patent monopoly, Day not only stirred the beehive of rubber licensees, but also touched on deep-seated fears about corporations, which were just then making their debut as manipulators of the U.S. economy. To some laborers and small business owners, corporations had no roots in family and geography and were creatures of malign legal fabrication that if left alone would crush competition and create monopoly. Their tendency to weld themselves to one another to form ever bigger and more powerful organizations struck an ominous note for smaller business owners.

It was these sentiments that Day planned to play on when, four months after the broadened patent was granted in December 1849, a group under his leadership submitted to Congress a memorial with a long, self-explanatory title:

> Petition to the U.S. Senate and House of Representatives from Manufacturers, Dealers and Workmen, Engaged in the Business of Fabricating India Rubber, in Reference to the Present Defective Patent Laws and the Recent Unlawful Re-issue of a Patent to Charles Goodyear, for Vulcanizing India Rubber, Dated December 25, 1849, Upon the Surrender of his Patent Dated June 15, 1844, Together with the Legal Opinions of Distinguished Counsel upon the Invalidity of the Acts of the Commissioner of Patents. SHOWING FRAUD and the Necessity of a Law for the Repeal of Fraudulently Obtained Patents.

Two hundred business owners and individuals signed the petition.

The main body of the petition consisted of statements from more than a dozen attorneys claiming that the reissued Goodyear rubber patent was a "palpable attempt to defraud the public, by appropriating to himself, what in truth is the common property of all." In it Goodyear is portrayed as a charlatan engaged in a rubber-covered deception. Goodyear "crawls up by degrees" to new claims which he "artfully edges in," wrote Providence attorneys Samuel Ames and Abraham Payne. "The slightest comparison between the original and amended patents, proves such art and contrivance on the part of the patentee, in weaving together the little he knew in 1844, with the much that everybody, without his aid, knew in 1849, so as to make two things, essentially different, appear to be alike, as of itself to indicate fraud."

The petitioners hinted at corruption and at gullibility on the part of the patent commissioner. "The nearest approach to invalidity on the face of the papers, is made by the evidence of gross fraud practiced upon the Commissioner, afforded by a comparison between the original and the amended patent; for we will not speak of connivance between the Commissioner and the patentee without positive proof." Goodyear had exploited the inexperience of the new commissioner of patents, the petitioners said. "The marks of fraud practised upon one, new to the duties of his office, are so strong, that it is difficult to pronounce that an intelligent jury or a sound judge, would not, upon a mere inspection of the papers, without further proof than they afford, be justified in finding fraud in the surrender and renewal of this patent."

Congress denied the petition, but Day was not through. He next turned his campaign to business newspaper ads filled with sarcasm. The text of the ad in the November 6, 1850 edition of the *New York Commercial Advertiser* begins:

> LATEST DISCOVERY IN RUBBER—NEW RECEIPT—Get patent "honestly if you can, but get it." If other people make discoveries which renders your patent obsolete, useless, throw it up—take out another covering everybody's discovery—not necessary that you should be the inventor, but swear strong-pay five, ten, even twenty thousand dollars to agents to get a re-issue; commence a dozen suits to annoy your neighbors. If defeated, try again, and again. If, in an interlocutory motion, your opponent is refused by the Judge get some name under which to publish, and boldly assert that your patent is sustained by the Court. Truth is not necessary under this new system, boldly assert that you have heavy suits, no matter if twelve or fifteen of the most eminent legal advisers in the country publish in newspapers that a decision is in your favor.

Day accused Goodyear and Judson of striving for monopoly at any cost by intimidating formerly independent rubber makers to join them as licensees, eliminating competitors. "Keep capitalists out of the business, and you will make a fortune, retire, and be perfectly respectable."

Finally, Day commented on the peculiar importance of public relations in creating the myth of the inventor: "A single word of caution: don't fail to make the world believe your man is a great genius; use his name, but keep him always out of sight."

If Horace Day was expecting Charles Goodyear to reply to these accusations, he was bound to be disappointed. The job of responding to accusations of monopoly, all the bellicose pronouncements, belonged to Judson and the licensees. Goodyear's patent may have nourished a tightly bound tribe of manufacturers whose revenue and power had grown rapidly, but people didn't realize that Goodyear did not make all products that bore the words "Goodyear's Patent" on them. Because of his financial improvidence, his need to raise money by selling licenses and his desire to remain a pure inventor, he was only benefiting from the monopoly indirectly. And while Goodyear may have been proud of the industries that arose from his patent, he certainly didn't feel as if he himself was an industrialist sitting atop a growing monopoly such as those ruled by Vanderbilt and later on by the railroad barons. Goodyear belonged to another world.

As soon as the new patent was granted, the Shoe Associates began filing new lawsuits against Day, his customers and his agents in five states. A final decisive legal confrontation was shaping up, but it wasn't clear how it would be fought. Nor was it clear that Charles Goodyear would be present for the showdown. A huge industrial exhibit had been planned for London the next year, in which Goodyear hoped to show that rubber meant more than just shoes and raincoats and suspenders.

CHAPTER EIGHT

A Trial for the Century

Horace Day was wealthy by the standards of his time, operating three rubber factories, employing three hundred workers and living in and moving among homes he maintained in New Jersey, New York and Massachusetts. He also held a number of rubber-making patents. But his confrontational nature was draining his resources. In 1847, not long after he had made temporary peace with Charles Goodyear, Day had built a dam along a river branch in his hometown of Great Barrington, Massachusetts, and opened another rubber fabric plant in a building on the banks. Although an engineer questioned whether there was enough water flow to power the equipment inside Day's plant, he began operations and for a while it seemed that rubber making might boost the Great Barrington economy. But soon after the plant's completion, the Berkshire Woolen Company claimed that Day's dam backed water up and slowed the flow powering the wool company's equipment. Its owners forcibly removed part of Day's dam, and Day promptly fixed it.

The conflict divided the townspeople of Great Barrington, with some favoring Berkshire Woolen and others backing Day. Local politicians ran several elections where the conflict was the main issue. When the matter ended up in a federal court in Boston in 1849, Day pulled out all the stops and summoned nearly fifty witnesses from Great Barrington and fed and housed them. But it didn't help; he lost the lawsuit and had to cut eleven inches from the top of his dam. He had too little power to continue, so he pulled out his equipment and abandoned the factory. The building in decades to come became a spooky ruin where Great Barrington school children found discarded rubber and chewed it as gum.

That Horace Day would even consider taking on other opponents while struggling with the Goodyear licensees showed his aggressively foolhardy determination to prevail in every arena. Yet he had never faced an opponent quite like the Shoe Associates—and William Judson. The lawyer's relentlessness was by now becoming more apparent. His influence over Goodyear was considerable—Day often said that Judson and Goodyear were for all practical purposes the same person—but Judson's additional ability to direct Goodyear's licensees made him even more formidable. Judson had abandoned all his other interests and clients to run the Shoe Associates and by this time had amassed a considerable fortune. Still, his appetite for battle was stimulated by Day.

As the trial approached, Judson and his team poured it on. They sought depositions from dozens of witnesses and testimony stretching back to the 1820s, with some witnesses giving their second or third depositions in the India rubber litigation. For a while Judson set up operations at the Boston-area house of William Trotman and from there coordinated the Massachusetts depositions, including all those from Goodyear's Woburn neighbors. In Connecticut, Nathaniel Hayward, who was himself now growing rich from rubber making, submitted to several days of interrogation between June 18 and July 11, 1851, answering 709 questions that when printed filled 92 pages of near-microscopic type. Day's legal team, led by a lawyer named Francis B. Cutting, was already on its heels. Judson arranged for thirteen separate witnesses to be deposed at the same time, in different cities, making it impossible for Day's lawyers or their associates to be present at every examination. Day's team went before the judges in Trenton and won a delay in the trial. The court appointed three commissioners before whom all testimony was to be taken.

Day's witness list concentrated on the possibility of a jury trial in which Day would challenge the validity of Goodyear's patents. To that end the witnesses were heavily represented by experimenters who had used rubber and sulfur and heat, and workers employed by Day. One of them, shoemaker Ford C. Skinner, swore he saw Day in 1827 or 1828 cooking rubber and sulfur in a tin pan. "I asked him what he made use of the ground brimstone for. He said it was to keep it from sticking. I asked him how he came to make use of the brimstone. He said it was because his aunt made use of it to bleach her hats and he thought he would make use of it to bleach his rubber." By 1834 and 1835, Day was so devoted to his rubber work, Skinner claimed, that "his whole soul seemed to be wrapped up in it; nothing seemed to daunt him." The only trouble with the sulfur was its lingering scent. It was believed to be a particular nuisance to women, who were thought to have a more refined sense of smell than men.

Day's strategy, in addition to indicating his own critical involvement in the creation of rubber-making technology, was to try to diminish Goodyear's stature by establishing the ubiquity of treating rubber with sulfur and heat among others who had tried to tame the substance. David Brown of Philadelphia testified that in 1813 and 1814 his brother William and a carriage maker in Salem, Massachusetts, name Abraham Fowler created a mix of gum elastic paints they called gum elastic cloth and that they used rubber and sulfur. William Beers of Woburn (owed money never paid by Goodyear) testified that he had suggested to Goodyear gradual heating of the rubber to prevent blistering, entitling Beers to a claim on the discovery. Hatmaker Elisha Pratt testified that he had used rubber, lead and sulfur in 1834 and 1835 to make cloth hats coated with rubber. The lead made the rubber "a body of more substance" and the sulfur was "a great dryer." A providential accident occurred when some hats were hung too close to a stove—not unlike Ely's and Goodyear's—which transformed the rubber, making the hats lighter and "very elastic and springy." The heat in the room was great but not so great that Pratt could not remain inside with the door closed.

A somewhat more compelling account of precocious rubber making was told by Richard Collins of Baltimore. He claimed to have heated a compound made of dissolved rubber shoes, sulfur and white lead in a wood stove in his one-room apartment. The experiment went well and Collins says he repeated it while working for various rubber companies in Massachusetts: "I did it secretly, so that no one should know." Over time he told his secret to three or four other people whom Collins had since lost track of. Collins' brother, John, backed his brother's story. He testified that Richard always kept the sulfur and lead locked in a chest so that no one would learn the secret. Eventually, Collins sold his secret formula to Leander Earle.

As soon as Collins' deposition was in hand, Judson's team heaped scorn and ridicule on him and his story, suggesting fraud. But there was much to fear in his tale; Collins had earned $1,000 a year working for rubber companies and thus had a good deal of professional credibility. And Collins had indeed managed to sell his secret to Earle. So Judson recruited Earle and paid him several hundred dollars to give testimony that would undermine Collins and his credibility. Of particular interest were the original receipts written out by Collins and provided to Earle for rubber cement, rubber and sulfur, and rubber and lead and sulfur, which Earle had stowed in an old trunk. The minute Earle unexpectedly indicated during deposition testimony that he would make the receipts available as exhibits in the case, Judson and his team turned on Earle and claimed he had no credibility.

At one point Day's attorneys tried to get hold of the books of the Eagle India Rubber Company, where Hayward and Goodyear both had worked and whose ownership Hayward had inherited as the company failed. (Day needed to establish that sulfur had been used before the patent was established, to show that the practice was common before Goodyear patented Hayward's sulfur method.) Day also wanted to blur Goodyear's claim on the patent by suggesting that Hayward, who once claimed to be the inventor, was the true father of vulcanization and that Hayward had sold out too cheaply and was cheated. Judson, with his usual expediency, got hold of the Eagle Company's books and kept them locked away from Day's lawyers.

While the legal battle was going well, Goodyear and Judson had not yet secured clear victory in the publicity campaign. They needed a way to neutralize Day's aggressive ads and articles in the *New York Commercial Advertiser* and other publications. The Goodyear licensees established a fund that Judson drew on to pay for anti-Day articles in newspapers in Washington, D.C., and Boston. In one arrangement, Judson hired a writer named D. F. Bacon to plant some of these stories in local publications. Judson told Bacon that Day was "a very bad, dishonest, mendacious and artful man who by misrepresentations published in the newspapers, had succeeded in creating a very general false impression in the public mind as to the character and history of claims of Charles Goodyear." According to Bacon, Judson said "it was difficult to obtain a fair and unbiased jury for the trial of the patent cases then in litigation ... and that it was necessary to disabuse the public mind of the false impressions and to set forth the true history of the inventions and patents." Whatever Bacon delivered, it apparently didn't satisfy Judson. Bacon sued him for failing to pay his fee of $1,750.

Tactical legal considerations now dwarfed all other concerns. In keeping with its effort to grind down Day, Judson and the Goodyear team had filed at least two separate lawsuits against him in federal court in New Jersey. Day's attorneys hoped to have Goodyear's suit tried "at law," or before a jury, believing their best chance at a favorable decision was to raise the issue of the basic validity of Goodyear's patent before a panel of laymen. A trial at law also would take the decision itself away from a panel of federal judges whose objectivity Day suspected could be compromised by the fact that one of the judge's sons was a counsel to Goodyear. If they could present their case to a jury, Day's lawyers could arrange for a procession of early rubber bakers to talk about their work and cast doubt on the novelty of Goodyear's original patent.

On the other side, Judson and his team hoped to try the case "at equity," or before judges, who would weigh the legal technicalities of the injunction they sought to prohibit Day from making non-shirred rubber products. A trial at equity would probably not involve the question of the patent's validity. Instead, Judson and his team hoped to argue that the matter was simply a breach of contract where one party failed to live up to its obligation to the other, and a patent infringement under which Day compromised Goodyear's legally granted intellectual property rights.

The "at law" suit against Day, which would require a jury trial, had been filed first, and Day's attorneys assumed it would be called to a trial first. At a conference with his lawyers in the weeks leading up to the trial, Day's legal team decided not to take depositions for the other case. No court, Day's lawyers believed, could ever force a final hearing on the equity side before all the jumbled facts had been reviewed by a jury. Thirty witnesses on Day's list who lived within one hundred miles of Trenton never gave deposition testimony for a trial at equity because Day's attorneys assumed that these same witnesses would appear in person at a jury trial.

Then, with a single dramatic stroke, Day grabbed the advantage. Looking for oratorical talent and political connections, he recruited the top trial lawyer of the age, former Massachusetts congressman and senator Rufus Choate, to deliver the key opening statements and summation. Choate was a Whig known less for his service in Congress than for his rhetorical mastery in winning judgments in civil and criminal cases. His physical presence was riveting: he stood six feet tall, and had olive-colored skin and mirthless, beseeching eyes. He also had a bald pate ringed by a wreath of untamable hair. "His contorted lips, disheveled locks, and somber expression gave him a weird, exotic appearance, as if he were the product, not of staid New England, but of some far-off planet," a reference book about great Americans would later state.

Choate often spent so much energy on his legal orations that after he had finished he was prostrate for several hours. But his efforts had produced historic victories. In one murder trial, he used somnambulism as a defense and won acquittal. In another case, he won the exoneration of a Roman Catholic priest accused by a girl of criminal assault, and he did it before a

Protestant jury. There were those who disparaged Choate's knack for setting free the apparently guilty, but that kind of criticism only seemed to expand his renown as "the Wizard of the Law."

Everything Judson had set up so far to make the Goodyear patent impregnable was now in trouble. But there was a man who could neutralize Choate's charisma, and that was the celebrated Daniel Webster, another Massachusetts Whig who was then U.S. secretary of state. Would a sitting cabinet member take temporary leave of his cabinet post to argue a commercial case? Would he interrupt his federal service to rent himself out to powerful interests to pick up large litigation fees? Ordinarily the answer would have been no, but Judson happened to know that Webster was deeply in debt and made him an offer he couldn't refuse.

Although taking the case would give ammunition to those who regarded him as morally bankrupt and mercenary, most Americans regarded Webster as a historical figure who had shaped the Republic. His speeches in Congress twice helped to postpone civil war, and his arguments before the Supreme Court in civil cases shaped the character of constitutional law. A capitalist and champion of big corporations, Webster's walk-on role in the Goodyear saga changed it forever. If Goodyear had submitted rubber to fire and brimstone, Webster would now submit Goodyear to history.

That is, if he still had the strength and mental dexterity to do it. In his prime Webster had been an intimidating, dramatic figure with dark, tangled eyebrows punctuating his massive face. But his burly form had shrunk with illness and age, and his voice had lost some of its resonance and cadence. He drank too much and often was ill and needed medical attention.

At first Webster said no to Judson's offer. He had too much work, and didn't wish to travel to Trenton in February or March when it would still be cold. The Shoe Associates then told Peter Harvey, Webster's colleague and friend, that the fee would be $10,000 for arguing the case and another $5,000 for winning it.

"That is an enormous fee," Webster told Harvey. "Can he [Goodyear] afford it?"

Harvey told Webster that it was Goodyear's business "whether he could afford it and that Goodyear was shrewd and that everything he had now was at stake."

"It's a hard thing to undertake," said Webster. "It is an unfavorable season of the year, and my duties at Washington are pressing; but really I do not see how I can forego the fee. This fee I must have, for it will pay fifteen thousand dollars of my debts, and that is what I am striving to do. If I can pay my debts, I shall die in peace, a happy man. I do not see how I can begin to do it so well as in this way. I shall go and accept the fee." George Griswold, a New York rubber manufacturer allied with Goodyear, sweetened the deal by offering Webster an additional $1,000 in the event he won the case.

As the legal antagonists began to prepare for battle, the key player was flat on his back in a New York City hotel. Goodyear had spent the previous months in London at the Great Exhibition staged by Prince Albert. It had been a triumph. Millions of visitors had passed his exhibit in the Crystal Palace, and he was one of only a handful of Americans to have won a precious Council Medal. He had proven himself the equal of his rival inventor Thomas Hancock. Even the jury, trying to walk a diplomatic fine line between the competitors, had helped to elevate Goodyear's stature: thanking Macintosh & Company and Hancock for the popular waterproof clothing, but noting Goodyear's "skill and perseverance" in producing waterproof rubber shoes. Hancock had discovered "anew" something Goodyear had already invented, and he had found that lead isn't needed to vulcanize rubber at a time when Goodyear believed it was "indispensable," the jury wrote. But Goodyear clearly was considered vulcanization's first father.

He had won acclaim at the greatest industrial exhibition ever held, and his name began to spread in Europe along with shoes made by his licensees. Dozens of new business prospects presented themselves, and that was good, because Goodyear's expenses were running high and his health was erratic. The costs and effort involved in keeping his family in London and recreating his exhibit in Sydenham, the site two miles north of London where the Crystal Palace would be rebuilt after the exhibition in Hyde Park closed, would also be great.

Goodyear was exhausted and the crossing from England had taken a toll, sending him to his bed again with illness when he reached New York. Clarissa tended to him as best she could. When Haskins, the friendly Roxbury Company founder who had always liked Goodyear, called on him at his hotel, he found the inventor confined to his bed. "If Mr. Judson wished me to go to Trenton, I must and will," Goodyear told Haskins, although he appeared to be in no position to go anywhere.

When Webster reached Trenton, he found the city as cold and snow-covered as he had expected. His presence was similar to that of a champion prizefighter and he was courted by civic leaders. He turned down a dinner invitation by the civic committee of Trenton but accepted one to address a special joint session of the state legislature. Goodyear, who had also arrived despite ill health, was attentive to Webster's comfort and placed a horse and carriage at the lawyer's disposal at the American Hotel.

Webster later recalled that Goodyear was particularly anxious about the transportation and asked him, "Do you like that horse, Mr. Webster?"

"I think he is a very noble animal," Webster replied.

Trenton at that time was emerging as a capital of iron and steel man-ufacturing. The Roeblings had opened the wire rope manufactory that would produce the cable strands to tie together the Brooklyn Bridge. Peter Cooper had invested in an iron mill and Josiah Bird and Edward Weld had pur-chased an axe factory and added a foundry. These ventures and their suc-cessors would blossom in the coming decades. But for now all the town's people could talk about was the Great India Rubber Trial scheduled for fed-eral court. The vying claims over rubber technology stirred interest mainly among business people and business newspapers, but the participation of Daniel Webster and his face-off against Rufus Choate excited a more gen-eral curiosity. Lawyers and visitors from other cities booked hotel rooms in town in anticipation of the rhetorical display to come, and ladies from New York in particular made their way to the courthouse. On the morning the case opened, March 23, the federal court in the statehouse was filled to over-flowing. Hale and healthy and full of long-smoldering resentment, Day took a seat. Goodyear, planted at the end of the plaintiff's table, "looked more dead than alive," according to Haskins.

Day's legal team pronounced itself ready for the jury trial that would unravel the tangled history of the manufacture of rubber, but the Goodyear side refused to press that suit and instead insisted that the equity case on Day's alleged infringement on Goodyear's patents be called. Motions and countermotions were made. (At one point a young lawyer on Goodyear's team named Dickerson, the son of one of the two judges hearing the case, stood up just as Webster was about to speak, and Webster was so insulted he refused to get out of his chair afterward.) Over objections from Day's team, Judge Grier said that no trustworthy jury could be impaneled in New Jersey because the facts on the origins of the new durable heated rubber were too tangled for laymen to sort through. "It is more than probable," Grier later wrote, "from the confusion created by the great length of the testimony and argument, and from the force and effect of those urged from interest, no verdict would be obtained, and most certainly none that would alter the present convictions of the Court."

The trial at equity—a victory for Goodyear—was to commence the next morning. This meant that Day's team was forced to proceed with a case for which it had failed to take much relevant testimony, failed to examine all the possible contingencies and probably failed to do adequate research. No witnesses were to be called to testify—the matter now hinged on interpretations of contract law and commercial agreements. If the judges wanted, they could consult the depositions and submitted exhibits, 1,300 pages of them. The Wizard Choate would have to work his magic on federal judges rather than on jurors.

With arguments about to get under way, Trenton schools closed and businesses were shuttered. Crowds thronged around the courthouse. A reporter for a local newspaper reached the courtroom at 11 A.M. and could not get inside. The judges moved the proceedings to the Trenton County Court, which seated seven hundred. On the first day attorney James T. Brady spoke all day for the plaintiff. Although there is no record of his presentation, he is likely to have argued that by entering into his pact with Goodyear in 1846 and becoming Goodyear's licensee, Day forfeited any future right to dispute the validity of Goodyear's patents. And further, that once Day took a license from Goodyear and entered a covenant not to infringe his patents, he admitted the patents' validity and was now prevented from claiming otherwise. As a symbol that compromise had been reached between Day and Goodyear, Brady pointed to Day's letter to Goodyear trying to arrange a deal before trial and the invitation Day extended for Goodyear to visit him at his home. Brady also described Goodyear's last-minute letter to patent agent Jones asking for changes to be made in the 1849 patent application. The changes seem to indicate that Goodyear didn't mean to expand his claim on all rubber making through the reissued patent, but meant to limit it to the heating of sulfur and rubber through "heated atmosphere" or "sulfur gas." In other words, Goodyear wasn't engaged in a patent land-grab, as Day's side had claimed. The letter was not introduced into evidence until the last minute, preventing Day's team from examining it in great detail.

One last element of Brady's presentation turned out to be especially clever. When he reached the great questions of originality and priority in the patent, he turned to the learned counsels for the defense and challenged them to name one man who deserved to be known as the heating method's inventor along with Goodyear. "If Charles Goodyear is not the inventor of vulcanized rubber, who is?"

The silence was pregnant.

Day's legal team then set down the main outlines of the defense: that the basic patent was invalid because the processes it described were already in the public domain; that Day knew everything there was to know and was using shirred fabric techniques two years before Goodyear's 1844 patent; that Day "meant to reserve his right" to manufacture, in any way he pleased, other items of rubber after Goodyear failed to protect Day's agreed-upon monopoly in shirred products. This last point involved the legal theory of estoppel, regarding the rights of people who make agreements.

On the fourth day of the trial, Friday, March 26, Choate spoke for five hours on the subject of estoppel, portraying Day as the duped victim of a monstrous business combination and its predatory attorneys. While the subject of combinations had not yet inflamed the American public the way it would fifty years later, there was a growing suspicion of their power and practices. The injuries they had delivered to Day were said to have nearly destroyed him as a human being.

Those in the courtroom considered it a great discourse, but the Wizard had been denied his wand, his chance to make an emotional plea before a jury of laymen. Not a word of his oration survived in court or historical records.

With Choate's effort focused on the issue of estoppel, the main summation for Day now was left to the less magnetic Francis Cutting, who took over after the Wizard had finished. For the next two and a half days Cutting described Goodyear as a self-aggrandizing johnny-come-lately to the rubber trade, riding the achievements of others, the puppet of a powerful cabal of lawyers and manufacturers who exploited him to justify their own profits. Goodyear wasn't even a legal plaintiff with standing to sue Day, Cutting argued, because he had sold large stakes in his patent to his lawyer. Judson was a rightful (though much less sympathy-inducing) complainant and should be listed as such.

Cutting said that Goodyear had violated patent law in several ways. First, he had kept his "secret" to himself and only much later applied for a patent, and second, he had patented a process, curing rubber and sulfur through "an atmosphere" in an oven, that is impossible to perform. "I call upon the learned counsel on the other side to put their fingers upon any particle of evidence which tends to show that any person ever did vulcanize rubber combined with the gas of sulfur."

At that moment Webster challenged Cutting by offering to have Goodyear vulcanize rubber right there in the Trenton courtroom. "The practicability of making good vulcanized rubber by the use of rubber and sulfur alone, can be exhibited in this court at any time," Webster interjected. Webster was taking a huge gamble. In the few weeks he had studied the subject he could not have known the difficulties of vulcanizing rubber in an oven, much less doing it as a command performance. The results could have been disastrous for Goodyear's case.

Luckily, Cutting backed away. "I must differ with my very distinguished opponent," he shot back. "But I must say that I know of nothing so deceptive, nothing so difficult of detection, as what he proposes. I have seen experiments made in court before. I have tried cases where the most perfect exhibitions were produced in open court, during the heat and bustle of a trial, were successful, not elsewhere to be accomplished."

"We do not press it, sir," Webster said. So the prospect of a risky rubber-baking demonstration in court disappeared—although raising it had damaged the defense's case.

Cutting resumed his argument, noting that when the original, ill-worded patent was superceded by the new one in 1849, it was like a settler staking a claim to more than one homestead. The new patent surrounded all of rubber making with an outrageously expanded claim of invention covering any kind of heat, including the well-known English method of heating with steam. "The evidence shows that Goodyear was ignorant of the use of steam in 1843; and knew nothing of it until informed by others, after his patent was taken out," the lawyer charged.

In his summation, Cutting nominated no less than half a dozen inventors of vulcanization, none of whom happened to be Goodyear. Richard Collins in particular, the rubber maker who had heated rubber and sulfur in his Baltimore apartment, was suggested as the true author, but hat maker Pratt, carriage maker Fowler, and Day himself also were possibilities. Then Cutting picked out his favorite: Nathaniel Hayward. Hadn't Hayward at one time claimed to be the inventor? Why else would Goodyear have had Hayward sign a sworn statement unless Goodyear was buying the invention from him? Why else would Goodyear favor Hayward with so many lucrative licenses? "What could have been the motive or reason for paying exorbitantly and enormously for a mere certificate of fact [with Hayward stating that Goodyear was the one true inventor], if that fact were true?"

After two and a half days of talking, Cutting told the judges that if they granted Goodyear his injunction, Day would be finished. Appeals would be fruitless because before they could be made Day would have suffered huge losses. And if after everything they had heard the judges had any doubt about the disputed facts, Cutting told them, the right thing to do would be "to send the case before an impartial jury."

Choate had eloquently defended Day's right to rubber after Goodyear's camp had apparently violated the pact, outlining the concept of estoppel with a fine-point pencil to show that his client was completely within his rights to make rubber products that seemingly violated Goodyear's patent. And now Cutting, perhaps more than Choate, had methodically explained the broader injustice so that even the most disinterested jurist would feel compelled to correct it. It seemed to observers that a miracle would be needed for an effective rebuttal. So many facts and nuanced legal theories would have to be overturned that the challenge seemed insurmountable. Even a healthy Webster at the peak of his abilities might not have been able to do it, and Webster was far from his peak. No one knew if he had absorbed the details of the case deeply enough to embed them in the compelling rhetoric for which he was famous. As he started to speak, with the haggard Goodyear sitting a few feet away, it was hard to tell whether the lawyer or his client was more physically unwell.

Webster began by apologizing for the "evil odor" that sometimes arose from the record of the case, a reference to the defamatory advertising against Goodyear and allegations of corruption. Then he explained that property rights of inventors are inherent and recognized in the Constitution. A patent is no odious monopoly, he said, but rather a man's intellectual lifeblood.

Webster launched into a narration of the natural history of rubber and its early uses. He described the 1830s rubber manufacturing boom in the United States. All the manufacturers failed and all the would-be inventors of vulcanization, Collins and Stoddart and Pratt, "the whole of them came to nothing." Then Charles Goodyear stepped into this landscape of failure.

Webster paused to comment on the suggestion made by Day that Goodyear first failed in the hardware trade and came into the rubber business as a refugee. This "odious statement," as Webster called it, hardly warranted repeating because everybody knew Goodyear was "a man of inquisitive, ingenious, laborious turn of mind." What was the state of the rubber industry, Webster asked, before Charles Goodyear went to work in it?

The statesman then wittily described his own experiences with frozen rubber clothing at his farm in Marshfield, Massachusetts. "A friend in New York sent me a very fine cloak of India Rubber, and a hat of the same material. I did not succeed very well with them. I took the cloak one day and set it out in the cold. It stood very well by itself. I surmounted it with the hat, and many persons passing by supposed they saw standing by the porch, the Farmer of Marshfield."

Webster reviewed Goodyear's "wanderings," carefully describing the episodes of poverty and reproach, "the destitution of his family, half clad." He pictured Goodyear "picking up with his own hands, little billets of wood from the wayside, to warm the household ... receiving indignation and ridicule from his friends." Webster took out a copy of Goodyear's letter from jail in Boston dated April 21, 1840, where Goodyear invited Haskins and Baldwin to call on him at his hotel, saying he felt some "anxiety on account of my family," then ending resignedly by saying that jail was "perhaps as good a resting place as any this side the grave."

Webster turned next to Clarissa. "In all his distress, in all his trials, she was willing to participate in his sufferings, and endure everything, and hope everything; she was willing to be poor; she was willing to go to prison, if it was necessary, when he went to prison; she was willing to share with him everything and that was his only solace." Tears gathered in many spectators' eyes. "May it please your honors, there is nothing upon the earth that can compare with the faithful attachment of a wife; no creature for the object of her love, is so indomitable, so persevering, so ready to suffer and to die."

But Webster hadn't finished squeezing the melodrama out of the Goodyears' past: "Under the most depressing circumstances, woman's weakness becomes mighty power; her timidity becomes fearless courage; all her shrinking and sinking passes away, and her spirit acquires the firmness of marble—adamantime firmness, when circumstances drive her to put forth all her energies under the inspiration of her affections."

Inventors, Webster said he had learned from personal experience, spend huge amounts of money, time and thought on risky plans that at any instant may be duplicated elsewhere. One inventor he admired was Nathaniel Hayward, who managed to keep his secret, that of using sulfur and rubber. "He made his discoveries in the arts as other people make discoveries—by experiments, by comparison, by watching the operation of natural causes." Webster compared Hayward's methods to Newton's and said Hayward "learned things step by step, and not by one leap."

The magnitude of Goodyear's achievement, Webster said, rested in the counterintuitive nature of vulcanization. If heated along with sulfur to 212 degrees, rubber softens and melts, as most people would expect. But through untiring experiment, Goodyear found that applying a much higher temperature hardens the "vegetable substance" and makes it "metallic." Who could anticipate this apparent anomaly in the workings of nature? Webster asked.

> And now is Charles Goodyear the discoverer of this invention of vulcanized rubber? Is he the first man upon whose mind the idea ever flashed, or to whose intelligence the fact ever was disclosed, that by carrying heat to a certain height it would cease to render plastic the India Rubber, and begin to harden and metallize it? Is there a man in the world who found out that fact before Charles Goodyear? Who is he? Where is he? On what continent does he live? Who has heard of him? What books treat of him? Yet it is certain that this discovery has been made. It is certain that it exists. It is certain that it is now a matter of common knowledge all over the civilized world.... If Charles Goodyear did not make this discovery, who did make it?

For the remaining hour of daylight, Webster pulled on every loose thread in Richard Collins' story of how he had figured out the secret of heating India rubber and sulfur, unraveling Collins' testimony about his whereabouts and the secrets he communicated to the mysterious Frenchman. After Webster had gone on about forty minutes Judge Grier told him, "You need not trouble yourself with the testimony of Richard Collins." Webster replied, "I am very much obliged," and indicated that since they were letting Collins go he proposed to similarly dispatch Elisha Pratt and Mr. Stoddard "to bear him company on his way."

The court adjourned until the next morning, when Webster began to earn his large fee and prove his reputation. He called Day a liar and a rascal and a potential criminal, too. In the event that he lost the trial, Webster claimed, Day had boasted that he would put his factories in the hands of friends and continue as before. Webster suggested that this was cause for a criminal inquiry by a grand jury. So it was plain that Day, not Goodyear, was acting inside a combination—the very word Day had splashed all over his anti-Goodyear newspaper advertisements.

As for Day's other claim, that Goodyear's dry-oven heating method was ineffective, Webster again offered to prove it in court with a demonstration.

He asserted that the heating method was irrelevant to the patent and that the patent rightfully encompassed both ovens and steam.

By noon Webster still hadn't finished and the judges didn't interrupt him for a lunch break. The lawyer had now returned to the subject of Goodyear's bankruptcy. Goodyear conducted himself in "exact conformity" with the law and was discharged from his debts, over $30,000 worth. "The first thing he did, when he began to realize anything out of this invention was to pay those debts, principal and interest," Webster said, ignoring the selective nature of Goodyear's repayment and the debts the inventor had continued to acquire in recent years. "I should have been glad not to have seen upon this record, an unnecessary averment, that he was a man who had failed in business, and threw himself from the desperate circumstances in which he was placed, into the rubber business."

Goodyear's name will be known long years to come, Webster promised. "The man who sits at this table, Charles Goodyear, is to go down in posterity in the history of the arts in this country, in that great class of inventors, at the head of which stands Robert Fulton, a renowned relative of my learned friend Mr. Cutting; in which class stand the names of Whitney, and of Morris, and in which class will stand *non post longo intervallo*, the humble name of Charles Goodyear."

Having unfurled his Latinate peroration, Webster thanked the court and the people of New Jersey elaborately, like a campaigning politician. He said the case would undoubtedly bring honor on both the court and the people, at which point Judge Grier interrupted to say, "You need supply no more proof of that."

Webster answered: "Then Your Honor will be excused from any more hearing today."

Spirits in the Goodyear camp ran high as court was adjourned. L. Otto P. Meyer, a German-born manufacturer who had just acquired a license from the Goodyears to make hard rubber products in a factory in New York City, recalled, "From the courtroom many persons, including myself, went with Mr. Goodyear to his private room in the hotel, where he showed us beautiful samples of soft and hard rubber articles, of almost everything makeable of rubber. On that memorable day nearly all the principal men interested in the Goodyear patent sat at dinner with him, my friend Conrad Poppenhusen and I sitting together. Joy reigned all around, tuned high by champagne."

Months later, on his return to his farm in Marshfield, Webster found the horse that had drawn his carriage during the trial, the one he had admired, waiting for him in the stable. It was a gift from Charles Goodyear. Webster named the horse Trenton.

Day's contingent celebrated at a local hotel. Horace Greeley, writing in the *New York Tribune,* where Day had advertised, didn't believe Webster had won the case. "Without doing any injustice to Mr. Webster we must say, it has fallen far short of our expectations. None of the great law points raised by Messrs. Cutting and Choate has been disturbed." In his adopted home of New Jersey, Day found even more comfort. A reporter for the *True American* wrote: "Mr. Choate and Mr. Cutting made out such an incontestable case on the part of the defendant, that even the eloquence, the reputation, the ability, the legal acumen, and the overwhelming influence of the 'god-like' Daniel himself was inadequate to the superhuman task of its overthrow."

The judges retired to their chambers and the wait for a verdict began.

The interlude between the trial and the verdict was hardly a peaceful one in the Goodyear camp. Charles' youngest brother, Nelson, passed away in July, leaving a wife and children. But instead of rallying to each other, Goodyear family members and their employees struggled to claim credit for an invention that Nelson had patented, the method of making hard rubber. The Goodyears used hard rubber to make combs and canes and heavily ornamental objects that might otherwise have been carved out of wood or bone. Charles Goodyear's decorative veneers and rubber furniture at the London exhibition had all been made of hard rubber.

When Nelson died, Austin Goodyear Day of Springfield, Massachusetts, a nephew of Charles whom he had employed as an assistant in performing experiments since 1841, claimed credit for having helped Nelson invent hard rubber. Lavius Andrus and George W. Homan, non-family employees of Goodyear, claimed credit, too. And Ellsworth David Sprague Goodyear, a cousin who had worked for Charles as an investigator and experimenter in New York and New Jersey, also made a bid for part ownership of the hard rubber patent. (Two years later he would be granted a patent for making hollow rubber balls, which because of their lightness and bounce would become a favorite among American children in the twentieth century.)

Henry Bateman Goodyear, now Charles' only surviving brother, emerged as the custodian of Nelson's hard rubber patent, apparently settling claims made by relatives and workers and beginning a longer fight to stamp out infringers. From the patent, Henry not only earned a living for himself but also produced income for Nelson's family. Among the most lucrative licenses were those sold to A. D. Schlesinger and his friend Conrad Pop-penhusen, who purchased licenses from the Goodyears for "artificial whale-bone" (hard rubber) to be used in making clothing and for combs, for a total of $30,000. Later Poppenhusen and his partner H. A. Meyer purchased a whipstock license for another $1,000, and over ten years the licensees paid the Goodyears another $70,000 in royalties. Meyer and Poppenhusen also joined with Henry to form an association that sued hard rubber makers who infringed their patents, following the business model successfully instituted by Judson and the Shoe Associates for Charles Goodyear's patents.

Almost fifty-two years old and ailing, Goodyear needed to press on with his own affairs. He had defended his patent. He had seen his reputation vindi-cated by one of the great statesmen and orators of the age. He was now widely known in business circles in the United States and among increas-ing numbers of Americans wearing "Goodyear patent" boots and shoes. But he also saw the future in the gray and cream-colored envelopes he received with the promissory notes that were coming due. He still owed tens of thou-sands of dollars to Steele and DeForest and to numerous small suppliers in New Haven. Just as America was discovering rubber anew, he had to go back on the road and carry his cause once again to Europe, seeking more licensees whose up-front payments would satisfy the immediate need for cash to pay creditors.

Of Goodyear's feelings about his property rights in England, where he still had not confronted Hancock in court, there was little doubt. All Goodyear wanted was justice, not money or glory. The exhibit at the Crys-tal Palace, like his placing his name on his licensed products, had nothing to do with "ambitious motives," as so many perceived. The exhibit and the use of his name on licensed goods were a defense against the Macintosh Company, which Goodyear believed had "wronged him in appropriating to themselves the advantages in England of the discovery of vulcanization." Righting this wrong in England was as important as the battle with Horace Day in America.

The Goodyears set off for England again by packet steamer in June 1852. They crossed safely, but with the usual seasickness tormenting Charles, and returned to a rented suite of rooms in the West End near Regent's Park.

Ellen, their oldest daughter, still served as her father's right arm and helped to teach rubber making. She traveled with the family to London. Charles Jr. at nineteen was active in the business too, but he remained in New Haven. Cynthia, their second-oldest daughter, reluctantly accompanied the family back to London, interrupting a courtship with a cousin, George Goodyear, that had flourished during the trial. She hoped that George would resume the courtship and propose in a letter so they could soon marry.

Clarissa re-enrolled Clara, now thirteen, and William Henry, age six, in school there. Of all the family members, she seemed the least enthusiastic to return to London. She had enjoyed seeing her husband attaining respect and notoriety after his successful English exhibit, but she was a stranger in town again with few friends except those she made at church. During the long trip to Liverpool, she developed a dull ache behind her left eye. She made a note to ask a doctor for chamomile, which she had been told would ease the headache.

Goodyear set up an office in Sydenham near the rebuilt Crystal Palace and his exhibit, now named Goodyear's Vulcanite Court. And there were new worlds to conquer. He established contacts through which he could license his processes in Germany and Russia. He reopened discussions with Hancock and the Macintosh Company. And just in case negotiations with Hancock fell through, he began writing up specifications for patents in England of applications for vulcanized rubber. Anyone who used vulcanized rubber would have to license the right from Hancock, but if they used an application patented by Goodyear they would have to pay him too. In October 1852, using the same patent attorney employed by Hancock, Goodyear was granted patents for rubber guns and pistols, telescopes and tubes, book covers and picture frames, trunks and knapsacks, pails and tubs, harness and carriage furniture, musical instruments and elastic ribs, sticks and fillet for umbrellas. The outburst of speculative patenting ended in November and brought Goodyear's total number of English patents to eighteen. He sold a five-eighths interest in the patents to William Judson in exchange for £12,000 in notes, with terms of one to three years but paying no interest.

Still there was no word from America about the trial verdict.

Illness and worry often drove Goodyear to his bed. Anticipating Charles Jr.'s arrival in London, Goodyear wrote that "he will be here and his bones will ache as bad as his Father's (I hope not with the gout)." But his illness was no laughing matter. When he suffered the slightest stimulus became unbearable. He spent hours in darkened silence, making his needs and wants known to Clarissa by some sign of the lips or eyes. The Reverend Peirce, his biographer, suggested that some people would have thought Goodyear was on his deathbed by his complete motionlessness, but Clarissa understood that her husband was actually trying to gather his strength for the trials that lay ahead.

When he felt better, Clarissa read Scripture or poetry to him. It's possible that she read him this section of a poem by Percival, later printed in his book, about the exquisite agony of stolen ideas:

> They find what they had won
> By long and earnest toil, by other hands
> Seized as their own, and shown with vain display
> As their own trophy, with not even a hint
> Whence they had stolen the prize.

Finally, in September 1852, word reached England that the judges had submitted a decision in the Trenton case. Judge Grier started his opinion by scolding the respective parties for spending so much effort on arguments irrelevant to the central points of the case. On the first important point, whether Horace Day deserved a jury trial at law on the validity of Goodyear's patent, Grier said he did not. Based on the volumes of testimony and arguments submitted by each side, Grier wrote that he and Judge Dickerson could determine matters of both fact and law themselves. And they had determined that the patent was valid and Goodyear was the inventor; the fact that the patents had been granted was prima facie evidence of it. Since the revised Patent Act of 1836, the Patent Office acted quasi-judicially in deciding whether to grant a patent, said Grier, and that lent substance to the determination.

Now Grier approached his main thesis, the key points of which were taken from the revised patent of 1849 and the argument made by Daniel Webster. Grier briefly retold the story of the rubber boom of the mid-1830s and the problems with the substance that caused the subsequent bust. A great variety of experiments and failures, many facts and processes were discovered during this time, but not vulcanization. Then Charles Goodyear went to work. After spending much money and time, "his family reduced to poverty, and himself immured in a prison," Goodyear persisted and "finally his faith and energy were rewarded by the discovery, the value of which this controversy most abundantly proves."

Grier, who later admitted that he never read the 1,300 pages of deposition testimony, was seconded by Judge Dickerson in finding for Goodyear. The two ordered a special master of the court to assess what tariffs and damages Day would pay. They also ordered Day to report regularly to the master and to open his books and premises for inspections, if needed.

The judges had done more than declare Goodyear the victor. Grier's stirring rhetoric lifted Charles Goodyear into the industrial pantheon where he would stay, despite the difficulties that still lay in his future, until rubber and steel gave way to binary code and computers. A more thorough defeat for Day could not have been imagined.

The Trenton decision flooded Goodyear with gratitude, the judges' words surpassing anything he could have hoped for. All his strivings and sufferings now seemed to have been vindicated. Horace Day was finished and the Goodyear licensees that had held back could resume paying their pennies-per-product tariffs. Clarissa wept. Goodyear led the family in prayer and then Clarissa bought a bottle of champagne, although neither she nor Goodyear drank, as neither was feeling well. Charles Jr. was planning to join the family in England and George Goodyear did propose to Cynthia, as she hoped, agreeing to travel to London for the wedding.

His U.S. patent now safe and his licensees and future income secure, Goodyear began to spend more freely. He might have thought he was acting in keeping with his new image as a gentleman inventor, but he behaved more like an India rubber parvenu. He bought a carriage and used it to travel from his spacious apartment in the West End to the Crystal Palace and other destinations. Burrows Hyde, an acquaintance in London, remembers talking to Goodyear as he sat in the carriage. Hyde presumed that the carriage trim was ebony, but Goodyear informed him that it was hard rubber. A driver and footman sat up in the box, their red livery uniforms brightening another drab and smog-choked London day. "He made quite a display," recalled Hyde later. "I remarked to him, the whole thing was pretty expensive, or something of that import."

Goodyear replied that he was trying to make an impression in London. He asked Hyde if he had seen his rubber display at the Crystal Palace in Sydenham and urged him to go. When he visited, Hyde remembered a room "furnished entirely with hard rubber, except the carpet," including a "highly wrought bedstead of hard rubber, picture frames and secretary." At their next meeting Goodyear told Hyde that he had spent several thousand pounds preparing the specimens for exhibit. "I saw him at several different times riding through London, once driving a two-horse team. I was attracted to him by the style in which he was driving; he always had a footman," said Hyde.

Goodyear acted rich even if he really wasn't, like an ambassador of some great, undefined cause that went beyond India rubber and marine safety. Goodyear wanted nothing to do with the abolitionist sentiment catching fire in his native New England nor with most other kinds of social reform, but he was dead against imprisonment of debtors. He went to hear Charles Dickens read and took the writer's address, hoping to tell Dickens about his arrests and jailhouse days. Although he kept the carriage and horses at Sydenham, Goodyear sometimes ordered a cab in the morning and made the cab and driver wait for hours at his door. When friends commented on the extravagance, Goodyear replied that he could afford it.

Urged on by friends, Goodyear attempted to set down in words a definitive account of his knowledge of rubber. After talking about the plant in its natural habitat, he turned to his own contribution. He staked his claim as the pivotal figure in rubber's industrial drama, insisting that until 1839 it was "never heard of" that India rubber could be prepared or remanufactured in such a way that it wouldn't stiffen in cold, soften in heat or dissolve in oil.

His brief, elliptical autobiography, written in the third person, repeated the story developed in his patents and legal presentations, a story of ruin and redemption and eventual triumph over adversity. He dramatized the change wrought in rubber by sulfurous gas and a high degree of heat in Woburn in the winter of 1838–39 as having been made "under circumstances of such a nature, that there could be no mistaking the facts in the case, or blending the results of the writer's labors with those of any other individual." At the time of his accomplishment he was "so completely insulated by misfortune, (seemingly courted by him, in persisting in what appeared to every one else an idle and foolish enthusiasm,) and all his acts and pretensions at that time were so censured or ridiculed, as to identify, in the most unquestionable manner, the inventor with the discovery."

The unspoken subplot is the link connecting Goodyear and rubber to God. In early life, Goodyear wrote, he inspected an imported bottle of India rubber, made by native peoples in South America, and he thought that if a way could be found to stop the rubber from sticking to itself it would constitute a beautiful fabric with many uses. This dream had become a reality, he asserted, and now rubber was revealed as a miracle material destined to replace substances used for millennia. "There is probably no other inert substance, the properties of which excite in the human mind, when first called to examine it, an equal amount of curiosity, surprise and admiration," he wrote. "Who can examine, and reflect upon this property of gum-elastic, without adoring the wisdom of the Creator?"

An entire second volume of Goodyear's book is a compendium of the more than five hundred applications for rubber that he envisioned, a galaxy of rubber clothing and household and medical and industrial devices that foretold the adoption of synthetics for use in everyday activity. Dryly narrated and illustrated with cleanly cross-hatched pencil drawings, the book credited Goodyear's "extravagant" predictions to his "presentiment of the future, quite common to inventors." In 379 pages Goodyear prophesied a rubber future and provided descriptions and manufacturing directions. His thirty chapters included Educational (maps, charts, globes), House, Ship, and Camp Ware and Utensils (washboards, bellows, ice-water tanks) and Medical Devices (ear trumpets, varicose stockings, nipple shields). The only uses Goodyear advised against were as a fabric worn tightly next to the skin or when sleeping, because of the problem of perspiration, and as a beverage (although South American Indians had been known to drink the sap, he said). Otherwise, rubber was predestined to supplant natural materials wherever durability, impermeability and elasticity gave it an advantage. Only high early costs had kept rubber's inevitable triumph from unfolding more rapidly.

Goodyear applauded some of the uses for rubber invented by others that had not yet found their way into general commerce. By setting rubber in a metal socket at the end of a pencil, Goodyear noted, the manufacturer had given the writer an eraser whose convenience surpassed everything known. He also predicted widespread popularity for the rubber band, first used in clothing by Hancock to close gloves and stockings and other garments snugly, and then replacing string and thread in tying together small bundles.

Other applications encouraged but not necessarily invented by Goodyear included the hot water bottle, "the merit of which is not commonly known" but which Goodyear was sure would become popular because "no means are so convenient and effectual for fomentation." Waterbeds, which Goodyear also believed held great promise in bringing comfort to the sick, were another application that would take time to catch on.

He envisioned a self-contained universe of rubber where furniture would be covered with a fine sheet of rubber veneer, saving the cost of good wood veneer, and where rubber dishes, like the ones he had made when he was poor in New York, would come into vogue because they would not break like crockery.

The uniformity and plasticity of hard rubber convinced Goodyear that rubber violins, rubber organ pipes and other rubber instruments soon would be common.

Durable rubber toys, Goodyear promised, could save "vast sums of money" over the current breakable versions. Rubber dolls could not "be injured by the ordinary play of children" who didn't resort to fire, violence or the use of "very destructive edge tools" to break things. Phrenologists would have to study the effect on children who would no longer be able to "destroy or mutilate" toys, Goodyear surmised. Care would be needed, however, to prevent a toy gun equipped with elastic springs from "becoming a deadly weapon."

In early spring 1853 Clarissa wasn't feeling herself, complaining about dizziness and fatigue and often bothered by "The Headache," as she called it, which seemed to have taken up permanent residence in her sinuses. She began to lose her concentration in supervising little William Henry and while talking to teenage Clara. She seemed to drift in and out of conversations with Charles as he chatted about his daily business meetings and ideas.

One day at dinner The Headache jabbed sharply into Clarissa's eye and sinuses, startling her and provoking a small cry. Charles rose in alarm. Clarissa rose, wavered, then excused herself from the dinner table to go up to her room. Sensing something serious, Goodyear asked a nanny to put the children to bed and followed his wife up to the room. He gingerly helped Clarissa remove her skirts and get into bedclothes. Her face, framed in gray hair that fell down to her shoulders, had contorted as she strained against the pain. One eye closed. Wife and husband now sensed something dangerous unfolding. Clarissa asked Goodyear to pray for her but before he did, he sent for a doctor. Clara came into the room to help and took her mother's hand. Charles sat on the other side holding her other hand.

While they waited in the familiar pose of nineteenth-century family life, holding vigil at the bedside of a dying loved one, Clarissa commented wryly that she was usually the caretaker ministering to Charles: "I feel like you should be lying here instead of me." Then she asked, "Where are William Henry and Clara?"

Clara was holding her hand and told her mother she was right there. "William Henry is being put to bed," Charles said. "You can see him in the morning." Clarissa asked to have him brought to her anyway.

A moment later a blood vessel behind her eye burst and she lost consciousness. When the doctor arrived, she was gone, and he said that a stroke had been the cause of death.

William Henry was inconsolable, screaming for his mother, and Clara crumpled in grief, weeping while still holding Clarissa's dead hand. Charles stared into Clarissa's face for half an hour before rising from his chair.

For the first time in his life, he could not bring himself to pray. Instead of returning to America with Clarissa's remains, he decided to bury her in England.

Charles Goodyear sealed himself off from the world of rubber for the next few weeks. When he tried to ease back into his business affairs he found he was distracted with decisions about family life with which he had never before had to contend. Clara and especially William Henry clung to him as never before. He took to his bed, the one where his wife had died weeks earlier, as the pain in his joints flared again. The children came into the room demanding his attention anyway. He missed business appointments and forgot what business had most occupied his attention on the night that Clarissa had died.

Finally he had himself driven to church. His gout was raging and he used crutches to get to his seat. In the front pew he wept quietly.

Over the next few months, a nineteen-year-old woman whose family belonged to the church took note of the grieving American who had recently lost his wife. Fanny Wardell recalled the first moment she saw him: "I shall never forget the impression made on my mind by the deep melancholy in the first tones of his voice that ever fell upon my ear, as, leaning upon his crutches, he was first presented to me." She also noticed Goodyear's well-turned-out carriage and later learned that he was a famed and ingenious inventor. By coincidence she remembered seeing his Vulcanite Court at the Crystal Palace. Immediately, she had an urge to take care of him.

Their relationship began, formally, with Goodyear's request to Fanny's father for permission to court his daughter. From Wardell's point of view, Goodyear was a respectable Christian gentleman, a good man who had tragically lost the love of his life, and so he had no objection despite the more than thirty-year age difference between him and his daughter. Charles began to call on Fanny and sit with her for tea and ride with her and sit in the park. He talked to her about Clarissa and about the children. He described the tragic losses of his brothers and parents and children, and the frightful poverty into which the family had sunk following the Philadelphia hardware store debacle. And then more passionately he spoke about his heated gum, the vulcanized rubber, and how Charles Macintosh & Company had taken it from him unjustly in England. Fanny listened raptly. Goodyear gave her flowers and rubber-framed watches and necklaces.

Fanny thought him very dear. Her father, believing Goodyear to be rich, thought the two were an excellent match and was already anticipating being relieved of responsibility for taking care of the girl.

In Fanny, Charles had found a youthful, compliant helpmate and a new young lover. In him, she had found another father figure who appeared to be quite wealthy and resourceful despite his chronic illnesses. A wedding date was set and a honeymoon tour planned that included travel in France, where Goodyear had business to conduct and where Fanny's ability to converse in French would come in handy.

Fanny Wardell Goodyear stepped into Clarissa's shoes barely missing a stride. She took charge of William Henry and Clara and Robert's daughter and slowly worked to win their love. She ran the household and supervised a nanny, a housekeeper and a personal physician who had been hired to care for Charles. There were the usual adjustments to be made by the Goodyear children to their new young stepmother. Soon enough, she was initiated into the family in the truest sense as she began to suffer with Charles the see-sawing fortunes that had characterized the prior twenty-two years of his obsession with rubber. And by January 1856, Fanny started feeling a little woozy when she woke in the mornings and soon a doctor concluded that she was pregnant.

Goodyear's spirits rebounded and he considered making a trip back to America. He wrote to his cousin Amelia in the United States and invited her to visit him at the family's new home, a comfortable house they dubbed Para Villa in St. John's Wood, outside of central London. What he really wanted was for Amelia to come to stay with the children in London while he and Ellen returned to the United States to do business. "I ought to have been frank with Amelia," he said in another letter to his brother, Henry. There was a playful note in the letter in which he joked about Amelia's potential visit by saying: "It is high time that the mother country was colonized by the sons and the daughters of her daughters."

Soon after Clarissa's death and his own remarriage, Goodyear again picked up his obsession with rubber. He told his brother that he was trying to settle peacefully a problem with the Boston Belting Company, a licensee that paid him a $15,000 fee in a prior year. As part of the agreement, Charles McBurney of the belting company and his partners promised to pay Goodyear one-quarter of the profits of any improvements Goodyear introduced into rubber belting. For some reason Goodyear felt the company wasn't holding up its end of the agreement and anticipated visiting McBurney at a future date to "see what can be done on the peace system." There was a catty, disdainful tone to his language. Goodyear seemed to feel his power, the way he had when he first journeyed to Boston armed with his acid method. Now he had legal weapons at his disposal, but decided to spare the Boston Belting Company the wrath of his lawyer. "There would probably be a Seven Years war between Mr. Judson and the Boston Belting Co., but life is too short to be spent in quarrelling (unless it is with Day, who would not be at peace with anybody any way)."

An agent he had engaged, a French-speaking American named Charles Morey, began to report promising possible licensing deals in Paris. With Goodyear's eternal hopes for a big pay day stimulated by Morey's optimistic assessment, the two men drew up agreements under which they would both be partners in any French licenses. Morey, like Judson, agreed to advance money to Goodyear, invest some of his money in their venture and contribute his services for a substantial share of any profits. Morey, accompanied by his wife, would go ahead to Paris to make arrangements and Goodyear agreed to join him there soon.

In the summer or early fall, Goodyear left for France and then, rather than travel on Sunday, decided to stop after a day's journey at Folkestone for a day of rest before sailing. The stop gave him time to read and answer some of his mail, particularly a troubling letter from his old friend and former tutor William DeForest in New Haven. DeForest had married Goodyear's sister Harriet, cementing the relationship between the families, after Harriet's first husband had died. In New Haven, DeForest had become a target of some of Goodyear's creditors while Goodyear himself was in Europe. The creditors, who may have included the New Haven stove dealer

Ralph Steele, understood that Goodyear's income now exceeded $30,000 a year—about the sum he owed DeForest. Word of Goodyear's English house, carriage and private physician may have filtered back to Connecticut. In conveying the pressure he felt from creditors, DeForest quoted Goodyear's own expression about the constant need for cash and suggested that Goodyear was unmindful of his trouble.

The implication that he had ignored DeForest's financial trouble stung Goodyear. In his response, he compared himself to a confessing Puritan who bares all his sin but fights back when anyone else ventures to criticize him. Debts still hung "like a millstone" around his neck, too, Goodyear reminded DeForest. "I am not rioting in independence," he wrote. As usual, Charles expected to extinguish his most recent debts with new licenses, in this case from France.

"As relates to your case, my feeling has been this," Goodyear wrote. "That having shown the good people of New Haven my disposition to pay, by paying them, they would indulge you and me with the liberty I have taken with them and you; and I had hoped with this indulgence you would be comfortable."

Goodyear also expressed pain that even his brother-in-law, his largest and friendliest creditor, failed to grasp the magnitude of his crusade. A new industry was a-borning; factories needed to be built and workers set to their tasks. And the only way in which such miracles would occur was if Goodyear showed the world that rubber could clothe them and carry them and cushion them from discomfort. Rubber now demanded his full attention, rising above the middling concerns of money. Hadn't he carried his cross long enough? So many had mistaken him for an egotist when he was really an idealist. "I feel that I have done all that mortal man could do, under the same circumstances, to recover from that pecuniary indebtedness to my fellow-creatures into which I fell in early life," he wrote. Personal advancement was never his sole objective; he had kept on going for all these years "to accomplish a great work for the good of mankind."

And so far, events supported his analysis. About five thousand United States citizens were now making rubber and rubber products, a remarkable recovery and growth spurt few could have foreseen in the dismal year 1835, when the Roxbury Company had buried much of the decomposing stock it had sold the year before. Millions had been invested and tens of millions had been returned to investors. And the flow of handmade imported rubber shoes had all but stopped as the manufacture of rubber products in the United States had exploded. In 1852 and 1853, more than two million pounds of raw rubber arrived at the Port of New York and another 250,000 pounds arrived in New Haven alone. Only 7,000 pairs of native-made shoes were imported into the United States in 1853, down from a peak of 190,000 pairs in 1849. "I need not tell you that I have been successful" in accomplishing a greater good, wrote Goodyear to DeForest. "Vast numbers of mankind already bear witness to this." Then he added magnanimously: "I only wish they could have known you and others who aided me."

Goodyear was now racing to finish his life's work. He had resigned himself to pestering and sniping from creditors and to the weight of debt he continued to carry, but he believed with a feeling "very much like faith" that he would be delivered from embarrassment and its trials before he died. As he rested at Folkestone, anticipating his trip to Paris and justifying his mission in life, his mind wandered back to the days of imprisonment in Philadelphia, Boston, Springfield, New York and New Haven. His twenty-year industrial odyssey had now put him within a day's travel of the French capital and promising new transactions. Judson, his licensees and his creditors all seemed distant. Europe and the continent could finally be—as he had always thought—the key to his release from decades of uncertainty. He remembered the neighborhoods where his family had scraped together fuel and food and where he had first been chastened for borrowing so freely. Kimberton, Washington Hill, Woburn Plains, he wrote, reciting the names like campaigns of a long war. There were also "the cells of gloomy prisons, and two visits to most of these," he wrote DeForest. "And yet, for the most part, my heart was light. Seldom a dark cloud, except from ill health, darkened my sky of hope. And why should there? The scene shifts, we may realize our hopes and worldly independence, and yet sigh for the former state, in which our cup overflowed with blessing. We murmured that God did not bestow all his blessing upon us at once."

Goodyear met with potential licensees in Paris and scouted various offices and apartments he was considering renting. On his return from Paris, he fared badly in the channel crossing and told a prospective new agent, Daniel L. Gilman, that he was "still in feeble health" and therefore couldn't report to his office. Five days later, Goodyear still couldn't go out but he arranged to meet Gilman in his lodgings. Once they had met, Goodyear scheduled a meeting at his rubber exhibit at Sydenham, but because he felt unwell, he switched to a meeting at his office or at his house the same day.

Goodyear continued trying to settle matters with Hancock and the Macintosh Company. The Shoe Associates had hit him with a flurry of lawsuits aimed at overturning his now ten-year-old vulcanization patent. By 1854 both sides intended to try the case. Macintosh had apparently sued Goodyear or a licensee for violating an English Macintosh patent and this case came close to trial early in 1854. At the last minute the Macintosh Company dropped its claim and Goodyear was "released from the annoyance" of having to appear as a witness. "They of course paying the defendant's bill of costs," he reported.

In February, Goodyear planned another visit to Paris to see Gilman prior to Gilman's departure for Russia with specimens both men hoped would win new licensing agreements there. Goodyear paid Gilman 500 francs to cover the costs of bringing his rubber products on the trip. Waiting to hear if Russia would provide his next licensing windfall, Goodyear scheduled a brief respite for a "wedding tour"—his delayed honeymoon with Fanny.

Tentative steps to establish a manufacturing operation in Russia came to nothing, but Goodyear's prospects in continental Europe had never looked better. While still fighting it out with Hancock in England, he received applications from Prussia and Belgium for the purchase of his patents. He planned his most exhaustive European trip to date: a three-city swing through Brussels, Vienna and Berlin that would last at least two months. He asked Gilman to meet him in Berlin with the samples so that he would have more to show in Prussia. He also arranged to meet Charles Jr., who had made the trip to Europe to help his father secure European deals, and Ellen in Vienna in August 1854.

The three-city trip would begin from Paris. Goodyear had signed a three-year lease for a house at 42 Avenue Gabriel on the Champs Elysées, opposite the French exhibition hall, which he would soon fill with India rubber furniture. Fanny, fluent in French, often served as translator. In summer 1854, the family settled into their Paris apartment and Goodyear kept constantly busy with business appointments and touring the sights.

He had always struggled with his gout, but now attacks that had been spasmodic returned with concerted force, bringing all his activities to a stop. The lead he had pounded into rubber over the years had entered his bloodstream and began to break down his health completely. Never a sound sleeper, on the night of August 14 he awoke in pain. The following day he felt well enough to keep his business appointments and he worked hard. At bedtime that night his throat "felt weak," preventing him from speaking, and the following morning, at 3 A.M., he "awoke in protest of great pain," as Fanny wrote in a journal. He had so little strength during the next six days that he didn't get out of bed.

Fanny called in new doctors to supplement the care provided by Charles' personal physician. They put him on a regimen that included constant wraps in cloths soaked in hot linseed oil and sprinkled with laudanum, a tincture of opium. Poultices, as such wraps were called, were common medical procedure at the time, as were medicated drapes on windows or around beds. (The medicated drapes in this case were not rubber only because Goodyear had already tried them and concluded that they didn't work.) With the latest attack, Goodyear's sensitive stomach went into full rebellion, leading his doctor to recommend Bordeaux wine with dinner and no milk products of any kind. This regimen appeared to work: His strength returned and his indigestion disappeared. But then, after another busy day of business meetings and Paris sightseeing with his family, he collapsed and couldn't leave his bed for a day. He needed his crutches to walk after that, and chest pains from indigestion also returned.

By October, Goodyear made his way back to London. His relationship with Gilman had begun to fray. Goodyear had paid him at least twice for reports he submitted in general terms about what he had learned in Russia. But Gilman had not stopped to see Goodyear in Paris before setting out for Russia again and the two men had not met since he returned to Berlin. "The consequence is, I am in ignorance of any detail, or names of parties or where the specimens are left, or to whom they were given," Goodyear wrote. Despite the fact that he hadn't provided these vital details, Gilman pressed earnestly for final settlement of his account. But Goodyear was accommodating and the two men apparently settled their problems in January 1855.

Although still suffering with gout and lameness, Goodyear soon returned to Paris to make preparations for a French industrial and decorative arts exposition that promised to rival London's exposition of 1851. He worked with Gilman, who spoke French and was crucial in preparing the show exhibit, although the subject of his payment remained a prickly one.

As Goodyear tried to drum up new licensees in Europe, his myth was growing at home. Americans framed images of him based on the stories told by Daniel Webster and repeated by Judge Grier after the Trenton trial. Barely a year after the decision, the *Illustrated American Biography* lionized Goodyear's "stout heart" and endurance of "lawsuits, duns, executions, sheriffs, and the sharp tooth of poverty." The encyclopedia quoted the most poignant lines by Webster and reprinted Goodyear's April 21, 1840 letter from debtors' prison in Boston, inviting Haskins and Chaffee "to call and see me at my lodgings" which are "as good a resting-place as any this side of the grave." Psychologists took an interest in his character. The *American Phrenological Journal* reported after an examination that Goodyear had "a swelling-out of the upper part of the organ of Constructiveness, where it joins Ideality, at the temple, which indicates the tendency for invention, experiment and discovery." His temperament was "a combination of the mental and vital, or Nervous-Sanguine" and his physical constitution exhibited "Warmth, zeal, sprightliness, and restless energy." Goodyear, the *Journal* wrote, ranked in stature with Robert Fulton, Samuel Morse and the western explorer John Fremont.

Goodyear eagerly embraced his emerging image as a larger-than-life figure. In fact, his account of his life and work, the two-volume *Gum-Elastic and Its Varieties,* showed him to be as adept in the construction of myth as of rubber products. Published privately in New Haven by the author, the book was full of blank spaces awaiting dates and names; references were made in the text to portions of the book nowhere to be found. All this suggested the book went to press without Goodyear's final review, but even in its sloppy, incomplete state, the book is a truer representation of its author than he ever intended. And even though the memoir was chaotic and unfinished, Goodyear indulged his technical showmanship again by crafting at least one presentation copy of the book all of rubber.

In two autobiographical chapters, Goodyear referred to himself most often in the third person as "the inventor." He wrote of the revolutionary steel hay fork that was the center of family pride, the tragic failure of the hardware business, the first trips to debtors' prison, the first interest in rubber and the precarious journey through poverty and misfortune. In tiny footnotes he gave perfunctory credit to key early supporters, such as Coolidge and Haskins. He also credited those who were less than pleased about unpaid debts, such as William Ballard and Ralph Steele. Even James DeForest, who sued William DeForest for money lent to Goodyear with William's guarantee, was thanked. Goodyear gave William DeForest warm praise. William Ely was not mentioned.

In several sections Goodyear argued that inventors are America's maltreated children, and he called for changes in patent laws to protect them. While at times he was defensive about his ambition and obsession with work, Goodyear nevertheless remained faultless in his own eyes and had not a particle of responsibility for the calamitous events of his life. On the other hand, there was no vindictiveness or retribution. Horace Day was not mentioned in the book, and Goodyear spared Hancock and all the other enemies who reviled him a final judgment. Such forbearance and magnanimity only furthered his legend and endeared him more deeply to his admirers as a man of exceptional Christian temperament.

While Goodyear's status continued to grow in the United States, the legal wheels kept grinding on Horace Day. While waiting for Judges Grier and Dickerson's decision, Day sold off his New Jersey rubber operations. After the decision, he squirmed to avoid the oversight of the court master assigned to keep him in line and assess damages owed to Goodyear. At first the Hudson River seemed to be enough of a shield to protect him from the Trenton-based federal judges. Day moved to New York City, where he had a shop and homes and friends, and started a new company in Manhattan in 1853 along with Samuel Armstrong, the former Roxbury Company manager, and Charles Gilbert, who had been an investor for a while in one of the early Goodyear-licensed Naugatuck rubber companies.

In theory, and under his court-enforced agreement with Goodyear, all Day and his partners and the men to whom he had sold his New Jersey factory could manufacture was shirred rubber. Yet he couldn't hold to his mandate. The federal court in New Jersey found Day in contempt of its orders to restrict his operations and report on his activities, and summoned him to Trenton for a hearing. He appeared without attorney. Judge Dickerson interrogated Day for hours and ordered him to present his business records. After several days the hearing resumed in Jersey City. Day's lawyer, Francis Cutting, was involved in a trial and couldn't attend; the Wizard Choate also was unavailable. Fearing a jail order, Day stayed away from the hearing but sent another lawyer to plead for a delay. Judge Dickerson's son, representing Goodyear, requested a contempt ruling and the father complied. But by moving to New York, Day had put himself beyond their reach. At some point the contempt order was rescinded.

Day's luck seemed only to grow worse. Along with a partner named Anson G. Phelps, he had a large Connecticut factory in Goodyear's hometown of Naugatuck. There they manufactured rubber railroad-car springs using steam-heating processes that Day believed fell outside the Goodyear patents. But the Goodyear licensees sued the railroad companies, and the railroads in turn insisted that Day and his partner stand in their shoes and defend them. Then the factory burned down and Phelps died, leaving Day to confront not just the Goodyear monopoly but the railroads. At this point, he believed he faced ruin and hurriedly paid all his debts. His hair, which he combed straight up from his head, went gray almost overnight.

Still, all the fight (and finance) had not gone out of him. He engaged an attorney to try to stop Goodyear's application to the U.S. Patent Office in 1853 to extend Hayward's patent (without which Goodyear's own patent was less valuable). Day's lawyer prepared a lengthy brief that resurrected all the chief arguments of the Trenton trial and claimed that that decision had been a grave error and injustice. Day also struck out against Goodyear licensees for using processes he claimed infringed his own patented rubber-rolling machinery, suing in federal court in Rhode Island. The key defendant was Isaac Hartshorn, a partner of Nathaniel Hayward's, whose Providence-based shoemaking plant used the methods in dispute.

One day after court adjourned, a witness for Hartshorn strolled near the house of the juror William Blaisdell, a veteran rubber factory mechanic, and struck up a conversation. Blaisdell told him that he alone among the members of the jury could grasp the complex technical matter of the trial. The witness kept talking. Blaisdell later said, "I then interrupted him, and endeavored to prevent his talking to me, but he kept on till I went into a grocery store to avoid him." A fortnight later, after Blaisdell's parents left his home to go to worship on a Sunday afternoon, the same man called at Blaisdell's house and entered. The man looked around at the "prospects and situation" and said it was a fine pleasant place and asked Blaisdell if he owned it clear. Blaisdell told him there was a mortgage. As people started filling the streets outside after the Sunday worship meeting had ended, the man stood up and put his hands on Blaisdell's shoulders and said, "If this case goes right, all things shall go well with you." He added that the case against Hartshorn was unjust and that "Day was going round buying up lawsuits." In coming days, the man continued to intercept Blaisdell as he went in and out of the court. After the jurors returned a verdict against Hartshorn, one of Hartshorn's lawyers turned to Blaisdell and said, "We are deceived in you, we relied altogether on you," or words to that effect.

After numerous attempts by English and American competitors to overturn Thomas Hancock's vulcanization patent, the Goodyear group and Charles Goodyear made one final attempt. English courts provided fewer opportunities for creativity than their U.S. counterparts because English civil complaints often were argued by the government's prosecutors, not charismatic attorneys like Daniel Webster. Hancock, on the other hand, hired Frederic Thesiger, a former solicitor general and attorney general with more than thirty years of legal experience. There was another important difference with the Trenton trial. Until the early 1850s, the plaintiffs and defendants in English civil proceedings could not testify as witnesses in the case. This was changed in time for Goodyear's lawsuit against Hancock and the Macintosh Company. Both Goodyear and Hancock would testify.

Hancock was no stranger to civil court, having defended his patents and pressed claims against patent infringers, beginning with those who took advantage when the secret of his masticator first escaped the walls of the Macintosh factory. Other skirmishes followed. But despite his past court victories, Hancock was a reluctant litigant. He had already buried his partners Macintosh and Birley and his colleague Brockedon, who passed away in August 1854. Hancock wished that his vulcanization patent "would now be allowed to run out its remaining days in peace" after seven years of consistent litigation with a variety of opponents. But in May 1854, a judge issued a writ for Goodyear's lawsuit. In essence, the suit charged that Hancock had committed fraud, that he was not the first inventor of the heating method, and that he didn't know how to vulcanize rubber when he filed his "deposit paper" with the English government in 1843, six months before finishing the specification. All Hancock had at the time, the lawsuit charged, were Goodyear's stamp-sized samples and the telltale scent of brimstone in his nostrils.

It isn't clear if Hancock and Goodyear might have come to an agreement except for objections by Hancock's partners (as Charles Jr. later suggested). Nor is it certain, as has been written, that Hancock offered Goodyear half the proceeds from the remaining years of the patent. What is certain is that Hancock felt unprepared to become a trial witness under the new English civil trial rules and was put out by having to gather evidence to support his account of the time and circumstances of his discovery. He "ransacked" his drawers, boxes and receptacles and found among his experimental scraps plenty of early ones that were vulcanized, but most had no dates. Then, fortunately, several bearing faint dates of August 1842 came to hand and, even more fortunately, another dated the fourth of June. Armed with evidence, Hancock clung to the story that he was the sole legitimate inventor of vulcanization in England.

The claim had to do with pride, not money. If Hancock prevailed, the Macintosh Company wouldn't be remembered just for the famous rubber raincoats (bearing his partner's name), but also for his own efforts in helping to transform material technology.

The trial took on elements of an epic contest in part because Goodyear, out of madness or principle, felt precisely the same way. God had not shepherded him this far in order to settle out of court the great matter that would help determine his place in history. He would take his chances with another lawsuit to prove that he was the man he claimed to be.

As with his other lawsuits, Goodyear needed a cash-rich partner. He teamed up with Hutchinson, Henderson & Company, which was making five thousand pairs of shoes a day in France using his heating method. This firm had filed a lawsuit to break Hancock's vulcanization patent in England, and Goodyear bought a 50 percent interest in the company's claim, contributing his expertise and prestige and allowing himself to be cast as the starring witness.

On the morning of July 7 both sides assembled in a courtroom at Guild Hall in London. A panel of jurors was seated and Sir Robert Campbell presided. In his opening speech, the defense attorney Thesiger described Hancock's thirty years in the rubber business and his quest to rid rubber of "its clammy adhesiveness, its liability to change from variety of temperature ... and its being affected by oil or grease." After telling the story of how Goodyear's samples were left with the Macintosh Company by Stephen Moulton in 1842, Thesiger called on Hancock to testify about how he had burrowed through the hundreds of old scraps to turn up the clinching pieces of evidence, the small test scraps with their faded dates written on them.

With cross-examination, the contentious nature of the proceedings became clear. Mr. Hill, the prosecutor for the Queen, walked Hancock through some of the particulars of how he had obtained the Goodyear samples that exhibited the elusive quality of cold resistance. Hill asked if the sample from Goodyear in 1842 with the traces of sulfur on the surface also carried the odor of sulfur. Hancock first indicated there was no odor, then changed his mind and said there was enough sulfur in the rubber to produce an odor and to leave a trace on his fingers. Then Hill asked if new samples from Goodyear brought by Moulton also arrived in 1843, and he asked whether these also carried the mark of sulfur. Hancock hesitated again.

Hill said testily, "Try to recollect, uncertainty is very inconvenient."

Still Hancock couldn't say. Finally, he admitted that the new Goodyear samples Moulton had brought in 1843 also bore traces of brimstone. "They had the same appearance on the surface. It came off," Hancock said, struggling to recall. "If I remember right. I am under very great difficulty if I am tied down to state ..."

"You found very little difficulty when my learned friend was examining you," Hill broke in. "Why should you find difficulty when I examine you?"

"I have no difficulty at all," Hancock answered.

Hancock's wavering had by this time exhausted Lord Campbell's patience. "I state to you with most perfect confidence Mr. Hancock that you had better simply answer the question."

Finally, Hancock admitted that the new Goodyear samples brought by Moulton in 1843 had the appearance and odor of sulfur and also were cold-resistant. In other words, Hancock had in two consecutive years indirectly received vulcanized samples from Goodyear. This strongly suggested that he had used the samples to figure out how rubber was changed.

For Hancock, the testimony was as arduous as any experience he had endured, particularly the way Hill, Goodyear's attorney, was "sifting, catching at every word—perverting or altering my language—urging me to state the minutest particulars during my researches and experiments." Still, in the end Hancock was pretty well pleased with the performance of his "failing memory," particularly how it was aided by the discovered scraps.

After several expert witnesses testified for Hancock, Goodyear took the witness stand for the first time in a career marked by litigation and brushes with the law. The Queen's prosecutor, Mr. Hill, led Goodyear through the story of his discovery and how poverty prevented him from quickly filing patents for it in the United States and England. The discovery itself, Goodyear testified, was a fortunate accident made possible by sustained observation. After the accidental contact between sulfur-treated rubber and the hot stove, and the change it triggered, the patch had to be analyzed by a discriminating eye. What he had achieved was not the result of blind luck.

Under cross-examination by Thesiger, Goodyear was made to appear more an opportunist than a stoic, long-suffering inventor. First, Thesiger established that Goodyear was not the original direct plaintiff in the lawsuit but a 50 percent investor in the lawsuit initiated by Hutchinson, Henderson. Then he asked: How many shoes a day does Hutchinson, Henderson make in France?

"Five thousand," Goodyear answered.

"Does Hutchinson, Henderson pay a dividend and have much capital?"

"I'm not a shareholder."

"At what temperature does India rubber become viscous?"

"India rubber turns viscous with the heat of the sun or sometimes exposure to the sun."

Thesiger conveyed surprise: "Cannot you give us the degrees Fahrenheit?"

"It depends very much upon the circumstances," Goodyear answered.

"The term vulcanization was Mr. Hancock's term and not yours," Thesiger remarked. "You call it metallic rubber?"

"Yes," Goodyear answered.

"Metallic compound."

"Yes."

"Metallic compound," Thesiger repeated, implying that Goodyear couldn't even provide a decent name for the invention.

Leading him down a dangerous path, Thesiger established through his questions that Goodyear could not convince his friends of the validity of the invention for two years after the discovery in 1839. Told that Goodyear didn't receive his final full U.S. patent until 1844, Thesiger cried, "What! From 1839?" How to explain the delay?

Goodyear said he was unable to manufacture or prove to people what he had accomplished. Thesiger asked if Goodyear understood what caused the result he had achieved.

"I did know," answered Goodyear. "It was due to the action of sulfur and heat in combination with lead."

The next question was meant to strip Goodyear of his remaining shreds of credibility, to brand him once and for all with the image of an interloper and opportunist.

"I believe you are no chemist," Thesiger commented.

"I am not," answered Goodyear.

"And you had not anything to do with chemistry," said Thesiger.

"No, except what I had learned," said Goodyear. Yet what he had learned wasn't chemistry at all, but the technology of taking natural substances and turning them into man-made things. In his journal entries, Goodyear compared vulcanization to the curing of hides to make leather, to the smelting of iron ore to make iron and to the baking of iron with carbon to forge steel.

Thesiger saw a chance to play on the improbability that a scapegrace hardware merchant who wasn't a respected man of science or industry could claim credit for this singular innovation. He said he believed some of the samples Goodyear sent to England were perfect—"Were they not?"

Goodyear answered, "Perfectly vulcanized, imperfect in as much as they showed the mark of sulfur, but most perfectly vulcanized."

So although he was not a man of science, Goodyear had managed to vulcanize rubber perfectly all by himself, his only error being that he had left the brimstone unmasked? The attorney left the impression that such a bumpkin could not have done it himself and that he was a predator now trying to swoop down to feed off the English rubber business.

Hill needed to repair the wounds inflicted on Goodyear by cross-examination, and had his chance when he called Moulton to testify. Moulton recalled that on his 1842 visit he had left Goodyear's vulcanized samples with Macintosh in Manchester. As he had admitted before in depositions, Moulton said the samples had been left on the understanding that they not be used "to the prejudice of Mr. Goodyear." He then returned to America. When he went back to England the next year, Moulton said, Macintosh and his partners told him they had subjected the samples to tests and the samples had withstood both cold and oil without deteriorating. From these tests all understood that the technology had been advanced. Moulton returned again to the United States and shipped more patch samples and samples of rubber goods, and continued written communication with Macintosh's partners in 1844.

At this Thesiger leapt into the discussion. "Then you must produce the letter, I am told that really is not so."

Lord Campbell tried to restore order. "We have gone on with great regularity on both sides ..."

Hill then resumed his examination and drew from Moulton explanations of how he had left additional samples with an agent at Leaf & Company at the same time he left samples with Macintosh in Manchester in 1842.

With his cross-examination, Thesiger sought to demonstrate just how nebulous were the terms on which the samples were left, but Moulton surprised him.

"Did you state upon the last of the two occasions that you were examined that you left the samples with them confidentially?" Thesiger asked.

Moulton assured him that he had. Then Thesiger asked what expression was used.

"The exact expression?" Moulton inquired.

"The exact expression," Thesiger affirmed.

Moulton said that he stated distinctly to Macintosh's partner, the elder Mr. Birley, in the presence of Mr. Birley's son, that he would leave the samples confidentially and that they should not be used to the prejudice of Mr. Goodyear. And then Moulton quoted Birley: "Suppose we should find out the secret without the assistance of Mr. Goodyear's sample?"

Neither Lord Campbell nor anyone else in the court had heard this before. "Suppose that they should discover the secret?" Campbell repeated.

Moulton then threw down his thunderbolt: "Yes, without the use of the samples," meaning discover the secret on their own. "I said I would leave that to his own honor."

Thesiger now recognized that his client's honor had been impugned for even investigating how the change in the rubber was made while the samples were on hand. "You have been examined twice before on this matter. Did you ever say one word before today of the last part of the conversation?"

"I never did," said Moulton.

"And this was Mr. Birley, who died?"

"I think it was." Moulton wavered slightly.

That was all Thesiger needed. He took the offensive, trying to limit the damage to his client's honor. He asked Moulton if he had any ownership interest in any India rubber manufacturing company now. Moulton did not. He asked if Moulton had any rubber patents. He did, just one. Thesiger wanted to know if Moulton had anything to do with the National India Rubber Company, an entity related to Hutchinson, Henderson. Nothing whatsoever. And did Moulton have a stake in the claim of the lawsuit? None.

At this moment, a juror stood up to address the court, which was allowed under the English system. "I should like to ask the witness one question. He says they were left without prejudice. He says he was told the samples had been subjected to a test that he raised no objection to and that he raised no objection when he was told that of their being tested."

"No, I did not," answered Moulton.

The jurors came back with a verdict for Hancock on the day the trial closed. Goodyear would never earn a cent from vulcanization in England nor from any of his other English patents.

CHAPTER NINE

"I cannot censure myself"

O ne night in the fall of 1855, French bailiffs arrested an American in connection with unpaid debt. They brought him to a fortress-like stone structure in a section of the city known as Clichy. That night the businessman's wife secured a judge's order for the prisoner's release the next morning. Unaware of what had occurred, the prisoner stared longingly through a window. As he stood there, a guard who was watching believed the American was attempting to escape. The guard raised his rifle and shot the prisoner dead.

The man was Charles Morey, Goodyear's agent and partner, and the debt that landed him in jail was one he shared with Goodyear.

Plagued by illness since his days as a teenage hardware store apprentice, Goodyear always expected he would be the next to die. Every tremor of indigestion, every stabbing pain in his joints seemed to confirm the expectation. Instead he outlived not only his parents but also two brothers and a sister-in-law, a niece, four children and wife Clarissa. Now his associate Charles Morey was gone, too, and with him the last hope for financial success on the Continent that Goodyear had yearned for much of his life.

France had promised to be different from the United States and England. Compared with the problems he faced in those countries, France had rewarded Goodyear from the beginning. The French government had granted him a patent on April 16, 1844, two months before his U.S. patent was issued. Through the effort of the French-speaking Morey, three companies had been formed to manufacture under license to Goodyear's patent, among them Hutchinson, Henderson. Around 1852, the licensees together paid Goodyear and his agent at least one and perhaps as many as three advance payments of $10,000 and tariffs based on a small percentage of sales. A legal challenge to Goodyear's French patent initially was decided in his favor, further boosting his confidence. Although other challenges were under way, his rights to heated rubber seemed safe, at least for a while. Morey had enriched Goodyear more quickly than anyone else he had dealt with in Europe so far. Goodyear and his agents were able to parlay his French licenses into sales in Brussels and Vienna. In 1854, while he was in Paris with his family, Goodyear dispatched Charles Jr. and Ellen to Vienna to instruct a licensee on how to compound and heat the rubber.

These favorable conditions encouraged Goodyear to borrow even more than usual. To finance the creation of the Paris exhibit, including the manufacture of products in France, he obtained funding by signing notes secured by future payments expected from his French licensees. Another expense estimated at being upward of $30,000 was incurred for shipping rubber goods from the London exhibit. Part of the exhibit would also consist of portraits painted on hard rubber of Charles Jr. and Daniel Webster, commissioned from the painter George P. A. Healy, who then had a Paris studio. Goodyear, who had been introduced to Healy by Daniel Webster at Webster's Boston home, planned to sit for a portrait as well.

In the weeks after the trial in England, Goodyear pressed on with the preparations for the Paris show. He advised Gilman on changes to a publicity pamphlet, reminding him to mention telegraph-line sheathing and "Philosophical Instruments"—medical and scientific instruments—in another pamphlet being prepared. Ever mindful of small details that might make a difference, Goodyear paid special attention to a Paris exposition juror who had also judged at the 1851 London exposition. He told Gilman to let the juror know how much he had helped him earn a Council Medal in London and instructed Gilman to "send him the umbrella with the India rubber cover."

Contrary to his spendthrift image, Goodyear seemed especially conscious of costs during the preparations in 1854 and early 1855, although he placed no upper limit on the expenditures. When Gilman, now sensitive to Goodyear's desire for more fiscal accountability, inquired what he wished to spend on the exhibition, Goodyear answered: "All that is necessary to do justice to the subject." He asked Gilman to send an estimate after which he promised to provide "more definite instructions."

In the meantime, Goodyear remained keenly interested in the manufacturing costs of the rubber products. Because he would be suggesting that the items shown had a broad appeal and that rubber was a viable and competitive material, he asked Gilman for general costs of making items in

France, including the price of raw rubber (12.5 sous per pound) and sulfur (2, 3 or 4 sous). The bigger the product, the lower the cost per pound of material. For example, large bas reliefs cast in moulds would have relatively low material costs, while small articles that required high-quality finishes, such as combs, would be much more expensive. Goodyear cautioned Gilman that the prices he was quoting were "cost prices and the first articles" put on the market would necessarily be much higher than the prices mentioned. Before leaving on a brief holiday at the Isle of Wight, Goodyear reminded Gilman of the "remarkable properties of the hard compound" and especially that it "bears a harder blow than metal without indentation."

After returning from his holiday on August 1, Goodyear again was confined to his bed. He was able to tell Gilman that he was willing to pay 5,000 francs for printing a program about his exhibit in Paris. Charles Jr., then in Paris, also pitched in on the exhibit preparations. He sought permits to exhibit some furniture and portraits painted on rubber for what the Goodyears were referring to as the Pavillion de Caoutchouc in the Palais de l'Exposition. In early September, Goodyear asked Gilman to interpret for him during an interview with the editor of a business publication, a role normally performed by Fanny, who was ill at the time.

The production snafus that had crippled the launch of Goodyear's U.S. licensees recurred in France. The French rubber workers had no experience in compounding and heating rubber. At some point it was decided that a new, experimental rolling machine almost as big as Chaffee's Monster, first built more than twenty years earlier in Roxbury, would be needed as a substitute for the calenders being used. Goodyear designed the machine himself and endorsed $5,000 worth of notes given to him by French licensees to pay for it. By tying up his own capital in a piece of equipment, he would be more directly involved in large-scale manufacturing than he had ever been.

Goodyear had to obtain special permission to exhibit as an American, although much of his exhibit's content was manufactured in France. Even before the exposition began, Goodyear's rubber exhibit won him the notice of Napoleon III and Empress Eugénie. As they toured the exhibits, the emperor mistook a stack of Goodyear's India rubber footballs, piled military-style like shells, for cannon balls. Soon Goodyear was invited to ride in a carriage with the emperor to the Bois de Boulogne to demonstrate rubber pontoons. The emperor admired an India rubber necklace with inlaid jewels that he had seen at Goodyear's exhibit and asked if he could have it for the Empress Eugénie. Goodyear demurred and said that the necklace was reserved for Fanny. Napoleon III persisted, so Goodyear had an identical one made for him.

Riding in a carriage alongside the emperor and the Count de Morny, the emperor's half-brother and prime minister, Charles Goodyear may have felt that he was beyond the reach of trouble and had endured his last trial. Although he had doubts about the propriety of life in Paris, a city that flaunted physical pleasure more freely even than London, he thought about settling his family in the city.

The question never had to be answered. Within a few months, Goodyear's French business affairs were enveloped in controversy. In September he had a deepening sense that his European efforts might net him little more than satisfaction that he had "advanced the arts" of rubber making in Europe without "realizing all the profit he had hoped for." Once again, he was undone by overeager attempts to make money from European patents by sending out samples with agents. In this case, he had sent several pairs of rubber shoes to businessmen in France. The French court, which was still weighing challenges to Goodyear's patent, ruled that by having sent the shoes to French agents Goodyear had placed his invention in the public domain and thus forfeited his right to the final two years of patent protection.

Without a French patent, Goodyear was unable to present himself as a secure credit risk. The French contractor refused to honor his notes guaranteeing future payments, including the ones used to secure the financing of the new rolling machine. The machine hadn't been finished, but Varill, Middleton demanded payment from Goodyear and Morey of the total amount outstanding, about $5,000.

When Goodyear could not pay, the contractor obtained court orders for his imprisonment, much the way creditors in the United States had in the 1830s. Goodyear and Fanny scrambled to hold them off. Morey also became a target. The French company demanded payment of 175,000 francs from Morey in London. He couldn't or wouldn't pay it. When Morey arrived in France, he was arrested and taken to Clichy, the Paris prison where he was shot.

A few days after Morey's death, Goodyear showed up at George Healy's studio with a large flat package containing a rubber panel. On it the artist was to paint Goodyear's portrait, and artist and subject began work at once. Goodyear sat in silence as Healy outlined his face and figure on the smooth panel. Both men were elated with the results and decided to continue the sitting the next day.

Goodyear told Healy he could be reached at his shop at 40 Rue Vivienne. "If I am not in, give the message to my partner, Mr. Morey," he said. "He's almost as interested in this as we are." Then he left.

A short while later, a boy delivered a newspaper to Healy's studio. Casually glancing through it, Healy saw the name Goodyear, and read an account of Morey's shooting. He realized that Goodyear knew nothing of what had happened.

With Morey dead, creditors focused their sights on Goodyear. The contractor Varill, Middleton went to court and three times during several weeks in November 1855 obtained orders for Goodyear's arrest. On the night of December 5, four uniformed bailiffs arrived at Goodyear's Paris hotel. One pair made its way to the balcony outside a suite of rooms. Another pair headed down a corridor and, as the two approached the door, one of the bailiffs rapped firmly on it.

When Fanny opened the door, she recognized one of the men from a previous meeting. They looked past her. *Je vous retrouve enfin! Le voilà!*" (I have you at last! Here he is!) one bailiff shouted. The other bailiff rushed into the suite, entered the bedroom and blew a whistle.

Roused from his bed and standing toe to toe with the bailiffs, Goodyear at first refused to be cowed. "Under what warrant were the officers acting?" he demanded. They showed him a special order for his arrest. "May I have some privacy in which to change?" The bailiffs refused and remained in the room as he replaced his sleeping gown with a shirt, a bowtie, a waist jacket and greatcoat. Fanny pleaded for the officers to allow her husband to stay in the hotel room at least until morning rather than bring him out into the cold, which would aggravate his illnesses. But they insisted that their prisoner accompany them immediately. Flanked by his captors and propped up on crutches, Goodyear boarded a cab along with Fanny and the bailiffs for the bumpy ride to a courtroom adjoining the prison. A judge, also roused from bed, processed Goodyear for confinement. Fanny asked to stay the night with her husband, but the judge refused. She accompanied Charles to the massive doors leading into the prison and he went inside. One of the bailiffs agreed to escort Fanny back to the hotel.

The next morning she applied at the prison office for a ticket to admit her for a visit. The clerks asked if her husband "was the Goodyear of caoutchouc, about whom there had been so much in the papers." Later that day she visited men with whom Goodyear had done business, seeking their aid to procure his release. All responded coldly, except one, who said he would see what he could do.

Fanny remembered feeling relieved by this tentative pledge to help, and she headed to the prison, where she was searched and admitted. Eyes fastened on her from behind the grated prison windows as she passed through the corridors. When she reached her husband's cell, he wasn't there. Another prisoner, described by Fanny as "a good-natured Italian," offered to go find him. In a few minutes the man returned to say Goodyear was on his way back. In another minute he hobbled in and greeted Fanny calmly and cheerfully.

Fanny asked her husband how he had passed the night. He took both her hands in his and looked in her face.

"I have been through nearly every form of trial that human flesh is heir to, and I find that there is nothing in life to fear but sin."

Husband and wife prayed together and then Fanny, who was in the early stages of pregnancy, gave Charles his business messages. In a few minutes, he and Fanny set out down the grim corridors to find two other Americans whom Charles had met that morning. All Goodyear wanted to do was to cheer them up and see what he could get for them.

Later, after Fanny had left and Charles had been locked in his cell, he had a chance to contemplate his French fortunes. He decided that God had sent him a message, and it had nothing to do with business practices or borrowing. Goodyear believed God was telling him not to settle down and raise his children in the iniquitous city of Paris. Why else would He visit such tribulations on an honest man?

Goodyear had already resolved to leave the country a few days later, when Charles Jr. came to visit bringing the Cross of the Legion of Honor. The emperor had awarded it to Goodyear for his excellent exhibit and products.

Goodyear's exit from France followed a familiar melodramatic script. He had to borrow $5,000 from a friend to secure his release from prison, which he did on December 21, 1855. He arranged to return to London a few weeks later. Charles and Fanny had already crossed the English Channel when French creditors, apparently unsatisfied with their settlement, obtained an order through which an English sheriff arrested Goodyear and jailed him before he reached London. Goodyear refused bail offered by English friends and for several days remained in jail until he could convince the sheriff that a mistake had been made, and he was freed.

This final indignity, the first time a creditor had reached Goodyear across an international border, triggered the same questions that had ricocheted through his thoughts for twenty-five years. Why was this happening to him?

A last trial of some sort, Goodyear concluded, had been orchestrated by God to test his faith. Satan, Goodyear recalled in a letter to Fanny, was once let loose in this way upon "poor Job; not that I presume to compare myself with that good man." In truth, Goodyear actually did consider himself the victim of a cosmic homily about suffering similar to Job's. Neither his lavish exhibit-spending nor the financing of the incomplete rolling machine could be interpreted as unwise or sinful: "Scrutinizing my conduct as closely as I can, I cannot censure myself for, or really regret, after what has happened, anything which I have done, which others might, in ignorance of the circumstances, suppose to be the cause of such persecutions, which often are occasioned by a man's own folly or imprudence." Instead, Goodyear and Fanny blamed the calamity on the frugal French, their peculiar patent rules and the late Morey's rash speculations.

After checking into an inn not far from his English jail, Goodyear sat down in the parlor. On the other side of the room he saw an engraving of a prisoner chiseling the image of Christ on the prison wall with a nail.

"How one would like to know that man!" he wrote to Fanny.

Thinking about everything that had happened to him in the last month, Goodyear settled his doubts like an accountant balancing the books. These troubles were for a purpose, a special purpose for the good of Charles Goodyear, or for his family, even if he couldn't tell yet what that would be. And that purpose would be fulfilled on this side of the grave, in the current life, not the next, he concluded.

Goodyear repledged himself to God. He prayed and wrote Fanny of his prayers: "Committing you and all dear to us to God's kind care, trusting that he will deliver us in every day of trial until we are safely brought to a happy death and immortal life through our Savior."

Goodyear's health, as it had so many other times, followed his business fortunes into decline. The family returned to a house in Norwood, near Sydenham, its third residence in the London area. Charles found it hard to keep up his business correspondence and appointments, although now there were discouragingly few new prospects. In the United States, Judson, to whom he had signed over a large interest in his patents, controlled affairs with licensees and the Shoe Associates. Goodyear's growing suspicions of mismanagement and self-dealing by Judson had led him to open up a similar working relationship with another attorney, James Dorr, who handled many of Goodyear's legal affairs on non-shoe patents in exchange for a full third of all of Goodyear's patent-license revenue.

Goodyear's joint pain from lead poisoning struck him harder than ever before, and once again he took to what appeared to be his deathbed. The family gathered around and waited. Goodyear sent farewell messages to his friends; but he again failed to die. He celebrated the marriage of his eldest daughter, Ellen, to Charles DeForest (possibly a relation of William DeForest). And in early summer, 1856, Goodyear became a father again, of his eighth child, Henry Wardell.

He remained so ill that it was decided to move to Bath, the city west of London whose hot springs had been favored by the Romans, and might, he hoped, soothe his gouty agony. For nine weeks up until his departure Goodyear lay stone-still in his bed. On April 8, 1856, he was moved gradually to a private carriage for the trip.

Even during these troubles, he managed to press ahead with his work. Sometimes at night he would rouse Fanny to ask if she was not too tired to record his thoughts. "I have not closed my eyes yet, for I believe I have thought of the true way of overcoming a difficulty," he would say to her. Commenting on a particular rubber application, he would say, "I have been studying that so many years," and mention the length of time. Then he would rapidly dictate exact specifications, letters and instructions. When his thoughts were committed to paper he finally rested.

As an autumnal mood of reconciliation came over him, he returned to his long preoccupation with maritime safety. Steam power and steam-boats had expanded the opportunities for travel both on the open sea and on inland rivers, but steam-powered navigation also generated ever-growing numbers of maritime disasters from snags, collisions and exploding boilers. "How can I sleep, when so many of my fellow-creatures are passing into eternity everyday, and I feel that I am the man that can prevent it?" he asked Fanny. Every few months, newspapers carried lurid reports of the latest mishaps, and publishers began to churn out highly popular compilations of maritime disasters, replete with eyewitness accounts.

Goodyear first believed he could end drownings with a universal garment or wearable safety device that could be fitted on every passenger, including those restricted to the lower deck who paid a reduced fare but were exposed to the greatest hazard. Taking another approach, he theorized that each ship could be furnished and fitted with rubber-made objects that could double as flotation devices and would be so thoroughly dispersed around the ship that no one need search long for one if disaster suddenly struck. That fantasy completed Goodyear's vision of a rubber-made world free from the hazard of drowning.

But Goodyear's own struggle to stay afloat in an ocean of sickness and debt seemed ever more hopeless. The winter of 1857 was "one of deep trial, constant sickness, acute bodily and mental distress, and great pecuniary inconvenience and anxiety," said Fanny. In the spring their infant son, Henry, died. Fanny, who was already pregnant again, barely had time to mourn for her little boy. Other cares pressed in and Charles' health was unpredictable. At times he reassured his young wife that all would turn out well, but at other times he fretted about ending up in the poorhouse.

In the spas of Bath, Goodyear's prospects were light years away from the grim realities he had dealt with in Woburn. His family could afford a private physician and respectable accommodations, and they no longer scraped for food or fuel. Yet rather than get out of debt, he had merely joined a better class of debtor. He was no longer trying to enter the upper classes by material purchases, as he was when he first arrived in London years earlier. Gifts for family and friends and rubber experiments were the only indulgences he permitted himself. Yet his debts continued to grow and his creditors at home had not seen in him years.

Fanny had another boy, Arthur, in May 1858. The Goodyears planned to return to America as soon as she and the baby were well enough to travel. They didn't have the cash ready to pay for their trip, so once again Charles pawned household property. He sold his watch chain, Fanny's gold chain and a diamond ring.

As he contemplated his return, Goodyear realized that although he had helped a new industry to grow, he had no home to return to. His only properties were intellectual.

During the crossing by steam packet Goodyear remained in his cabin most of the time, fighting seasickness and eating little. Fanny and the children slept in the ladies' cabin behind the engine room. Occasionally Goodyear would join them on the promenade deck and in the dining room, but with his lingering illness he could not avail himself of the small pleasures of an ocean crossing. The Goodyears stayed on board the steamer until it had docked at Washington, D.C., where they checked into a hotel.

Upon returning to the United States for the first time in six years, Goodyear faced a new crisis with the looming expiration of the fourteen-year term of Patent No. 3633, on June 15, 1858. Lawyers began to make the rounds again taking depositions in preparation for the hearing before the patent commissioner. One of Goodyear's most generous supporters, the New Haven stove dealer Ralph B. Steele, now fifty-seven years old, dutifully recalled in his testimony for Goodyear that the inventor had dedicated himself to his rubber quest at the expense of all else and that the deep prejudice against rubber in New England had made the task more formidable. Goodyear made great sacrifice of his patent interests, selling off equity to defray costs of litigation, Steele said. He told his interrogators that he had lent Goodyear $40,000 over the years, of which $35,000 remained outstanding. Goodyear had paid back the first few thousand borrowed, but in the last three years Steele had "not received a dollar from him."

William Ballard, the New York knife maker and manufacturer who had been replaced by William Ely as Goodyear's most important early bene-factor (and who had been given a footnote of thanks in Goodyear's book), made an even more curious witness. Ballard had been deposed for Goodyear for the Trenton trial, but this time he testified for Goodyear's opponents. Before Goodyear had left for England, Ballard said, he would see him occa-sionally in New York and the inventor would tell Ballard "as I was his best friend, he would remember me." Yet Ballard had never collected a dime.

Goodyear's formal application for the patent extension contained a sworn statement from the inventor, continuing his tale of woe where the heartrending account given by Daniel Webster at the Trenton trial left off. During his whole time in England, Goodyear said, he had been and was still "out of health" and was much "embarrassed in pecuniary debt." In France, Goodyear continued, he was so embarrassed as to be imprisoned for debt until he was "liberated" by loans from friends who were as yet not repaid. Subsequently, Goodyear said, he was incarcerated in London for four days on the false oath that he would leave the country. Despite this plague of mis-fortune, Goodyear was proud to have established the reputation of India rubber fabrics made according to his improvements. He had obtained numer-ous honors, including a medal presented from the Emperor Napoleon while incarcerated. Yet in England he was deprived of the benefits of his invention by Thomas Hancock, who used eminent chemists to find the secret to the vulcanization process used on Goodyear's samples.

At all times, Goodyear claimed, he was a model of fiscal probity. Every dollar received was spent in applying his invention to new uses and for exhibitions and necessary family expenses. Only in Paris did he, for one year, pay more than $600 per year in rent since obtaining his patent. Part of that time, he had had to bear the additional burden of caring for his nieces and nephews after his brothers had died. He swore he used "proper discretion and sound judgement" in his expenditures. Various members of his family devoted their entire time to aiding him and "all of them by reason thereof are in a similar pecuniary position to that of your applicant and he is under moral obligation to make them compensation therefore."

From his efforts, Goodyear proudly proclaimed, an industry that employed five thousand people had taken root. Since his patent and especially beginning in 1849, when investors started pouring in more capital, rubber making had expanded into a lucrative and well-oiled industrial engine. Between 1823 and 1844, 100,000 to 500,000 pairs of unvulcanized rubber shoes had been exported to the United States from Brazil. By 1852, the seven members of the Shoe Associates made 2.25 million pairs of vulcanized shoes and boots, using home-grown American labor, and probably could have made more had they not tightly controlled production through quotas that artificially propped up prices.

Only Thomas Hancock, who sent a lawyer to fight the patent extension, and Horace Day, still burning with resentment, threatened the picture drawn by this narration. Day still operated rubber factories in Manhattan, where Samuel Armstrong and Charles Gilbert were his partners. His hunger to bring down Goodyear drove him to new excesses. After William Ely—Ballard's successor as Goodyear's partner and backer and the accidental discoverer of how fire and brimstone could cure rubber—had died sometime in the mid-1850s, Day managed to gain ownership of some of his personal papers, including forty letters from Goodyear to Ely during the 1830s and 1840s. In the letters were many intimacies, both business and personal, and Day now searched these letters for revelations of the evil he had convinced himself lay at the core of Goodyear's being. He used the letters to buttress and develop themes that he had been sounding since Trenton: that Goodyear was not the real inventor of temperature-stable rubber (Ely or a great many other people deserved credit); that a jury had never passed judgment on the rightfulness of the patent (as legal custom required); and that Goodyear had lived in a world of luxury and ostentation while bluffing poverty and abusing his creditors.

According to Day, the letters told the story of how Goodyear, realizing Ely had stumbled upon a valuable secret, attempted to manipulate the younger man with "tales of doleful suffering, privation and doubt, and hope deferred" even as his letters to patent agent Jones in Washington, D.C., bespoke another reality. These letters "assumed the rich, bright picture of the traffic with princes and kings, and visions of untold wealth and personal aggrandizement," said Day. He found the letters "ingenious, very natural, and one by a master spirit. They would be really touching—even pathetic, if they were indeed true." He was able to make this charge only by engaging in some manipulation himself, excluding the most pathetic letters from his legal brief, among them one in which Goodyear told Ely of the death of the second little William Henry.

As part of the hearing over the extension, the applicant had to produce evidence that he had not yet reaped all the reward—adequate remuneration—to which the law entitled him as patent-holder. In other words, if he could show that he was shortchanged somehow or that there was a hardship or extenuating circumstance, the patent commissioner could tack a few more years onto the patent to allow the inventor time to make money.

In trying to unravel whether Goodyear had been adequately remunerated, Judson prepared a statement that fixed Goodyear's receipts since 1843, when he declared bankruptcy, at $162,894. Most of the money was license fees and percentage-of-sale tariffs from licensees. The statement also totaled Goodyear's expenses at a prodigious $129,535.46, which meant that his net income for the roughly fourteen-year period of the patent was $33,358.63, or slightly more than $2,000 a year, a respectable but unspectacular income at that time.

The government didn't accept this accounting at face value. The examiner of patents, Dr. Thomas Anticell, was given the task of reinterpreting the exhibits and information supplied to him and collating it with the testimony submitted. This required him to sift through data on deals for rubber cloth, blankets, car springs, belting and packing and steam-engine gaskets. He also had to consider deals relating to all the other uses to which the world had put vulcanized rubber. Anticell's calculation of Goodyear's revenue from his patent came to $162,894, the same as Goodyear and Judson's statement, but with related debts and costs only half of those stated by Goodyear and Judson, he estimated profit at $114,128, a small fortune at the time.

Strangely, even after reassessing Goodyear's income, the examiner judged this amount not "adequate remuneration" in keeping with the spirit of the patent law. Although he blamed Goodyear for selling his licenses too cheaply, Anticell counted Goodyear's sacrifices in legal expenses, experimentation and lost health and peace of mind on the expense side of the imaginary ledger. Once that was done, Anticell reasoned that Goodyear was entitled to an extension.

Not unexpectedly, Day performed his own analysis with vastly different methods and results. He reported that Goodyear's profits had been in the millions, and that dozens of deals and fees and streams of income had simply been left out of the report drawn up by Judson and ignored or overlooked by Anticell. Any extension of the patent, Day claimed, amounted to a tax on the public that would put countless millions more into the hands of Goodyear and the attorneys who shared ownership of the patents, especially Judson.

Goodyear's attorneys, backed by Anticell, didn't need to argue much about the financial analysis. They erupted briefly at the scandalous introduction of Goodyear's letters to Ely, demanding but never receiving an account of how the letters came into Day's possession. Ultimately they succeeded in portraying the publication of the private letters as further evidence that Day was a scoundrel. For the most part Goodyear's lawyers stuck to the basic story of trial and suffering that had worked for so long.

Goodyear's hopes for relief from his misery now rested on the extension. The day before Patent Commissioner Joseph Holt's decision was due, Goodyear wrote a letter to Fanny. She never made its contents public but simply described her husband as entrusting his fate entirely to God. "The letter is almost a psalm of thanksgiving," Fanny later told a contemporary biographer, "without one word of anxiety or suspense." In the letter Goodyear recounts "the mercies and deliverances of his past life."

To the family's relief, Commissioner Holt not only decided to extend Goodyear's patent another seven years but rivaled the Trenton decision in sentimentality. After dismissing Day's objections to the novelty and originality of the patent, Holt excused Goodyear's inability to supply records of his finances: "Inventors ... have ever been distinguished" by poor business habits; because they are "completely engrossed by some favorite theory, they scorn the counsels and restraints of worldly thrift, and fling from them the petty cares of the mere man of commerce as the lion shakes a stinging insect from his mane." Holt described Goodyear's dedication to his task as one of "almost superhuman perseverance.

> Not only were the powers of his mind and body thus ardently devoted to the invention and its introduction into use, but every dollar he possessed or could command through the resources of his credit, or the influence of friendship, was uncalculatingly cast into that seething cauldron of experiments.... The very bed on which his wife slept, the linen that covered his table, were seized and sold to pay his board.... His family had to endure privations almost surpassing belief.... We often find him arrested and incarcerated in debtor's prison, but even amid its gloom his vision of the future never grew dim, his faith in his ultimate triumph never faltered....

He then concluded: "With such a record of toil, of privation, of courage, and of perseverance in the midst of discouragements the most depressing, it is safe to affirm that not only has the applicant used that due diligence enjoined by law, but that his diligence has been without parallel in the annals of invention."

Goodyear could rest comfortably knowing that the patent had been renewed, but his Job-like personal woes continued. The family stopped in New Haven, where Charles Jr. lived, and while they were there the new baby, Arthur, died. Fanny was devastated by the loss of a second child in as many years, while Charles, who had learned never to trust an infant to grow to childhood and therefore hadn't yet admitted the baby fully to his heart, suffered less. In any case the rubber business was now for all of them a life-and-death matter.

In the winter of 1859 the Goodyears set up a permanent residence in Washington, D.C., in a house within a fifteen-minute carriage ride of the Patent Office and other federal agencies. Goodyear intended to patent new inventions and probably also lobby federal officials to adopt the life-saving maritime devices he designed. (The federal government had, since 1852, begun to play a greater role in enforcing safe commercial navigation and trying to limit the appalling losses from steamboat accidents and explosions.) Goodyear set up a workshop in one room, with a large bath for testing life preservers. His youngest children, Clara and William Henry, were now eighteen and twelve, respectively, and Fanny was pregnant for the third time.

With seven years added to his patent and the promise now of more license income, some of Goodyear's torments began to subside. He told Fanny that he "had never made his experiments with so much ease and success before," and later on she remembered him saying that he "had never had so much rest, or taken life so easily." Fanny later interpreted the new calming not as the result of success but as a "foretaste of that eternal rest which he was so soon to enter."

By setting up in Washington, D.C., Goodyear placed some distance between himself and the licensees in Connecticut, New Jersey, New York and New England. He distanced himself from the continuing legal skirmishes with Day, and relied more and more on Charles Jr., who was in Boston and married to Henrietta Colt of New Haven, to make up his rubber samples. The contacts in Washington seemed promising. Charles met a Colonel Roberts of the U.S. Army, who was making some experiments with shotguns in which he thought India rubber could be used to advantage. "You will do whatever is in your power to forward his views," Goodyear instructed his son.

Goodyear continued to be harassed by his illness, but at times an unfamiliar, almost eerie, peace prevailed in his life. He looked old now, with a nest of mostly white whiskers projecting from his chin. The hair atop his head covered his ears with uncombed tangles. Instead of being deep-set with melancholy, as in the past, Goodyear's eyes looked simply tired, the skin beneath them pleated in purple-gray folds. On April 25, Fanny gave birth to their third child, a girl also named Fanny. During this time of transition she detected in Charles "a marked ripening for glory; a growing gentleness and forbearance; an increased spirituality of mind, and a superiority to earthly care and anxiety."

But this mood did not prevail for very long. On May 30, a letter arrived informing Goodyear that his daughter Cynthia, who was thirty-two and living in New Haven with her husband, cousin George Goodyear, was very ill. Charles immediately boarded the steamboat Montebello accompanied by his physician, Dr. Bacon. Seasickness weakened him. During the trip he wrote a note to Fanny saying that he was ill, but characteristically noted that "Providence always smiles in the storm as well as in the sunshine."

On reaching New York harbor, Goodyear saw his son-in-law George at the dock. Cynthia had died on May 31. A funeral was scheduled in New Haven, but Charles' own illness, exacerbated by grief, laid him low. He was carried to the Fifth Avenue Hotel, on West Twenty-third Street and Broadway. Word was sent to Fanny that he was very sick. Goodyear also rushed messages to New Haven to brother-in-law DeForest, who arranged Goodyear's chaotic business affairs as best he could. When DeForest showed up in New York, Dr. Bacon told him, "This is the last!" He made it clear that he fully expected Goodyear to die within hours. When Fanny arrived in New York on June 7, Charles was too weak to speak although he let her know that he recognized her. Other members of the family gathered at the hotel. Twice they convened for prayers at his bedside, and as they did he blessed each person by name. He also instructed Fanny and Charles Jr. to have Clarissa's remains brought back to the United States from England to be buried alongside him. As hours passed he repeated, "God knows." Looking at Fanny with an intense gaze he modified the phrase: "God knows all." As family members and friends reminded him of his accomplishments, Goodyear answered, "What am I? To God be all glory."

There would be no anticlimactic recovery this time. Goodyear hung on for a month as people came and went from the room, ministering to him as best they could. Fanny later claimed the last words that Goodyear spoke expressed forgiveness for "a person from whom he had suffered much." He never indicated the exact identity, and although many took it to be Horace Day, it could just as easily have been Thomas Hancock. On Sunday, July 1, as church bells called worshippers to service, Goodyear half-raised himself from the pillow as if he saw someone entering the room, then sank back again and died.

The newspapers of the day took only brief notice of his passing. The *New York Times* acknowledged Goodyear's "great discovery." In what is probably a reference to the popular use of his name in a patent, the newspaper noted that Goodyear had been "very constantly before the public in connection with the manufacture of articles of all kinds, to a door-mat or a child's toy out of India-Rubber." The *New York Daily Tribune* observed that Goodyear "felt the honorable obligation which his patents imposed upon him, and, with complete disinterestedness, kept himself poor that he might enrich the world."

Goodyear's body was taken to New Haven for funeral rites at Charles Jr.'s house and then buried at the Grove Street cemetery.

Set free from the ambiguity of his business life, Goodyear's dogged resourcefulness and stoic disregard for adversity inspired new tributes. In church services and memorial services in New Haven, the Congregational clergy picked up the themes of Goodyear's triumph codified years earlier by Daniel Webster and knitted them into a new, reverent version of the noble Christian technologist. The Reverend Dr. Dutton, Goodyear's minister in

New Haven, recalled his generosity and gratitude: "When the days of his prosperity at length came, he remembered those who had aided him in his adversity and extremity, and he was not satisfied with a full payment of their dues. But when any of them were in a pecuniary misfortune he aided them with a princely generosity. Indeed, some of them with their families were really supported by him for years." According to Dr. Dutton, Goodyear provided jobs and careers to many friends and relatives: "In his manifold experiments and through his influence in connection with the extensive manufactory under his patents, a large number of them have been employed, and have found avenues to lucrative and independent business for themselves. And for all the objects of benevolence he had an open heart and hand, giving to them cheerfully and unsparingly whenever he had money at his disposal."

Goodyear's estate told another story. The $30,000-per-year income suggested by his lawyers in the 1858 patent extension exhibits turned out to be pretty close to the mark. But as Goodyear had always believed, it was the future that held his riches. While the unfolding Civil War crippled some commercial enterprise, the Lincoln administration equipped the federal Army with an unprecedented $27 million worth of rubber boots, raincoats, ponchos, tents and pontoon boats, virtually all of it from Goodyear patent licensees and their subsidiaries. From 1861 to 1865 the Union Army bought 1,893,007 rubber blankets and 1,596,559 ponchos at a total cost of $17 million.

People who could not or would not pry their money from Goodyear's living hand finally rushed forward to wrest it from him now that he was dead. By the end of 1862, 101 claims against the Goodyear estate had been filed, the majority by small businesses and suppliers of goods and services. Not all were easily categorized. To the Connecticut Savings Bank and Bank of Metropolis, Goodyear had loans outstanding of $6,644, while $7.50 was owed to the Continental Hotel and $3.63 to the Warren Chemical Manufacturing Company. Dozens of other businesses and individuals filed claims for sums ranging upward from C. Wilcox's near-trivial $3.33 (a good day's pay at that time).

The claims by family members were led by William DeForest's $30,000, but a separate claim was filed by DeForest's wife and Goodyear's younger sister Harriet, for $4,500. Sons-in-law Charles T. DeForest and George Goodyear claimed another $2,300 and $5,300, respectively. Stephen Bateman, a cousin on Goodyear's mother's side, claimed $1,200. Licensees Jonathan Trotter claimed $4,898.42 and Leverett Candee put in for $3,367.72. Even portrait artist G. P. A. Healy, who had been painting Goodyear just as disaster struck in Paris, was owed $670. Altogether Charles Jr. allowed claims of $188,871.71 in the first years after his father's death.

This was only a fraction of the total amount claimed. Benjamin Coburn and L. S. Maring, who felt cheated by Goodyear during his Roxbury rubber period, wanted a total of $421.68. Edwin Chaffee, the inventor of the Monster, his partner William W. Brown and other owners of the Providence Rubber Company were suing (or countersuing) Goodyear for almost $100,000 in federal court in Rhode Island, trying to invalidate his patent. The Riders, who had purchased licenses from Goodyear early in his rubber career, were suing for about $10,000. And a French company called L. Brun, which may have helped build the Paris exposition exhibit, claimed $32,000.

Finally, gullible William Ballard, by then an old man, put in a claim for several hundred dollars. He had called on Goodyear at his home in Washington, D.C., trying to collect on the $5,000 to $7,000 in promissory notes that Goodyear had given him more than twenty years earlier. Instead the two men had agreed that Ballard would take $100 in cash and $300 later, but of course the $300 never came.

The money collected for the estate by Charles Jr. between 1861 and 1863 from the Shoe Associates and Naugatuck-based licensees remained relatively modest in the last few years of the patent. Only Leverett Candee's flourishing boot and shoe company, which grew with advertising of its canvas and rubber croquet sandals (which in the 1870s became known as sneakers), made a comparatively strong showing, with a payment of about $9,000. The industrial licensees, on the other hand, pumped a river of cash into the estate during 1861. The New England Car Spring Company, whose coiled shock-absorbing devices had been able to cushion the discomfiting bounce of railroad travel, paid about $17,000. The New York Belting & Packing Company, which helped trap the steam and increase the power and efficiency of the century's revolutionizing power equipment, tossed in another $16,000. The windfall would have been substantial had not Goodyear assigned a full third of this income to his lawyer James Dorr.

The suspicion that Judson, as agent for Goodyear, had cheated the family surfaced during the legal activity after Goodyear's death. Executor Charles Jr. asked Judson for an accounting of the money paid and due to his father. Judson dragged his heels and produced no report and in the summer of 1863 Charles Jr. filed suit in federal court for the money owed. In a petition filed two months later, young Goodyear said Judson was indebted to the estate for "more than $100,000" and held and controlled large amounts of property and that the court should without delay force Judson to post security of $100,000. A person at Judson's place of business had informed Charles Jr. that Judson was "preparing to leave the U.S." for Europe. Judson didn't flee, but he delayed his answer five times between August and December. On February 10, 1864, Judson asked the court for still more time to prepare his report of payments to Goodyear.

In the four years since his father had died, Charles Jr., although not yet thirty, had experienced several lifetimes worth of legal woe settling his father's estate. Now his father's famous Patent No. 3633 was due to expire again, on June 15, 1865, and Charles Jr. embarked on yet one more legal campaign to have it extended again. The twenty-one-year-old patent had lived longer than most and the patent commissioner, having once extended the patent, could not do so again. An act of Congress was necessary. Charles Jr. hired the Boston law firm of Blatchford, Seward & Griswold to prepare a petition, and he and Fanny headed to Washington with their lawyers.

With Goodyear dead the legal contest over the extension lacked the fairy-tale quality of the previous patent extension hearing and the great Trenton trial. A latticework of shifting and secret alliances, augmented by dirty tricks, began to take form. Backroom bargaining and paranoia fueled by planted stories and half-truths replaced oratorical flourish.

Scientific American magazine, which opposed the Goodyear monopoly, reflected some of the anti-corporation sentiment beginning to appear in post–Civil War America. It suggested that a broad conspiracy had been undertaken through which the Goodyear patent-holders had teamed up with owners of expiring patents on Woodworth's planing machine, Fitzgerald's safe, Adams' Janus-faced lock and other inventions. "We are informed that the parties who support these claims have formed a sort of combination of interests, and mean to 'push their cases through,' if money will do it. We warn the people to look sharp after these corrupt schemes and to use their best efforts to beat them." Other publications also took sides against the Goodyears. The *New York Herald* chided the correspondents of the Associated Press for failing to expose the attempted extortion of public funds represented by the patent extension petition. If the correspondents "were worth a button they would do so without a hint from any quarter," wrote the *Herald*.

There had been precedent for congressional intervention in patents. What was unusual was that conflicts of interest and connections to the rubber

industry disqualified two of the five members of the Congressional Committee on Patents. Its chairman, Thomas A. Jenckes of Rhode Island, was
a former federal judge who also had at one time been an attorney for Horace
Day fighting the Goodyear patents. But Jenckes now was an investor in a
rubber company and he favored the new extension. And a rubber company
had hired another member of the five-man patent committee, Leonard Mey-
ers, to work as an attorney. That left three voting members of the committee.

The intrigues suggested furtive alliances. At one point, a T. J. Mayall,
of Roxbury, Massachusetts, who had several patents for manufacturing rubber fabric, met with a Mr. Lyman at Young's Hotel in Boston. Mayall told
Lyman that he couldn't use his rubber fabric patents until the Goodyear
patent had expired and that certain parties in England had offered him more
than $200,000 for his help in defeating the extension. Mayall "took out a
bundle of papers and letters which were loose in his pocket, and shuffling
them over showed me several envelopes apparently containing letters, which
envelopes had what appeared to be English postage stamps on them," said
Lyman. Mayall had also met with Judson in New York City, ostensibly to
discuss how to prevent the patent extension.

Judson now opposed the extension of the patent as a way to get Charles
Jr. off his back. Perplexed by Judson's opposition, which appeared to have
no other motive than retaliation, one of Charles Jr.'s new lawyers, James T.
Brady, theorized that Judson was preparing to team with Mayall "to organize some other gigantic monopoly, as it will be in effect, to take the place of
those which are now, as it is supposed, successfully being carried on."

By suing Judson, Charles Jr. may have inadvertently nudged him closer
to his old rival Horace Day. Judson held substantial stock in many of the
Goodyear patent licensee companies and had formed a new company with
Conrad Poppenhusen. In 1862, their company bought out all of Day's rubber-making plants for $371,000. Day finally was out of the rubber business
with a huge bank account, and he was willing to use some of it to get even
with Goodyear posthumously.

One Goodyear biographer, P. W. Barker, interpreted the buyout as an
effort to eliminate a chronic infringer. He noted that Day received "more
money as a nuisance fee to desist from infringement than the inventor
[Goodyear] had realized during his sixteen years as patentee." But the deal
showed something else. It indicated that whatever loyalty Poppenhusen or
other licensees might have had toward the father, that loyalty did not extend
to Charles Jr., especially now that he was suing Judson, who with his partners

and licensees now controlled more rubber-making assets than ever. That gave Charles Jr. something to think about: who would be his licensees should he succeed in winning an extension, if Judson and the existing licensees lined up against him?

The family's petition for extension followed a familiar story line: the impoverished inventor who persevered at all costs until his discovery was secured, never realizing significant financial gain during his lifetime. At his death he "left a widow, who is in feeble health; five children, the youngest now only four years of age; one grandchild, the daughter of a deceased daughter; and one adopted child, who are nearly all, if not all, wholly dependent upon the settlement of his estate for their pecuniary maintenance and support."

According to another new family lawyer, Clarence A. Seward, America, as a rising industrial power, owed a debt to all its great inventors. "We, of to-day, would not permit a descendant of Columbus to live in poverty on our soil," Seward said, drawing a parallel to the country's great literary and scientific discoverers. "Look in what direction you choose, and where can you find, in any civilized community, a human being who has not realized the blessings of Goodyear's great invention," he went on, arguing that the duty conferred by the Constitution on Congress to promote the progress of "Science and the Useful Arts" meant that Congress should act as the guardians of inventors' families, and the defenders of their memories, "at least so far as to protect their property till it pays their debts, and secures a competence to those whom they leave behind."

An extravagant response to the Goodyear petition was submitted by Day, who labeled his old antagonist "the original confidence man." Essentially, Day argued that a great financial hoax was being perpetrated on Congress and the country through which the people of the United States would have to pay $75 million dollars more for rubber goods during the life of the patent extension. Of that, $5.5 million would go to Charles Goodyear's heirs and another $4.5 million would "go directly into the hands of two lawyers who own 45 percent of all Goodyear's patent interests," referring to Judson and Dorr. A Goodyear attorney replied that Day's accusations against Goodyear "brought back to my mind the forms of Webster and Choate, and Cutting, the living and the dead"—a not-so-subtle jab at Day's spiritualist activities and séances.

On Friday afternoon, March 11, 1864, lawyers for both sides reassembled in New York and continued deposing Charles Jr. He had testified that he had no knowledge of the numerous phantom payments Day claimed were

left off of the summary of his father's income and that his father lived mod-
estly and never had employed a driver, or at least not one who wore a livery
uniform.

Still trying to reverse Trenton, Day, representing himself, began the
cross-examination. After asking a harmless question or two about Goodyear's
book, Day quickly switched to a more personal line of questioning. Name
your schools and the places you lived as a child, he demanded. Charles Jr.
declined. Give the place and the name of your teacher, Day asked. Again
Charles Jr. curtly replied, "I decline to answer." This ritual was repeated five
times within the first minute of personal questions.

Day asked, "Do you refuse and intend to decline to answer any questions I may put to you on this examination, touching your occupation and
residence previous to your becoming twelve years of age?"

"I have no settled intention on that point," Charles Jr. replied.

And then as Day asked Charles Jr. to name his residences and schools
at the ages of thirteen, fourteen, fifteen, sixteen and seventeen years of age,
Charles Jr. quickly said again, "I decline to answer."

On some points, Charles Jr. replied briefly, saying that he had "an indis-
tinct recollection of having attended school—might be termed an infant
school"—in Roxbury. Day then wanted to know where the family lived, and
Charles Jr. replied that he thought it was called Norfolk House. But then
the cat-and-mouse game resumed, with Day asking why Charles Jr. declined
to answer to some dates about where he worked in rubber factories. Charles
Jr. then declined to say why he declined to say.

The personal questions were not purely vindictive. Charles Goodyear's
personal life, his poverty and his always-changing number of dependents
had been a critical part of the legal arguments. Asked how many siblings he
had, Charles Jr. said he had two brothers, two sisters, one half-sister and one
adopted sister. Day asked for their ages and Charles Jr. declined to answer.
Then Day asked, "what countrywoman did" his father "marry for a second
wife?" Charles Jr. declined to answer. What about the children born by the
second wife? Day wanted to know. Again, no reply. Day asked Charles Jr.
about the money owed to William Ballard, and Charles Jr. said Ballard gave
the old promissory notes to his Uncle Henry to bring to his father in Washington, D.C., but that when Charles Jr. asked his father, Goodyear said he
never got them.

Congress turned down the Goodyears but the legal battles continued.
One of them involved Edwin M. Chaffee, one of the founders of the Roxbury

Company and the designer of the Monster. After the Roxbury Company folded and Goodyear had filed his patent, Chaffee and his partners started the Providence Rubber Company but not as Goodyear licensees. With Chaffee's long experience as a rubber maker, he believed his techniques were not Goodyear's property and the Providence Company won the first round of the battle, in federal district court in Providence. The Goodyear side appealed and won a review by the Supreme Court. The Providence Company had, like Day, tried to invalidate Patent No. 3633. Four years after the patent's expiration, the U.S. Supreme Court ruled in favor of the Goodyear team, upholding a damage award of $310,757.72. "In every instance the patent was sustained" during previous challenges, wrote Justice Swayne. "We have examined the question by the light of the evidence found in the record and have no difficulty in coming to the same conclusion."

Patent No. 3633, which passed into history on June 15, 1865, had proven sturdier than its author, and not just because it outlived him. As years passed, the patent's mystique gathered new weight as the symbol of a great struggle by a great man. In coming decades it would attain the status of an industrial myth and burn the name Goodyear even deeper into the public mind.

EPILOGUE

"Grandfather's life was faithful, just and righteous"

Few of those connected with the strange saga of Charles Goodyear were left by the turn of the century. William DeForest, Goodyear's staunch friend who had married his widowed sister, Harriet, retired with her to an elegant and hospitable home in New Haven. Their nest egg was enlarged by the $30,000 recovered from the Goodyear estate. DeForest outlasted his wayward friend by nineteen years and died in 1879, at eighty-three; Harriet followed him five years later.

Nathaniel Hayward, Goodyear's partner, employee, dupe, antagonist and successful licensee, died one month after the Goodyear patent expired, in July 1865. Hayward was many things Goodyear could have been, including a reliable and successful industrial manufacturer. With a partner he had set up a rubber shoe business in Colchester, Connecticut, in the mid-1840s, and while Goodyear and other licensees still were scuffling to make ends meet, Hayward figured out a way to make rubber shoes that shined like leather. He and his partner kept the method secret for two years, giving them a running start on the other licensees, and they sold their shoes in England under license to Thomas Hancock. In 1847, Hayward sold a large portion of his equity in the venture at a nice profit, continuing as an owner and president while engaging in other businesses.

Thomas Hancock, who outlived all his partners, died three months before the Goodyear patent expired, in March 1865. He went to his grave as the undisputed giant of the English rubber industry. His claim as the first and true English inventor of vulcanization remained very much in doubt, however, with many in England eventually acknowledging Goodyear as the source whose sample guided Hancock's vulcanization effort.

Horace Day could have retired in comfort many times during his fitful manufacturing career and he could have taken some satisfaction that the

Goodyear patent finally had died in 1865 (even though the Supreme Court upheld its basic validity in *Goodyear vs. The Providence Rubber Co.* in 1867). But the restless Day worked himself more deeply into the world of spiritualism. He had provided space for a periodical, the *Christian Spiritualist,* in a lower Manhattan building he rented that served as a sort of headquarters for mediums. The *New York Tribune* said Day was "rather fond of producing and reading articles on finance and other subjects, which he claimed had been written at the dictation of spirits from the unseen world." He claimed to have made contact with the spirit of Daniel Webster, and had a rubber medallion struck with Webster's image on it.

As early as 1856, Day circulated pamphlets and had newspaper articles published about the development of an industrial park on land along New York's Niagara River, whose turbulent flow, some believed, would power machinery. The estimated force of the water at the time was said to be 170,000 horsepower, or an amount believed by some to be equal to the energy produced by all the coal mined in the world for a year. Day believed that businesses could be induced to move to this unusual location. Others had started the excavation of a 100-foot-wide, 10-foot-deep canal that began a half-mile above the falls and terminated one-quarter of a mile below it. After Day took over as the sole owner of the Niagara Falls Water-Power company, he finished one mile of the canal project and bought an island for a harbor, spending $700,000 in all.

But Day had worked himself into a corner. The huge development costs forced him to set rental rates way beyond what manufacturers and mill operators believed they could afford. When a New York firm offered $20,000 a year for a section of the land, he stubbornly rejected it as too low. The project foundered and his only tenant was a flour mill operator. Day took out mortgages until his total debt and unpaid taxes came to $60,000. The lenders eventually foreclosed and sold the property at auction for $130,000.

Undaunted by his wasted fortune, Day conceived another idea that involved harnessing the mighty Niagara. With the water driving giant fans, Day believed he could propel a current of air strong enough to power machinery all the way to Buffalo. When he finally died in the summer of 1878 in Manchester, New Hampshire, Day had been at work devising a machine for grinding bark, from which the acids needed to tan leather were squeezed.

Charles Goodyear Jr. and his brother William (youngest son of Charles and Clarissa) admitted that their father's estate eventually netted $200,000, supporting Fanny Goodyear and her young child and stepchildren.

Within a few years of Goodyear's death, the family and some Congregationalist ministers in Connecticut advanced an airbrushed version of the inventor's life. Instead of the destitute merchant yearning for release from his debts, Goodyear was said to be indifferent to wealth. "It is this wholesale scorn and indifference for social distinction, show, luxury, contempt for money except as a means to one single end, that makes him unique," wrote William. His father "created and despised wealth at the same time" and was "a Puritan Monte Cristo."

In trying to repair the image of his father that had persisted in the minds of some who had known him as a techno-hobo in a tattered rubber jacket, William dispensed altogether with the fiction of his father's poverty. Goodyear's youngest son asserted that his father was "a rich man after 1844, rich for those days, and rich enough, if the expenditure of thousands, up to some fifty thousand for some single given enterprise (like the Paris exhibit of 1855) can be considered indicating riches." By devising new applications and preparing them for manufacture, then selling them for a bonus and royalty, Goodyear alternately created and liquidated several fortunes, "successively and inevitably" spending them, in William's words.

This picture was far preferable to that of Charles Goodyear as a financial incompetent who ever since he was thirty found it psychologically convenient to ride the wild fluctuations of his cash flow. William preferred to see in his late father the stoic whose few indulgences included a brougham and driver and a physician and not much else. He was more comfortable with the idea of his father as a gentleman-technologist, a conservative southern political sympathizer in a maroon waistcoat.

The son who knew Charles Goodyear far better, Charles Jr., said much less on the same subject, but he too never uttered a critical word about his father in public. Charles Jr.'s sale of the Goodyear name in the year the patent expired was one of his last recorded activities as executor, most of which were devoted to cleaning up the legal mess his father left behind. The son admitted his father had confused matters to the extent that he believed he owned his late brother Nelson's hard rubber patent, but this was hardly surprising given the complexity of their affairs. As his father's closest family business associate, Charles Jr. admitted his father kept no records of any kind even when this would have been prudent. But that was a grudging admission of culpability.

In so many ways Charles Jr. was his father's son. Living in Stamford, Connecticut, at the time the estate was settled, he took up the life of an inventor and probably used capital generated by his father's patents to seed his own fortune.

Schooled from boyhood in the rubber and rubber footwear business, Charles Jr. was approached by James Hanan, a member of a Brooklyn shoe manufacturing family, who was working with August Destouy on a machine that stitched light soles. Hanan wanted Charles Jr. to develop some new machinery, and Charles Jr. ended up buying or buying an interest in Destouy's innovation. He set up the Goodyear Welt Shoe Machinery Company, bought another patented shoe machine and hired its inventor. He also brought in a team of machine builders and paid them to solve the three-dimensional riddle of designing machines to sew together a comfortable shoe.

Since the Middle Ages, most shoes were crafted inside out. Young Goodyear's new system of machine sewing brought together an outer sole, an inner sole and the upper part of the shoe without having to turn them. Few of the existing shoe manufacturers believed these machine-made shoes had much of a future.

Although the basics of an effective machine were known by 1874, Charles Jr.'s hope of profiting from his plan wasn't realized until the 1880s, when his team devised a way to sew shoes together by a completely machine-made method. In what came to be called the Goodyear Welt method, the edges of the upper are stitched to a rib in the insole, and also to a welt, a narrow strip of leather. The machine next sews the outer sole to the welt. This method of joining the upper to the soles leaves no stitches on the inside to irritate the feet. The Goodyear Welt became famous for producing sturdy, comfortable, premium shoes and boots, and is used to this day.

The Goodyear Welt Shoe Machinery Company eventually yielded enough profit to allow Charles Jr. to buy homes in New York and North Carolina, and an estate in Florida. He died in 1896, leaving his wife, Henrietta, three sons and four daughters.

Charles Jr.'s younger brother, William, shared his father's capacity for long-range vision. After graduating from Yale as a history major in 1867, he was studying Roman law in Germany when he became ill and traveled to Italy to convalesce. There he became interested in classical architecture and art. During visits to Syria, Italy and Greece, William detected bothersome irregularities in what everyone had assumed was the rectilinear geometric perfection of much classical architecture and the great buildings of the world. In Pisa, with foot rule and plumb line, he surveyed numerous bends, leans and curves in apparently straight surfaces in the cathedrals. Architects made mistakes, people assumed, but William showed that many of these presumed mistakes were deliberate esthetic refinements. In 1874, he published his idea: in a nutshell, that until the Renaissance, mathematical regularity in the great buildings was the exception. The idea immediately catapulted him to center stage in the world of artistic scholarship.

Two decades would pass before he could verify his theories through organized tests in the field. During this time William distinguished himself as a writer and scholar in art and ethnology, and curator at the Metropolitan Museum and at the Brooklyn Museum. He also organized the Children's Museum of the Brooklyn Institute, which still exists. In 1895, with financial support finally in hand, he began a painstaking survey of the great buildings of Europe that proved his theory correct.

William and his wife and children lived in a small brownstone on Park Avenue in Manhattan, and his fame as an Egyptologist, author and lecturer landed him on the cover of Sunday newspaper supplements. His daughter, Rosalie, says she first became aware of her father's stature when she was eleven; he traveled so often he was not much of a factor in her life until then. "It was an overwhelming discovery, making my childish ego dwindle, yet when my teacher at school asked me what my father did for a living it gave me a wonderful opportunity to reply: 'He lectures, writes books and goes to Egypt to sleep with the mummies. Mother says he walks around the Nile digging up old queens and climbing pyramids to look at Fair Ho.'" When a Sunday supplement ran a photo of William standing before the pyramids, Rosalie assumed that the caption—"One of the seven wonders of the world"—referred to her father, not the monuments.

On one of the trips William made to Europe and the Middle East, his young nephew Nelson, Charles Jr.'s son, came along to assist in making observations and taking photographs. Nelson was so moved by his studies of the Michelangelo design for St. Peter's basilica, the Pantheon at Rome and the mosques at Ispahan and Cairo that he formulated his own theories of where architecture and cathedral design in particular had gone wrong. The problem began, he believed, with Sir Christopher Wren's St. Paul's in London, where curtain-wall and curtain-roof construction rang in an era of falseness. Nelson maintained that structure should be openly expressed.

"Goodyear carried the idea of constructional truth to a point of believing that a vault covering a church, which certainly looks like its roof from the inside, should be its roof in fact," wrote *Architectural Record* magazine. Eventually, Nelson turned his attention to chemistry and designed numerous uses for acetylene, including torches or buoys used to illuminate the Panama Canal. He died suddenly of pneumonia in 1917.

In Naugatuck, the Goodyear-licensed enterprises prospered even without the protection of a patent. Propelled by strong sales throughout the Civil War, the rising rubber industry gradually grew to overshadow the buttons and Yankee notions that Amasa Goodyear had relocated to the Fulling Mill Brook to manufacture. Men and women turned away from decorative buttons on their waistcoats and dresses, and small shops powered by water just couldn't compete with bigger operations.

A worker was particularly fortunate to have a job in rubber. The rubber makers paid unskilled laborers $1.50 a day in 1880, 25 cents to 50 cents higher than other kinds of factories. Among the rules binding workers at Naugatuck's rubber glove factory, for instance, were that employees "attend strictly to their work and give a good example of correct deportment to others" and "attend some place of Public Worship on the Sabbath." Scarcely a word of complaint issued from these workers at a time when unrest was roiling other segments of labor. A lockout in 1880 was settled with the employer announcing that in the future a particular type of work that was the subject of dispute would be given only to women and "any man wishing his old job back should go home and put on petticoats." Many workers stayed twenty and thirty years.

Drawn by Naugatuck's skilled rubber workforce, six more rubber companies opened up in town. Two of them were absorbed by the original powerful Goodyear companies, which threw in with the members of the Shoe Associates in a merger in 1892 that created the United States Rubber Company. The glove company joined it in 1894.

Ironically, one thing the United States Rubber Company and the West Coast Goodyear Rubber Company never made nor sold was tires. But in 1898, a farmer's son with a penchant for risk named Frank Sieberling bought a lot with a couple of old factory buildings in Akron, Ohio, for $13,500 and decided to go into the rubber business. Other rubber makers, such as Benjamin Franklin Goodrich, already had operations in town. Sieberling named his enterprise the Goodyear Tire & Rubber Company "to honor Charles Goodyear," who "died penniless" in 1860. This homage became the company's rationale for glossing over the fact that Sieberling had appropriated the name to give his products and business an added cachet.

Had they checked carefully, the men who founded the Goodyear Tire & Rubber Company in Akron in 1898 would have discovered that a Goodyear Rubber Company already existed, having been established in San Francisco in 1865. Its founders had legally purchased the right to the Goodyear name from the estate of Charles Goodyear when the company opened for business on the opposite side of the country, far from the other Goodyear-name licensees in Connecticut, New Jersey and New York. The Goodyear Rubber Company had developed numerous branch offices and subsidiaries. A company catalogue from 1901 (when Goodyear Tire & Rubber was still in its infancy) proclaimed the Goodyear Rubber Company "the largest manufacturers and dealers in rubber goods in the world."

Along with machinery belting and packing, the Goodyear Rubber Company sold hose, cuspidors, spittoons, furniture fenders, currycombs and Mackintosh *(sic)* cloth hats, pants and raingear. All of it was emblazoned with the company's gold seal, further proof of its authenticity. The company was proud of its name but also conscious that it was far from the only firm using it. "We are the original and only Goodyear Rubber Company," said the company's letterhead. "No connection with other firms using the name 'Goodyear.'" And, like the Midwest's fledgling Goodyear Tire & Rubber, the West Coast company had no direct connection with the inventor himself.

The use of the name established a pattern of contempt for the intellectual property rights of patent monopolies that was in keeping with Charles Goodyear's long travail and came to characterize Sieberling's new company in its early struggle to survive.

To be sure, the bicycle- and carriage-tire businesses were locked up by patent-license monopolies. According to a Goodyear corporate autobiography, Sieberling didn't know carriage tires had been covered by a patent until he read a newspaper article on Christmas Day, 1898. The article told him that one of the carriage-tire patents, the Grant patent, had been voided by a court decision. Despite the adverse court ruling, the owner of the Grant patent, a company called Kelly-Springfield, notified Sieberling that he had to become its licensee anyway to continue making carriage tires. When he applied, Kelly-Springfield denied him a license. An angry Sieberling ordered his workers to keep making carriage tires in the method outlined in the patent. When Kelly-Springfield filed suit and won a desist order against Goodyear Tire & Rubber, Sieberling had to borrow to post a $250,000 bond until the matter was settled.

After obtaining the bond, Sieberling called in his head of carriage-tire sales and sent him out to win business from the three largest carriage makers in the country. Their plan was to gain customers by selling at the lowest possible price.

What use were patents anyway, the Goodyear Company wrote, but as protective shields for odious monopolies that strangled legitimate enterprise? Kelly-Springfield's hold on carriage tires was especially firm because it controlled the tire-mounting machinery. Tire makers produced long, serpent-like lengths of rubber that had to be sent to Kelly-Springfield plants to be mounted, but Kelly-Springfield had stopped mounting Goodyear's tires. So Sieberling devised his own method of mounting tires and began to "break through the patent blockade," in the words of a later corporate history, with new products. The effort "made Goodyear." The company had to put all its carriage-tire profits in escrow pending the outcome of its lawsuit with Kelly-Springfield, but despite its troubles Goodyear had $500,000 in sales and $35,000 in earnings in its first full year.

About this time trouble broke out in the bicycle-tire business, where Goodyear worked under a license. The owners of the Tillinghast patent withdrew Goodyear's license, but Goodyear decided to sell its tires anyway and made as many as four thousand every day. Tillinghast sued but Goodyear kept right on selling the tires until it had outlasted Tillinghast, which withdrew its lawsuit.

The new company hired a twenty-five-year-old named P. W. Litchfield, who would go on to become the chairman of Goodyear Tire & Rubber. Litchfield concentrated on the smaller but promising market for automobile tires, a field in which Goodyear was limited to 2 percent under a license from the Clincher Association. The Clincher method involved stretching the tire over the rim, making it difficult to change after the frequent flats and blowouts. Litchfield believed a radical new approach to auto tires had to be found, and he searched for a tire with a bead strong enough to be locked on the rim, instead of stretched on, so that it would be easy to change tires. He turned to an inventor named Nip Scott, from Cadiz, Ohio, who proposed using braided wire that could be cured into the tire bead. That would allow the tire to lock tightly on the rim yet remain flexible on the road. By changing the design of the tire rim and the way the tires locked onto it, Goodyear simplified the cumbersome process of changing tires and decreased chances for punctures while making the change. The new rim design produced a 10 percent increase in the tire volume, which increased capacity, and along with redesigns that strengthened the tire itself (among them, braided piano wire in the tire bead), resulted in far fewer blowouts. The company now had a clear advantage in car tires, even after a disappointing loss to Dunlop and Michelin in a European race (the Goodyear tires were a little too strong and lacked some flexibility, which was soon designed into newer versions).

The Grant patent litigation at last was approaching a final court decision, and the Goodyear company's future—all of its earnings from carriage tires—was at risk. Goodyear won, and all the escrowed money came pouring back into the treasury. Goodyear was on its way. Auto-tire production at the company grew from thirty-five thousand in 1908 to seven million in 1920, and sales from $2 million to almost $200 million. Goodyear, the company with the borrowed name that had broken patents to finance its growth, had crossed another threshold.

With the explosive growth of pneumatic car tires, the name Goodyear, which first won fame as a patent marked on boots, capes, pen casings and balls, gained an intangible value far beyond the multiple of its earnings. Inevitably, the Goodyear Rubber Company and the Goodyear Tire & Rubber Company clashed over the right to use the name. The confrontation climaxed in 1927.

Although it was by far the bigger company, Goodyear Tire & Rubber settled rather than fight to the end. The two companies drew up a pact under which Goodyear Tire & Rubber agreed to refrain from using the gold seal trademark and to pay the West Coast Goodyear Rubber Company $10,000. Both companies acknowledged the other's right to use the Goodyear name and the Goodyear Rubber Company agreed not to use the name on any items that related to tires and inner tubes. In this way, Goodyear Tire & Rubber, which had helped itself to the Goodyear name and violated established tire patents in its struggle to survive and grow, seemed to be clear of any challenge to the use of the name. It would never have exclusive control, though, and it would always be sensitive about other potential legal claims on the name.

As the Goodyear name was beginning its meteoric afterlife in the hands of men who had never known the eccentric inventor, the blessing and burden of being a biological Goodyear fell unevenly on Charles' grandchildren. In December 1929, a physician in Mount Vernon, New York, Andrew F. Currier, wrote to P. W. Litchfield, who by then was the top executive of Goodyear Tire & Rubber, about his concern for Charles Goodyear III, one of Charles Jr.'s sons, who lived outside Boston in Auburndale. Caretaker of his invalid wife and cousin, Clara, Charles III had been the executor of his father's estate but was now destitute, living in a house provided free by relatives and, in an echo of the past, fearful of "the poorhouse." Charles III and Clara knew nothing of Currier's letter on their behalf and tried to scratch out an existence selling Clara's decorative calendars. The Goodyear Company "in particular" benefited from Charles Goodyear's discovery, the doctor noted. Would Litchfield be willing to provide "a resting place" for the couple's remaining years? ("It cannot certainly be for a very long time.") The company eventually agreed to provide a $100-a-month pension, and Clara Goodyear, too proud for pure charity, insisted on sending decorative calendars in exchange.

A different sort of struggle engaged William Goodyear's daughter, Rosalie. She watched her surroundings being stripped away when her father divorced her mother and the family's possessions and Park Avenue house were sold. Rosalie and her mother went to live with her grandmother in another part of New York in the Bronx. Her mother became depressed and ill, and Rosalie was shipped first to live with unloving old Aunt Clara and later with her first cousin, Agnes. The loss of her mother's care and the experience of being passed from one family member to another, like a refugee, were hard on Rosalie. She was a dreamy, romantic soul who hoped to be a dancer or an actress. When she turned eighteen, William Henry Goodyear cut off any financial support for her, according to the terms of her parents' divorce. At an age when she believed she would have been "due for my Uncle Charles' legacy," she was told to support herself.

Rosalie explained her predicament by blaming relatives for cheating her out of the family fortune she was certain existed. Even her cousin Charles III, who was wasting away in poverty near Boston, "was evidently swindling us all by various speculations. Had he been wise he would have retained his father's holding and we all might have been counted in the millionaire class."

Perceptions that she shared the "Goodyear wealth" followed her like a ghost.

"Are you related to the Goodyears in the Goodyear Tire & Rubber Company?" she was often asked.

"No," she would answer, blushing. "There are no Goodyears in the company, but my grandfather invented rubber. The company appropriated grandfather's name for their advertising purposes I believe."

"What an outrage. Why don't you sue the company?"

"On $8-a-week wages?"

Rosalie dedicated much of her life to pacifism and defense of persecuted dissidents. She wrote and published poetry, married a writer named Raphael Doktor and championed the cause of the obscure American impressionist painter Arthur Goodwin. As the Great Depression settled over America, in June 1931 Rosalie wrote to P. W. Litchfield, offering to sell Goodyear Tire & Rubber two rubber cufflinks "worn by grandfather while at the court of Napoleon 3rd." She said that she hadn't worked for eight months although she was registered with numerous employment agencies. A Goodyear official who evaluated the correspondence wrote to Litchfield that "this is a tough one," noting that Rosalie was probably ignorant of the money being sent to her cousins in Boston and "we probably don't want to mention this or she would feel that she would be entitled to something."

In 1939 the Goodyear Company organized a combination fortieth anniversary and vulcanization discovery centennial celebration in Akron, and the organizers reached out to the more respectable descendants of the inventor. One of Rosalie's sisters, Mrs. Nelson Goodyear, represented the Goodyear family at a ceremony attended by hundreds of Akron business leaders and politicians, with Governor John W. Bricker of Ohio heading a delegation. Radio broadcasts carried speeches by industrial leaders from around the country. A statue of Charles Goodyear, holding a wad of rubber in his hand, was unveiled at the center of a park in downtown Akron.

Rosalie smarted at being left out of the Akron celebration and another held in Woburn, where a plaque commemorating the discovery of vulcanization was dedicated. In a letter sent to the company and others, she swaddled her invective in some lofty pronouncements about justice for inventors and protection of family names, but her underlying purpose was to vent rage over fortunes long lost by her forebears: "Grandfather's life was faithful, just and righteous, but our family has had no evidence of concrete tribute being paid to us either for Goodyear's name or process, which has been used for some 60 years." Apparently unaware of the limited nature of patent protection, Rosalie asked rhetorically if any of the eight living grandchildren "ever received a penny for the use of his invention and remarkable name? We are sorry to say 'no.'" Then she touched on a matter on which the company still might have been vulnerable. "Why are rubber companies permitted to use grandfather's name" and his life for advertising? she asked. And then a question that must have made the company's attorneys wince: "Have they title to it except by appropriation?"

A Goodyear official wrote that the letter had been sent to various periodicals, probably with a view toward "shaking them [Goodyear Tire & Rubber] down for a dime." No reply was sent and at least two Goodyear grandchildren who could not attend the Akron celebration wrote the company that Rosalie's views didn't represent their feelings.

As the centennial of the discovery approached, proud residents of Woburn, Massachusetts, planned their own ceremony. Finding a place to dedicate a plaque commemorating the famous accidental discovery led town officials into something like a wild goose chase. As they dug into the details of the winter of 1839 they never considered that they might be chasing a phantom. The chairman of the Woburn Committee for the Charles Goodyear Centennial and the town librarian mounted valiant efforts to overcome strong local traditions that said—despite Goodyear's own words to the contrary— the discovery had been made in a store. A historic sites committee had previously placed a marker at a house at 280 Montvale Avenue where Goodyear had lived. The current resident, Carl Carter, who was fifty-six, told the librarian in a "prompt and positive" way that he was quite sure the discovery had been made in a room on the ground floor of the house. But an earlier Woburn historic sites committee, in 1892, believed the discovery had been made at Bowen Backman's store in the center of town, two miles from the house. As the 1939 anniversary approached, Goodyear biographer P. W. Barker admitted to Woburn residents seeking his advice that he had no idea where the discovery took place, even after both he and the town officials parsed the testimony of the 1852 Trenton trial for clues. The local historian tried hard to "get a straight story," but nothing definitive was confirmed. It wasn't until another fifty years had passed that another local historian, Tom Smith, made a reasonable case that the discovery had occurred in the still-existing attached dwellings that had been used as a workers' residence by the Woburn Agricultural and Manufacturing Association.

At the ceremony in Woburn, Agnes Goodyear Gould, one of Charles Jr.'s daughters, said that her grandfather Charles Goodyear thought always of "home and children as he centered all his thoughts on how to make rubber. Charles Goodyear loved the beautiful things in life and saw to it that his children were well-educated.... While he suffered many disappointments, he had great faith in his own destiny."

On an afternoon in March 1938, a ninety-one-year-old woman looked through her window in North Haven, near New Haven, in the direction of the highway traffic passing outside. According to a reporter, she was "thinking of the days when all the revolving rubber tires were just potentialities." The woman was reflecting on the work of her long-dead cousin, Charles Goodyear. Ellen M. Goodyear was the last living Goodyear to have enjoyed the company of the inventor. She was the granddaughter of Simeon Goodyear, Amasa Sr.'s brother and Charles' uncle. Like so many others in the family, Ellen had married a cousin.

She recalled as a teenager sitting down to breakfast with Charles Goodyear in New Haven. He wore a morning coat lined with yellow satin. Ellen talked of Goodyear's achievements and of his rubber jewelry, including four bracelets he gave to her, two plain bangles edged in gold and others made of jointed segments and decorated with locket-shaped rubber hearts. "I still wear them with short-sleeved dresses," she said.

Ellen remembered her cousin as a generous man, kindly and affectionate in his disposition. She emphasized his preoccupation with preventing drowning through rubber life preservers. But the automobile—and the tires on the turnpike spinning outside Ellen's window—had more to do with the rise of rubber than life preservers ever would. In 1870, U.S. rubber consumption was four thousand tons. In the later years of Ellen's life, so much rubber was used in tires that five thousand tons scraped off onto the surface of U.S. roadways during a single Sunday of driving.

The American enchantment with automobile travel translated into an insatiable demand for rubber tires. By 1941, the United States consumed two-thirds of the world's annual global rubber output, half a million tons per year, ten times as much as the Japanese.

As World War II broke out, scarce supplies of rubber made it the second-most critical strategic commodity, after oil. America's crude rubber supply was concentrated in Malaysia and the Dutch East Indies, including Java and Sumatra. Singapore protected those locations, and after the surprise attack on Pearl Harbor, Singapore was directly in the path of a Japanese army. This meant that discovery of synthetic rubber became a critical element in sustaining the U.S. war effort.

The pathway for this innovation had begun at the giant I. G. Farben chemical conglomerate in the late 1920s. A team of organic chemists at the German company had homed in on the secrets of polymer structure until they had refined their techniques to the point where they could synthesize a new polymer every day of the week. (A polymer, as defined by German chemist Hermann Staudinger, is composed of molecular chains of practically limitless length and molecular weight, held together by conventional covalent bonds.) It fell to an American disciple of Staudinger, Wallace Carothers, to press forward with basic research at Dupont in the late 1920s and provide irrefutable confirmation. Working with colleague Arnold Collins, Carothers directed research into the polymer divinylacetylene (DVA). While isolating it from impurities, Collins recovered a liquid that spontaneously polymerized into a new, unknown compound. Collins described it as a "white, somewhat rubber-like mass." Later it became known as Neoprene. Efforts were soon under way to synthesize polymers of even higher molecular weights.

The Japanese march on Singapore exposed America's vulnerability to overseas rubber supplies. The "arsenal of democracy" was in danger of screeching to a halt as the dwindling supply of rubber deprived it of tires. Tire sales to ordinary civilians were banned and scrap rubber drives were promoted.

"Rubber caused more serious headaches in the defense and war-production agencies than any other single material . . . ," recalled Donald Nelson, chairman of the War Production Board. "We knew we would have to fight a highly motorized and mechanized war or a losing war. We knew we could not mount a highly motorized, mechanized war [without] rubber."

The only comfort was that the Nazis faced a similar shortage of this strategically critical material. But the Germans had by now developed a synthetic rubber, Buna, which Adolf Hitler's government scheduled for gradually increasing use up to the critical year 1939. On the eve of the Polish invasion, Hitler crowed to a hypnotized crowd at a Nuremberg rally, "We have definitely solved the rubber problem!"

The Nazis attempted to meet their demand for synthetic Buna rubber with slave-constructed plants, but fell far short of their goals. In the United States, a crash program to construct fifty new synthetic rubber plants surpassed its production goals by the target date of mid-1944. In five years, from 1939 to 1944, the production of synthetic rubber rose from 1,750 to 800,000 tons. The synthetic rubber producers achieved in five years what the natural rubber industry took seventy years to accomplish.

On May 6, 1937, nearly a hundred years after Charles Goodyear began his pursuit of the miraculous secrets of rubber, the German airship *Hindenburg*

suddenly ignited and crumpled to the ground, while a radio reporter's anguished description turned the news into a national trauma. The disaster in New Jersey brought an end to the airship as a promising mode of passenger transportation.

If the explosion of the *Hindenburg* was a major setback for the German government, which had made the silver dirigible into a propaganda flagship, it was also a disappointment for P. W. Litchfield, chief executive of the Goodyear Tire & Rubber Company. He had nourished dreams that the company he led could play as central a role in air transportation as it had in automotive travel. That wistful, long-range vision endured despite the disasters that had overtaken Goodyear Tire & Rubber's own hydrogen airships. The first disaster, in 1911, involved what was called an "airship envelope" that plunged into the ocean off New Jersey, killing the pilot and several crewmen when an engine spark had set off a fire. The second one occurred in 1919 and involved the Wingfoot Express, a small blimp carrying passengers on a public relations excursion over Chicago. A fire broke out inside the ship's hydrogen-filled bag, and the Wingfoot Express plummeted through the skylight of a bank, killing ten people inside. The pilot and passengers tried to parachute to safety but flaming debris burned their parachutes, and they died, too.

But risk-taking was part of the corporate character and part of the heritage of the Goodyear name. Litchfield had built the company with innovative, high-quality products and a knack for clever marketing. When the company decided to make auto racing a priority again in the late 1950s, after abandoning the sport more than thirty years before, Goodyear Tire & Rubber relatively quickly dislodged its smaller cross-town rival Firestone from the dominant position. The only area in which the company had flopped was aviation, but soon that too would change.

Goodyear made airships, or blimps, for military purposes until 1962, when the Navy stopped flying them. Then the company faced a question about whether to dispose of its mothballed fleet. An enterprising public relations director, Robert Lane, believed the blimps still had use as "billboards in the sky." Their ubiquity at national sporting events in the next decades provided a currency for the name Goodyear unimaginable in the nineteenth century. The successful linking of the Goodyear airships to athletics came at a time when Goodyear was the largest U.S. tire and rubber company and a rubber conglomerate that made shoe parts and plastics and chemicals and automobile components. Goodyear, in the words of one manager, "seemed to have no competition" and "so much money we didn't know what to do with it."

The uneasy relationship between Goodyear Tire & Rubber and some of Charles Goodyear's descendants continued into the 1960s. The company bought out for $15,000 paintings and artifacts that two Goodyear descendants had lent to the Smithsonian for many years. Among the paintings were portraits on rubber panels of Charles and Clarissa Goodyear and Daniel Webster. Then, in 1983, a cantankerous sixty-one-year-old Goodyear cousin from the western United States contacted Goodyear Tire & Rubber. He offered to sell the company a hard rubber figure of the Venus de Milo, a squirrel rifle once owned by Charles Goodyear and a painting of young Charles with his two youngest children on his lap. The cousin said he wanted to sell the items because he was on limited income and getting on in years. "I understand you do have a museum," he wrote on August 14, 1983, in a letter to Chairman Robert E. Mercer.

Goodyear executives first tried to handle the situation with diplomacy. In his first reply, Mercer said he regretted that the descendant hadn't had a sales career with Goodyear Tire & Rubber. With Goodyear's products and the Goodyear name the cousin would have been "invincible with customers," he wrote.

The friendliness sparked a new enthusiasm and the cousin wrote back requesting a job. The added income would help, he said. So the company dispatched its public relations manager to meet with the Goodyear cousin at his home. The company wasn't interested in the rifle but found someone on its staff who was willing to buy it. For the hard rubber figure and paintings, the company offered $1,000, plus shipping costs. The cousin expressed amazement at the low offer, did some checking and claimed to have found that the paintings and figure had considerable value, about $15,000. He wouldn't take no for an answer and wrote directly to Mercer again, adding that he was "looking forward to a ride in the blimp" that the company had offered him. Finally in 1985, after extended negotiations, a deal was struck for $1,000, although the cousin said $1,200 would be better as he needed new glasses and dentures.

The Goodyear Tire & Rubber Company willingly served as the custodian of the Charles Goodyear legend and always took care to treat it respectfully.

The full story of his revolutionary discovery "remains open to debate," the company wrote in the introduction to its corporate autobiography, *The Legend of Goodyear*, published in 1997 just prior to the centennial of the company's founding. The book repeats the "most delightful version," in which Goodyear hurriedly heaves a concoction into the oven to hide the mess from his wife.

Although interest in rubber as a revolutionary technology had faded by the days of the Internet, the Goodyear company reserves for the inventor a corner of its World of Rubber exhibit at its headquarters in Akron. Schoolchildren and other visitors thus are indoctrinated in the legend. A Goodyear statue greets them at the center of a small rotunda. Beyond the entrance to the exhibit, painted models of rubber-making equipment, along with some models of raw and partly processed rubber, are on display. The company shows off the tires it made for the Apollo 14 moon flight.

At the back of the exhibit is an old, glass-topped display case containing Goodyear notebooks, medals and rubber figures. Presiding over the case are portraits of Clarissa and Charles Jr., and at the center, the bearded portrait of Charles Goodyear at thirty years of age, with Ellen and Cynthia on his lap. It is Charles Goodyear the hardware merchant, before the store failure and debt, before rubber and its tragedy and triumph, still full of innocence and love.

Opposite the portraits and the display case is a fake log cabin whose interior displays an aproned Charles Goodyear mannequin busy cooking his rubber, with a spaniel nearby for just the right touch of domesticity.

At the press of a button, a projector whirs to life and beams a face onto the mannequin, which begins to speak.

"Quiet, boy," Goodyear tells the yapping spaniel. "These are friends. How do you do? My name is Goodyear, Charles Goodyear, a familiar name to you I'm sure."

The mannequin speaks with a touch of the New England patrician in its accent. "But back in 1832, when I first began experimenting with rubber, the only people who knew my name were the people to whom I owed money. I was always in debt it seems, but to me money was not important. Rubber was. So I kept experimenting, kept trying different ways of treating rubber, to make it more usable. Other people had tried and given up. My rubber would never amount to anything, they said."

The mannequin then reviews the effects of heat and cold on rubber. "Still I kept on trying, even when they sent me to jail because of my debts,

I kept trying. You see, I was sure I could get rid of the stickiness by mixing some kind of powder with rubber. I was right too, I made a better rubber, but it wasn't good enough, I still lost money. Finally, in 1839, after seven years of trying and failing, it happened. One day, right here in the kitchen, I was mixing some sulfur powder with rubber, and I spilled some of the mixture on the stove. That did it. It was the heat that made the difference. Accident or not, I discovered it."

Then the mannequin claims credit for the term that the real-life Goodyear had to adopt from one of his rivals. "So I named it vulcanized rubber, and it was better than all the other attempts."

The mannequin continues: "During the next twenty years of my life, as I refined the process and developed new uses, the news of my discovery spread. Many countries honored me with medals." Then it finishes on a familiar note of irony. "Fame and fortune, you say? I got the fame all right, but not the fortune. In 1860, twenty years after my original discovery I still owed more than two hundred thousand dollars. Poor? Yes. But millions of people today live richer lives because what I was doing was more important to me than money."

The projector switches off and the figure falls silent.

AUTHOR'S NOTE

With the record of his life scattered and the value of his accomplishment obscured by better-known inventions, Goodyear presented an elusive subject. The difficulties explain why there has been no adult biography of him for more than sixty years. Previous books all contain reasonably reliable accounts of primary sources for which I could not locate originals. The first book, *Trials of an Inventor: Life and Discoveries of Chas. Goodyear,* by the Reverend Bradford K. Peirce, is a short work that portrays Goodyear as an exemplar of Christian stoicism. It is based partly on memorial sermons and an 1865 article by the Reverend James Parton in the *North American Review.* Peirce enjoyed the cooperation of Fanny Wardell Goodyear and Ellen Goodyear, who shared memories and letters. The book is available in major research libraries and from used and rare book stores.

The first full-length biographies of Goodyear didn't appear until 1939 and 1940, in conjunction with the hundredth anniversary of the discovery of vulcanization. In one of the books, *India Rubber Man: The Story of Charles Goodyear,* rubber historian Ralph F. Wolf expressed his disdain for Peirce's Sunday school approach and took a more skeptical point of view. Unfortunately, his skepticism lived only in opposition to the supertext of the vulnerable and lovably eccentric inventor besieged by unscrupulous rivals and colleagues. To his credit, Wolf collected important information through contact with Goodyear's grandchildren and by digging out correspondence buried deep in the legal record. His book is available at many libraries.

P. W. Barker, a Commerce Department economist, was another admiring biographer who admitted his trouble in writing "in a detached and disinterested manner." *Charles Goodyear: Connecticut Yankee and Rubber Pioneer,* has fewer sources and details than *India Rubber Man.* But it does provide some new information about Goodyear's exact whereabouts at different times (no easy task), about his licensees and about the rubber industry and its origins. Barker theorizes, and I agree, that Goodyear suffered from lead poisoning. His book is available mainly from used and rare book stores.

Charles Goodyear and Thomas Hancock provided their own accounts of their lives and work and the American Chemical Society republished them in a single volume in observance of the 1939 centennial of the discovery of vulcanization. The book encompasses Goodyear's two-volume *Gum-Elastic and Its Varieties* and Hancock's Personal Narrative. In his book, Goodyear presents himself as the long-suffering hero of rubber technology. When myth-making took precedence over fact, as with Goodyear's touching of the rubber patch to the stove and Hancock's alleged rediscovery of vulcanization, the rivals engage less in active fabrication than strategic vagueness.

To strip away myths, I tried to use information about Goodyear that had not been published before. His chief American rival, Horace Day, turned out to be a useful if biased source. In his Captain Ahab–like pursuit of Goodyear, Day collected and published letters, affidavits, testimony and legal transcripts that previous Goodyear biographers either considered tainted or ignored. Forty-three letters from Charles Goodyear to William Ely were submitted by Horace Day to the patent commissioner in 1858 and about half of them were put into the public record again in a petition submitted in 1864 and published in *Goodyear Before Congress* (New York, 1864), a compendium of important legal documents related to Goodyear that is available at research libraries. The rest of the letters are available at the National Archives, College Park, Maryland.

The copies appear to have been carefully made and show no evidence of fabrication. They reflect Goodyear's quirky humor and give him a "voice" he never had before. Without Day we would know a good deal less about Goodyear.

We would also know less about the mysterious William F. Ely. In his 1864 petition, Day printed information that partly corroborates his claim that Ely, not Goodyear, had the providential accident involving rubber being touched against a hot stove. The fact that the testimony came from Day's allies and future partners casts some doubt on its reliability. But Ely's complete absence from Goodyear's book, Goodyear's vague description of the accident and his practice of taking ownership of technical breakthroughs achieved by others all point to a cover-up. Although Goodyear took pains to say the breakthrough was the result of informed observation, not luck alone, he allowed the impression to remain that he, not Ely, accidentally touched the rubber to the stove because he understood the story's emotional value in supporting his claim as the miracle material's inventor. That's how I see it.

The other area that remained somewhat mysterious was Goodyear's family life. I found no letters to or from his wife or parents, so to fill in the blanks in a few instances (indicated in the notes), I substituted estimates of what people did and thought based on their characters as described by others and the customs of the time.

I am indebted to many people for help in completing this book.

Editor Peter Collier has given me many gifts. In addition to recognizing the relevance of Goodyear's fanaticism to today's technology pioneers, Peter saw Goodyear's story as a chance to illuminate a frequently overlooked, pre–Civil War segment of U.S. industrial history. His guidance in shaping the manuscript and deft editorial hand helped turn the mass of material that I initially submitted into a coherent whole. His wit and goodwill helped sustain me through the rewrites.

It would have been much harder to write this book without the help of Woburn historian Tom Smith, who is also the assistant to the mayor. Smith's short book, *Goodyear: The India Rubber Man in Woburn* (Woburn, Mass.: Black Flag Press, 1986), provides a streetwise description of key events in the Goodyear saga and is available at the Woburn library. Smith personally guided me to the remaining Woburn sites where Goodyear and Nathaniel Hayward pioneered rubber technology. He also lent me research material.

Fred Haymond of the Goodyear Tire & Rubber Company in Akron has been generous in providing access to historical material and images of Goodyear and his family. John Miller of the University of Akron Archives also gave me access to historical records of Goodyear Tire & Rubber, a company that other than its name had no formal tie to the Goodyear family.

My chemically knowledgeable cousin Sari-Beth Samuels gave me scientific sources and my linguistically skilled friend Brett Kline helped with the French. Four authors—Stephen Fenichell, David Cohen, Donna Rubenstone, and David Kohn—gave me advice and ideas. Two passionate scholars, Frank Braconi and Jay Rosen, have backed my efforts for many years. Amy Dunkin of *BusinessWeek* has given me numerous journalistic opportunities, as has Frank Flaherty at the *New York Times*. And special thanks go to another longtime supporter and talented editor, Pat Lyons. He was my editor for a *New York Times* story about patent warfare that stimulated my interest in Charles Goodyear.

Two people who have expressed confidence in my future work are my new agent, Jim Levine, and my attorney, Susan Golenbock, who has been a source of inspiration for many years.

My present and former colleagues at *Engineering News-Record* have nurtured me in many ways and collaborated with me in countless journalistic adventures. They include Howard Stussman, Jan Tuchman, John Kosowatz and the peerless William Krizan.

My family has guided my development, too. They include my brothers-in-law and sister-in-law and nieces and nephews but particularly my sister, Rachel Tolkoff. My mother-in-law, Florence Silver, has been especially supportive, as was my late father-in-law, Solomon Silver. My father, Leonard Korman, has given me his love of culture and my mother, Allegra Korman, has given me enough encouragement to last through several lifetimes of writing.

My son, David, and daughter, Natalie, have allowed me to talk through Goodyear's story—and recreate Goodyear's obsession—many times in the last two years. To them I'm forever grateful.

And to my wife, Elaine Silver, I want to express immeasurable gratitude for brilliant guidance and resourceful assistance in all phases of this project. My joy in completing it is great especially because it is part of a life we live together.

—September 2001, Orangetown, New York

SOURCE NOTES

Abbreviations

Names
CG—The first Charles Goodyear
CG Jr.—Charles Goodyear Jr.
WE—William F. Ely
HD—Horace Day
TH—Thomas Hancock
WD—William DeForest

Archives and Libraries
NACP—National Archives, College Park
NANY—National Archives, New York City
UAA—University of Akron Archives, Akron
GTRC—Goodyear Tire & Rubber Company, Akron
CSL—Connecticut State Library, Hartford

Documents
GBC—*Goodyear Before Congress*

*Prologue**

My descriptions of the U.S. exhibitors draw heavily on David Freeman Hawke's entertaining *Nuts and Bolts of the Past: A History of American Technology, 1776–1860* (New York, 1988). There is no record of the Goodyears walking around the Crystal Palace, but the scene I have described is based on details of the hall exactly as the Goodyears must have seen them.

1   "much-moved": Queen Victoria's diary, as quoted in John Allwood, *The Great Exhibitions* (London, 1977), p. 20.

---

*Numbers at left indicate page numbers

1   The King of Prussia's concerns: Letter from Prince Albert to the King of Prussia, quoted in Allwood, p. 18.

2   Attendance figures: John J. Tallis, *History and Description of the Crystal Palace, and the Exhibition of the World's Industry in 1851* (London, 1852), p. 92.

2   Crime statistics: Ibid., p. 92.

2   "more like the fabled palace of Vathek": *The Great Exhibition: A Facsimile of the Illustrated Catalogue of London's 1851 Crystal Palace Exposition* (Avenel, New Jersey, 1995), p. xxiii.

2   "That majestic palace of iron and glass!": J. F. Shaw, *The World's Great Assembly (1851)* (London, 1851), pp. 12–13, as reproduced on The Victorian Web (landow.stg.brown.educ/victorian/1851/crystal1.html).

2   the English industrial exhibits: L. T. C. Rolt, *Victorian Engineering* (London, 1970), p. 157.

3   Number of U.S. patent applications: John Leander Bishop, *A History of American Manufactures from 1608 to 1860* (Philadelphia, 1868), p. 482.

3   Evidence of this future greatness: Merritt Roe Smith, in Carroll W. Purcell Jr. (editor), *Technology in America: A History of Individuals and Ideas* (Cambridge, 1990), pp. 45–60. Contains a discussion of Eli Whitney and the American system of manufacturing and states that in the years after the Great Exhibition governments sent teams to investigate U.S. industry and, although little noticed, "these events signaled America's coming of age as an industrial power."

3   the metal coffin equipped with a pump: Robert Stephenson, *The Great Exhibition: Its Palace, and Its Principal Contents* (London, 1851), p. 162.

3   Hobbs flabbergasts and Colt shows off: David Freeman Hawke, *Nuts and Bolts of the Past: A History of American Technology, 1776–1860* (New York, 1988), pp. 251–255.

4   "providentially linked": Gordon S. Wood, *The Rising Glory of America* (New York, 1971), pp. 237 and 18. Wood writes on p. 237 that Americans came to identify technological progress with the promise of their history: "Political and physical science seemed to be providentially linked, and technology became as important as virtue in achieving America's realization of itself as a moral republic."

5   The new age of synthetics: Richard C. Progelhof and James L. Throne, *Polymer Engineering Principles: Properties, Processes, Tests for Design* (Cincinnati, 1993), pp. 3–4.

5   set a new standard for quality: Charles T. Rodgers, *American Superiority at the World's Fair* (Philadelphia, 1852).

5   "do away with the risk of corns": *London Illustrated News* as quoted in Rodgers, p. 87.

Chapter One

I based much of the history of Naugatuck on Constance McL. Green's excellent *History of Naugatuck, Connecticut* (New Haven, 1948). For more information about early Naugatuck see Fred Engelhardt's *Fulling Mill Brook: A Study in Industrial Evolution, 1707–1937* (Brattleboro, Vermont, 1937) and William Ward's *The Early Schools of Naugatuck* (Naugatuck, 1906). Also, some key dates in Goodyear family history are noted in Helen S. Ullmann's *Naugatuck, Connecticut, Congregational Church Records, 1781–1901* (Bowie, Md., 1987). All are available at Naugatuck's Howard Whittemore Memorial Library.

8   Many New Englanders simply left the land: James Truslow Adams, *New England in the Republic*, vol. 3 (Boston, 1927), p. 191.

8   Return of ship-carried trade: Ibid., p. 303.

8   Experiences of one Olney Burr: Connecticut State Library. General Assembly, 1806, Microfilm II:123ab.

10   The town of Salem: Constance McL. Green, *History of Naugatuck, Connecticut* (New Haven, 1948), p. 88.

11   "So completely has the article formerly used been superseded": *Gum-Elastic and Its Varieties, with a Detailed Account of Its Applications and Uses and of the Discovery of Vulcanization* (originally published in New Haven for the author, republished by the American Chemical Society, 1939, in a single volume with Thomas Hancock's *Personal Narrative*), p. 95. Goodyear also claimed his family's spring steel hay and manure forks were "universally considered in the United States one of the greatest improvements ever made in farming implements."

11   Amasa bought an interest in a button-making patent: Certified copy of transfers of patent rights (Washington, D.C., 1816). The volume is in the Rare Book and Manuscript Library of Yale University and its contents are listed online in the National Union Catalogue Manuscript Collections.

12   Little sympathy for violent attacks: Rev. Bradford K. Peirce, *Trials of an Inventor: Life and Discoveries of Charles Goodyear* (New York, 1866), p. 20.

13   Parker's complaint: Rev. Daniel Parker, *Proscription Delineated, or a Development of Facts Appertaining to the Arbitrary and Oppressive Proceedings of the North Association of Litchfield County in Relation to the Author* (Hudson, 1819). All the material and quotes from Parker come from this book-length description of the conflict. A reply to Parker's book was published by one of his rivals in Sharon, Connecticut, the same year.

13   He asked to be dismissed: According to Sharon, Connecticut, historian Jeanne Magedalany, Daniel Parker was ordained May 26, 1802, and dismissed April 18, 1812.

14   "greatly disappointed by being obliged to abandon the idea": *Gum-Elastic*, p. 94.

17   "I have quit smoking": Peirce, p. 31.

18   "They were unsuccessful at the time": *Gum-Elastic*, p. 98. Goodyear promises to describe the stella rota and self-winding clock in another section of the book, but never does. They apparently contained rubber components, most probably a strap or band.

18   "too great an extension of paper credit": Arthur M. Schlesinger Jr., *The Age of Jackson* (Boston, 1953), pp. 74–87. The discussion of the Second National Bank of the United States is based largely on these pages.

19   The Goodyears turned to Charles' old tutor: Letter from an attorney for WD (third page and signature missing) to CG, April 15, 1840. Yale University Library Archives, New Haven. The letter contains DeForest's account of the meeting with CG.

21   Problems and reform of the patent system: Paul Israel, *From Machine Shop to Industrial Laboratory: Telegraphy and the Changing Context of American Invention, 1830–1920* (Baltimore, 1992), p. 12. The discussion of the patent system is drawn from the first chapter of this book.

21   "shake off the epithets of inventor": *Gum-Elastic,* p. 98.

23   "If any one is desirous": Ibid., p. 96.

Chapter Two

25   Brazilian Indians were among the most skilled: *Gum-Elastic,* pp. 44–45.

25   A looping trail: Glenn D. Babcock, *History of the United States Rubber Company: A Case Study in Corporation Management* (Bloomington, Indiana, 1966), p. 3. This study synthesizes a great deal of information about rubber in describing the company that evolved from Goodyear's original licensees.

25   "incredibly into the air": Ralph F. Wolf, *India Rubber Man* (Caldwell, Idaho, 1939), p. 41. See also Howard and Ralph F. Wolf, *Rubber: A Story of Glory and Greed* (New York, 1936), pp. 304–305

25   "remarkable national ineptitude": T. K. Derry and Trevor I. Williams, *A Short History of Technology: From the Earliest Times to A.D. 1900* (New York, 1993), p. 524.

26   "It soon became evident": Thomas Hancock, *Personal Narrative of the Origins and Progress of the Caoutchouc or India-Rubber Manufacture in England* (London, 1857; republished by the American Chemical Society, 1939), p. 10.

27   Statistics on imports: *Personal Narrative,* pp. 158–165

27   "the impetuosity and daring": *Gum-Elastic,* p. 54.

28   "had baffled all the efforts": Ibid., p. 101.

28   "It was at this time": Peirce, p. 66.

29   "Do not make up your mind": Ibid., p. 29.

30   "The job was so completely done": *Gum-Elastic,* p. 103.

30   Steele regularly endorsed Goodyear's notes: Testimony of Ralph B. Steele, 1858 patent extension hearing, National Archives College Park.

32   "It was at his suggestion": Affidavit of William Ballard, quoted in Argument of Horace Day, submitted to Congress' Committee on Patents, April 22, 1864, and reproduced in *Goodyear Before Congress* (New York, 1864). Copies also exist with the records of the 1858 patent extension hearing, NACP.

33   "did not know how to rub": Peirce, p. 73.

33   "William, here is something": Ibid., p. 74.

36   "Mr. Goodyear frequently told me": Affidavit of William Ballard, Argument of Horace Day, GBC.

36   "at the mercy of the pawnbroker": *Gum-Elastic*, p. 109.

37   "Give me ten dollars, brother": Peirce, p. 87.

37   "Hilltops blazed": quoted in Wolf, p. 54.

37   The Monster saved: P. W. Barker, *Charles Goodyear: Connecticut Yankee and Rubber Pioneer* (Boston, 1940), p. 20.

38   "The invention of this machine resuscitated": *Gum-Elastic*, p. 111.

Chapter Three

39   "good hearts": CG journals, Goodyear Tire & Rubber Company. Also, *Gum-Elastic*, p. 8 and ch. 7.

39   "Whether I shall come off": CG to WE, February 28, 1837. Argument of Horace Day, GBC.

40   Agreements between CG and WE: *Goodyear vs. Day*, National Archives New York.

41   "I conclude India Rubber destroys the memory": CG to WE, September 21, 1837, GBC.

42   "I have come here to avail myself": Ibid.

42   "Keep cool": Ibid.

43   "I am not sure but a stock" and "We only want a stock of goods": CG to WE, September 26, 1837, GBC.

44   "Don't tell Mrs. G. I write you first": CG to WE, September 21, 1837, GBC.

44   "Your favor with $140, is at hand": CG to WE, October 14, 1837 (second letter of that date), GBC.

44f   "I do not know that you yet understand": CG to WE, October 14, 1837 (first letter of that date), GBC.

45   "When may I expect them": Ibid.

46   The move to Norfolk House: *Gum-Elastic*, p. 114; Peirce, p. 92.

46   Bombazine dress: Peirce, p. 93.

46   Little Willie's shoe: Ibid., p. 106.

46   Family regained its ballast: This is supported by the fact that Amasa Jr. marries Melinda Hine. Grace Goodyear Kirkman, *Genealogy of the Goodyear Family* (San Francisco, 1899). One serious error in this book is that Nelson Goodyear, one of Charles' brothers, is reported to have died in 1841; he lived until 1852.

47   "I know of nothing in the way now to be genteel": CG to WE, October 21, 1837, GBC.

48   "was poor, but meant to be rich": affidavit of L. S. Maring, GBC.

48   "They came into the office": affidavit of William Armstrong, GBC.

49   "The prejudices of the public gave way": *Gum-Elastic*, p. 114.

49   "Another New Thing under the Sun": *Boston Courier*, June 19, 1838, reprinted in Wolf, p. 84.

49   Sales of acid-gas licenses: Barker, p. 32.

50   "Goodyear would get tired of building castles in the air after a while": Wolf, p. 78.

50   "By considerable excitement": deposition of Nathaniel Hayward, August 30, 1851, for the Great India Rubber Trial, quoted in Wolf, p. 87.

51   "could depend on being well rewarded": Nathaniel Hayward, *Some Account of Nathaniel Hayward's Experiments with India Rubber, Which Resulted in Discovering the Invaluable Compound of That Article with Sulphur* (Norwich, Conn., 1865), p. 4.

52   "occasionally lay down their common sense": author's interview, September 2000.

53   "Mr. Goodyear, of the fancy rubber establishment": Letter from Jacob Richardson to NH, March 27, 1838, Argument of Horace Day, GBC, p. 29.

54   "At one of his visits to my factory": Hayward, *Some Account*, p. 7.

Chapter Four

My description of vulcanization draws heavily on Richard C. Progelhof and James L. Throne, *Polymer Engineering Principles: Properties, Processes, Tests for Design* (Cincinnati, 1993), pp. 2–4. I also used a website with a section called *The Story of Rubber* (www.psrc.usm.edu/macrog/esp/rubber/bepisode/vulcan.htm), The Polymer Science Learning Center and the Chemical Heritage Foundation. For more advanced information on polymers and heavy chain molecules, please see Bruno Vollmert's *Polymer Chemistry* (New York, 1973), pp. 1–32. To understand how complicated vulcanization is, see also p. 329. For background on the historic advances in chemistry's understanding of vulcanization see W. A. Gibbons, "The Rubber Industry, 1839–1939," *Industrial and Engineering Chemistry*, October 1939, p. 1200.

57   Rose up in rebellion: James Parton, "Charles Goodyear," *North American Review*, July 1865, p. 80. "His friends, his brothers, and his wife now joined in dissuading him from further experiments." Although Parton doesn't make his source clear, he is the only contemporary writer to describe a family schism that I believe is finally culminated when the two Amasas make their ill-fated journey to Florida.

57   Continued to work as blacksmiths: Testimony of Nelson Goodyear, *Goodyear vs. Day*, January 26, 1852, NANY. Nelson states that Amasa Jr. was a blacksmith. He also says that Charles and Henry were in the mercantile business and that Charles had been a manufacturer of buttons and pitchforks.

57   "As had happened on former occasions": *Gum-Elastic*, p. 118.

58   "Ely appeared to be a good deal excited": Testimony of Samuel Armstrong, 1858

patent extension hearing, quoted in Argument of Horace Day, GBC. In 1848 Armstrong insulated telegraph wires for the Morse Telegraph Company using gutta percha.

58f   Kekulé's dream: The National Academy of Sciences, *Polymers and People* (Washington, D.C., 2001), a website that supplies context for Goodyear and Kekulé's achievement at http//www4.nas.edu/beyond/beyonddiscovery.nsf. For more discussion of creativity and Kekulé, see Robert Weisberg, *Creativity: Beyond the Myth of Genius* (W. H. Freeman, 1992).

59   Polymers, thermosets and spaghetti: Richard C. Progelhof and James L. Throne, *Polymer Engineering Principles: Properties, Processes, Tests for Design* (Cincinnati, 1993), pp. 2–4

61   "perfectly cured": *Gum-Elastic,* p. 119.

66   "my potatoes are not nearly enough": CG to WE, February 5, 1840, NACP.

67   "How do you think I manage to get on?": CG to WE, January 7, 1840, GBC.

67   "I suspect I am quite as able to pay": CG to WD, December 15, 1840, reprinted in Barker, p. 47.

67   "I sometimes think they intend": CG to WE, January 1, 1840, NACP.

68   "It is true, that I am on Staten Island": CG to WE, January 29, 1840, GBC.

69   "After the current sets that way": CG to WE, April 21, 1840, GBC.

70   "We think the God of Love smiles": Prison Discipline Society, *15th Report, 1840,* p. 477. The Prison Discipline Society advocated penal reform.

70   "Gentlemen: I have the pleasure to invite you": CG writing to Luke Baldwin and John Haskins, in all likelihood from debtor's prison, Boston, April 21, 1840. Quoted in numerous sources.

70   "nearly indestructible": Ibid.

71   "Close confinement": CG to WE, May 19, 1840, GBC.

71   William Henry calls out to his father and then dies: CG to WE, June 24, 1840, NACP. In the copy of the letter Goodyear writes, "I was sent for and have laid in the grave little Wm. Henry he died of the Fever on the Brain calling on me to help him." The rest of the description of Goodyear's return home, the bedside vigil and moments following the death of William Henry are based on my estimate and imagining of what occurred.

72   Goodyear summoned the children: Peirce, p. 128.

73   "You know me": CG to WE, March 8, 1840, GBC.

76   "Most of the goods": Henry B. Goodyear, testimony, *Goodyear vs. Day,* NANY.

78   "knew more about rubber in half an hour": *Some Account,* p. 11.

79   "I assure you that I place a high value": CG to WE, January 16, 1841, NACP.

79   Federal and state bankruptcy laws: Peter J. Coleman, *Debtors and Creditors in America: Insolvency, Imprisonment for Debt, and Bankruptcy, 1607–1900* (Washington, D.C., 1999). For a discussion of imprisonment for debt and the emergence of the speculative type who borrowed from tradesmen, storekeepers and craftsmen, all of whom relied on imprisonment as a method of debt collection, see. p. 267.

80   "odious": *Gum-Elastic,* p. 128.

80   Goodyear's debts: Copies of Goodyear's bankruptcy petition and lists of creditors are in the 1858 patent extension hearing file, NACP.

81   "Never had cause to regret": *Gum-Elastic,* p. 128.

Chapter Five

Most of the information in this chapter on Thomas Hancock is from his *Personal Narrative of the Origin and Progress of the Caoutchouc or India-Rubber Manufacture in England* (Boston, 1939). The information on Horace H. Day is drawn partly from Charles J. Taylor's *History of Great Barrington (Berkshire County)* (Great Barrington, 1882) and Bernard A. Drew's *Great Barrington: Great Town, Great History* (Great Barrrington, 1999). The latter book is available at the Mason Library in Great Barrington, where genealogist Sue Farnum generously assisted in research.

82   Attic at Stoke Newington: *Personal Narrative,* pp. 92–107.

84   "Suppose we find the secret": *The Queen vs. Hancock and Others,* Court of Queen's Bench, Guildhall, July 7–9, 1855. Copies of the proceedings are in the 1858 patent extension hearing file, NACP.

84   "I will leave that to your own honor": *The Queen vs. Hancock,* Moulton's testimony, pp. 215–221, NACP.

84   "I thought that": *Personal Narrative,* p. 93.

86   "for a time [he] relinquished the use of sulphur": *Personal Narrative,* p. 99.

86   "struck out the first spark of the 'change'": *Personal Narrative,* p. 100.

87   "No analogy or reasoning": Ibid., p. 104.

88   Horace Day's early life: *Berkshire Courier,* August 28, 1878.

89   Buy the secrets from Horace Cutler: Much of this information is quoted in *Speech of the Hon. Daniel Webster in the Great India Rubber Suit* (New York, 1852), pp. 34–39. Webster reproduces letters and quotes directly from Cutler's deposition and includes all the appropriate citations.

90   "It's so hot Cutler, let me toast awhile": Ibid., p. 35.

91   "He said he was well-acquainted": Ibid., p. 39.

91ff Patent No. 3633: Specification forming part of Letters Patent No. 3,633, June 15, 1844, Improvement in India-Rubber Fabrics, Charles Goodyear, of New York, N.Y., Records of the United States Patent Office, National Archives, College Park, Md. A copy of the patent is in the UAA.

93   Rise in number of patents: Bishop, *A History of American Manufactures,* p. 482.

Chapter Six

94   The Lewises: Green, *History of Naugatuck,* p. 23.

95   Ellen's clothing and tools: I base these on what was typical of the time.

96   Profitability remained elusive: Testimony of Henry B. Goodyear, 1852, NANY.

97f Description of rubber-making difficulties: Affidavit of Benjamin F. Cooke, clerk at the Naugatuck Rubber Company, NACP.

99   Recommendation from Presbyterian church: Note dates February 14, 1846, manuscript no. 125, New Haven Colony Historical Society.

99   "callers pouring in upon him": Peirce, p. 149.

100 Charles' preoccupation with business: In Peirce, Goodyear's secretary A. S. Hunt says his employer's "business was his religion." Also, Goodyear traveled incessantly and, based on his letters from Woburn, I believe he frequently left the family for days and weeks at a time. Clarissa's response to his travel and business obsession is my conjecture.

100 "He could not look upon want or suffering": Peirce, p. 145.

101 Gift to the lame man: Ibid., p. 146.

101 Robert and Cynthia's deaths: Goodyear several times in later years referred to the burden of raising his brother's children, but the exact number of them isn't clear.

102 *"beau idéal":* Emmett Saunders' description of DeForest and Goodyear appears in Green, *History of Naugatuck,* p. 148.

103 "in a frolicksome mood": *Gum-Elastic,* p. 141.

105 Agreements between CG and William Judson: NANY.

107 "You must keep still": Wolf, p. 157.

108 "come up to scratch": Argument of N. Richardson on behalf of Horace Day before the commissioner of patents, in *The Great Day and Goodyear India Rubber Extension Case* (New York: Narine & Co., Printers, February 4 and 5, 1853), p. 77. The hearing concerned the extension of Goodyear's patent of Hayward's sulfur innovation. Richardson is quoting an account of the discussion provided by Halsey Bower, a former Day employee hired away by Judson and Goodyear.

108 "Goodyear had the impudence": Ibid., p. 158.

108 "Do you think you are a scoundrel": Ibid., p. 158.

108 "From what I saw": Ibid., p. 158.

109 "It would give me a great deal of pleasure": CG to WE, March 24, 1845, GBC.

109 "My care and perplexities": CG to WE, October 28, 1845, GBC.

110 "I think if you was in New York": HD to CG, November 2, 1846, *Speech of Hon. Daniel Webster in the Great India Rubber Suit* (New York, 1852), p. 46.

110 "Make a visit at my house": HD to CG, November 15, 1846. Ibid., p. 46.

Chapter Seven

113   "A volume might be written": *Gum-Elastic*, pp. 317–323.

115   "It was a cloth impervious to water": Parton, *North American Review.*

115   "What! Must men continue to be drowned": *Gum-Elastic*, p. 233.

116   Gold rush creates market for rubber products; promoted products to the California-bound: P. W. Barker, *Charles Goodyear, Connecticut Yankee and Rubber Pioneer* (Privately printed by Godfrey L. Cabot Inc., Boston, Mass., 1940), p. 55.

116   Text of rubber boat ad in *New York Commercial Advertiser*: Barker, p. 74.

117   Shirred goods market falls to $20,000: *Hunt's Merchants' Magazine and Commercial Review*, vol. 34, no. 3 (January-June 1856), p. 321; also p. 319.

117   "The whole litigation": *Hunt's Merchants' Magazine*, p. 323.

118   Hancock's licensees and their products: *Personal Narrative*, p. 114.

118   Bullet-shield experiment: Ibid., p. 118.

119   Steam heating is always uniform in every part of a boiler: *Personal Narrative*, p. 111.

119   "take some energetic steps": Testimony of Charles Gilbert, Argument of Horace Day, GBC.

121   "The leading feature": Argument of Horace Day, GBC, p. 3.

123   "Latest discovery in rubber": Barker, p. 74.

Chapter Eight

Much of the information in this chapter is based on two sources: the often-quoted Trenton trial Argument of Daniel Webster and the frequently overlooked Francis Cutting's Argument against Daniel Webster, counsel for Charles Goodyear, in the Great India Rubber Case, held at Trenton, N.J., 1852. Webster quotes much testimony and evidence and includes an appendix with documents. A copy is in the collection of the New York Public Library.

125   Day's dam dispute: Charles J. Taylor, *History of Great Barrington (Berkshire County)* (Great Barrington, 1882). Also see *Berkshire Courier*, August 28, 1878.

126ff The Testimony of Skinner, Pratt, Collins and Beers: cited in Francis Cutting, Argument Against Daniel Webster. Also cited in Argument of Daniel Webster.

129   "His contorted lips": *Dictionary of American Biography*, p. 88.

130   Webster's illness and debts: Robert V. Remini, *Daniel Webster: The Man and His Time* (New York, 1997). See p. 710 for Webster's illnesses in August 1851; see pp. 754 and 755 on his illnesses in the summer of 1852 and Webster's condition of being "constitutionally opposed to or incapable of meeting his financial obligations."

130   "That is an enormous fee": Peter Harvey, *Reminiscences and Anecdotes of Daniel Webster* (Boston, 1921), pp. 103–104. Also Remini, pp. 730–731.

139   "tuned high by champagne": L. Otto P. Meyer, "Some Memories of Goodyear," *The India Rubber World,* August 1, 1901, p. 328. Copy in UAA.

140   The gift horse Trenton: Barker, p. 72.

140   "Without doing any injustice to Mr. Webster": Greeley's comment appears in Barker, p. 72.

140   "Mr. Choate and Mr. Cutting made out such an incontestable case": *The True American,* quoted in Wolf, p. 201.

141   Still owed tens of thousands of dollars: CG to WD, quoted in Peirce, p. 159. Before departing for Europe, Goodyear borrowed another $1,000 from a friend in Boston and accepted $3,500 from another acquaintance, probably Luke Baldwin, in exchange for a note.

142   English patents: Some of Goodyear's patent drafts are in his journals, GTRC.

143   Extract from Percival: *Gum-Elastic,* p. 75.

143f   Verdict for Goodyear: Decision in the Great India Rubber Case of *Charles Goodyear vs. Horace H. Day,* delivered September 28, 1852 (New York, 1852).

144   Grier never read the deposition testimony: Argument of Horace Day, part 1, p. 34, GBC. Day quotes from proceedings before Judge Grier on motions and court orders subsequent to the decision in the Great India Rubber Case, when a lawyer says he will refer to some parts of the record in *Goodyear vs. Day.* Quoted is Grier's reply.

144   Clarissa wept: Her tears and the celebration are as I imagine them.

144   "He made quite a display": affidavit of Burrows Hyde, argument of Horace Day, GBC.

145   Charles Dickens: The author's address appears in Goodyear's journals, GTRC. I surmise Goodyear's attendance at a Dickens reading and interest in talking to him.

145   Goodyear attempted to set down in words: Goodyear wrote that he wanted to preserve "much information that would otherwise be lost." Goodyear journals, GTRC.

147f   Clarissa's illness and death: only brief mention exists in the record so I created a fairly typical nineteenth-century death for Clarissa and used conjecture to recreate Charles and the children's immediate response to her passing.

148   "I shall never forget the impression": Peirce, p. 174. Virtually all that is known about Fanny Wardell Goodyear comes from Peirce and the quotes and descriptions he got from her. Some of my observations about their relationship and her family's impression of Charles are my conjecture.

149   "I ought to have been frank with Amelia": Letter from CG to either Henry Bateman Goodyear or William DeForest, July 23, 1853. GTRC.

150   Trip to Folkestone: Peirce, p. 159.

151   "As relates to your case": Ibid., p. 161.

152   "cells of gloomy prisons": Ibid., p. 162.

153f   Illnesses in France and medical care: Fanny's journal entries, GTRC.

154   Relationship with Gilman begins to fray: Letter from CG to D. L. Gilman, October 13, 1854. CSL.

154   References to continuing illnesses. Letter from CG to D. L. Gilman, January 17, 1855. CSL.

154   Preliminary details of French show. Letter from CG to D. L. Gilman, February 6, 1855. CSL.

154   "stout heart": *Illustrated American Biography*, vol. 3, 1853–1855. Photocopy in UAA.

155   "a swelling-out": *American Phrenological Journal*, 1856, p. 125. Photocopy in UAA.

156   Choate was unavailable: Day never held it against him. Day wrote the *New York Tribune* a letter that appeared in the February 11, 1875 issue: "I have employed many lawyers, but I have had but one lawyer who was wholly unselfish, and that was Rufus Choate. His memory I have occasion to cherish with more satisfaction than that of any man I ever met." Quoted in Samuel Gilman Brown, *Life of Rufus Choate* (Boston, 1879), p. 430.

157   A witness for Hartshorn strolled near the house of juror William Blaisdell: GBC, Part 1. Argument of Horace H. Day, GBC, pp. 54–56. Affidavit submitted to Rhode Island District, in Providence, May 23, 1855, by William Blaisdell.

159ff   Trial testimony: All of the dialogue is from *The Queen vs. Hancock and Others*, 1858 patent-extension hearing file, NACP.

Chapter Nine

164   Shooting of Morey: Marie De Mare, *G. P. A. Healy, American Artist* (New York, 1954), p. 176.

165   Introduced by Webster: Ibid., p. 158.

165f   Goodyear's keen interest in manufacturing costs: CG to D. L. Gilman, July 20, 1855, CSL.

167   Riding with Napoleon III: Wolf, p. 251.

167   "advanced the arts": Letter from CG to Benjamin Silliman, September 1855, Cadwalader Collection, Pennsylvania Historical Society, Philadelphia.

168   "If I am not in": De Mare, *G. P. A. Healy*, p. 177.

168   "Under what warrant": Peirce, p. 183.

169   "I have been through nearly every form": Ibid., p. 187.

170   "poor Job; not that I presume": Ibid., p. 193.

171   "I have not closed my eyes yet": Ibid., p. 196.

171   "How can I sleep": Ibid., p. 197.

173   "not received a dollar": Testimony by Ralph Steele, May 17, 1858, patent extension hearing of 1858, NACP.

173   "as I was his best friend": Ballard testimony, patent extension hearing of 1858, NACP.

173   "out of health": Goodyear's application to patent commissioner Joseph Holt, patent extension hearing of 1858, NACP.

174   Statistics on the Shoe Association: Babcock, *History of United States Rubber.*

175   "tales of doleful suffering": Argument of Horace Day, GBC.

175f   Patent examiner's report: Argument of Horace Day, GBC, p. 47.

176   "almost a psalm of thanksgiving": Peirce, p. 201.

178   "This is the last!": Peirce, p. 216.

181f   Charles Goodyear Jr.'s lawsuit against Judson: *The Estate of Charles Goodyear vs. William Judson,* NANY.

182   Opposition to the patent extension in *Scientific American:* the magazine had followed the Goodyear patent controversies since the Trenton trial and printed articles against the extension on March 5 and 19, April 9, 16, and 23, and May 7, 1864.

183   Judson buys out Day: The irony was noted in "India-Rubber Stretched out at Last!" *Scientific American,* June 16, 1860.

185   Day cross-examines Charles Jr.: The fascinating confrontation between Day and CG Jr. is recorded in GBC, part 2, p. 26, testimony of CG Jr., March 12, 1864.

Epilogue

187   "elegant and hospitable home": Kirkman, *Genealogy of the Goodyear Family.*

187   Hayward's other businesses: Ellen Levin and Thomas Mahlstedt, Middlesex Fells Reservation Historic Land-Use Study: Cultural Resource Management Study Series No. 1, Metropolitan District Commission, Reservations & Historic Sites Division (Boston, 1990), p. 14.

188   "rather fond of producing and reading articles": *New York Tribune,* August 27, 1878, p. 8.

188   Sold the property at auction: *Berkshire Courier,* August 28, 1878.

189   "It is this wholesale scorn and indifference": William Henry Goodyear, *The Architectural Record,* May 1905, p. 433.

189   "a rich man after 1844": Ibid.

191   "It was an overwhelming discovery": Rosalie Goodyear, *Defiant Dreamers,* unpublished manuscript, Archives of American Art, Smithsonian Institution (Washington, D.C., 1964), p. 10.

192   "Goodyear carried the idea": John Mead Howells, "Nelson Goodyear, Architect and Inventor," *The Architectural Record,* September 1917, p. 259.

192   Rubber overshadows Yankee notions: Green, *History of Naugatuck, Connecticut,* p. 154.

193   "to honor Charles Goodyear": Jeffrey L. Rodengren, *The Legend of Goodyear* (Fort Lauderdale, 1997), p. viii. This book is a corporate biography prepared in cooperation with the company.

193   Goodyear Rubber Company: The History of Goodyear Rubber & Supply, website at www.goodyear-rubber.com/history.html. Goodyear Rubber & Supply was incorporated in Oregon on August 19, 1893. It was originally named Goodyear Rubber Company and operated as a branch of the Goodyear Rubber Company

of California, which opened in San Francisco in 1865 after acquiring the right to
the Goodyear name from the estate of Charles Goodyear.

193   Pattern of contempt for intellectual property rights and patent monopolies: Rodengren, *The Legend of Goodyear,* pp. 26–27. See also Hugh Allen, *The House of Goodyear*
(Akron, 1936), pp. 16–25.

194   "a $250,000 bond": Rodengren, *Legend of Goodyear,* p. 27.

194   "break through the patent blockade": Allen, *House of Goodyear,* p. 17.

196   fearful of "the poorhouse": Andrew Currier to P. W. Litchfield, December 29,
1929, UAA.

196   "was evidently swindling us": *Defiant Dreamers,* p. 10c.

197   "Grandfather's life was faithful, just and righteous": Rosalie Goodyear to Clifton
Slusser, March 10, 1939, UAA.

197   "ever received a penny": Ibid.

199   Ellen M. Goodyear: "When Fashion Decreed Rubber Jewelry: Relative of Inventor Recalls When Goodyear Startled World with Experiments Here and Opened
New Industry," *New Haven Register,* March 6, 1938.

200   "Rubber caused more serious headaches": Stephen Fenichell, *Plastic: The Making
of a Synthetic Century* (New York, 1996), p. 182.

203f   Goodyear Tire & Rubber Company Exhibit: Author's visit, February 2000.

INDEX

acid-gas process, 47, 55, 56, 67
  flaws of, 48, 53, 56, 67, 89
A. Goodyear & Sons, 15–19
  financial crisis, 18–20
  see also Goodyear, Amasa
Albert, Prince, 1–2
American Phrenological Journal, 155
Ames, Samuel, 122
Andrus, Lavius, 140
Anticell, Thomas, 175–76
Architectural Record, 192
Armstrong, Samuel, 42, 47, 48, 50, 58, 60,
  89, 156
autobiography (CG), 155–56

Bacon, D. F., 128
Baldwin, Luke, 63
Ballard, William, 32, 34–35, 36, 173, 181
  debt to, 81, 155, 183
bankruptcy, 79–81, 139, 175
Barker, James, 70
Barker, P. W., 183, 198
Bateman, Stephen (cousin), 180
Beers, H. M., 64
Beers, Isabel, 80
Beers, William, 66, 127
Berkshire Woolen Company, 125
Bird, Josiah, 132
Birley, Hugh, 84, 158, 163
Bishop, James, 110
Blaisdell, William, 157
Borden, Gail, 6, 7
Boston Belting Company, 150
Boston Courier, 49
Boston Post, 55

Bradshaw, Thomas, 34
Brady, James T., 133–34, 183
Bricker, John W., 197
Brockedon, William, 84, 118, 158
Brontë, Charlotte, vii, 2
Brower, Halsey, 107
Brown, David, 127
Brown, Jane, 80
Brown, William W., 127, 181
Burbank, Daniel, 64–65
Burr, Henry, 105, 107
Burr, Olney, 8–9
Byington, Jared, 10

Calhoun, John C., 18, 40
Campbell, Sir Robert, 159, 160, 162–63
Candee, Leverett, 180, 181
  cloth business, 19
  patent licenses, 78, 104–5, 106
  shoemaking, 116, 120
Carle, Silas, 31, 39, 80
Carothers, Wallace, 200
Carter, Carl, 198
Chaffee, Edwin M., 27, 37, 42, 47, 52, 67,
  181
chemistry, 52, 58–60, 87, 161, 199–200
Choate, Rufus, 129–30, 132–34, 136, 140,
  156, 216
Clark, Luther, 49
Clay, Henry, 40
Coburn, Benjamin, 78, 181
Collins, Ahira, 12
Collins, Arnold, 200
Collins, John, 127
Collins, Richard, 127–28, 135, 136, 138

More Praise for
The Natural Mother of the Child

Named a Most Anticipated Book of the Year
by *The Rumpus* and *The Millions*

"Parenthood is full of the questions we don't always know the answers to, and in Krys Malcolm Belc's *The Natural Mother of the
Child*, Belc's courage to ask his questions frankly and unflinch-
ingly is riveting. These beautiful moments of intimacy, many
written to loved ones, help us explore the history of a family, a
community, and the expectations of who we call Mom and who
we call Dad." —DUSTIN PARSONS, author of
Exploded View: Essays on Fatherhood, with Diagrams

THE NATURAL MOTHER OF THE CHILD

The Natural Mother
of the Child

A Memoir of Nonbinary Parenthood

KRYS MALCOLM BELC

COUNTERPOINT
Berkeley, California

The Natural Mother of the Child

Library of Congress Cataloging-in-Publication Data
Names: Malcolm Belc, Krys, author.
Title: The natural mother of the child / Krys Malcolm Belc.
Description: First hardcover edition. | Berkeley, California : Counterpoint,
    [2021]
Identifiers: LCCN 2020016501 | ISBN 9781640094383 (hardcover) | ISBN
    9781640094390 (ebook)
Subjects: LCSH: Motherhood. | Surrogate mothers. | Adoption—Law and
    legislation. | Parenthood. | Gender-nonconforming people. | Transgender
    parents.
Classification: LCC HQ759 .M328 2021 | DDC 306.874/3—dc23
LC record available at https://lccn.loc.gov/2020016501

Jacket design by Dana Li
Book design by Jordan Koluch

COUNTERPOINT
2560 Ninth Street, Suite 318
Berkeley, CA 94710
www.counterpointpress.com

Printed in the United States of America

10 9 8 7 6 5 4 3 2 1

To Samson Ryan Belc, for teaching me me

In order for something to be handed over a
hand must extend and a hand must receive.
We must both be here in this world in this
life in this place indicating the presence of.

—CLAUDIA RANKINE

CONTENTS

The Machine   7
First Seen in Print   53
Breasts: A History   143
How to Photograph Your Newborn   169
In the Court of Common Pleas   201
Wild Life   235

Acknowledgments   281
References   285

THE NATURAL MOTHER OF THE CHILD

When, in big groups, I am asked to pick out a fact no one would guess about me, I pick this one: My first athletic competition was in Irish dance. Yes, I say, I had the big blue dress in a protective sleeve in my closet, sets of pink foam rollers, gillies and hard shoes, and so many pairs of crinkled white socks. Sometimes I think I do this to break the tension of not knowing if people can tell, about me, what I am.

In Rockaway Beach we danced, everyone danced; we were all Irish and every girl I knew danced. We practiced at St. Francis de Sales on Beach 129th Street. At least half the girls were named Caitlin. Krystyn is not an Irish name. I remember the hard click of the tape player, tapping my hands against my gym shorts, looking around, waiting for all the other legs to start moving. I was always athletic but never good at any sport in particular. I liked Irish dancing, all the jumping and pounding, the tight black laces against my calves, the bang of hard shoes on the floor. My first sport. Our teacher had long black hair and freckles and played the reel from a black cassette player in the middle of a gymnasium. It was always the same tape, the same jig the same reel the hornpipe that came on just as my practice was ending and the bigger girls came in with their duffel bags and long skinny freckled legs. I did not know, then, that being freckled and redheaded was unusual. At home when I closed my eyes in my room I could still hear the music. I try to remember what it was like then, when I was four and five and six, if I was unhappy. I am supposed to remember being unhappy, but mostly what I remember is what it's like to stand there knowing the dance is about to start.

This is a story about something I don't entirely remember but I believe that it happened. In a family as big as my family, six kids, children have their signature stories and this is mine: I was five when I got up on the stage at my first feis. The reel started and I just stood there and I did not dance. I held on to my skirt as I had been taught. The floorboards rattled with music. It was raining lightly, but we were under a tent. Or maybe I just remember rain because this is supposed to be a bad memory. I remember the feel of cloth in my fists because, when I was that age, that was the only way I could keep my arms from moving. People say I am competitive. Too competitive, just like my father. Like my brothers. But in this story I did not compete. I look back through a lifetime of fighting but think of this moment most of all, this standing still. Everything slowed. My father is angry in so many of my memories but he was not angry that I did not dance. He came up on the stage to get me. Did he carry me or take me by my hand? If I had never seen a picture of him holding a baby I'm told is me I would not believe he ever carried me.

I know I used to dance because of the stories and the pictures and because I still know how, all these years later, although I've never shown anyone. I'd rather do almost anything. Why this story? The girl, standing on the stage, waiting for the dance to start, though it has already started, and everyone waiting for me to do what I'm supposed to.

The Machine

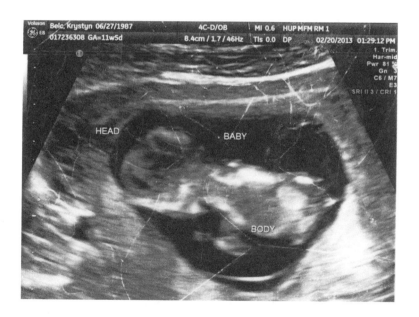

The women in the waiting room were not happy to see me. I sat waiting for a blood draw, Christmas Eve morning, five-month-old sitting in my lap. Every time Sean made a sound, a gurgle, a hiccup, just the rustling of restless baby legs, the women in the waiting room turned to watch him. Why was I here if I already had a baby? But he wasn't mine; I wanted to hold a sign that said: *My Partner Made This One.* In this waiting room for women who had no babies, I was an invader, androgynous, a trans parent in this space for women trying to conceive. I tried to sit as still as possible, to breathe quietly, to feel my insides, to decide if my uterus was empty or not. After the nurse took my blood and saw that there was enough hCG in it to make her say *The numbers look good* they said I had to come in for an ultrasound. They never said *You're pregnant.* They never mentioned *The pregnancy.* There was, of course, no present or future *baby.* They just said *The doctor would just like to make sure it's not ectopic.* I was just twelve days past ovulation. I told them no thanks, I'd wait a few weeks, and they said an ectopic pregnancy could kill me. I said I knew, but I refused, not wanting too many exams, too many interventions. I didn't put on gowns for just any occasion. Before I'd gotten pregnant, the fertility doctor demanded I get a pelvic exam, my first in over a decade. People like me don't get pelvic exams unless under threat of something. I didn't want to see those parts—women's parts—and know they were abnormal, or normal, or even there.

I weighed my desire not to be examined, not-yet-five-weeks, probably-pregnant, probably-for-good-this-time, against the small potential of pipes bursting, a flood of blood in my abdomen. Shock. Death. Ectopic: *out of place*. Wasn't this true, regardless? *I guess I'll tell your doctor*, the nurse said. I stood at the checkout counter waiting with Sean beside me, resting on the floor in his car seat. I rocked him with my foot while the nurse spoke with my doctor about how hard to push me to come in as soon as possible. Refusing standard testing was something that made me suspicious to them. They had protocols. Recklessness didn't risk just my life. Then, after some negotiation, I agreed to one follow-up appointment instead of two. The nurse back in the window, the clicking teeth, the paper shuffle, typing, an appointment in a week and a half to see tiny new life.

The first vaginal ultrasound took place at the fertility doctor's office. I was six weeks, five days pregnant. I had a thick lubed wand inside me. I held my breath, held Anna's hand, spread my legs. The doctor never looked at me; she only looked at her screen. Watching the screen I wondered at the shagginess, the furriness of my insides. I held my breath. She moved the wand in me, and then we saw it. A globule clinging to my uterine lining, its ragged racing heart. It wouldn't be real unless we heard something. Fetal heart rate increases from around 85 to approaching 170 beats per minute between five and ten weeks. We heard the flutters, saw the number: 124.5 beats per minute. A blurred dot that would, most likely, become a baby. *This looks normal, good, etcetera*, the doctor said, with the blandness of a server rattling off dinner specials.

The embryo first lives the life of a plant, secondly the life of an animal, and third the life of a particular species. Men have as well an intellective power, which derives not from matter but from the heaven. It is infused by the celestial forms, and from these celestial forms the end and perfection of all forms existing in the inferior realm derive. Now it is the custom among medical authorities to say that the first life is hidden and secret, the middle apparent and manifest, and the last indeed excellent and glorious.

Women are so full of venom in the time of their menstruation that they poison animals by their glance; they infect children in the cradle; they spot the cleanest mirror.

—ALBERTUS MAGNUS,
De secretis mulierum (Women's Secrets)
late 13th/early 14th century

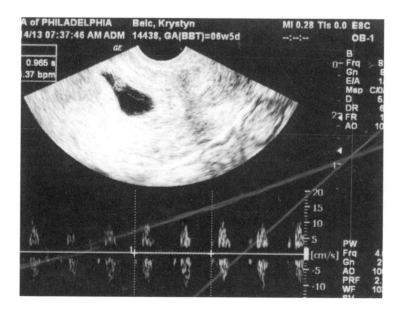

The cover art of Albertus Magnus's *De secretis mulierum* shows two adults, each with an ambiguous figure, ambiguous genitalia, a soft body and a hard face, holding the hands of a huge baby between them, a baby half their size, a toddler really, and yet with an adult's face, a terrifying face, and what an enormous baby. This book was an early treatise about how the reproductive system might work. The set of conjectures and speculations was meant as an instructional guide for monks, a textbook about women's bodies, but it became widely read throughout the medieval period, influencing many people's ideas about how we came to make new humans inside us. At my first prenatal appointment Sean lay in Anna's arms nursing while the midwife asked me a lengthy series of questions about my health history. I was eight weeks pregnant. We were at a birth center outside the city, in an examination room directly above the room where Sean had been born. It was January, icy and gray. We'd tried to make this appointment feel special by stopping at the Wawa across the street for snacks, but Sean had screamed the entire hour-long car ride, strapped into his car seat, and once in the store we tensely selected snacks at random.

I remembered the night he was born, how when Anna was asleep I'd come to the same Wawa late in the night to get her an Oreo milkshake and me what I consider the Wawa special: half black coffee, half thick, sweet hot cocoa from the machine. Sean was born on a muggy July night and yet the cocoa coffee was so right. After a full day of my stomach twisting as I watched Anna in pain, I welcomed the warm, sugary liquid once it was over. She lay in bed in the birth center with Sean while I walked their cord-blood sample across the street to a laboratory for testing. After I dropped off the sample I was a parent for the first time, alone in line at the Wawa. I walked across the wet birth center grass and into my new life.

Sean was named after my brother and yet had nothing to do with our blood. The new baby inside me was the size of a pea pod. Everything online compares fetal growth to the sizes of common fruits and vegetables. At my first birth center appointment the midwife took my blood pressure; she had firm, strong hands. She was the same midwife who delivered Sean. I remembered her sitting on the edge of the bathtub downstairs in the birthing room, looking calm as my wife cried out in pain on the bathroom floor. *I can see this much of the baby's head*, she'd told Anna at one point, making a tiny diamond shape with both hands. *I know how big a baby's head is*, Anna replied. I was generally healthy but the midwife slowed down, way down, at the mental health section of her questionnaire. She ticked boxes, took notes. I was anxious; had a history of eating disorders; struggled with gender dysphoria. *And how's this been for you?* she asked. *Okay so far,* I said, thinking of how a pea pod grows after not long to be a watermelon. At the expanding I was undergoing everywhere. Becoming more woman where a woman was never supposed to be. The midwife nodded, looked at me and Anna and back at me again. *You know, Anna could nurse your baby, too. If that's not for you.* She got it. She typed on an old computer. The birth center didn't have an ultrasound machine in the office; I'd have to go to a hospital if I wanted an ultrasound: *It can make you feel better but also can increase your anxiety,* she said. I said, *Yes, I'll make an appointment.* I still felt wholly untethered to the baby, had no idea how I could even be doing this, and where was my bag of snacks, anyway.

The baby was underwater. So small in such a vast space. I felt like I was, too, floating in and out of weekdays at the high school where I worked. I bookmarked a How Many Days Until website with the baby's due date plugged in: September 6. Every morning I checked it, aware that I was counting mostly how long I'd have to be pregnant, that my thoughts were focused on my body, not the baby's. E-mails mixed among those from my coworkers and students' parents: *Track your baby's development! Your baby is forming hands and feet! Click here to find out more!* On our first weekday off together after seeing the midwife Anna and I went to Buy Buy Baby, touched things we did not need. Onesies, baby hats. Sean was still an infant, and we had more than enough. She held shirts up against my belly, where there was still no sign I was pregnant. But I felt spreading hips, despite the baby's size—a cherry. Tender breasts, tingling at odd times throughout my workdays. Anna was nursing Sean, who woke up many times a night screaming for her, and the sleeplessness and nursing affected her sex drive, but I was almost desperate for sex, for proof that pregnancy hadn't taken me as far from androgyny as I imagined. Had I made a mistake that would change how she'd see me forever? Was I even the person I thought I was? *You look fine, you're sexy, I'm still into you*, she said, just before rolling over and falling asleep.

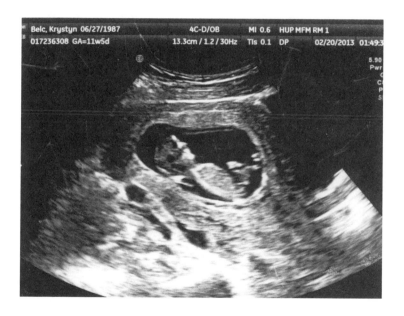

The second ultrasound was as far away from the floor Anna worked
on as we could get in the hospital. We walked the wide, glass hallways, pushing Sean in his red stroller. In my hospital gown and my
socks I looked in the mirror and thought that maybe this would

be it, the moment I'd feel happy to have a baby inside me. I left my work clothes—the size-up khakis and button-down, sneakers, a tie—in a locker outside the ultrasound room. Maybe after today I'd stop slowing down outside the Planned Parenthood by work. Stop walking away disgusted with myself. I'd gone out of my way to make this baby I so badly wanted out of me. Each morning I drank a rooibos tea and put my head down on my desk for a few minutes. My coworkers asked how I was feeling, and I had to say *Fine*. Anna bought me cases of lemon seltzer on Amazon to settle my stomach. *Who buys seltzer on Amazon?* I asked. I never said anything to her about my pregnancy. I pretended the big problem was being sick. It seemed pointless. The thing was done. After the ultrasound we celebrated with Shake Shack. Over crinkle fries and chocolate shakes she kept asking me how I was feeling. *Good*, I kept saying. *Happy*. I was pregnant and felt perfectly justified dipping every salty, greasy fry into my open milkshake. The next day, I sent a copy of my ultrasound picture to my mom, inside a card. *How do you think she'll feel?* my boss asked. *Surprised*, I said. *Because Sean's so young?* she asked. *I just don't think she thinks of me as the kind of person who carries a baby*, I said.

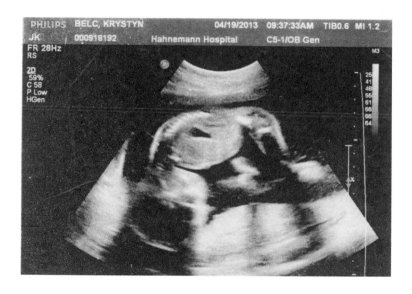

What is it about the image that makes us think we will
know, that we will connect?

Anna kept the scans in a gray box, underneath photos of me as a kid. I'd assumed my ultrasound images were long gone. They're not the sort of thing I would keep. They were under pictures of my mom with thick red glasses, me in a walker, my dad with his mustache, me in a crib buried under Bert and Ernie and Big Bird and Elmo, my brother Michael in his high chair covered in carrots, the backyard in Long Island, a bib that says *Irish Baby*, Michael in a walker, my dad watching me learn to walk, sitting in a lawn chair, Jets cap just so, just like I wear now.

When I'd thought of my uterus, which was not often, I thought of a barren, wintry forest: untouched snow, thin, struggling trees. Harsh winds. The years in my teens and twenties when I didn't have a period were almost a point of pride, evidence that I wasn't a woman after all. There was nothing going on inside; I did not work properly in just the right way. At fifteen I'd stopped eating, starved my body into submission. At Hahnemann University Hospital in Center City, Philadelphia, I told the technician

I did not want to know if the baby was a boy or a girl. I was shown a brain, a heart with four chambers. Two arms, two legs. A spine, completely on the inside, where it should be. The technician thought we were sisters, cousins, friends. I wonder if it was because of the people she was used to seeing—women, alone—or because of how we acted. Anna, sitting in the corner of the room smiling blandly, unsure now about how having two babies just a year apart was going to work out, always unsure how to support me. She rocked Sean's car seat with her foot. How to touch—how to be with—this wild, untamed body, growing, fuller each week, halfway to bursting now. That night in our kitchen in West Philadelphia, the one with the tiny, crooked oven, I made bee sting cake: yeasted batter, almond crunch, pastry cream filling. The baby rolled around inside me as I spread the pastry cream to the edges of the cake with an offset spatula. It looked like a cake in a bakery case. It shone. The almond crunch cracked as I cut into it, this cake just for me. I stood at the counter eating cake, staring at this image. *The second half goes faster*, Anna said, sipping a beer and nursing Sean to sleep.

Endless leading questions: *You look great; do you feel great?*
Are you so excited?

A few days after the twenty-week ultrasound: Anna's birthday. In the morning we went to IKEA and had cinnamon buns and bought new plates. Everywhere we went people looked at us, trying to figure out who we all were to each other. This woman, this infant, this strange pregnant person in ball shorts and a tank top. Since we'd met, Anna and I had joked that IKEA was like an extension of a lesbian bar, but our family never neatly fit into that, and we were now somehow both closer and farther away from it. Queer people had children, but I almost never saw pregnant people like me. Alone at night, I sometimes placed my hands against the baby inside me and felt at peace, like we were in this together, and yet whenever I was outside the house I was aware of the publicness of my body, the unexpectedness. *What are we doing*, I couldn't help thinking. Many days passed this way, without the feeling that my body made sense. I made chicken-fried steak, mashed potatoes, gravy for Anna's birthday dinner, served it on our new plates. Sean put the entire bowl of mashed potatoes on his head. I had a few sips of beer but it tasted wrong, full of danger and shame, the opposite of relaxing.

The picture of the baby inside me, upside down, sat beside our picture of Sean at the same gestational age. We knew, then, that Sean would be assigned male. In the days since the ultrasound I'd started regretting not finding out the baby's sex. Every day the regret got worse, and the guilt about the regret along with it. It was something I thought little about before the ultrasound; of course I didn't *need to know*. But maybe I did. What did it say about me, my buying into the notion that the ultrasound could tell me something, that that something would make me feel more or less excited about the baby?

We hired a babysitter for Sean, got takeout milkshakes to drink in the car on the way to South Jersey's number one 4D/HD private ultrasound facility. This was most certainly a place in which I did not belong. A place for people who throw gender reveal parties, and yet. The facility was deep in the suburbs, a polished, stiff residential building. Everything was pristine, private. Designed to feel nonmedical, and yet the rooms were dominated by their machines. The machines were the only reason this place existed. The facility advertises the ability to determine the baby's sex at fifteen weeks so that families who cannot wait until the standard twenty-week ultrasound can *find out* early. There are packages: 3D image, 4D video, a teddy bear that could play your baby's heartbeat. The most popular package: find out the baby's sex as early as possible, come back a few weeks later for a video to see how the baby has grown, changed. There were pink and blue frames and souvenirs. This went against everything we believed in, and only the babysitter knew we were there. Everything about this pregnancy, I thought as I lay back, was mired in shame. The shame of a masculine pregnancy. The shame of wanting to know the baby's sex. Would happiness come? We got the minimum package, a few images. I was twenty-three weeks pregnant. I pulled up my shirt. How much can you hate a system you pay to be a part of?

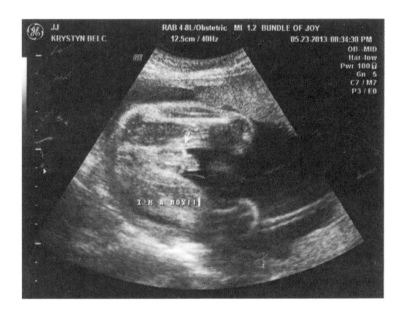

There was only so much we could know by feeling the round, hard outside of the fetus's home. Long before asking *How are you feeling*, people would ask me. *What are you having?* They expected me to know. They thought the ultrasounds meant something. My parents did not find out if I was a boy or a girl. When my mother was pregnant in 1987, it was far less common to find out a baby's gender. I have asked them why they named me Krystyn Marie, and they have not provided a satisfactory answer. No one bearing either name on either side of our family. No good friends with either name. According to the Social Security Administration, thirty-one American girls were given the name Krystyn in 1987. *I just liked it*, my father said. *Don't take the drugs*, my mother said. *You're the only one I took any drugs with, and I felt out of it for hours after.* This, her response to *Why was I named Krystyn?* On the other hand, all of my brothers were named after family members. Michael Thomas. Sean Patrick. Ryan Joseph. It has always made me feel like my parents were expecting someone else that summer Saturday when they made the trip from Flatbush to Manhattan to meet me. A Michael Thomas. I wonder how they got to the hospital: what tunnel, what bridge they took. The Brooklyn, the Williamsburg: these things matter. How late it was, how dark. We must have been in my father's white Honda Civic. I remember when that car was totaled in a garage flood in Rockaway in 1994, filled to the brim with water alongside boxes of dusty pictures and documents. I am not someone who is usually concerned with looking back at images, and when a friend asks me if I know where my ultrasound images are, the ones from the baby I carried, I wonder if my mother kept any images of me. There have been so many of us that they've never told me anything about the day I was born. Fetal ultrasound technology had only been around for about thirty years then, but had already completely changed how we view and experience pregnancy. Before my generation there was nothing to hold on to but hope, when you were pregnant.

The earliest ultrasound machines required the patient to submerge their body in a pool in order to work. There are images of shirtless men standing in chest-deep water; next to them, a technician sits on a stool, beside a metal box the size of a washing machine. They are fascinating, enormous machines. Modern ultrasound machines are much friendlier; they look like computers on top of narrow desks. Ultrasound does not capture an image so much as it uses sound waves to imagine the fetus. The machine does not see a baby, but rather detects where the baby begins and ends. Early in the history of obstetric ultrasound the machine could only capture an image of a fetus's head. Researchers have now calculated normal ranges for nearly every part of the developing fetus. According to John E. E. Fleming, an engineer who worked on early ultrasound machine development, the degree to which we can imagine the fetus through ultrasound *has probably reached more or less the pinnacle of its acuity.*

The machine told us that the baby was a boy. Looking at the machine, we thought we were seeing a body but we were just seeing a reflection. Images of a structure created by sound range. Sound waves directed into me. The machine told us we could know something this way. That we could see something in this dark reflection. Something important. Vital, even. A moving picture: arms waving, baby flipping, legs spread. A baby photographed from the bottom, midflip. When fetal ultrasound was discovered, doctors noted the presence of fetal movement. As if we didn't know. As if we couldn't feel. *I'M A BOY* the machine said. The baby flipped and flipped, became new in the imagination. *BOY.* I didn't want anything to change, but it did. I felt jealousy everywhere, deep in the pit he called home. He was so lucky.

After seeing his images, the midwives were concerned the baby's kidneys were too large. In an office at the birth center, the midwife sat across from me with her hands on her knees, her boots tucked in her stool's metal ring. I was wearing Converse sneakers, basketball shorts, a tank top. I had shaved legs, a shaved head. She asked me to lie back. Paper cranes dangled from the ceiling by strings. I see you're still training for birth, she said, and smiled. She seemed amused I was still doing CrossFit. Not worried at all. Her hands were warm and soft. She pressed a measuring tape up against the baby. Usually that was it. *We'd like you to go to a maternal-fetal specialist,* she said. *Just to make sure the kidneys are okay. What's the chance something is wrong?* I asked. *I'd really like you to go*, she said again.

In the late eighteenth century Lazzaro Spallanzani discovered that bats can continue to fly confidently even if they lose their eyes; they cannot, after all, see in the dark. Not everything can be seen. This was the beginning of discovering what was in the dark places: in the caves of our bodies.

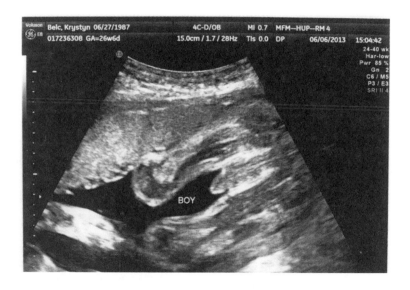

The kidneys were fine everything was always fine they
said. I never knew what I was looking at without a label.
I had no idea how I worked on the inside.

While teams in Minneapolis and Denver failed to bring ultrasound technology to useful diagnostic fruition in the 1950s, the Glasgow team led by obstetrician Ian Donald succeeded. Malcolm Nicolson and John E. E. Fleming, who wrote an account of ultrasound's development and implications, write that ultrasound largely succeeded there because Glasgow was a major shipbuilding center, a site full of equipment for what they call the nondestructive testing of military equipment. In early investigations of the potentials of ultrasound, Donald and engineer Tom Brown used industrial flaw detectors. Industrial. Military. Shipbuilding. When they looked at the baby inside me they weren't looking for what was going right. Industrial flaw detector. The first ultrasound machines looked like they belonged on a shipyard; they were large and imposing, like early computers. The only people who could operate them understood the technology: how sound currents change the piezoelectric crystals in the machine rapidly, causing sound waves to emit the electrical currents that give us the numbers. The early operators of the machine were scientists, not technicians. The machines were large gunmetal boxes. The enamel casing and electronics logos came later, when ultrasound technology became ubiquitous, around the time the medical establishment had finished convincing us that everyone was safer giving birth in a hospital.

One midwife measured my belly, and then she called another over. They got the same number: thirty. I was thirty-three weeks pregnant. *You're measuring quite a bit behind,* they said. *We'd like you to see a maternal-fetal specialist. Again?* I said. *I just saw one.* I imagined another hospital, another gown, another long row of plastic chairs lined up outside examination rooms. The room where they measured me had a wooden rocking chair in the corner. The birth center was like that: a strange mix of medical and homey. When our first son was born, I'd memorized every print on the walls of the birthing room; they were in mismatched thrift store frames. The large bed had a floral spread; the medical instruments were mostly hidden in drawers. There were no straps; there was no beeping; they stuck a handheld Doppler into the bathtub to listen to Sean's heart. Anna pushed for over three hours, and I learned every crack in the floor, every wrinkle in the sheets. It was a long day. When the midwife put on that gown, a mask, we knew it was almost over. What amazed Anna was how quickly they cleaned, how the instruments and measures retreated back into their drawers and we were left feeling like we were in a small-town bed-and-breakfast again. I scheduled another high-risk ultrasound, at a different hospital. *We're touring every hospital in Philly,* Anna joked. And we thought we were doing something different, choosing a birth center.

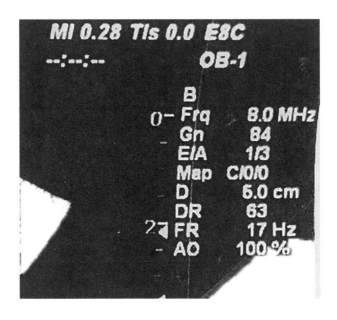

Diagnostic ultrasound provided an entirely novel way of seeing the body, exposing its cavities and soft tissues to the medical gaze in an unprecedented manner.

—MALCOLM NICOLSON and JOHN E. E. FLEMING

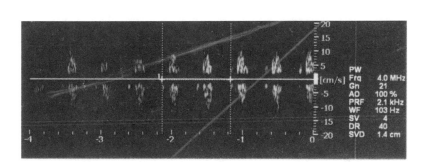

I was sixteen the first time I went to a gynecologist. My mother took me to hers. Dragged me. I wasn't having sex, but my period had stopped for a year and my mother said something had to be done. I was so nervous and ashamed that I cried out when he tried to insert a speculum. I had never read books about my body. I had never masturbated. I had never looked with a mirror. I was not connected with myself in that way and was scared and tense. Ashamed. He only tried one more time before he switched to an ultrasound. That was when I saw my uterus for the first time: the empty, fuzzy landscape that would be my baby's first home. I looked at the machine, my eyes blurred by furious tears. He put me on birth control pills so my period would become normal again. A decade later when they showed it to me again I remembered how against having children I was at that age. Sixteen. I was so thin I barely had breasts, barely had a stomach. I was barely a body. So small, half-starved. *So why am I still here?* I thought, lying on an examination table with my legs up.

When Anna had Sean, I couldn't believe how much he looked like her. He had thick, full black hair and an upturned nose, just like he'd had on the machine. I was drunk the night I told her I wanted to name him Sean, right after her twenty-week ultrasound. I wanted to feel connected, too, but was embarrassed to say. That it was hard, not being a part of our baby. The moment he was born I immediately loved him, like he was an extension of her, much more so once they were disconnected. I didn't cut the cord; our friend Jaclyn did. I didn't want to cause that breakage, that forever disconnection. I hoped I'd feel the same way about my baby, too, once he was on the outside. That had been the point—to feel that way earlier, to do what Anna had done. We wanted two babies close together. To have each other, always.

If I said anything during my first gynecology appointment, at sixteen, I don't remember what it was. When I think back on my pregnancy appointments I hear my voice as it is now, although I hadn't transitioned yet. Steady. Deep. Sure. The way it was always supposed to be. This baby helped me know the person I had to become. Now no one ever thinks I've carried a baby. I never want to remember my childhood voice, high, scared. Not a match. I'd been strong to take this body with me for another decade after that day. To make this person Anna and I wanted so badly in our family. To sit with so many doctors, so many machines, just to make sure our bodies were okay, were still working together to bring him to the outside. Samson, we decided to name him. He who killed a lion with his bare, strong hands.

Back at the first hospital, the one where Anna worked, long color-coded hallways, a locker into which I stuffed my sneakers and clothes. Signs everywhere: *Maternal-Fetal Medicine.* An exam room, the machine. Measurements: the head, the brain, the heart. Arms, legs. *Normal*, they said. *He's in the fiftieth percentile in everything,* the technician said. *He's just sitting a little low in the pelvis,* she said. *I could have told you that,* I said. She held out a handful of ultrasound photos, payment for my troubles.

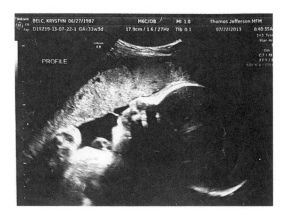

I was nearly eight months pregnant when we closed on a new house and moved across the city. Our old apartment was barely big enough for one baby. It had no closets and was impossible to childproof. We paid for nontoxic paint so I could make the boys a bedroom. Alone on a weekday night I lugged paint up the row-house stairs and got to work. I was in amazing shape from three CrossFit workouts a week. I did clean and jerks, burpees, ran endless laps around Philadelphia streets. Moving the body. Punishing the body. If I was to survive pregnancy, I had to do it in movement. Exercising, painting bedrooms, packing enormous boxes of books and kitchen appliances, these things made me feel like I was still in control of my own body. It was mine.

A good friend lived across the street. One day, while sweeping his stoop, his next-door neighbor approached him.

You know that new couple across the street?
Yes.
Well, I think the man is pregnant.
Yes, I think so, too.

Hot Philadelphia nights. With the windows open we could hear the neighbors yelling, teenagers riding illegal dirt bikes, the ice cream truck hours after we put Sean in bed. School ended. Then came the long, endlessly long days walking around Fishtown with Sean. We'd stop for cans of seltzer, corner store Popsicles. He still took two naps a day, and I took them with him, lying in my bed in our scorching room, holding a pacifier in his mouth. Everywhere I went the same: *When are you due?* September 6. *What? You're so small!* But every day I felt stretching, pressure. I stopped trying to wear sports bras tight enough to hide my breasts. The baby grew out, down. He started to eclipse me, and I wanted to get myself back.

Wild fetal movement whenever I stood or sat still. I dragged Sean with me to the gym to pass time. He sat in a corner in that red stroller while I pressed, squatted. A workout with a hundred dumbbell thrusters, dozens of burpees. The baby inside me was still as I lurched down Montgomery Avenue. After, lying under

43

the pull-up rig in a pool of my own sweat. Friends crouching down to make sure I was all right. That we were all right. Dessert runs multiple nights a week. When Anna suggested that Sean's difficulty sleeping might have to do with his two lengthy naps a day, I said we should just keep him up late. We walked around the city, sometimes till ten, pushing his stroller, passing time. The new ice cream shop, the new frozen yogurt place. We let Sean lick our cones, laid him down long after our new street was dark.

Thirty-four weeks. Thirty-five weeks. Nearing the end. A Fourth of July party, key lime pies. Walking down Cumberland Street to the store for condensed milk for the pies, teenagers leaning against their bicycles shouting—*Look at that, a pregnant man!* We took the pies to a party in West Philly. Everyone else drank while Sean and I ate plates and plates of watermelon wedges. There's a photo of me holding him at the party. He's propped up on my hip, almost straddling my belly. Tipsy people came over, offering him more watermelon, making playful faces. Around our friends, mostly queer, nothing was awry. We were Anna and Krys, and we all knew one another from college, and everyone had always known we'd be the first to have kids. We left first, before it even began to get dark, laughing on our way back to the car.

Sean's first birthday. I made two cream cheese pound cakes, froze one. *We can celebrate when we bring the baby home*, I said. I spent afternoons at the very end melted into the couch watching Sean, who could not stand or walk yet, lie on the floor on his belly flipping through books. He could look at books for a straight hour, spend another hour eating a single piece of toast. Overnights while Anna worked, standing in the window pressing Sean against my belly, trying to rock him to sleep. Then, back to my bed, where the baby would roll around inside me, awake. A sense of peace, those last few weeks. Books about birth emphasize thinking of the contraction as a wave, something that feels most unbearable as it is about to crest.

There is a picture of my belly just before Samson was born. I have no head, no legs, just a belly in front of a shiny refrigerator with an ultrasound picture affixed with two magnets, one yellow, one blue. Why is my head cut out? As if to suggest the baby could exist, in that moment, without me. One of my hands grips my hip, my thumb pressing firmly into my skin. Seven times I saw him on a screen and none of them made him feel any more real to me. These thin black-and-white images were a symbol of what I was supposed to connect with, but it was at night in the stillness of Sean's bedroom, rocking my son back to sleep, that I realized I was as close as I could come to knowing this new person my thumb pressed against in the picture. Being a gestational parent was still a great unknown to me. The ultrasound pictures didn't matter, those words—*I'M A BOY*—didn't matter. My mother had a single ultrasound when pregnant with me, and she did not find out whether I was a boy or a girl. What difference would it have made if she did? The image would have been as wrong as the doctor who delivered me. *Kids are always a surprise*, Anna said the day she stuck Samson's ultrasound picture to the refrigerator.

My body made a baby though I thought it was barren. For years I wished I had told that gynecologist when I was sixteen to do nothing, just let me be, I didn't need that part anyway. I had no reason to believe that except that it had to be because I was a man, because I thought I could wish the possibility of parenting away. But I was wrong. I kept looking at this baby's pictures next to the pictures of the baby my partner made and they were the same. Inside we were the same. The midwives tried to help me imagine pushing him out; they asked me for a *birth plan*. I said *To leave with a baby*. I knew it would be different with Samson and I was scared. Could a person like me, someone who was not a woman, perform the actions I'd seen Anna perform over the last year? Could I do what my mother had done? Had these women been more prepared than I was? The baby kept me up at night nudging me from the inside, swirling around gently like I was his hot tub. When he moved roughly I could barely stand to look down; his limbs pressing against me weirded me out. He was trying to have more space. One night after CrossFit and a late-night barbecue dinner and one of our aimless waddling walks around Philadelphia, I fell asleep to the baby swirling and woke up to pain. I woke Anna up. *This is . . . I think this is . . .* She said to take a bath and see if it stopped. It didn't stop. He was on his way out of me. I had done it: the fertility appointments, the ultrasounds, all those machines, the pictures of body parts moving in the black of me. I was excited to meet the baby. I was ready.

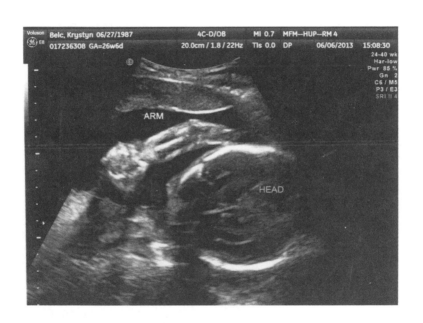

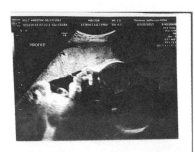

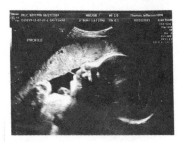

They saw my face but they wanted to be surprised, they said.

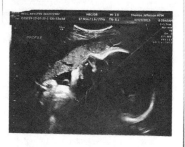

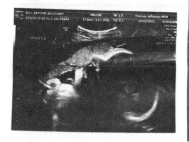

Patient: Krystyn Belc (
Review Date: 8/30/2013 8:42 PM
Order Date: 8/30/2013 8:31 PM
Report Date: 8/30/2013 8:42 PM
Performed Date: 8/30/2013 8:40 PM
Procedure [Final, Reviewed]: Delivery Summary
Diagnosis: TBC--NORMAL VAGINAL DELIVERY (650.)

Patient DOB: 6/27/1987
Reviewed by:
Ordered by:

Birth Summary
  Estimated Due Date: 9/6/2013
  Admission Date/Time: 8/30/2013 4:30 PM
  Birth Date/Time: 8/30/2013 7:34 PM
  Type of Delivery: SVD
  Birth Site: TBC
  Birth Attendant:
  Birth Assistant:
  GBS Status: Negative
Maternal Transfer
  AP or IP Transfer: N/A
Stages of Labor \ First Stage
  Onset Early Labor Date/Time: 8/30/2013 3:00 AM
  Onset Active Labor Date/Time: 8/30/2013 7:00 PM
  Onset of Pushing Date/Time: 8/30/2013 7:28 PM
  Problems First Stage: No
  Family Reaction to First Stage: very supportive
Stages of Labor \ First Stage \ Labor Induction
  Labor Induction: None
Stages of Labor \ First Stage \ Labor Augmentation
  Labor Augmentation: None
Stages of Labor \ First Stage \ ROM Details
  ROM Date/Time: 8/30/2013 7:20 PM
  Fluid Color and Odor: Clear
  Mode of ROM: SROM
  Comments: no VE after ROM
Stages of Labor \ First Stage \ Medications First Stage
  General Medications: None
  Analgesia: None
  Anesthesia: None
Stages of Labor \ Second Stage
  Presentation: Cephalic
  Position: Direct OA
  Problems Second Stage: No
Stages of Labor \ Delivery Details
  Maternal Delivery Position: Squatting(in bathroom)
  Nuchal Cord: Loose, X1(reduced easily after delivery)
  Operative Delivery: No
Stages of Labor \ Third Stage
  Expulsion of Placenta & Cord: Spontaneous
  Cord Vessels: 3
  Appearance of Placenta/Cord: Grossly intact
  EBL: 350 mL
  Date/Time of Placental Delivery: 8/30/2013 7:47 PM
  Problems Third Stage: No
  Family Reaction to Delivery: tearful, joyous
  Stem Cell Collection: No
Stages of Labor \ Third Stage \ Episiotomy/Laceration
  Episiotomy: None
  Laceration: Perineal 2nd repaired
  Anesthesia for Repair: Cetacaine Spray, 1% Lidocaine IM
  Suture Type: 3-0 vicryl
Stages of Labor \ Third Stage \ Medications Postpartum
  Medications Postpartum: None

First Seen in Print

VR 133 - M - 109024 - 120M -(86)

DOCUMENT NO. A 094766

| City of New York | Department of Health | Bureau of Vital Records |

CERTIFICATE OF BIRTH REGISTRATION

Below is an exact copy of a certificate of Birth registered for your child. It is sent without charge. If the certificate contains any errors return this copy with the correct information to the Bureau of Vital Records, 125 Worth Street, New York, N.Y. 10013. You will be advised how to have the record corrected. It is important to do this at once.

The reproduction or alteration of this transcript is prohibited by Section 3.21 of the New York City Health Code.

Notice In issuing this transcript of the record, the Department of Health of the City of New York does not certify to the truth of the statements made thereon as no inquiry as to the facts has been provided by law.

MAYOR   COMMISSIONER OF HEALTH   CITY REGISTRAR

CERTIFICATE OF BIRTH   156-87 - | | 7 8 0 8

Birth No.

DATE FILED

07 JUL | P 2: 40

1. FULL NAME OF CHILD (Type or Print) First Name: Krystyn   Middle Name: Marie   Last Name: McIlraith

2. SEX: Female
3a. NUMBER OF CHILDREN born of this pregnancy 1
3b. If more than one, number of this child in order of birth
4a. DATE OF CHILD'S BIRTH (Month) (Day) (Year): June 27, 1987
4b. HOUR: 9:35   ☐ AM ☒ PM

5. PLACE OF BIRTH: NEW YORK CITY
5a. BOROUGH OF: Manhattan
5b. NAME OF HOSPITAL, if not in hospital, street address: Lenox Hill Hospital
5c. TYPE OF PLACE: ☒ Hospital ☐ Home ☐ Other

6a. MOTHER'S FULL MAIDEN NAME: Helen Bridget Dougherty
6b. MOTHER'S AGE at time of this birth: 27
6c. MOTHER'S BIRTHPLACE, State or foreign country: Brooklyn, New York

7. MOTHER'S USUAL RESIDENCE a. State: NY b. County: Kings c. City, town or location: Brooklyn d. Street and house number: 1358 East 38th Street e. Inside city limits of 7c? Yes ☐ No ☐

8a. FATHER'S FULL NAME: Gerald James McIlraith
8b. FATHER'S AGE at time of this birth: 28
8c. FATHER'S BIRTHPLACE, State or foreign country: Brooklyn, New York

9a. NAME OF ATTENDANT AT DELIVERY: Peter Maran   C.N.M. R.N. D.O. M.D.

9b. I CERTIFY THAT THIS CHILD WAS BORN ALIVE AT THE PLACE, DATE AND TIME GIVEN.   C.N.M. R.N. D.O. M.D.
Signed
Name of Signer: Peter Maran, M.D. (Type or Print)
Address: 1430 Second Avenue, NYC
Date Signed: June 27, 19 87

Information added or amended
(Reason)
Date   City Registrar

BUREAU OF VITAL RECORDS   DEPARTMENT OF HEALTH   THE CITY OF NEW YORK

Print here the mailing address of mother. ➝
Copy of this certificate will be mailed to her when it is filed with the Department of Health.

Name: Mrs. Gerald J. McIlraith
Address: 1358 East 38th Street
City: Brooklyn   State: NY   Zip Code: 11234

I. KRYSTYN MARIE McILRAITH

(Type or Print) First Name	Middle Name	Last Name
Krystyn	Marie	McIlraith

Rockaway Beach looks like every other neighborhood in Queens except for the thin layer of sand covering everything—the sidewalks, the houses, the decks and lawns and cars. In the summer neighborhood kids bust the fire hydrants open and beige sandmud rolls down the sloped streets. Each afternoon when we come home from the beach my mother lines us up and hoses us off, cold water jet stream setting, no holds barred, our fleshy thighs rippling and throwing sand back at her. She makes my brothers pull down their pants out front on the sidewalk and they say, *Ma, here?* And she says yes but says nothing to me. I am left to creep through the house, soaked with icy hose water, my bathing suit bottom filled with sludge, until I am in the bathtub alone. Somehow with all these people living in the bottom of a two-family house I am always alone. On the weekends I ride my bicycle around the corner with the girl next door. Our wheels crunch down the city sidewalks. Her name is Kristen, too, and her bike barely works. My parents think her dad pulled it out of a trash heap. My father is always talking about the ways that we are not like them. One day Kristen asks me why I am such a boy. I don't know what to say, so I say I don't know. When we are eight she gets her period and I am the first person she tells. We are sitting in my garage eating Pop-Tarts and she says, *I have to tell you something big.* She doesn't have the words, though, and when she tries to write it out on a napkin she writes B-L-U-D. *Blued?* I ask. I hold the napkin up into the sun. We don't go to school together, and I had no idea she could not read and write as well as I could. *No*, she says, pulling me down into her parents' garage, which is beneath their house, at the end of a short, steep driveway, just like ours. *Blood. It's something that happens to us*, she whispers. *My mom says it happens to all of us. It comes . . . out of you.* It is all happening: coming at me like a wave. A body the neighbors can't see, a body untamed, the wrong kind of boy's body. Where we live you can never feel clean. Sand and grit cover everything. It is the Irish Riviera. New York's playground. Rockaway Beach.

(Type or Print)   First Name

Krystyn

Middle Name

Marie

Every day my mother drags us to the beach while my father is at work; we sit in the sand from sunup till midafternoon. To get there, I pull a wagon and she pushes a stroller the four long blocks from our house. People stop us to ask if we are all hers. When we get there, the babies nap on towels, umbrellas pitched over their heads or second towels draped over their pale faces. My mother slathers us nearly every hour with sunscreen, rubbing it into our scalps and the cracked, sandy bottoms of our feet. *You all have your father's skin, every one of yous*, she always says. One day some neighbors who live on the corner of 125th and Rockaway Beach Boulevard ask if I can stay longer to play, say that they'll walk me home around dinnertime; my mother looks at the stroller and the wagon and me and says yes, but only if I help her get everything onto the sidewalk first. I've so rarely been anywhere without her. There's an electricity to watching her walk down the street, away from me.

Marie has two brothers who like to push us around and throw sand on us. They are tall and thin and their swim trunks keep sliding down; as they run toward the ocean they wrap their hands in their waistbands and tug. Marie and I run after them for hours, past rainbow towel rows past rickety lifeguard stands past neighbors sitting on colonies of beach chairs past Italian ice vendors dragging enormous white coolers through thick sand, their ropy bronze muscles sweatslicked and pulsing. Marie and I don't catch the boys; their brown backs are always just steps ahead. I memorize those backs—wide shoulders, long bumped spines, tans. They are beautiful and I don't know why they make me sad. The pain and longing of chasing, little stubborn feet digging into molten, churning earth, July sun pounding us. As I run my swimsuit tugs in all the wrong places, the elastic trapping sand, rubbing welts into thighs. I don't stop. We run all afternoon, me and Marie.

When my mother sees me she says, *Oh, Krystyn Marie, I forgot to remind her to put your sunscreen on.* She almost never says my whole name; it is a foreign thing. Most children do not need sunscreen as often as I do. Over the next few hours, my skin blisters; the next day I lie in bed, in so much pain I forget my own name. My skin becomes scaly, then wet and sticky as the blisters pop. I lie in bed and believe with my whole self that it was worth it. The aloe is cold but my mother's hands are rough beneath it; she rarely uses oven mitts. *I don't have time for that*, she will say, grabbing a sheet pan or a meat loaf straight out of the oven, plucking a dropped spoon right out of a bowl of boiling chili.

2. HELEN BRIDGET DOUGHERTY

6a. MOTHER'S FULL MAIDEN NAME

Helen Bridget Dougherty

Your mother is telling a story. She is telling a story in English because *Please*, you've told her, *No Polish, please try to remember to speak in English.* She stops in the middle of a sentence and starts gesturing like she's trying to reel words forward from the back of her mind and when she can't remember the phrase in English you give her permission to say what she's trying to say in Polish. You translate, give her the words she needs. *Aha!* your mother says. We all laugh, me and you and your mother. At the evasiveness of our shared language, at trying to help one another understand. You drink tea and I hold a full, hot mug I don't really want. In this house you are not allowed to say no and you have to try everything, *Just one bite to make her happy, it's cultural*, you said in the car on the way from my parents' in New Jersey. The sugar bowl is in the cabinet; I can't decide whether to ask or rise myself. No one here uses milk. Everything is in translation. *This is stupid*, I said, sitting in traffic on the George Washington, the city slowly growing closer and bigger. I held my breath as we crossed into New York, saw the dark state line on the GPS. Your family changed this city for me—the beauty, the roar, the closeness of all those people to one another, the closeness of me to you in my car. I was eight when we left Queens and going back, with you, the magic was lost. Them, waiting, in a stuffy apartment in Queens. Forty minutes past the open sky above my parents' house I stepped out of my car, braced for the miscues and misunderstandings of your family's dinner table. The quiet. So much unspoken. How I took their daughter. Who only dated men, before me. Real men. Everything forced, everyone pretending we are family for one day. I am not their daughter, not their son. I am someone who never drinks the tea. From Queens I imagine my mother desecrating the family's turkey, hacking slices of breast straight off the bird, after it spent too much time in the oven, after it spent too little time resting. She never listens to me, never. *Cut along the backbone to remove the entire breast, then slice,* I reminded her before we left. *Use a thermometer. Don't pay any mind to that white pop-out thing.* She *Yeah yeah yeah*-ed me and told me *Have fun at the in-laws'* and winked. I always know exactly what my mother means when she speaks.

I draw the map as quickly as I can, on the back of a student's homework, in marker. I am late for work. I am stressed because I do not trust your mother with our children but she is all we have today. When you were little, she took you and your brothers across Poland by herself on the train. I try to imagine it: you and Pete and Jack and your mother with your backpacks, your child-hood bangs and hair plaited behind you, but I can't. I have never met that mother. Your mother asks me what to feed the kids for lunch while I am putting on my shoes and I say *Peanut butter and jelly*. She asks how to make it. I tell her, *You take two slices of bread and you, oh, never mind, I'll just do it* and I do, Samson hanging from my legs and Sean asking when I will be back. *Three forty-five at the latest*, I say, as if that means a thing to a three-year-old. To him a clock is just a circle on the wall. Today is just another day when his parents don't have enough time. I am always rushed, always inattentive, and it feels like my whole salary goes to our babysitter who cannot be here today. To Sean today is not Mon-day, it is just today, and his grandmother has arrived unexpectedly from New York to keep him alive. *Your* babcia *is going to take you to playgroup*, I say. *It will be fun*, I instruct him. Playgroup is the place you go to make parenting easier. All the weary moms and nannies nursing free cups of tea. A roomful of old plastic toys you hope your kids won't lick, circle time, plates of Goldfish crackers and raisins. Time ticking by. I think about giving your mother verbal directions to the old brown-brick church on Montgomery Avenue, but then I decide to draw a map. It is harder to get to playgroup than it is to make a peanut butter sandwich. *When peanut butter came to Warsaw*, you told me, *nobody knew what to do with it. We thought maybe it was like butter, that you used it on a ham sandwich. Then we realized it wasn't like butter, but we would use it with butter, like it was the ham.*

Here's Frankford, I say, drawing a fat road going north and south, ignoring that it is one of Philadelphia's narrowest main streets, *and here's Montgomery*, drawing a thin line where she'd turn east, toward the river, the highway, the church. *You turn away from the train tracks.* Your mother takes the map in her hands, looks at me with watery blue eyes. *Thank you*, she says. I cannot quite pin down what bothers me so much about her. I imagine it's mostly about me but these days I do not have time for much introspection. At three forty-five I rush in the door after a day of teaching everyone else's kids and Sean tells me they did not make it to playgroup. Babcia *turned the stroller the wrong way*, he says, *and I think we went to where the wild things are.* The tunnel past Lehigh, the graffiti and discarded needles, the ominous shadows and pieces of concrete strewn on the sidewalk. No stores, no other strollers, no playgroup. It's all blown out up there. Weeks later she will go to her local ER when she gets lost coming home from the grocery store. There will be a mass. Until most of it is taken out, your mother will not know what it is, glioblastoma multiforme, the worst possible news. MRI can provide a map to the tumor but only tells us so much about what it might be. We can only really know once we're there.

I'm just starting to make caramel in my parents' kitchen in New Jersey when my mother pulls a great big hamper of laundry up to the counter across from me and starts folding it. I measure some sugar and some water into a pot with high sides and turn on the flame, a real flame here, no glass stovetop. My mother tells me that somebody in the family has jacked up the joint Netflix account by watching every gay movie they could find. *Every gay thing imaginable*, she says. *Can you believe that?* she asks, tossing a shirt she'd started to fold into a crumpled heap on the counter, and I tell her *Yes, I can really believe that.* She picks up the shirt again. *I think it was Michael. Your father and I think he may be gay.* This shirt she is holding is going through the wringer, picked up and plopped down again like a prop in a poorly acted play. *Oh*, I say. *I've never thought much about that*, I say. And it's true; it never occurred to me that a second queer child would matter after me. You're at home in Michigan with our kids. I drove over a thousand miles to visit the East Coast, to feel like myself again, to be with my five younger brothers and sisters and other people who've known me more than a few months. In my mother's beautiful kitchen I scrape a spatula around the sides of the pan so the sugar-and-water mixture, the caramel, doesn't stick and burn black. In the car for sixteen hours, through all of Michigan and Ohio and Pennsylvania, I thought a lot about what my mother would see when she looked at me for the first time since testosterone really took hold inside me. When I got my first tattoo, a gift to myself a few weeks before our wedding, she was devastated. In the months since we moved to Michigan my seventeen-year-old sister has gotten a tattoo on her foot—her friend hand-poked it—and as far as I can tell no one is all that surprised. *She says it's a shark fin*, one of my brothers told me, over beers in the backyard, *but it just looks like a triangle.* They have all learned that there are worse things than tattoos. My mother is still messing with this same shirt and I step away from my caramel and pick up another shirt and fold it neatly, perfectly, like in a store in the mall. Then I head back to the stove and swirl the pot of boiling candy gently. In college, I took the acting course mostly to impress you. In the scene I performed as my final exam, I had to be a woman arguing with her husband while peeling a cucumber with a paring knife. As I talked to this husband—who, in the play, is secretly gay—I slid the cucumber's waxy skin down into one curled strand hanging by my knees. *Your lines are good*, the instructor said as I practiced, *but don't you think your character would be a lot less skilled at peeling that cucumber?* The caramel starts to smell burnt, burnt in the right way, the just-past-cooked way, and I pour the butter and cream in. I stir as it bubbles up; it always bubbles way up, so you have to use a pot with high sides. *A lot of people watch movies about gay people*, I say to my mother. *It's Netflix, not a porn site.* When I would talk to you about my acting class I called the boy in the scene The Statue because of how hard it was to get a read on his face. We had to kiss, in the scene. He had soft lips but nothing in his eyes, nothing. I think of a man I saw on the Second Avenue subway yesterday. Can you believe there is a Second Avenue subway, after all those years talking about making one? This man was pulling long black hair into a messy bun, like all the girls at Catholic school wore. I did, too. He was sitting right across from me; he was cute, and his jeans fit so flawlessly, and I tried to catch his eyes. In the small town where we live now everyone always looks you dead in the face. Everyone says hello. The beautiful man on the subway wouldn't look up, because you're really not supposed to, when you ride the subway. I remember that much. I've known you for over ten years, and it wasn't easy, in the beginning, with my parents. I was their first daughter. That was a long time ago. And yet, back at home for the first time in a year, I want this man on the subway, the man with the bun who will not look into my face. *And so what if he is?* I ask my mother as

I flake sea salt into the pot. *So nothing*, she says. *I was just saying*. She gets back to folding. The caramel is done. It is perfect, darker than anything you can buy in a jar, salty and bitter and achingly sweet.

The other day you came home from work and reported that a new doctor in your ER told you her father died of a massive heart attack, peacefully, in his sleep, at a roadside motel on his way to Florida for the winter. It must have felt like a blessing, talking with someone about death like that: a clean, easy death, in an emergency room where no one meets an easy end. Your coworker's mother went to the front desk to ask what state they were even in. *My husband is dead in his bed.* Your mother never got to be old. She was a gym teacher, not even sixty, tight and lithe and full of energy. She had thin, muscular arms and strong hands that were bigger than mine. When you told me twelve years ago that your parents were searching for a house in Colorado, you paused, then added, *Not that kind of Colorado. Like, middle-of-nowhere Colorado. Cheap Colorado.* It was their first real home together. Your mother had an apartment in Warsaw because she grew up in an orphanage and an apartment was the state's compensation for such a childhood. Sometimes you try to talk about how small the apartment is but in every tale it gets smaller until, when you tell of it, you can press the walls apart with your hands. Your mother used to tell a story about getting a broken watch as a gift and still showing it off; it was one of the only things she owned. She was proud when anyone asked her the time. You asked her to stop telling that story but she wouldn't. Their apartment in Queens felt sterile, like they'd never moved in. Like a hospital. *They've been here a decade*, you said. *But they don't think of this as their home.* Your parents kept renting their little place in New York, waiting for their trips to Colorado. Our first time in Bailey, Colorado, was my first time on a mountain. The house was beyond the middle of nowhere. After we had sex I was so dizzy, and I kept waking all night wondering if I was dying for lack of air. We started doing it on the floor because I thought the few feet would help and it was creepy, doing it in your parents' bed. I was nineteen. They were back in New York. You told me about how your whole childhood they dragged you up seemingly every mountain in southern Poland and you hated it. Your mother lived to hike. I'd never been hiking and thought it was at least worth a shot. By the back door of the house your mother had left two pairs of boots; we all had the same size feet. She had a stack of maps of the mountains of Colorado, and some mantras scrawled on index cards that she taped by the door, so she'd see them right before she went out hiking. They were all about how nature would and could crush us if we weren't wary. When she'd get depressed you worried she'd die up there by herself on purpose, going out when she knew there was a storm coming, throwing herself off the side of a mountain, even. She was an expert navigator and you'd know she meant it, if she did. And so what? Why should somebody have to die the way we want, to give us the story we want to tell?

3. WORDS FIRST SEEN IN PRINT IN 1987, ACCORDING TO *MERRIAM-WEBSTER*

1. potty-mouthed

: given to the use of vulgar language

When we met, you warned me you liked to curse. Maybe it was more brag than warning. It reminded me of my mother; with her, I was always waiting and cringing. You were brash. I liked it and hated it. It made me remember. My mother cursing at the sink; my mother cursing as she folded our laundry. My mother waiting for me to say, *Mom!* on the other end of the phone after she said something vulgar. When we met, you wanted to get your doctorate in psychology. You wanted to get your doctorate in theater. You wanted to be a psychiatrist. You wanted to move to London and write plays. And smoke cigarettes, you said. That part was very important. You were so tall and wanted so many things, but I only wanted you. My mother, too, wanted big things; she was a hardscrabble tennis champion who grew up in Flatbush. *We were the Bad News Bears*, she said, of her team playing the suburban kids. I had never seen the film but I knew what she meant somehow. She got into Cornell and could not go. It was the money. *I grew up with nothing*, she said. *I was embarrassed to bring my friends over to our apartment. You don't know how lucky you are.* My mother cleaned and cleaned; I can hardly remember her doing anything else. Nothing ever shone enough. The six of us were not allowed to curse. I disappointed my parents greatly, my whole life, but I never cursed in front of them. You did not get your doctorate. You did not write any more plays. You became a nurse. My mother was thrilled. *Nursing, wow, I should have done that,* she said mournfully, folding laundry and looking out the window.

2. BFF

informal

: a very close friend

Our college rugby team met to make T-shirts. It was silly: the beer, the paints, all of us coloring with fabric pens and signing one another's creations. You left yours behind when you went to work, draped over an auditorium chair. *Oh, crap, Anna's shirt,* a friend said, holding it up to me. *I think she said she was on her way to work,* I said. As if I didn't know for sure. As if I didn't know your hours. We were becoming fast friends, I thought. No one knew; we didn't run in the same crowds. Your e-mails were a secret I didn't know how to explain; our carefully faux-accidental run-ins were electric. At the circulation desk I felt everyone's eyes on me as I placed my elbow on the counter, leaned over the scanner to hand you the painted shirt. Where we went to school the library was always crowded, even on a Friday night. People watched me visit you at work. You've always loved to work the latest shift, making money while others relax. Running out the door in your scrubs while I give our kids their after-dinner baths. Saying goodbye as I say good night. Dinner-leftovers Tupperware at 3:00 a.m.

I'm so glad you brought this back, you said, stuffing the T-shirt into an enormous purse: you always carry your books in a crammed over-the-shoulder bag, never in a backpack. Girls' school, women's sports: my whole life I'd been falling for my best friends. Legs running downfield, hands that reached into backpacks when I needed to borrow a pen. The way I felt so many friendships obscured by hiding and quietly wanting. Shame and denial. *Everyone must feel this way sometimes*, I told myself. A group of girls getting ready to go out, a group of girls lacing up to play basketball, big hard shoes over delicate feet, the perfume, the makeup, the swigs of alcohol stolen from someone's parents. The high-pitched laughter and hugs I tried to avoid. *If they ever find out, I don't want them to think back on this moment*, I always thought. I'll sleep on the floor. I'll be the designated driver. Always an intruder. The first time we slept together I used your toothbrush in the women's bathroom of your dorm. We stood side by side at adjacent sinks, you washing your face, me brushing my teeth. You laughed. *I guess this is one benefit to sleeping with another woman*, you said. I laughed, too. I always have. When people ask how we met you are sure to tell them we were never friends. This was always a pursuit for you. It's not that it was easy; it is never easy. But you learned this about yourself in college. Pursuit was a freedom. You were never hiding. Nearly eleven years after I brushed my teeth in your dorm bathroom we pull off the Hutchinson River Parkway and enter an impossibly small rest stop. The line for the women's room snakes along the wall, and I walk right by it into the men's room. I laugh.

3. selective serotonin reuptake inhibitor

: any of a class of antidepressants (such as fluoxetine or sertraline) that inhibit the inactivation of serotonin by blocking its reuptake by presynaptic nerve cell endings

The medication made you not want sex. I was not angry that you were depressed. How could I be angry at that? It was that I needed you even though you said I could go get it anywhere, from anyone. *You're still in college*, you said. *Go find it somewhere else.* You were sad, and you needed the medication, but I was angry. While I studied with my friends or sat alone in my dorm room, headphones on and stacks of books beside me, you stayed in your apartment crying. Your first adult apartment, on Baltimore Avenue. I stained a plain wooden table you bought at IKEA; you had a picture of a couch taped on your living room wall. *It looks like a ballet studio*, you joked. We ate on the floor off paper plates if you had two dinner guests; you only had two chairs. You had a handful of mugs and no glasses. I remember all those late-night drives to keep you company in your ballet studio. The sex we'd have before I went back to college in the morning, back to class and my dorm. It is embarrassing to admit that I never came with myself before I came with you. You taught me this body was okay. You taught me how to make it work. You grabbed me where I learned to grab myself. It wasn't that I had never tried before, but all I felt was too much flesh in all the wrong places. Fat like what you trim off a roast. Fat for the trash. Fat for the dog's bowl. Fat you peel back, pull taut, slice. *Can I grab you here?* you asked. *Can I grab you like this?* you asked.

4. beer goggles

: the effects of alcohol thought of metaphorically as a pair of goggles that alter a person's perceptions especially by making others appear more attractive than they actually are

You took me out for my first beers when I turned twenty-one. Yards Philly Pale Ale at Standard Tap, a hipster bar across town from your former ballet studio, which now had a beat-up brown couch and walls I had painted Strawberry Rhubarb. We waited by the El tracks looking west at the whole city. *Which way does the train come from again?* I asked, tipsy.

We slept with the woman in your anatomy and physiology class because she and I were drunk and you were curious. At her party everyone trashed her galley kitchen. I remember bottle caps and crumbled tortilla chips, cigarette butts and the smell of spilled wine and bodies.

Her bed was public. Curtains separated the living room from her massive bedroom, or maybe it was just a flimsy sliding door. I remember a bed with no bedside tables and too many pillows. I remember her name and that she had a big, fluffy cat. Everyone at the party was queer or at least could have been. So many of us in one place. Getting up, cotton-mouthed, to pee. I threw up and went back to sleep next to you, tangled together on the other side of the bed. It is the only time in my life I ever woke up still drunk.

5. degenderize

: to eliminate any reference to a specific gender in (something, such as a word, text, or act)

When I am no longer your girlfriend I don't just become your boyfriend. I am in between and I intend to stay that way. I am a *partner* but come on, people just think that means lesbians, right? I am a lover but people our age do not say that in any kind of seriousness. I have never been a wife or a husband. When my mother has trouble remembering to use the right pronoun you advise: *Just say his name a lot. That's what I do.*

6. in-line skate

*: a roller skate whose wheels are set in-line for greater speed
and maneuverability*

One of our last dates before you got pregnant was to that roller
rink in Camden. You rented a pair of tan roller skates with orange
wheels and I paid the extra dollar for black Rollerblades. You were
no good; you looked like a Japanese spider crab on wheels. All
limbs and giggles. Smooth hardwood, pop music, lights flashing,
crowds of kids. I couldn't help but smile. We had soggy cheese
fries and Cokes and watched the kids with their parents, so impossibly happy, you and me almost like everyone else for at least
an hour or two.

In-line skates have been around for a long time, maybe centuries.
At the National Museum of Roller Skating in Lincoln, Nebraska,
you can see skates dating back to 1819. At your high school in New
York City they were supposed to offer Rollerblading Gym your

junior year but then September 11 happened and they canceled it. They moved your whole school of over three thousand kids to another borough, to another school that had nearly five thousand kids already. You showed me where you would have bladed, along the Hudson River. When you came back, the Chambers Street subway stop was still full of concrete dust and you signed up for Swim Gym, came early each morning to hit the pool and showed up to your next class with wet, chlorinated hair. It was amazing to me, a school like that just an hour from my high school, which was a big semicircular building in the woods of Bergen County, New Jersey. A giant Jesus perched outside, watching us come and go. Sometimes when I closed my eyes to go to sleep, hours away at the liberal arts college where I reinvented myself as your lover, I would remember walking down those halls, my kilt and knee socks, feeling so out of place. Soon after I met you, we were in bed and heard the metallic whoosh of a low-flying plane on its way to Philadelphia International Airport, which was ten miles from my dorm room, and you lost it. I was shocked; you sobbed and shook, your heartbeat would not slow down, so sudden like that, something I could not understand. Two people, learning to be, in one bed.

I got my first pair of Rollerblades after we moved to the suburbs, around the same time I got my first Sony Discman. Rollerblades were made to get us somewhere, but at eleven and twelve and thirteen I skated the same hundred yards back and forth at the end of Clover Lane. Our house on the edge of eleven acres of marshland, our vast front lawn a wooded bog. Years later, at thirty, and home to visit, I tell my mother how I cannot stand Manhattan, how it always feels like the worst kind of crowded airport, how everyone is always ready to yell at me if I hesitate for just a moment getting onto or off the subway, and she snorts. *You grew up at the end of a cul-de-sac*, she says.

7. messenger bag

: a rectangular bag that is large enough to carry papers, books, etc., and that usually has a wide shoulder strap and a flap that typically covers the opening and much or all of the front of the bag

My mother sends me a backpack for school every year, even the years I am a teacher and not a student. You say that you do not like to think of me as a child. *It is too sad*, you say. But I was not always sad; children are resilient. It was not all bad, and so I try to look back for the times my mother said yes. No to the Air Jordans for school. No to slacks and a shirt for church. No to short haircuts. No to repainting my room red or blue. No to a denim duvet like the ones my brothers had. It made their blankets so heavy, rooted them to their beds. But she said yes to the messenger bag I wanted, instead of a backpack, for the sixth grade. It was silver. In the checkout line she kept asking if I was sure. *It's going to hurt your shoulders, you know*, she said. *It won't,*

I said. Maybe we were never quite mother and daughter but in some ways we might have been. I learned to cook by sitting at the counter watching her while my brothers watched cartoons in the basement. Every afternoon after school she watched TLC's *A Baby Story*, a show in which each episode featured a woman's pregnancy and birth. I watched too. I don't remember much from the year of the messenger bag. I got my first Parental Advisory CD, Mase's *Harlem World*, and hid it in my underwear drawer. I forged my mother's signature on a failed science test and it wasn't even close, but I handed it back in to Mr. Gardner anyway and got caught. My mother had to talk to my French teacher once a week on the phone, to make sure I was doing my homework. One day my mother came to the school to find all the sweatshirts I had lost and in front of my entire class she emptied my locker onto the floor. *Will you believe this?* she asked everyone, looking around as she sifted through an unimaginable pile of junk, bewildered that we could even be related. But it was true: I came out of her body, on June 27, 1987. We were both there. She was right. The bag hurt my shoulder. I could only really fit one textbook in it, which made it way less likely I'd get it together as a student. The problem didn't last, though; the messenger bag was poorly constructed, the fibers connecting the strap to the bag slackened slowly, then snapped, leaving it unfurled on the bottom of my locker one day.

8. FAQ

: a document (as on a website) that provides answers to a list of typical questions that users might ask regarding a particular subject ("check the FAQ")

Your father wants to know how I chose my middle name. *Was it after Malcolm X?* It is an accusation. Your father wants to know when you *knew.* Your father wants to know if our kids understand, and if so, how? How do they understand me? Why did I bring them to a march? Why did I bring them to a rally? Why can't we just pretend to be normal? He wants to know if you're sure you've known I'm trans for as long as you say you have. It is another accusation. He wants you to know that, in his opinion, my being trans has its benefits. In a way, I have opened a new closet for us to step inside. He asks, *Doesn't this mean no one has to know you're different now?* I mean, look at me. Look at me. I almost look normal. Just young. A little soft. Just say this is the way it's always been, that you married a short, impossibly young-looking man. Your father doesn't hug me ever again after I ask you to tell him to call me he. If you liked men so much why didn't you just?

Someone at your job sees a picture of the five of us, our family, pauses, and asks: *How did you get your kids?* I am surprised when you tell me this at breakfast, over pancakes, after your night shift. No one asks anymore; we are just a mom and a dad and some kids. No one sees anything unusual. Some kids look like their moms; some look like their dads. Sean and ZZ look like you, Samson looks like me, and when the three of them sit in a row they look like brothers. Joined by their other genetic half, a man with his own family who lives across the country. *Did your partner have to go off testosterone for that?*

Call your mother, Samson demands one day while I lie on the floor playing Sean's Nintendo DS. I play *Super Mario 3D Land* and remember the good things about being a little boy. The pings of coins collected, the surprised sound Mario makes when he jumps from wall to wall, surprised at what his little body can do. *Why?* I ask. *I need you to ask her why she made you so HAIRY,* he says. *Your legs are hairy. Your belly is hairy. Your face is hairy. Why did your mother make you so hairy?* His older brother bangs on the bathroom door with both fists while I'm in the shower. *What are you doing in there?* he calls out. Samson joins in. *Yeah, what are you doing?* he yells. *Washing your VAGINA?*

9. thirtysomething

: *having an age of 30 to 39 years old*
thirtysomething *parents*
also: of or relating to people in their thirties
Just the usual thirtysomething *decor—Persian rug,
book-shelves, abstract paintings, glass coffee table, . . . and
a few exotic trinkets picked up on foreign junkets.*

—MARLY SWICK

You ask me if you should tell your new therapist that your husband
is transgender. You always say *husband* when you think *partner*
will be too awkward. *My problems are not about you,* you say. Your
mother has been dead for three weeks. Sometimes you feel like our
kids took away your sense of self. Try to read a book and somebody needs their nose blown. You can only drink so many cups of
cold tea. Feels like a lie to leave it out, the stuff about me, but what
therapist can resist thinking this is everything? The woman who
used to be, who should have been, who never was. You married

her knowing she was a figment of everyone else's imagination. You said forever when you meant never. Breasts smashed beneath denim shirts, a reluctant dad who still goes by his first name. At home he is just himself with no hoodies, no binders, nothing at all, just boxers and socks. Letters that come from our sons' school with his old name on them sit on the counter. Friends who haven't seen us in years forget he won't look anything like they remember. There is no way this could be anything but the most important thing in your life—right? We moved cross-country for me to go to graduate school and we do panicked math in the checkout aisles, trying to buy groceries. We can only buy the tiny jars of peanut butter even though each spoonful is more expensive that way. The men who live in our house in Philadelphia are getting a divorce and we will need to find new tenants. As far as we can tell one is cheating on the other. We liked them; they decorated and always paid us on time. They fixed our yard door. It is a luxury for millennials to own anything at all, even a house so far away; we know that and desperately want to keep it, our little corner of the world. Your mother never understood or accepted you and now she is dead. You want to know whether you should say something about me to your new therapist in this town a thousand miles from home.

10. deathcare

: of, relating to, or providing products or services for the burial or cremation of the dead

I did not see your mother when she died. I only saw her in her living coffin, a bed in the middle of the living room where she slept away most of the day. As far as we could tell she was not in pain; her brain went out slowly, like Christmas lights on a string, dimming one by one. We'd never had much to talk about and this day was no different, somehow. I sat in your parents' living room in Queens building an airport out of DUPLO blocks, cleaning up as our kids moved from one of your childhood toys to the next. Your parents have never had cable, but the boys found a jar of a hundred tiny Pokémon and dumped it everywhere. Eevee, Magikarp, Mewtwo, Charizard rolling like dice and banging against the foot of the hospital bed. One of my mother's biggest lessons: when you don't know what to do, clean. You kept feeding the kids fruit: quartered grapes, tangerine segments. Each kid took a turn snuggling your mom in her bed. I knew it was my final goodbye when I shuffled our kids out the apartment door, into the hallway where we put our shoes back on. I only waved and said goodbye like always; your mother thanked me for coming, like always. I've always felt that your parents feared I might take you away and never bring you back home. They will never accept that it already happened a decade ago. I could not be at the funeral but my mother could; she texted me because she could not remember your mother's name. I called her back to tell her. I had never said it aloud: *Ewa: brings life.*

4. GERALD JAMES McILRAITH

8a. FATHER'S FULL NAME

Gerald James McIlraith

Everyone says Samson looks like my father. Big, round heads; small, flat noses. *Pig nose*, my mother used to say. We were living at my parents' house for the summer, all of us, me and my partner and our three kids, and my father snuck Samson upstairs every morning while getting dressed for work. Sat him in front of cartoons while putting on that dorky white underwear, a V-neck Hanes tee, slacks and a polo. A watch—nice, but not too nice. Practical. My father plopped down next to Samson, put on some socks and shoes. He thought I didn't know. But I saw him grab a handful of M&M's and Samson's tiny hand while I spread jam on three slices of toast. Who is my father behind a closed door? I don't think I've ever seen him get dressed. *Where were you? Your toast got cold*, I told Samson when he came back. His thin, straight body. A human Tootsie Pop. Sweet, easy to love. *My big guy*, my father always calls him.

The first person who referred to fatherhood like I might know what he was talking about looked nothing like my father. He had a warm face, wire-rimmed glasses, like a patient math teacher. I could see his delicate hands gingerly drawing a parabola on a whiteboard. He had a cheap-looking gold watch, one I imagined matched with a short-sleeved oxford, a thermos of soup for lunch, a spiral-bound grade book on a tidy teacher's desk. At the hotel breakfast I could not possibly have enough arms for all the things my three boys needed; I turned waffles, poured juice, shook cereal out of cheap plastic dispensers. The kids spent the morning lounging on the hotel couch, watching cartoons. This is their luxury: sugar cereals, a bedroom with a television. Their first hotel stay. The man walked toward us in the middle of my first sip of sad, watery coffee. I steeled myself. I knew what I looked like. And yet. *When my boys were around that age, I took them fishing. I'm so glad I have a picture of that day*, he said. We were both fathers, he thought. Two of the same thing. *Well, so long!* he said soon after, shuffling away, surprised by his own boldness, approaching a strange man at the hotel breakfast, a man who reminded him of fathering young boys.

Samson was lost at his preschool's family dance party. One minute I saw his blond head spinning in the middle of the dance floor; the next, he was nowhere. As I milled around, I heard his voice. *I'm looking for my dad!* In the corner of the room there he was, tugging on a teacher's shirtsleeve. *Who?* she asked him.

My dad, I'm looking for my dad, he said. She looked around the room; eventually we locked eyes. Would she have seen me if Samson didn't have my face? Did I look anything like a dad?

Not many kids were made by their dads, right? Samson asks every once in a while. I nod. *That makes me special, right?*

I never told Samson to say *Dad.*

When I was five a man approached me after basketball practice at the local gym to ask if I was related to Mary McIlraith. *She's my aunt,* I said. I told my father as we left St. Francis de Sales and began the four-block walk home. *He said I play like her,* I told him. *That's quite a compliment,* he said, tousling my hair, jostling a few hairs free from my ponytail. There were three of us kids then, but my brothers were at home. For a moment I felt like his son. So fast, so strong, someone had noticed. Thick calves, my first pair of ball shoes. My new basketball tucked under my arm, round and fresh and leathery. I could be a good son.

My mother says the rift between me and my father started my freshman year of high school. He would drive me to school on his way to work, dropping me in the circular drive in front of Immaculate Heart Academy. I'd sling my backpack on, pull up my knee socks, and tense my whole body, ready to head in. An all-girls school. After a few months there I told him I wanted to transfer. Catholic school was not working out; could I just go to the public school? He said no. *We don't quit things just because we don't like them*, he said. *We*. He'd said the same thing before, about clubs, sports teams. *You don't understand*, I said. It wasn't like that. I'd take the same classes. Geometry, Honors English, Honors French. The same, just in a different building. After his final no, we rarely talked in the car. We listened to *Imus in the Morning*, New York traffic reports. My mother says he's still hurt over it, fifteen years later. *All those quiet mornings in the car*, she says. *What was he supposed to think?*

When I was a few months old, Dad's brother, John, tried to convince him to throw me in the pool, like John did with his own daughter. John was convinced this was the only way to teach a baby to swim. But my father couldn't do it. When it was time for me to learn to ride a bike, he waited until John was in town, visiting their mother who lived upstairs in our Rockaway Beach two-family. My father found himself unable to release me and my sparkly pink Huffy down Beach 125th Street. Uncle John's big hand held the back of my white bicycle seat, steered me half-way down the block, let go, released me into the summer sun. The street was sandy; everything was sandy, but I held on. I don't know whether my father watched.

At the hotel breakfast, I'd been on testosterone for about three months. We were on our way west from Philadelphia, moving to Upper Michigan. Once we left Philadelphia, I was never mistaken for a mother again.

The one thing my father and I always had was *Law & Order*. I have a thing for procedurals. I get into a rhythm with them; they allow my mind to be still. The body, the case, the trial. The body the case the trial. The fiction of it all; the false New York that is the show's setting. Not the Rockaway Beach where I first longed to be his son. The courtroom felt like an extension of our living room. Jack McCoy's speeches. My father and I could never talk politics, religion. Only sports. There wasn't that much to say. Jack McCoy talked for us. We didn't need *How was school? How was work? What is it you do again? What is it you study again?* There was McCoy: *Your grief might seem a little more real had you not just admitted you cut off your wife's head.*

The nurse practitioner who prescribed my testosterone and I were friendly right away. I know how to do happy chill trans guy, and she and I both laughed at my jokes. We chatted CrossFit, my job, my third baby, who was only six months old. Samson was three, old enough to understand, his mother and I thought. My partner would tell him, *When Krys was born, the doctors guessed who he was based on how he looked, but they were wrong.* The NP looked at a checklist, back at me. *You're not, like, a super-angry person, are you?* she asked, pen ready, scanning my face. Looking. At me: Small, upbeat, dressed in nice slacks and a striped shirt. A pair of Chuck Taylors. A pasted-on smile. After *How's heart health in your family?* and *Are you thinking of having any more children yourself?* this was what she wanted to know, about my anger. I thought about the person I am, about all I've done, and I said, *Well, my wife says I get a little ragey merging onto the 76.* She laughed again. *We all do,* she said. *Your blood work looks great.* My prescription was ready for pickup.

I always thought my father wished I was a boy, but by the time I was it was too late.

Why does Uncle Sean like to fish? Samson asked me once at the beach. Sean never catches anything, just sits there staring at the water, holding a beer. *It's something he learned to do with your grandfather,* I told him. My son, whom I made, watching my brother fish. I never could. Year after year, they packed for the fishing trip in Montauk: their coolers and dusty old rods and goofy hats. *The guys' trip,* they said. My sister Kathleen sputtered in the doorway, called them sexist. She wanted to be with them. I wanted to be them. I tried to unlearn longing. It was wrong. I convinced myself: I never much cared for the smell of the ocean, the salt buildup on my face, the fishy wind. The roar of an engine, the sound of men and boys laughing. I said nothing, instead asking my mother if we could go out for a special dinner, her and my sisters and me. We bought ice cream. Ate it out of bowls, with sprinkles, crowded into her king-size bed, us girls.

There are years smeared over with anger: high school, college, my first few years of teaching. Those quiet high school years, starving myself, sitting silently in the car. Early in college, I led a hyper-disciplined life that helped me manage my anger and my anxiety. I was the first in the dining hall at 7:30 a.m., went to bed by 11:00 each night. I'd only talked to a handful of people about liking women, with mixed success. *This is just a little weird for me*, one friend said. Inexplicably, I went to the Catholic services on campus. Only a handful of us met, and I paid little attention to what the priest said. I wasn't there for the words, but rather for the stillness, for sitting quietly around other people, for handshakes from strangers, for a space where I felt like I came from somewhere, like I belonged to something.

Anna and I met playing rugby. Rugby was my new church. It was a realm in which people like me, people who had wanted touch and pain in their lives in an organized way, converged. Being queer on a college rugby team was a nonevent. Our teammates chided, then celebrated us. For a moment, when our relationship became serious, I thought she was the solution to my anger. A calmness came over me, but then there was the realization that I was the same person in a relationship as I was outside it. She could not have only the life I had started to make after leaving home. We broke up, got back together, because when we fought, no matter how trivially, I'd become so angry, angry beyond reason, and in a few hours we'd say we were done trying. I could not set aside an enraged life because I loved someone.

Once, years before Anna and I had children, one of our neighbors called the police on me. After the policeman left our apartment she told me, *I don't want this to be my life.* I was just out of college. I had screamed at her and kicked the bedroom door. Cracked it. Another fight about nothing that became about what an angry person I was. Someone, a neighbor, must have thought she was in danger. We lived on the fourth floor in a one-bedroom apartment overrun by mice. We hated our jobs. Not only can I not remember what this fight was about, I can't remember a single fight we had in those years. The officer looked at me, then at her, then at me, and then he left. After the police came to our apartment I saw a therapist who worked a few blocks from my job. After school, I'd park on Germantown Avenue, walk down the cobblestoned street to her tiny office, sink into the couch she had. When I get mad, I explode, I told her. I sat in her attic office listening to the hum of blood boiling, biting down on the insides of my cheeks. Seething.

Samson kicked the refrigerator when I told him *Yes, you have to nap today.* The way he clenched his fists at his sides, kicked over a kitchen chair, and then said he was sorry. The way he looked at his foot after, the reddened big toe, the shock at what he had done. I've felt this all before.

My father was not the kind of dad I am. Weeknights he often came home late, ate dinner only with my mother. He worked more hours than I ever have, ever will. On the weekends he did projects, cleaned the garage, napped in his cotton shorts and long socks. We'd play catch on the lawn. I was always the best at sports; he wanted more for my brothers, but none of them have the rage it takes to be great. In the evenings all eight of us crowded along the dinner table, ate even our most loathed foods. No was not an option. He referred to the seat next to his as *striking distance*. My brothers sat there, especially Sean and Ryan; we girls had it easier. I was in the corner, choking down chalky lima beans.

When we had Sean, Anna went back to working nights just a few weeks after. Sean was so small, and looked so much like her, and cried so much. In the afternoon I'd bounce on a yoga ball with him, rewatching the entire first season of *Law & Order*. At night I sat in the chair in the nursery feeding him bottles of her breast milk, staring at the neon lights of the bar across the street. Some nights he cried every hour. My hands were rough, strong, conditioned to boxing, to gripping up Brazilian Jiu-Jitsu partners, to doing pull-ups and to flipping tires. Anything to keep them busy. I'd pick the baby up from his crib, half-asleep, tired of the wailing, feeling every baby rib between my fingers, so angry at him, irrationally, unbelievably angry, scared of myself. He was so light, so small. My boy.

I can never turn off season 1, episode 9, "Indifference," the story of a respectable-looking psychotherapist who batters his wife so severely she in turn abuses their children. Compared to the garden-variety dysfunction I grew up with, the scenes of terror and despair Detectives Logan and Greevey uncover in the home of Dr. and Mrs. Lowenstein revealed to me that everything in my home was fine, that I should be happy, that I was lucky that my parents were just occasionally a little rough. But when asked what should happen to the Lowensteins, whose toddler dies, Assistant District Attorney Ben Stone says, *Put 'em in a dungeon, put 'em on a wheel, and annihilate 'em. Mmm*, the District Attorney says, nodding knowingly.

I ate two pieces of pie in the car while Anna drove on the highway. We were pretty sure I was in labor. Samson didn't move much; he was calm under the pressure. It was a simple Pioneer Woman pie: Cool Whip, cream cheese, peanut butter, powdered sugar, a marshmallowy peanut butter pillow in Oreo crust. I always had it in the fridge the summer I was pregnant. I started baking in high school, to have something I could do right. A finished product. Anna says there is nothing feminine about it, my drive to perfect and provide. Visiting my parents on my sister's birthday, I asked Samson to help me frost the cake, plopped him on a stool. *I see you like to help your . . .* my father trailed off. He doesn't say *father*; he doesn't say *he*; he says nothing.

Samson was our second, so they let us skip the video about shaken baby syndrome and sign a waiver. My legs were still shaking from the adrenaline of birth. I was so happy to have him on the outside. I lay in bed at the birth center. Wrote my name next to *Mother* on his birth certificate. The only appropriate space. I never told the midwife I'd googled it many times before, this way of being so angry you hurt your own child, terrified of my middle-of-the-night anger at his older brother, at how I'd shouted, *STOP CRYING*. At how I'd sat on the iron staircase outside our house, my hands trembling, in the brisk Philadelphia winter night, terrified by how close I'd come to shaking him. His mother worked so many long nights; he wanted her. He wanted his mom. I wasn't a mom, wasn't a dad. Taking long naps with Sean changed me, changed us. I became gentler, less afraid of myself. I wrapped my pregnant, bloated body around his. Held him. Slept. Waited for Samson.

My father liked Ben Stone, but I preferred Jack McCoy. He was amused by this, by my tolerance for Jack's obviously problematic relationships with his women colleagues. On the other hand, I could never get over how many episodes we watched together in which McCoy delivered impassioned speeches against people just like my father—wealthy people, people who will intimidate to get what they want. Kill, even. Jack McCoy believed the world was a just place, where if you killed someone, no matter who you were, no matter why you did it, the full weight of the state should come at you. The world of *Law & Order* is not the real world, where poor folks always get caught, even if they didn't do it, and rarely see a trial. We never talked about that. *What do you think is going to happen?* my father would ask, breaking the silence. *I don't know; this is a tough one,* I'd say back. We'd reach into the same bag of sunflower seeds, plop our shells onto a paper plate. I look at Jack McCoy and see my father's face.

When I was growing up my mother always complained that my father never told any stories about his childhood. *It's like he remembers nothing,* she'd say.

When my brothers cried, he would mimic them. When my sisters cried, my mother would comfort them. I only cried alone, and rarely. I was the oldest, the leader of the six of us, and yet separated, as if watching them through a fogged shower door, wanting to fit into either camp, wanting them to know how to relate to me, wanting to feel like I was doing right. My hands pressed up against the fog, these angry hands.

Samson keeps punching me in the head, my oldest son says, often. Samson is slight, waifish even, still swat-able. Their mother wants to know what we should do about this, about the constant fighting. Growing up, it was the same. *Mom, Sean and Ryan are fighting in the garage,* I would tell my mother, coming in from outside even though we were supposed to stay out until dinner. *So let them kill each other,* she said. *And don't ever wear your Rollerblades in my house again.*

The first time I thought of myself as a dad I was in the checkout at Super One. It was four days before Thanksgiving and I was spending our last money on food so that my in-laws wouldn't know how broke we were. Samson wore a poufy purple princess dress over his regular clothes; it was slightly too long, holding us all up as he tripped down the aisle, wet boots squeaking on the linoleum. ZZ was strapped to my back in a baby carrier and Sean trailed behind us. Every time the checkout woman scanned a potato or a can I creeped a glance at the screen to make sure we could afford it. *You know, I'ma write about you on Facebook when I get home,* she said as I handed a pacifier over my shoulder. She was a woman in her thirties, probably a handful of years older than I was. *The Awesome Dad,* she mused. I told her, *Thank you. That's very nice of you to say.* I always go to the store; Anna can't do it without a list. *The Awesome Dad.*

My father didn't have a father for much of his childhood; my grandfather was an alcoholic, left when my grandmother was pregnant with her seventh child. No one talked much about him. His name was John. Jack McCoy, too, lives with the legacy of violence and drunkenness and Irishness; that's one of the reasons I can't look away from *Law & Order. My old man,* Jack always says, after work, after the trial, at the bar, when he's about to tell a story. He has bushy eyebrows and a rare, disarming laugh, like my father.

According to the CDC, most victims of shaken baby syndrome are boys. Most perpetrators are men—biological fathers, stepfathers, and mothers' boyfriends are responsible for the majority of cases, followed by mothers, they note. Once, I gripped Sean by his denim shirt and it ripped. He just wouldn't listen. When I unclenched my fists they were full of torn collar. I turned them over; these white-knuckled things could not be a mother's hands. Of 167 mass shootings committed between 1966 and 2019, 98 percent of the 171 perpetrators were men. Adam Lanza killed twenty children at age twenty; I am much older, but no one knows that. I look like a kid. Testosterone made me a kid. My soft blond mustache, soft, short body, soft smile. Sneakers and joggers. Once, Anna took me to a shooting range in South Philly, a warehouse by the Delaware River. I had thought it would be a good idea, a fun date, but the gun's textured butt and sleek trigger terrified me. I had all this power, all this anger. Next to me two men shot a giant gold-plated handgun. They laughed, giggled almost, like little boys. Each shot made me jump. I held the gun and tried to keep my eyes open while I squeezed the trigger. Angry people like me should not be trusted with guns. Couldn't anyone see that? *Do either of you ladies want to buy a gun?* The man at the register looked at me and Anna, knew we'd say no. Just a couple of lesbians, testing it out.

Samson and my wife cuddle at nap time most days, her long limbs encircling his tiny ones. She works till dawn and for her, Samson's nap time is the middle of the night. One day I decided to lie down in his empty bed with a book; uncovering the blanket I found a sword. And another sword. And an ax. These plastic weapons. Becoming a dad, accepting that's what I was, made me gentler, calmer. I think about what I am doing, who people see when they see me. They feel the fear I feel when I am alone in a roomful of men, when a large man approaches me to ask the time or to offer a warm comment about my children. I think men are coming for me. There is something inside us that scares me. Samson pretends to be a ninja. He pretends to be a soldier. He flips; he is so careless with his body. He and his brothers sword-fight, whine for toy guns. Anna and I made these men. Sometimes I have to pull them apart, like animals, by the scruffs of their shirts.

Men are more likely to assault. To murder and be murdered. When I think of my brother Michael I think of the sick crunch of my fist against his face. We were young, thirteen and eleven, maybe. Puberty: my worst time. That was when it felt final: I was never going to be the person I was meant to be. Michael was mad at me and hit me from behind; I turned and swung. There was more give to a face than I expected. My ears rang. *You broke my nose!* he screamed. Blood everywhere. I was happy. A hot blanket of calm came over me. I watched him stumble backward, call for my mother.

She and I would scream and fight. There were many *I hate you*s, drawers and doors slammed. She threw a glass of milk at me across the dinner table, pulled my hair, stomped on and broke one of my toes. She took off her shoe, tossed it at me in the back seat of the car. We called each other bitch more than once. But I've never been afraid of her, not one moment in my life. My mother got *frustrated*, even *pissed*, but she did not get *mad*. Everyone says I write about her with a warmth. *A surprising warmth*, Anna says. In my writing she is always in the kitchen, always by the window washing dishes, folding hot laundry at the counter, zippers burning her hands. My professor asks where my father is, in my writing. I say *I don't know. We're not estranged*, I say. *We don't not talk. We just don't talk. Am I making sense?*

Geometry 1 was a struggle. It was a hard year, my freshman year, realizing I had to be a girl, in a girls' school, realizing I had to separate from my father, that he would never understand. Like Samson, I was never really one for numbers. My teacher talked a lot about building sandboxes; we were fourteen-year-old girls. He'd draw them on the board, these rectangles with numbers hanging by their sides. The teacher had big glasses, nice eyes. He smelled good, like wood and the ocean. I liked to go to his room during lunch even though I was a poor student. He always looked happy to see me. If I finished a homework assignment behind his back while he walked around the room to check, I felt bad. I didn't like hiding. I wanted him to like me.

When I was in the third grade, I went to the archdiocesan math bee. My mother and I drove behind Sister Barbara in our wood-paneled van. My father was already drilling me at Samson's age—five—already quizzing me on arithmetic, showing me flash cards. *Spell your name backwards,* he'd say. There was no option but to do it right. I never thought about fatherhood when Anna was pregnant, or when Samson was growing inside me. I knew I wasn't a mother. How to fit? I always said *parent.*

Sometimes I step to them and they step back. They are so little, just learning how to be. Sometimes I grab them a little too hard, forcefully put them into their beds when I've had enough. I am often not the person I want to be. I stopped crying when I started taking testosterone. It's been years. I feel my father inside me, through the tips of my rough hands. I chose to accept becoming a dad. I am glad they are not babies anymore because now they cannot ever be shaken babies. I have never hit them but sometimes they think I am about to. Everyone thinks I am a kind, gentle dad. I try to be. But they are afraid of me, in a way they are not afraid of their mother. I sat and watched Anna sweep up the glass, said nothing when she said, *Better an oven than . . .* and trailed off. *The oven is broken,* they pointed out the next morning at breakfast. I didn't tell them I'd kicked the door, shattered the glass, while they slept.

Detective Lennie Briscoe doesn't realize all that he's done wrong with his daughter, Cathy, until she's murdered by her drug-dealing ex. As the cast turned over and over, my father and I kept watching. Twenty seasons; we've both seen them all. *I can't believe you can watch this again,* my mother said, huffing and leaving the dark living room.

We love this one, my father said, as the opening scene unfolded, with yet another homeless man stumbling over a discarded corpse.

In a hotel room in central Pennsylvania my father told us to stop fighting—stop fighting so he could spend time with our mother. I know that feeling all too well now that I have my own kids. We had adjoining rooms, our parents in one and the kids in the other. But we didn't stop. We could never stop fighting. It was our language. We were excited because we would start the day early in the morning at Hersheypark. We fought over a park map, arguing about which roller coaster to ride first. We yelled, pushed. He came through the door for me; I was the oldest; I was in charge. He caught me by the leg as I was trying to crawl into the bathroom cabinet to hide. I don't remember what happened next. It doesn't matter. What matters is the scrambling, looking for somewhere to hide, knowing the anger was coming for me.

My brothers and I started a roller hockey league in our neighborhood. There were three teams. My brother Ryan picked all his friends, hugged everyone at the end of a game. He has always been like that; I want my sons to be like that. My brother Sean and I were brutal. The neighborhood dads took turns refereeing but my father always had to step in when our teams played each other. The gloves came off multiple times every game; everyone watched as we swung wildly, tackling each other on skates. My mother stood in our street holding jugs of lemonade, yelling:

Gerry, do something. Our fighting was always about nothing. It was the only way we knew how to be.

I love my brothers, but I am mad they got to be boys. I dream about going back, about the day when we were in the backyard playing Wiffle Ball. Someone made fun of Sean for getting beat by a girl. Me. He laughed. For years, I've dreamed about going back and throttling him like a brother would have done. A slug in front of all his friends. When my father would pick them up by their collars, hold them up against the wall, when he was mad, I would think, *Why not me?* I always had it easier, and yet. I wanted my kids to be boys, too. All three of them. I thought it'd be easier, but now I'm not so sure. There is something to fight, and it is not coming for us; it is in us.

Anna wants to know what I dream about when dreams wake me up and won't let me go back down and I lie to her, tell her that I died in my dream. Samson, you should know that sometimes it is best not to say everything to your mother. But you: This you need to know. In my dreams my father kills me. I hear it coming, someone breaking into the house: the lock unclicking so quietly that it might not be happening, the knob turning; by the time I sit up I am gone. A single shot. Your grandfather's fear of guns loomed large in my childhood; we could never have them as toys. Even finger guns were suspect; *We don't play like that*, he always said. *Guns are not fun.* He wanted to protect us, in his way. My mother said that he saw a friend blow his hand up with a firework as a child and never recovered; it was my only indication that he had any weakness inside him. He never told us the story himself.

My mother also said once that if he had a gun, he'd shoot her over some dumb argument; she was kidding, and I never saw him raise a finger to her, but a temper like ours comes back to get you in your dreams. As teenagers your uncles hid paintball guns in their underwear drawers, covered their welts at the dinner table. When we fought we fought hard, in the basement or garage, until we were heaving and a mess of bruises. Nobody ever told us when you love someone you aren't supposed to hurt them. I don't want you to think your grandfather wants me dead; that would be too simple. Once when I was elbowed straight in the face at a basketball game he ran onto the court, a reflex. Even with the ref standing behind him screaming to get off the court he kept running toward me, his face open and caring.

I didn't know I'd have to be a dad.

At the gym I stand in the squat rack and watch groups of boys bounce basketballs and I think of him then, before we had nothing to talk about, the way we could each remember every play from every game we'd ever played together. When I missed a buzzer shot at thirteen he laid his hand on my lap in the car as I cried. He has not touched me in years. I never cry anymore. Samson, when you wake up at night you say, *I'm sorry but I had a bad dream.* I ask, *Why are you sorry?* You say, again, *I'm sorry.*

Jack McCoy speaks occasionally about his daughter, Rebecca, but the viewers never catch a glimpse of her. Is Rebecca real, or does she just represent McCoy's hope for a daughter, hope for fatherhood?

5. SEX: FEMALE

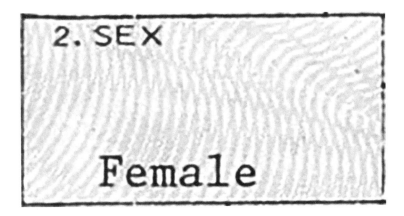

I look for evidence that what happened on that day, in that hospital in Manhattan, was wrong somehow. I was wronged. We were wronged. But really it is as simple as it is on paper. The paper says what happened. My parents were twenty-seven and twenty-eight. Newly married.

In all the pictures of childhood I am happy, smiling impossible smiles. Everyone who flirts with me wants to know the story of my name. There's no story, I say. It's just Krys. All traces of the little girl born in Manhattan are gone. I am just a boy with a strange name.

The pictures of me and Samson are the same as this picture of me and my father at the rocking horse. I have the same open mouth, the same round head, same muscled arms, same blond hair all over my face. His story follows in my wake. Smile wide, Samson. Say cheese.

Check my ID. Ask to see it. Ask to see it because sixteen-year-old white boys are always coming in this shop trying to buy beer and you've had it. Ask to see it because I must be the butchest woman you've ever seen. It's from Pennsylvania. The Keystone State. Keystone: wedge-shaped piece at the summit of an arch. Take it from my small, soft hands. Look at it. Turn it over and look at it some more. Look at it next to the credit card. Those names: those are women's names. They have to be. Ask me where I live. The city. The street. But it doesn't sound how it looks—*Could you spell that for me?* I spell it correctly. Ask the zip code, my birth date, a date thirty years ago, but that can't be right. I speak with the wrong voice: too strong, too deep. I am buying two beers: one for me and one for my wife. They stand together on the glass counter, their labels sweating on each other. Anna said she had a bad day today, so here I am with a single stout and a single IPA and a Snickers bar. She's sitting at home in her scrubs, waiting, but you don't know that. You only know the giant binder of fifty states and their IDs. Find Pennsylvania: after Oregon, before Rhode

Island. Look me right in my face and ask me to spell my street name again. Sepviva. The Norris family, whose wealth came from rum and sugar plantations in Jamaica, named their plantation Sepviva in the eighteenth century. They freed their last slave in the 1740s; they were Quakers, peaceful people, they said, and yet. Keystone: something on which other things depend. Sepviva Street is not beautiful; it is just a street in Philadelphia with row houses smashed together, but it's my street. A street a thousand miles from this small Michigan town. Look at the picture again: it's this same face three years ago. *If you were born in 1987, why are you wearing a Class of 2011 sweatshirt?* I look down at my hoodie. *I was a high school teacher in 2011*, I say, and think, But don't say that the class of 2011 is well over drinking age now and you just want me to admit I'm a liar. Confusing people, people like me; we must be lying about something. Keystone: a species on which other species in an ecosystem largely depend, so much so that, if removed, the entire ecosystem would collapse. Tilt my card, looking for who knows what. The face on the card: a sadder, gentler face. Pause a long long time. *Sorry*, you say, *lots of people try to jerk me around in here.* But it is not a real sorry; people like me aren't owed real apologies. We do this to ourselves. Take my money. Give me my two beers and my candy. Watch me walk out into the crisp evening.

Maybe it is not an accident that I lose it again and again, this record, the certificate of my birth. My father will only give me his extra copy when I am nearly thirty. I have three children. A house. A master's degree. I coordinate special education services for 140 elementary school children. *I don't trust you not to lose it,* he says. As if it is something real, something precious, something to be believed: this record of how I began in a hospital room in Manhattan.

CERTIFICATE OF BIRTH   156-87 - 1 1 7 8 0 8
                        Birth No.
DATE FILED
   87 JUL 1   P 2: 40

Last Name

McIlraith

It's usually not the one wearing the suit changing their name, is all I'm saying, my father said. It's the only thing I remember him saying at my wedding.

When people back home ask what winters in Marquette are like you cut me off before I can say cold or endless. You say, *It's just so beautiful. It's nothing like city winter.* We are used to heavy gray slush, sliding through unplowed streets, everyone shuffling down the sidewalk with hands in their pockets, slipping on thick ice in wet sneakers. That feeling, that fear, heart pounding, that you're about to eat shit in front of the neighborhood. I remember that winter you and I refused to wear anything other than old Chuck Taylors with holes in the soles. My feet were always numb. When they called snow days we'd just hide inside all day eating through our pantry. Spaghetti with garlic and olive oil. Little tins of almonds. Peanut butter and honey sandwiches sitting on our old brown couch. Even jury duty was canceled.

A thousand miles away nothing could be as quiet as a bright white blizzard night. You're at work and the snow has stopped for now. I should shovel. I pull on the shiny purple snowsuit my mother sent from New Jersey when we moved here, the one she wore in the nineties. I look fabulous. In Marquette I have learned that, when properly dressed like this, one can really work up a sweat no matter the temperature, really get warm inside, and I work my way along our car, down our sidewalk, shoveling inches and inches of powder into neat little piles when I hear the footsteps behind me. It is our neighbor, a small, wiry, angry man in sweatpants and a T-shirt. It's freezing. *Listen, faggot bitch*, he says. It is so dark, so quiet, so beautiful. My children are asleep inside. My neighbor and I are truly alone. *Don't shovel any snow onto my property.*

Seconds pass. I feel my heart pounding. With each pump it moves more blood through my body and I am still alive. In one day, my blood moves the equivalent of four trips from coast to coast of the United States. Blood rushes through me all day. It would take about two hours at this rate to make it home. Why do I only feel my heart when I am scared? In this town the sidewalks are clean, stamped with reminders not to spit. I have never seen a needle or a dead rat or a dirty diaper or a piece of torn hair anywhere, and yet here I am. Since I started testosterone I cannot scream anymore; my vocal cords are so scarred I can barely even be stern when my kids won't put on their socks. *No wonder your kids don't listen to you; have you heard yourself yell?* one of my siblings said to me once. I can't remember which one and I am going to die here, shoveling in the starry night in this beautiful quiet town in the Midwest, making perfect plush piles of snow.

I want our neighbor to go inside because I have just started the life I want, one in which I cannot yell and in which I am suddenly a faggot. I've never been called that before. Lezzie, lesbo, dyke, queerbo, even, I've been called all of those and more. But I am finally a faggot and I step back, walk back, afraid. I have wanted to be seen as a man my whole life. I want you to come home from your work, in the emergency room, saving the sick and injured people of Upper Michigan. Do strong men scramble backward like this, thinking of our three little boys in bed, how quiet it is, how no sound will even come out if this man continues forward. My neighbor steps toward me. His name is Brian and I imagine he has hated many people before he met me. I am not special. I am just here, living next door to him in a crappy little apartment we keep talking about leaving. There is nothing special about my heart. My heart, such a beautiful and temporary thing. Trying to keep me alive, second by second, liter by liter. If they take me to your hospital, if I don't make it, I will be just as dead as anyone else.

We could talk about how easy television chefs make it look to strip thyme off the stems. It never comes off like that, in a neat pile, does it? I'm sure we can agree that laundry pods are a useless invention, that the world still needs magazines, that nobody's feet look sexy in Birkenstocks. I'd like to discuss how the train tracks in this small town are not just for show; you used to be able to get somewhere from here. It should be easy, this kind of talking about nothing, but it is not so easy for me to meet anybody anymore. I'm afraid now. I see you trying to look through my clothes and I don't mean in a good way. You and I are the kinds of people who should make small talk at the grocery store or the library, should nod when we pass each other with our strollers. But you will try to look through me, try to learn my insides, not whether my heart has four chambers or whether my capillaries can move the blood between arterioles and venules. They can. Italian biologist Marcello Malpighi first observed the capillary system, in a frog's lung. He discovered several structural elements of kidneys; that blood clots differently in different areas of the heart; that invertebrates do not rely on their lungs to breathe. Let's talk about him when we cross paths in Target, buying our children mittens because first snow came early this year; winter always seems to be coming in Michigan and yet parents never seem to be ready for it. Target is the same everywhere and I could be anybody in Target. In the 1600s, when Malpighi worked, it was easy to trailblaze, to conquer and map the human body. A man and a microscope, a yearning to know what is inside. You, too, want to know. You try to undress me but you can't. You get to have clothes that are just clothes. A shirt with a crumpled collar. A T-shirt from your high school graduation. But mine are an elaborate covering: covering binders, covering curves, covering the poor posture of a lifetime of hiding. Shielding me from eyes that wander during small talk. You probably wish you were my neighbor. He has seen me naked dozens of times because I am not as careful as you think someone like me ought to be. One evening after he got into an argument with my wife over pushing his gigantic lawn mower too close to our toddlers, he stood in his window watching us eat dinner. He was lit from behind like a Halloween decoration. He crossed his arms and watched me serve stew into five bowls and I could just see that he knew, knew everything underneath my sweats and my T-shirt. It is possible that Malpighi was not the first person to see red blood cells, that he was the second. But he saw a lot of things first. Is knowing what's inside when it is already known to somebody else the same? The fluid, the rush, the noise of the body: dilation, contraction, a system working perfectly, moving as if by design, something worth talking about.

Our new apartment is on the ground floor of an old house. The man who lives upstairs with his girlfriend is named Sammy. As winter slowly fades away Sammy spends more and more afternoons lying out on the roof on a towel, sunbathing. He gets there by climbing out his bedroom window. He's lithe and has long blond hair pulled back into a ponytail. He's in his early twenties, I think. He gardens shirtless in the sun. The boys decapitate dandelions, ride their scooters around the block, write BUTT and POOP on the driveway in sidewalk chalk, and Sammy pleasantly ignores them. This man's resemblance to my projection of how Samson will look in twenty years is uncanny. Those muscles, that goofy smile, that same ponytail. All that yard work. It endears me to him, though we've never spoken more than a few words to each other. He and his girlfriend come and go at regular hours; we can hear their door close, their feet on the steps behind our kitchen. They drive a clean gold Jeep. They play soft music. I never hope that Sammy is home, or that he's not home. Sometimes I forget to lock the front door for hours, days even.

We are a five-minute walk from our old apartment; I heard the old neighbor, the scary neighbor, got evicted from his place for harassing somebody else after I moved out. Once, his landlord came to my house to make excuses for not evicting Brian after the third time I called the police on him. He stood in the doorway, hat in his hand. *He's never actually hurt anyone, you know?*

the landlord said, avoiding looking at me. After he left, I looked myself over, wondering if this landlord thought I deserved to be harassed, or asked for it, looking the way I do, with my tight pants and my little black earring and my voice, gay as it is.

Whenever I walk down our old block I am terrified I will see him, though he hasn't lived there in months. It is a nice town, quiet, with gardens in front of nearly every house. Nothing chained down like where we used to live, in Philadelphia, on a street lined with shackled benches and chairs and flowerpots. DO NOT SPIT ON THE SIDEWALK this Marquette sidewalk calls out to me. I heard the neighbor got a job butchering at the local grocery store and I hold my breath each time I step up to the counter. A few weeks ago the kids and I were scootering down Third Street and I saw him, the scary neighbor, step out of his forest-green pickup outside the shoe-repair shop. *Slow down*, I hissed at the boys. *Let's turn here.* They wanted to know why. *I just saw somebody I don't want to talk to*, I said. We turned. In May if it is warm enough to scooter around town everyone is outside, and I found myself looking around the side street for someone to help, if he'd seen me. What kind of person would help somebody like me?

When we met you told me some of your friends called you Anna Worst-Case-Scenario Belc, and that is not me, yet whenever I think of Brian I think of the scissors you carry in the breast pocket of your scrubs to cut maimed people's clothes off when they get to the hospital. In the weeks before we moved away from him if I walked home after dark, from writing in a coffee shop or at a bar,

I would open up my phone and dial 911, my finger hovering over the call button as I passed his house. What was the anger about, how would he hurt me if he could? Not knowing was the worst part. All my life people have hated the way I look so much, and it used to be because I was a woman who looked the wrong way, but what it is now? I've imagined Brian hunting me, hurting me so many ways. You tell me that you did not realize how anxious you were about him, about my stalker, until we moved. I would peer between our shades multiple times a day, at all hours of the day, and somehow he was usually standing there waiting for me to look. Our new block is quieter and he is not here.

Still, some nights I stand in our apartment's entryway holding a basket of laundry wondering whether to find a binder, or at least a sports bra. We share laundry with Sammy and his girlfriend in the basement. It's late when I do laundry, ten, eleven at night, and you are at work. There is no reason for Sammy to know anything about me, and in the doorway I am stuck considering whether I should learn from previous neighbors to be more stealth. It is often in moments like this that I remember I am trans. In our last apartment, we learned too late to put up curtains. Being a good trans neighbor seems to mean nobody knowing I am trans at all. Sometimes you must be reminded to warn me if a friend is coming over to the house so I can find my binder. One of your friends from work points to our wooden *Happy Wife, Happy Life* sign. *Why do you have that?* she asks. She does not take us to be people whose relationship is structured by traditional gender roles. *Oh,* you say. *It used to be funny.* And now you and I both agree that it's funny still. A gift from someone attending what she believed to be a lesbian wedding. But there is no simple way to explain why without explaining everything. Our plan is to move back to Philadelphia in a few months. Our neighbors there have not seen me in three years. You look exactly the same, and then there is me. There may not be a place where things are truly not weird with the neighbors. The other night soon after you left for work Sammy showed up with two pizzas Domino's had brought to his door by mistake. His knock was surprisingly firm; I am afraid that every knock at the door will be Brian. But it wasn't; it was the kind man who lives upstairs and wants to give our kids his pizza. The kids had just eaten, and so I said *No, thank you,* my arms held tight across my chest, not because I wanted to be hostile, not because I wasn't thankful, but because I was wearing a tank top with nothing underneath.

A new doctor's intake form has a line for *Name* and a line for *Previous Name.* And yet when the nurse steps out into the waiting room looking for me she yells:

Krystyn?

I was my grandmother's first grandchild. My mother was her only daughter. We share many cells, she and I. I can only imagine how happy she was when the doctor grabbed me from between her legs and said

It's

a

NORTHERN MICHIGAN UNIVERSITY

ADA B. VIELMETTI HEALTH CENTER
1401 Presque Isle Avenue
Marquette, MI 49855-5301
906-227-2355 | 906-227-2332
www.nmu.edu/HealthCenter

Re: Krystyn Marie Belc

May 3. 2017

a/k/a : Krys Malcolm Belc

DOB: 6/27/1987

I declare under penalty of perjury under the laws of the United States that the foregoing is true and correct.

I have been seeing and treating the above-named person as a patient, and we have an established physician/patient relationship.

He is in the process of gender change, from female to male, and has been taking clinically appropriate hormonal therapy, which has been ordered and closely monitored by me, in accordance with recognized and published medical standards. He is very well informed and compliant with therapy.

He would like to officially change his gender designation on official documents from female (Krystyn Marie Belc) to male (Krys Malcolm Belc). I am in support of this request as he continues the necessary hormonal therapy with excellent results. Please let me know if any further information is needed or if I can assist you or him in any way. Thank you.

███████████ MD (Board Certified Family Medicine)

███████████

███████████

Michigan License number: ███████████

FIRST JUDICIAL DISTRICT OF PENNSYLVANIA
COURT OF COMMON PLEAS OF PHILADELPHIA COUNTY
TRIAL DIVISION—CIVIL

IN RE: Krystyn Marie Belc :
(a/k/a Krys Malcolm Belc) : January TERM, 2017
    :
   Name change : No. 2386

DECREE FOR CHANGE OF NAME

AND NOW, to wit this ~~28~~ day of _APRIL_ 2017, upon hearing of the within Petition and upon motion of ▃▃▃▃▃▃ Esquire, attorney for Petitioner, and upon satisfaction of publication requirement together with proof that there are no judgments or decrees of record or any other matter of like effect against the petitioner, and it appearing that there is no legal objection to the granting of the prayer of the petition,

IT IS ORDERED AND DECREED that the legal name of Krystyn Marie Belc be and hereby is changed to Krys Malcolm Belc.

BY THE COURT:

Abbe F. FE

J.

CERTIFIED FROM THE RECORD OF **MAY 0 9 2017**
ERIC FEDER
DIRECTOR, OFFICE OF JUDICIAL RECORDS
PHILADELPHIA COUNTY
BY _Theresa M Taylor_

In Re: Krystyn Marie Belc-ORDER

17010238600011

DOCKETED
MAY 0 2 2017
N. SWEENEY
JUDICIAL RECORDS

COPIES SENT PURSUANT TO Pa.R.C.P. 236(b) P. DIVON 05/03/2017

Breasts: A History

My sports bras shred in the dryer, from overuse. I wear them layered over each other until I feel squeezed enough, like a lemon that's given up most of its juice. *I don't understand what you even do to these things,* my mother says, peering through the holes.

Breast: *A person's chest, especially when regarded as the seat of the emotions.*

At fifth-grade lunch, boys shout out the number on Sydney's shirt that appears over her enormous breasts: *1892* for Abercrombie & Fitch, *1969* for Gap. She is the first girl in our class to have boobs. In her book *Master Breasts,* Francine Prose writes that breasts are *a body part that we didn't start out with ... whole new organs, two of them, tricky to hide or eradicate, attached for all the world to see ... twin messengers announcing our lack of control, announcing that Nature has plans for us about which we were not consulted.* I read Judy Blume's *Are You There God? It's Me, Margaret* like everyone else, stuffing it in my backpack between chapters so my mom won't see, won't ask if I have any questions. I read about the impending doom, dreading them. I feel my chest to make sure they haven't come yet. I want to stay flat.

I'd be happy to show it to you, but I also have to tell you it doesn't work, Blume says in a video interview over forty years after she published the book. She pulls back a vest to reveal breasts even smaller than mine. She is demonstrating the famous exercise—*I must, I must, I must increase my bust*. It looks sort of like the chicken dance. She laughs: a bare, open thing. *Not only doesn't it work, she says, but know what? You find out it doesn't matter.*

Nora Ephron disagrees. In "A Few Words About Breasts," she writes angrily about her small chest: *What can I tell you? If I had had them, I would have been a completely different person.*

My second sister Kelsey has huge boobs. *Like my mother*, my own mother says. *You could see hers before the rest of her turned the corner.* In Paula Vogel's 1997 play *How I Learned to Drive*, the lecherous grandfather makes the same tired joke: *She'd better stop being so sensitive. 'Cause*

five minutes before Li'l Bit turns the corner her tits turn first.
Asking why his granddaughter wants to go to college, he
says: *What does she need a college degree for? She's got all the
credentials she needs on her chest.*

My sister Kathleen and I are tiny; my mother calls us
unlucky, how she sees herself.

It fascinates me how differently we view these body parts.
As mine grow, toward the end of middle school, I give
them stern looks in the bathroom mirror, the equivalent
of a talking-to. *That's quite enough,* my eyes tell them. My
parents make me and my siblings leave the room when
anything we're watching has a sex scene. Leaving the
room causes more of a scene than the scene itself; by the
time my brothers and sisters and I have left, the clip is
ending. From the other room we hear my father say, *That
was barely anything.* From my mother, *You want our kids to
see those huge, fake things?*

*Everything from cutting one's nails to cutting off one's leg
falls somewhere on a spectrum of moral or ethical judgment.*
—Susan Stryker

The first time I really try to rid myself of them I am
fifteen. At the clinic intake, I am asked to step on a
scale. My feet are cold; everything is cold. They make

me take off my clothes. I have four dollars in quarters in my pockets. I am wearing an underwire bra. Every piece of material will make me seem more okay, heavier. The criteria state: *Disturbance in the way in which one's body weight or shape is experienced, undue influence of body weight or shape on self-evaluation, or denial of the seriousness of the current low body weight.* I weigh 98.5 pounds. They ask if I have a goal weight. *I just want to disappear,* I say.

At fifteen, Janet Mock started taking Premarin, estrogen pills made from pregnant horses' urine. Her transgender friend gives them to her. *This underground railroad of resources guided me during the years of uncertainty,* she writes. But I am completely alone. I do not know at fifteen that what I feel is a thing that many other people feel.

I go to an all-girls Catholic high school. My high school religion teacher tells us again and again that people like me are called to what she terms *the single life.* When she gets cancer, they take her left breast; she comes back to school looking more or less the same, except for one day, when I see it: the fearsome lopsidedness, how huge the right one looks with the left completely gone. This is the first time I really realize that breasts do not have to be forever. I feel an electricity, the hum of possibility in this teacher's misery. A classmate hangs around after class to point toward our teacher's off-balanced chest, to tell her: *I'm sorry if this is inappropriate, but I needed to let you know that you forgot something.*

Breast: *The part of a garment that covers the chest, i.e., breast pocket.*

About losing her breasts to cancer, Judy Blume writes: *My dense, small breasts aged well. They stayed perky while other body parts sagged. I'd become quite fond of them.* But immediately after that, she admits it was easy to decide to excise them, once they became infected. It's a horrible feeling, wishing mine were, sometimes. Infected. When I move away to attend college my mother calls me and says she's had a dream. *You became a man, she says. You even cut off your boobs,* she says. I laugh. *How odd,* I say. *How's everyone?* I ask. She begins going through her other five kids, one by one, recounting their recent missteps, the ones that did not take place only in a dream.

Somehow, I continue to eat. I do not will myself to disappear. I remain whole. But in my dreams I melt them off with giant candles. Or I wake up without them; the doctor says: *There was an accident.* But what accident could end like this? Hippocrates believed breast cancer was caused by menopause. In the Middle Ages women believed that breast cancer could be caused by bumping into something with one's chest. My grandmother died of breast cancer; it ate her slowly, took years. Will they take mine because of that?

After her mastectomy, Audre Lorde wrote: *Any amputation is a physical and psychic reality that must be integrated into a new sense of self. The absence of my breast is a recurrent sadness, but certainly not one that dominates my life. I miss it, sometimes piercingly.* She rejects reconstruction and prosthesis, wishing to bear her body as a witness to highlight the visibility of survivors of breast cancer: *going flat*, it's often called now. Before the creation of reliable implants, if someone miraculously survived mastectomy, there was no way to be anything but flat.

Maggie Nelson, pregnant when she flies to Florida with her partner for his top surgery, writes: *Flipping channels on a different day, we landed on a reality TV show featuring a breast cancer patient recovering from a double mastectomy. It was uncanny to watch her performing the same actions we were performing—emptying her drains, waiting patiently for her unbinding—but with opposite emotions.* I first hear those words together—*top surgery*—when I meet a trans person for the first time. He has a blog, linking to other blogs, and other blogs. I start reading and I can't stop.

Hitler called him *the most dangerous Jew in Germany.* One of the earliest advocates for transgender surgeries,

Magnus Hirschfeld helped arrange the first sex reassignment surgery, for a woman named Dora Richter, in 1931. He was the first person to stand up and say that we are people in need of care, of assistance, of acceptance. In the most famous image of Nazi book-burning, they are destroying the library at the Institute for Sexual Science. Our library; our way of learning how to become.

When I first start researching top surgery, the only real information about surgeons and results is on Transbucket, a crude website where transgender people post before and after photos of their procedures. I stare at the long semicircular scars underneath their chests, at the blackened, scabbed nipple grafts sewn back onto them. The bags of bloody fluid hanging next to raw chests. With shirts on, these are simply people with flat torsos, but here they choose to show me how they have changed.

Although they have been performed since antiquity, breast surgeries were rare—and largely unsuccessful—before the development of anesthetic and antiseptic techniques led to innovations in mastectomy, including the Halsted method of radical mastectomy, introduced in the 1880s, in which the breast, lymph nodes, and pectoral muscles are all removed. Before that, cauterization and crude amputation were the norm. Breast cancer was a terrible secret, a punishment, hidden. In 1811, the novelist, diarist, and playwright Fanny Burney, a rare survivor of early mastectomy, wrote a letter to her sister detailing her torture at the hands of a team of doctors as they performed a radical mastectomy in her home near Paris: *I then saw my good Dr Larry, pale nearly as myself, his face streaked with blood, & its expression depicting grief, apprehension & almost horrur.* For weeks after I read her letter, when I try to close my eyes at night I see scalpels dipped in bowls of water at my bedside, a group of men beside my bed, ungloved fingers. I roll over, hold my girlfriend, run my hands under her shirt and around her small, firm breasts. I fall back asleep.

Breast: *A joint of meat or portion of poultry cut from the breast of a bird or mammal.*

It is not easy to say no when, tipsy and uncharacteristically impulsive, I somehow find myself making out with my childhood best friend one night in our hometown. I'm twenty-one. She grabs my hair, tells me she misses it long. *You were so beautiful,* she says. She smells like beer.

In the dreadful moments between hearing what she's said and feeling her teeth on my breasts I realize I have let someone who does not know me at all take off my clothes, put her hands all over me. She bites down again, though I know she heard me say no. She is over six feet tall. She outweighs me by fifty pounds. By the time I say it a third time her hand has made its way almost inside the body I have never wanted less to be mine. We are in her parents' basement in a town with no streetlights, no sidewalks, nobody who could ever understand what this is. After, I have to ask her to drive me home.

My college girlfriend and I get back together for good and we become more serious. After two years together, I tell her I am not a woman. It is something I've never told anyone. We have just had sex. She has nothing to say, so I put my clothes back on and pretend it is still a secret.

In my desk at the high school where I get my first teaching job I keep a copy of Adrienne Rich's *The Dream of a Common Language*. It reminds me of a high school teacher—at that all-girls Catholic school—who, waiting until the other students had left, recommended it to me quietly. Recognizing in me someone who needed something.

In "A Woman Dead in Her Forties," Rich refers to a beloved friend's postsurgical chest as a *scarred, deleted torso*. I look at the words during my lunch, recovering from a student asking, *Why you wanna be a man, miss?* I look at the words again, at my browser history.

Since it killed my grandmother, my mother tells me I should find out if I, in particular, am susceptible to this cancer, and others. My father survived rectal cancer. My mother survived melanoma, twice. But I don't find out. I don't do anything. I don't go to doctors if I can help it. In my apartment after my mother reports back on her recent mammogram I look online at the torsos of brave people who've posed to show what they look like postmastectomy. Removing a cancer is not at all like shaping a chest to look like a man's chest. It is a functional reimagining—a shaving-off of bad is all they have in common—but without consideration of how one might look in a locker room.

My mother says it hurt more than usual—this mammogram—because, as a recent birthday gift, she's received a boob job from my father. She sees my look of surprise, says, *Don't judge. You don't know what it's like, after kids.* The unsaid: *You never will.* Also unsaid: *How can you be so unlike what you are supposed to be like?* And finally, still unsaid: *Why can you not appreciate what you have?*

The first person to get a successful modern silicone breast augmentation didn't really start out wanting it. In 1962, Timmie Jean Lindsey went to a Houston clinic looking for someone to remove a large tattoo on her chest. When she encountered a surgeon looking for volunteers to receive an experimental breast augmentation surgery, she told him that her real issue with her appearance was her large ears, which, in her words, *stood out like Dumbo.* She wanted otoplasty—surgery in which the ears' position is changed, in her case to have them pinned back—and received it along with the experimental implants. I wonder about trades: What I would let someone put in my body to fix them. What I'd let someone pull out.

I say successful because Timmie Jean Lindsey is still alive. The implants stayed where they should. I say first because Timmie Jean Lindsey is a woman. Before her there was a dog—Esmerelda—the first real victim of implants. After a few weeks, she'd chewed at the stitches so viciously that they were removed. Aside from hatred of the implants, Esmerelda had no ill effects, and implants were declared ready for us.

When our first son is born, Anna is so sad. She's sad like she was only once before, after college, when she saw the psychiatrist she described only as *The tall doctor with the bright orange hair,* when I was not enough and books were not enough and parks were not enough and she had to take pills to help her get to work. When Sean cries she looks at him, and at me, and at him again, like she does not understand what this all means. *Feeding him is literally your only job,* I say, disgusted with her and with having to pressure her, to control her breasts in this way. To tell her to give her body to someone else, whenever he wants, sometimes hourly. She lifts up her shirt and feeds him, before she hands him back to me to take away.

At night she takes care of some of Philadelphia's sickest people, men and women with tubes and wires hanging everywhere. A patient who needs her to do everything for them is said to require *complete care*. Anna doesn't write anymore, doesn't act anymore. She is no longer the woman I met in college. Having this baby, feeding this baby, has changed her. When she comes home and sleeps through days, I sometimes lay the baby against her body, pull up her shirt, and let him drink.

A large percentage of breast cancer is found by the owner of the breasts: *Get to know your body after surgery*, one top surgeon cautions. My breasts are small, soft, with one regular nipple and one inverted, dented in and sad looking. It seems an oddity of form, not function; I have no plans to breastfeed, until I do.

A day before Thanksgiving and two weeks after first injecting myself with a friend's sperm I wake up with sore boobs, pins and needles that begin in my nipples and radiate through my entire breasts. I take a pregnancy test, hold it in a variety of lights, and decide the second line is faintly there. We've decided our children should be close together—Irish twins, even, but breastfeeding means Anna does not ovulate, and we move on to the next best uterus. Two days later the line is gone. I bleed. I feel my breasts constantly throughout the day, there is less pain every hour, and I mourn its loss.

The baby who could have been, borne from the body that should never have been. He would have been born in July.

But this body has at its foundation a strong will to carry out its biological destiny. Some people may have been born in the wrong body; I was not. I was born in a body that gave me the freedom to carry a baby, one who stays around this time. I am not quiet in bed, but I hesitate for the first time asking my partner, my lover of seven years, to touch my pregnant breasts. *They just feel . . . different. Like in a good way.* She once balked when I told her I was not a woman, and now she balks at these: these large areolas. Bull's-eyes to help our not-yet-born second son find them, when they're his.

Breasts are unusually susceptible to cancers. Inside they are porous, thirsty for toxins. As the world allows itself to be poisoned, those of us with them are poisoned first. The FDA claims that, in its current levels in our food, bisphenol A (BPA) is safe. Many studies find otherwise. The water fountains in Philadelphia schools are not safe, so I often purchase bottled water on my way to work, from a pizza shop across the street from school called Paulie's. Perinatal exposure to BPA in rats can cause malignant, metastatic mammary tumors. Breast cancer. The FDA says maybe, if you're concerned, seek alternatives to plastic and cans. Pregnant people need to drink water, and a lot of it. There is no safety in having this body in this world.

When Anna tells friends or people at work that I'm pregnant, they say things to her like: *Wow, you're so lucky. Krys must really understand you.* At home she admits she hates this, this assumption that to be queer is to be more easily understood, that a uterus and breasts make our experiences the same.

Pregnancy protects the breasts, and so does breastfeeding. The younger you have children, and the longer you use your body to feed them, the better the protection. Strange, the choices I make. Strange, the protection they offer from this sickness. Everything online refers to *breastfeeding women, breastfeeding moms.* But I'm not a woman, not a mom. I google *What does breastfeeding feel like?* and, at nine months pregnant, find no satisfactory answers. Most responders take this as an opportunity to share why breastfeeding did not work out for them. I stare grimly into my future: me, a human vending machine.

When Samson is born I weigh 175 pounds. When filling sausage casings, if you press a thumb firmly into the sausage, an indent should remain when you pull your hand back. Otherwise, it is overstuffed and will burst. Contractions make my abdomen a casing pulled too tight, the membrane fit to tear. I am worried about what to wear. I pack clothes of all kinds, but somehow, these hours are some of the only ones in my life in which I forget I have breasts at all. My shirt comes off seconds after I get to the birth center.

In truth, when I'm breastfeeding Samson it feels like he is a vacuum and I'm an especially dusty rug.

The detachment of the placenta is what signals the body to begin lactating. As it rips from the uterine wall the body experiences a sharp decline in progesterone. Soon after, if a baby is placed to the breast, the establishment of supply can usually begin. I didn't have a birth plan except to say: *I don't want to see my placenta.* I have no desire to see my organs on the outside. Placenta, from the Latin: *a flat cake.*

Typically, a baby has to suck at the breast for a few minutes before letdown, the ejection of milk, occurs. The second Samson's mouth touches one of my nipples, milk shoots forcefully out. There isn't just one hole; one of the ways in which humans differ from cows is the number of streams we have. They have one. Our ducts lead out through multiple ductal orifices, creating teams of tiny synchronized jet streams. I'm not sure how many I have. I never try to count, too busy trying to contain the flood. If I press on one nipple like an elevator button, nothing will come out and we will all be safe while I think of what to do.

At night I lie next to my infant son—and then toddler—in bed. For two long years he nurses, gripping the side of my breast in his fist like I'm a coffee mug, gulping me while I try to sleep.

My stomach is white and smooth, snaps back to its old self weeks after Samson is born. My breasts are different; every day they grow bigger. Along their sides there are angry purple stretch marks. I put weight on with Samson slowly, day by day over nine months. But a week after his birth my A cups are at least a D. Every morning when I wake up, they feel bigger, welled up and fit to erupt.

Breasts: *Either of the two soft, protruding organs on the upper front of a woman's body which secrete milk after childbirth.*

I am on my way to a Brazilian Jiu-Jitsu camp in Massachusetts with a friend when I have to stop to pump in a Dunkin' Donuts bathroom. It's been too long; they feel firm and gravelly by the time I sit on the toilet, manual pump in hand. I maneuver the pump with one hand, pressing down on its plastic like an old-fashioned water pump, massaging the bright white milk out with the other. Begin at the top of the breast with an open palm, smoothing the milk down and out through the ducts. Squeeze in an even, controlled motion; never pull. After fifteen minutes I emerge with two warm bottles and hold them up to my friend, an offering. She laughs, too.

They are for food, right? History is full of debates over whether the animalistic way we feed our infants is best for them. And if it's best, how best is it? Did I need to do this? My partner, the labor and delivery nurse, thinks it really is that important. She starts taking college courses so she can sit for her lactation consultant exam. I pick up one of her papers off the kitchen counter, spend a moment reading it. *Maybe*, I mention after, trying to sound casual, *you should say parent. Instead of mother. When you talk about nursing.* But Anna glares. *It's a paper for a stupid class. Don't take everything so seriously.*

My entire life I think it is going to be surgery first, and hormones later, if ever. But I am not ready to commit to six weeks of not lifting a baby—not now and not for years—and so I find myself in a queer clinic on a hot April afternoon. *You'll need two hands to push it; it's thick*, the nurse who teaches me how tells me. He is pretty. *You'll need to inject it somewhere fatty*, he says. *The stomach is perfect*, he says. Right here. He places a thick finger next to my belly button. Going to extremes to look good isn't anything new, I think, as I push the syringe of heavy, pus-colored oil into a knob of pinched belly fat.

Some estimate that as many as 4 percent of American women have breast implants. After a severe dip in the 1990s, boob jobs are way up again, with nearly 300,000 breast augmentations performed in 2019. Recently, a procedure called fat transfer augmentation has again become popular; in it, someone can get fat suctioned from one place on their body injected into their breasts. Previously, only an average of about four and a half ounces of fat could be injected into the breast. With pre-expansion, by which the recipient of the surgery wears a suction bra for weeks to vacuum space into their breasts before surgery, that number has soared to nearly eight ounces. I look at my chest in the mirror, remember when it was big, like that: wonder at the choices we make, the changes we pick.

I am aware I am moving away from something and toward something else. It fuels me. In this liminal space I walk around the house in my underwear, not caring who sees me. I lean in front of strangers in the elevator to press the correct button, ask them, *What floor?* aware that this new body takes up just the right amount of space. And I smile. To disrupt class one of my students breaks out in song and I find myself dancing. *Miss, you crazy*, he says.

A friend of a friend, a woman in her twenties who belongs to my gym, finds out she has breast cancer. When she returns months later, after a mastectomy, I try to stop myself from watching our coach figure out what this woman's new body can do. She puts her arms up and to the sides, testing. After a few minutes she sits beside a pull-up bar, her face in her hands. When I do pull-ups the bar sometimes grazes my nipples. I take mental notes about range of motion, for later, and feel a sick jealousy. I want mine gone; I want to give hers back to her.

I buy my first binder only a few months before the publication of the first big study about chest binding among queer people. The binder is slippery and comes shrink-wrapped in a little plastic sleeve. Wearing it feels like trapping myself in a permanent inhalation. The study says that clinicians should compare the physical harms caused by binding with the mental health or quality-of-life benefits reported by the patient. We are not supposed to wear our binders to swim, to sleep, to work out. One hot Saturday in April I don't listen. I wear a binder to the gym, run in the heat next to an upbeat woman. I struggle to breathe, to pull air in, to fight the nightmare in which I pass out here and everyone finds out what is underneath the layers.

Not all of the results posted online are good. Many are accompanied by warnings. We must submit our bodies to this. No one knows what the hormones really do; I signed a paper acknowledging I know they may make me infertile, despite knowing multiple people who took them for years before carrying children. Decades after Hirschfeld's library burned and we are still experiments. No one knows the true risks of all this. My breasts are shrinking. As my fat redistributes it settles in my belly and leaves my chest. They look like whoopee cushions someone sat on.

Some trans people use the phrase *gender euphoria* to describe the feeling of someone using the right name, the right pronouns, the feeling of looking in the mirror and seeing changes, the feeling of layers of bandages removed to reveal not a new self, but a more real self. After Transbucket comes YouTube, hundreds of videos of top surgery reveals, people crying and laughing as masked surgeons unravel them. I watch these videos after my children are in bed, feeling a familiar compulsion and revulsion. A friend adds me to a Facebook group for top surgery questions and answers. It has ten thousand members. Most of them write that surgery is a means to freedom, but I am trapped by the questions: the *Will I?*, the *When will I?*, the *How will I learn to live without them?*

Each of us struggles daily with the pressures of conformity and the loneliness of difference from which these choices seem to offer escape. —Audre Lorde

We usually do a breast exam? the nurse at Planned Parenthood says. I've moved to a small town, a thousand miles away from where I cracked up my midwife by shouting, *I'm not pregnant anymore!* seconds after giving birth. *We usually do a breast exam?* It's said like that: a question I'm supposed to answer. *I still have them*, I say. I motion toward my layers: a binder, a T-shirt, another T-shirt. *They're under here somewhere.* She's relieved at the joke; I said it like that for her.

How to explain that for some, or for some at some times, this irresolution is OK—desirable, even (e.g., "gender hackers")— whereas for others, or for others at some times, it stays a source of conflict or grief? —Maggie Nelson

A young man approaches me at the gym and I am worried he will yell at me for hogging the equipment, for reading multiple pages on the bench between sets. *What's that?* he asks. Oh, I say, holding up Florence Williams's *Breasts*. He takes a moment to consider whether he still wants to flirt with the man at the gym who reads an entire book about breasts—books upon books, is what he doesn't know.

One by one the guys in my transmasculine support group get their top surgeries. We talk about their phone consultations, their calendar arrangements, taking leave from work: how to do it without saying the surgery you're getting, how to tell your coworkers no when you're back at the office and they ask you to replace the water cooler's thick, full bottle. Every week they tell us how many more weeks they have left until their breasts are gone. They fight their insurance companies by e-mail, over the phone, by e-mail again. Appeals are filed. We are outraged on their behalf; only we are outraged on their behalf. And then, for weeks, they're gone, and we know that when they come back, they will finally be unburdened.

No one in the group talks about what one does if one cannot decide whether to keep them or not. If it is normal to harbor both intense gratefulness and revulsion toward them. No one in my group has breastfed a child. No one talks about wishing they were sick, about the decision being out of their hands. No one talks about whether it is normal to touch them when masturbating, to walk around the house topless, but to feel fear and shame when thinking about the people one knows, but doesn't *know*, finding out they exist. No one does, and so I don't either.

My last memory of living in Philadelphia: four months on testosterone. Ninety-one degrees and counting. I leave the gym covered in a wet shirt. I take it off, walk down crowded Frankford Avenue in my sports bra, drinking iced coffee from a sweating cup. Every day my shoulders are bigger, the hair on my legs a touch thicker. But I am the least of the strange things one can see here on a Saturday morning in Fishtown. It is gender euphoria.

Breast: *(verb) Face and move forward, against, or through.*

How to Photograph Your Newborn

I. THE AUTHOR'S FIRST FEW MONTHS (1987)

When you bring the baby home from the hospital, you're supposed to put it down in a bassinet. But before the baby comes, the bassinet just sits there, waiting. In the corner it looks profoundly empty, unsettling almost, before there is anyone to place inside.

The emptiness follows you around the room while you shuffle back and forth folding tiny baby laundry, stacking swaddling blankets just so, changing again and again which is on top, which will be first. Open and close the new hamper just for baby clothes to make sure it, in fact, opens and closes like it should. Stand looking inside, trying to decide whether to open a package of pacifiers now, whether to open a baby thermometer, wondering if these are silly things to do before there is even a baby.

When the baby comes home, swaddle it. The nurse showed you how. Don't bother with the stack of blankets beside the changing table; grab the one they gave you at the hospital. It's scrunched up inside the baby's car seat. The blue and pink lines. On top of your bedspread lay the blanket out flat, then fold corner to corner. Lay the baby's head just above the blanket's edge, marveling at the little crushed ears, pointed at the tops like elf ears, red like they've just been out in the sun, red like when you lie or drink too much. Try to remember how to do it, remember those fast, experienced hands. It was so late at night when she showed you, and the baby was so new, and you were so sore, and so tired. Everything felt slow and confusing. The nurse placed two ibuprofen tablets in a cup on the nightstand and wrapped the baby up tight, roughly almost, before taking your blood pressure and urging you to get some rest. You picked up the wrapped baby and put it to your breast, feeling a deep pulling inside, where there was a baby just hours ago. Now you are the thing that is empty. And here you are, at home now, next to the impossibly empty bassinet, tugging with hesitation, folding the blanket over your baby, hoping it holds, laying the baby down to sleep. Was there something to hold on to inside? Where is this baby trying to go?

Having a summer baby is lucky because you do not have to dress it in so many layers. Dress the baby in one more layer than you'd wear, the nurse says. Dress the baby the same as you, the baby's pediatrician says. You are bleary and leaking and only half listening each time you're given advice and are not sure you've really heard any of it. No matter; it is so hot you'd rather walk around in your underwear, so you select an undershirt, three-month size, so large and baggy you can see the baby's entire diaper sticking through. It is not a cute look. You mistakenly think no one will see a baby, shoved inside an enormous perambulator like this, but the head of each person you pass swivels back to look inside. You have made something everyone wants to see. As you walk down the sidewalk, listening to the ice cream truck wailing and the open fire hydrant roaring on the corner, you hum a little, because the baby

is asleep and you are for once alone with your own thoughts, the sounds of your new unswollen feet shuffling along toward nothing, away from home, from the rocking chair, from the couch where you've spent the first few days nursing. A baby cries out from a neighbor's window; under your T-shirt your breasts leak sweet, hot milk. Your mother warned you about the pain and tingling of letdown, but in the beginning there is so much milk that it just falls out of you all the time, sliding around all sides of your breasts if you lie flat, falling between you and the baby if you lie together nursing. There is so much; how can the body make so much food and never grow too tired to make more? Your legs push forward. It is like walking on the beach, this walking so soon after having a baby. Hot and hard and deeply satisfying. You slow down and lean against a light pole, catch a breath, snap a picture; it is hard to get a good one when the baby is always either asleep or attached to you.

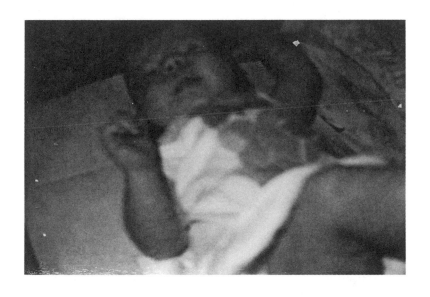

When awake, the baby flails around as if lost underwater.

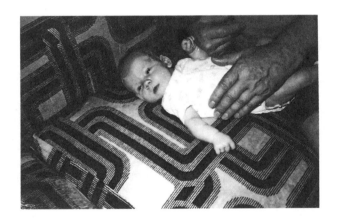

We now know that the fetus begins to hear in the second trimester, around nineteen weeks. At first, it mostly hears your heart, slow and calm as you rest, and fast as you try to keep jogging, keep moving, even as you get bigger. It's noisy in there. But in 1987, nobody knew for sure how noisy. You haven't seen it, this baby; you just know it was a baby you were not ready for, with a boyfriend you were not so sure you were going to marry. And then you did.

You're pregnant just four years after scientists discovered consistent fetal responses—forceful blinks—to sound at twenty-eight weeks. But you know the baby can hear; you just know. When no one else is around, you talk to it, not sure how loud you'd have to be for it to hear you. Tell the baby it will be your parents' first grandchild; that it must root for the Mets, how they just won the World Series. Describe the way the vacuum never works quite as well as you want it to, how it always releases an unpleasant musty odor into the basement apartment. *We're in Flatbush*, you say. *But hopefully not for long. We don't want to raise a baby around here*, you say. You want to believe the baby knows your voice, before it's even here.

Ask someone to lay hands on the baby, to steady it on the sloped cushion. Whose hands are they—brown, swollen, sunspotted. Hard, fat hands with nails that need a trim. Hands the size of your baby's torso. Grab the camera. Your baby knows your voice. Say your baby's name.

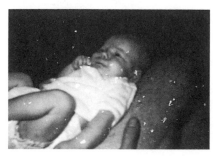

Lay the baby on a lap. They like that, this other lap. Watch TV together, a family of three. The game. *Matlock*. Hold the tiny hand next to you; tamp down the jealousy that it is not your lap. Eventually it cannot always be you. Next to you feels so far away; for the better part of a year, you shared one body. You never stood in a long grocery line, sat on hold for an hour, clipped your toenails, woke up in the middle of the night alone. Make faces at the baby during commercials. *What does the dog say? What does the elephant say?* There, do that one again.

Your mother came to this country by herself as a teenager. Maybe, she thought, she'd become a nun. A few years later she was married to the monsignor's brother and had your brother, Joseph. After that came the miscarriages, the stillbirths. By the time you and your twin brother were born eight years after Joseph it was settled: Every baby who lives is a miracle. You were a miracle. The way you and David danced inside, that you kept it up on the outside, too. There aren't many pictures. You and David in your baptism outfits, one in each parent's arm, who knows which is which from that far away. The Flatbush church behind them. Your mother short, smiling, smiling at the wonder of it all. Two live babies. How hard it is, how much they cry, it meant nothing. You both lived. Your mother never had much to say about the years before she came to Brooklyn. She tried to make it sound beautiful, where she grew up, but then there was how she left all by herself, the mournful way she said the word: *Ireland*. Her soft accent and wet eyes. There is one more picture, the one of you two lying next to each other in a bassinet. You're screaming. How babies scream sometimes. Eyes closed, mouth open, back arched. David sleeps beside you, his lips loose and limp. You've always been you, even then.

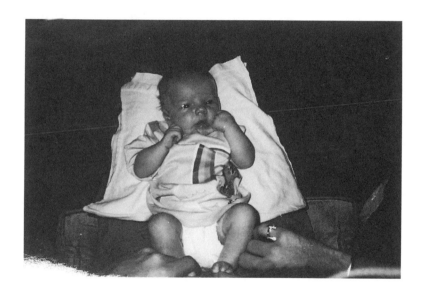

Sometimes the baby can't be made to smile for the camera. Fresh diaper, fresh milk, that beloved other lap, big hands wiggling tiny toes: *Look, look here, what does the elephant say?* Say the baby's name and this is all you get back, this vacant stare. *Mail me a picture!*

your mother says over the phone. She wants to know how things are going. *How is the baby eating? How is the baby sleeping?* Everything is good, everything is fine, smile for the camera, baby, look over here, right over here.

II. THE AUTHOR'S CHILD AS AN INFANT (2013)

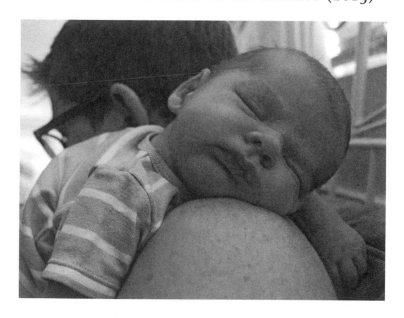

There aren't any pictures of newborn Samson with both eyes open. We brought him home twelve hours after I had him, after eating bagels in bed and having the nurse check him over— his tiny, flat red ears, skinny legs that stretched wildly when he lay flat on his back. Poppy and sesame seeds spilled over onto wrinkled white sheets. *He's a sleepy little guy*, Anna said. The room smelled of cleaning solution and last night's Indian takeout; I'd been so happy to give birth at dinnertime, to wobble my way to the shower and back to bed again, happy to have the warm bag of food in my hand. Anna let me eat almost all the garlic naan; I swiped it through both our curries while she held the baby. I remember the crisped bits of garlic, the way the bread breathed steam into my face as I tore it apart, cilantro leaves catching in my teeth. I bit down on a whole cardamom pod buried in my rice. The perfume exploded in my mouth. *Blech*, I said, spitting it into a napkin. I was sore, so sore whenever I talked or laughed or moved. I throbbed where the baby had come out of me, this little black-haired baby. He looked exactly like a squashed, red-faced version of my father. I shoveled food into my mouth with a plastic fork, leaning my head over the container of saag paneer. Nothing had ever tasted this good. *Now all I need is a beer*, I'd joked, taking ibuprofen from a little paper cup beside the bed. When Anna had given birth to Sean, I'd laughed at this offering, two tiny orange pills sitting beside all her half-drunk bottles of Gatorade and water, some ibuprofen after hours of roaring pain. After dinner the nurse explained to me how you take care of a baby.

What color their poops are supposed to be. How much nipple pain is okay. How I might feel cramping while nursing the first few days. *Do you think you'll need this?* she asked, motioning to a little bassinet beside the bed. *No*, I told her, *he'll sleep right by me.* The next morning we laid him on the bed so we could eat bagels and so Anna could pack. I lay there watching her shuffle around the room, shifted a little in bed. *Where do you think you're going*, she accused me. I sat back. *Can you hand me the camera?* I asked. *I have a feeling we won't get a lot of cute sleeping-baby pictures after today*, I said.

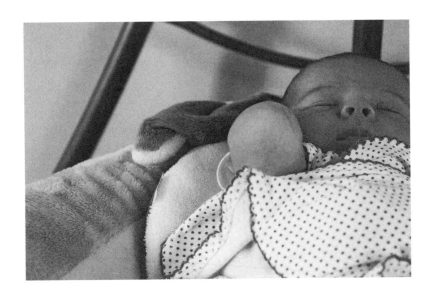

But he slept and slept. Every day his sleeping face was more like my face. In the dark I could not see it next to me but I knew it was growing more and more into the face I could have had. I look at pictures of me as a baby, lying on my father's lap on the couch, lying in a stroller being pushed through the Brooklyn summer sun, and wonder if you ever knew you were photographing the wrong face, not your daughter's face. Do you look at those pictures and see me? *You all look so much alike now*, you say, but you don't mean my sisters. You mean me and Michael and Sean and Ryan. Your four sons. *The baby is not your daughter*, I want to tell you, the woman behind the camera. *Don't say that name*, I'd tell you. *Say your baby's real name.* I'd whisper it in your ear. Krys Malcolm. *The photograph will come out better in the end*, I'd say, *if you say your baby's real name.*

We have all these pictures of Samson in a bassinet, but I don't remember ever laying him down like this. I only remember him sleeping curled up next to me, a tiny comma hanging from my breast. There is no way I took this picture, is there?

I always knew how happy it would make you to see me pregnant. When I met Anna you told me it made you sad, how my life would always be hard now. You still thought I was your daughter then. Often other trans gestational parents I know ask how to handle it when family members won't stop calling them Mom, wishing them Happy Mother's Day, even calling them their old names after years of studiously avoiding it. *People see you as different after you carry a baby*, they say. When you had a daughter, a daughter first, I am sure you thought ahead to this, to me sitting on stoops in the middle of our walks in my Philadelphia neighborhood to catch my breath. To folding tiny newborn-size onesies into a drawer. The enormous globe of me, full with your grandchild. So much possibility there, that I could really be the daughter I was supposed to be. I thought so, too. When I sealed my ultrasound picture in an envelope and sent it to you, I felt happy for a minute, like maybe I didn't need to transition to be happy with this body. But after he was born Samson only made me more sure: his face a copy of mine, of my brothers'. He lay there with the life ahead of him that I wanted for myself, if he wanted it. Nothing about being pregnant made me feel feminine. This body is what it is: not quite man, not quite woman, but with the parts to create and shape life. To expel and care for that life. Creating Samson, given such a strong name because I felt I had done something strong, made me ready to be me. *The best name in the world*, Anna says, though we have two other sons. *Your best present*, she says.

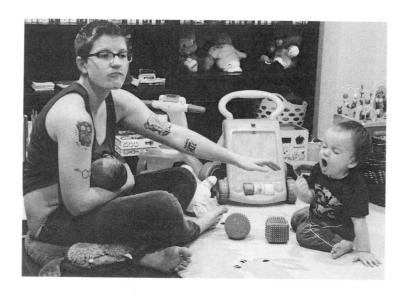

I encouraged Anna to take a shower, to take as long as she needed. I told her I had it under control. I put on jeans for the first time since I'd had the baby, put a big stuffed walrus pillow on the floor, limped over and sat. When she came downstairs, she grabbed the camera.

It is good we took so many pictures because I remember almost nothing from those early weeks. I remember the new iPad Anna bought me—my push present—and how I watched endless hours of television in bed, nursing a half-sleeping baby. I don't recall what I watched. Crime television, probably. Rapes, stabbings, murders. My choice. Each episode beginning gruesomely and ending with a clean resolution, the calming rhythm of imaginary killers and detectives. With Anna, it had been *The West Wing*, Sean's long head turning toward the opening theme each time a new episode began. I think he knew the theme song from before he was born. Hours of White House staffers talking and talking, walking down the halls, how did they all talk so fast all the time? With my baby, I couldn't sit on the couch; otherwise, Sean would scream for my attention, throw toys at me, steal my lunch. I couldn't move fast. I'd had a tear. So I spent most of the day upstairs, in bed with the iPad and sleepy Samson. I was so sore that Anna, the nurse, froze medical gloves filled with water, wrapped them in gauze, and handed them to me to stick inside my underwear. *Padsicles*, I later heard a woman call them. Samson had been born after only six minutes of pushing. With Sean, I supported Anna through endless hours, but with Samson, I stood up out of the bathtub, yelling for help getting out, the rush of the midwife pulling on gloves and a mask. *This is really good*, Anna said after the first push. *Oh shit, this already burns*, I said, and then he was out. Born in a bathroom just before dinnertime. *My stitches itch*, I told Anna, days later in bed. *That's what they do*, she said. *What if they're not healing right?* I said. *I mean, I'm happy to look. Won't you never*, I said. *You know*, I said. *Want to look at me again, after that?* She laughed. *Are you kidding?* she said. *I'm a nurse. You know how many gross things I've seen. Don't call me a gross thing*, I said. *I wasn't*, she said. *I definitely wasn't.*

These are the things I remember. I barely remember Samson, how he was like or unlike my other children, the ones Anna made. He slept more. He's asleep in every picture. When I look at pictures from that time I can't believe how young I look, how large and full my breasts were. No baby could possibly need this much milk, I thought. My nipples were red and puffy, many shades darker than ever before; the breasts had purple stretch marks everywhere. When Samson cried, they leaked. When Sean cried, when he screamed at me as we played together on the rug, they leaked, too, though he had never lived inside me, never nursed from me. I sat on a giant walrus-shaped pillow because I was torn up. Now, after pregnancy and nursing and years of testosterone and binding, my breasts are a ghost of what they once were, empty, floppy sacs. My stitches healed perfectly just like Anna said they would.

This looks perfectly normal, she said. Normal: transgender, postpartum, in bed hiding from a screaming thirteen-month-old, hiding from having to leave the house, my floppy belly, giant breasts. No one would call me sir like this, not ever. In the grocery store the older woman at the checkout laughs at how I pull out my ID at the same time I present her with a bottle of wine. *You knew that was coming,* she says. *Where do I find the birth date on this thing?* she asks, searching my license. *June 27, 1987,* I say. *I know I look young,* I say. *Damn,* she says, *you're not kidding. You're thirty?* When I take my shirt and my binder off at night I see this aged chest, used to bits but still here; I don't remember anything about the baby in the pictures, only the self, who I was then, just trying to make it through another day in the absolutely wrong postpartum body.

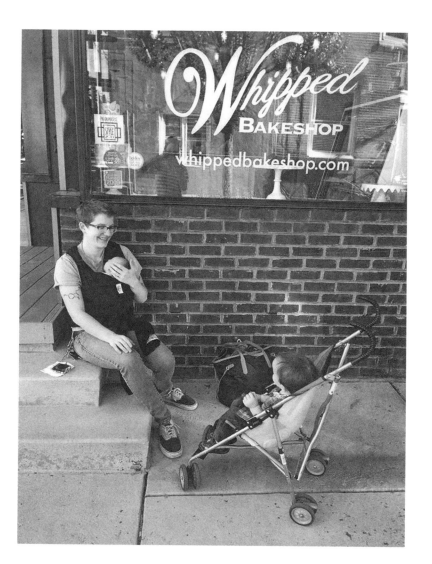

Wait, Anna said. *This is exactly where we took that other picture. What picture?* I said. *You know,* she said. *The other one. The other time we came here to get brownies. Just sit right there on that step,* she said. She parked Sean's stroller beside me and Samson. *No, Sean, you can have the brownie in a minute,* she said, stepping back into the middle of Belgrade Street, holding up her cell phone. *Don't freak out, Sean, you're going to get the brownie. Just let me take one picture of your Krys just like last time.*

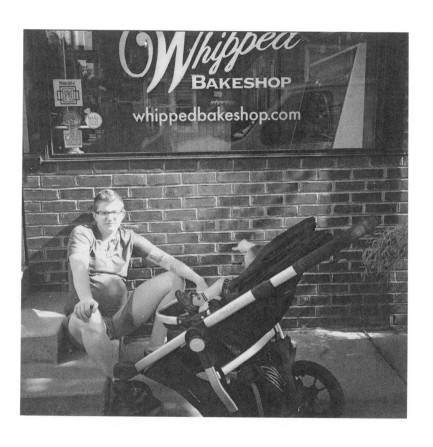

In the Court of
Common Pleas

---

1. The documents in this essay surround the second parent adoption of
my second son, Samson Ryan Belc, who was born August 30, 2013,
at the Birth Center in Bryn Mawr, Pennsylvania, and was subse-

quently adopted in Philadelphia's family court on July 20, 2016. Before this proceeding, Samson had one legal parent.

    a. This often led to Anna's claims that she had no legal obligation to change Samson's diaper or to scrub yogurt out of his hair.

    b. Although to this day I am unsure why this is the case, in Samson's adoption, I also had to provide information about myself, such as fingerprints, background checks, and testimony, even though I was his birth parent and had custody of him from the moment of his birth.

    c. I changed my name to Krys Malcolm Belc April 6, 2017.

2. When our first son, Sean Silas Belc, was born in July 2012, he was adopted just five and a half months later, in December 2012. At the time of his adoption in 2016, Samson was two years, ten months old.

    a. This was entirely our fault, as we had the money and legal support to complete Samson's adoption, and yet the paperwork sat incomplete in our e-mail in-boxes for two years.

    b. The motivating factor rushing us the first time around was feeling uncertain whether, if my wife died, her parents would consider me Sean's parent.

    c. When we married, Anna's father asked whether he should dress up to attend the wedding, and also inquired whether we thought people would *actually show up*.

    d. Nearly a decade later people often ask why I married so young, and they are nearly always straight and cis and cannot possibly understand marriage as a protective act.

    e. Queer folks who are not both genetic parents of their children must, in the United States, engage with the court system after their children are born to secure their parentage.

f. Because his date of birth was before the 2015 legalization of same-sex marriage, Anna and I were not married in Pennsylvania, Samson's birth state, and could not be listed together on his original birth certificate. Instead, next to *Father:* was *Information Not Recorded.*

g. Samson was adopted simultaneously with our third son, Sullivan Isaiah "ZZ" Belc, born November 22, 2015. ZZ is not my genetic child, bringing us back to 2a.

IN THE COURT OF COMMON PLEAS OF PHILADELPHIA COUNTY
FAMILY COURT DIVISION
ADOPTION BRANCH

IN RE: :   _____ TERM, 2016

ADOPTION OF: SANSOM RYAN BELC[3].   NO.

PETITION TO CONFIRM CONSENT .

TO THE HONORABLE JUDGES OF THE SAID COURT:

1.   The adoptee, Sansom Ryan Belc, was born on August 30, 2013, at The Birth Center in Bryn Mawr, Pennsylvania. The Adoptee has resided with the Petitioners: Natural Mother – since birth; adoptive mother-since birth.[4]

2.   The natural mother of the adoptee is Krystyn Marie Belc (McIlraith).

3.   The natural mother was born on June 27, 1987, in New York, New York.

4.   The natural mother resides at   , Philadelphia, Pennsylvania

5.   The natural mother is of the Caucasian race and Catholic.[5]

6.   The natural mother was married at the time of the birth of the adoptee, Sansom Ryan Belc.[6]

7.   The natural mother, Krystyn Marie Belc (McIlraith) is a Petitioner and has not executed a consent.

8.   The natural father is

3. Sansom Street is one of the smaller thoroughfares in Philadelphia; it runs from Front Street on the eastern end through most of the city and into Delaware County. This was never my son Samson's name, but throughout the adoption process we found that our own attorney and multiple court employees spelled his name this way.

4. Just before his adoption, Samson came home from school crying after he learned that a child in his preschool class had two mothers. This child's mothers had come into school to read the class a book for their daughter's birthday. My children love their mother and they felt jealous that other children could have two of them.

   a. Because Sean and Samson have summer birthdays Anna and I chose an alternate day to visit the classroom. We were introduced as *my mama* and *my Krys*.

   b. I read the class *Madeline*, Samson's favorite book.

5. I stated in the original interview with our attorney that I had been raised Catholic, but didn't object to this in the final petition.

   a. I last received communion in 2007, at a family event. It was a few months after I met Anna.

b. Anna and I sometimes marvel over how two people who are so different can be together, but are two people who have endured decades of stare-offs with their mothers over church attendance really that different?

c. Both our mothers forced us to receive the sacrament of confirmation. We were each fifteen, though Anna was in eighth grade and I in tenth. Our churches were thirty-one miles apart. We were born over four thousand miles apart. Her college dorm room was about seven thousand yards from mine.

6. See marriage certificates later in text.

9. The natural father was born on ⌐   in Bryn Mawr, Pennsylvania.

10. The natural father's mailing is ⌐   )

11. The natural father is of the Caucasian race and he is Atheist.

12. The natural father was single at the time of the birth of the adoptee.[7]

13. The natural father did execute a Consent to Adoption in accordance with Section 2711 of the Adoption Act on September 4, 2012. An original Consent is attached to this Petition and marked as Exhibit "A".

14. If natural father's identity has not been revealed, an affidavit executed by the natural mother regarding why his identity has not been revealed". Not required as natural mother has identified natural father.

15. A "no claim of paternity" statement is attached and marked hereto as Exhibit "B".

16. Statement of Parent form executed by father is attached hereto and marked as Exhibit "C".

17. A period in excess of thirty (30) days subsequent to the execution of the Consent has expired and the parent has failed to proceed with a Petition to Voluntary Relinquishment.

18. The Report of Intention to Adopt was filed on N/A. This is a kinship adoption.[8]

19. The Report of Intermediary was not filed as this is a kinship adoption.

20. Consent to Accept Custody executed by adopting parents is attached hereto and marked as Exhibit "D".

WHEREFORE, your Petitioners request this Honorable Court to hold a hearing to confirm the intention of the natural parent,   to voluntarily relinquish his parental rights and duties to Sansom Ryan Belc, as evidenced by the Consent to the adoption and to grant a Decree of Termination of parental rights and duties.

7. Well, not exactly. He may not have been married, but he was partnered and raising his partner's child. He had even had his name legally changed to take her last name, something I did in 2012 when I legally married Anna in New York State. I had been using her name for two years, but in New Jersey when we had our wedding in 2010, a nonresident of New Jersey could not change their name during the process of obtaining a civil union.

8. Most people I know refer to this kind of adoption as a *second parent adoption*, or SPA. In my work at a school for youth in foster care, we used the phrase *kinship adoption* when a child's parents were unable or unwilling to care for them and a family member such as a grandparent, aunt, uncle, or sibling legally adopted the child.

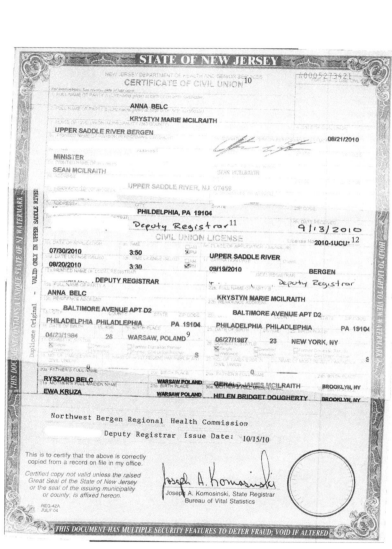

STATE OF NEW JERSEY

NEW JERSEY DEPARTMENT OF HEALTH AND SENIOR SERVICES

CERTIFICATE OF CIVIL UNION

ANNA BELC

KRYSTYN MARIE MCILRAITH

UPPER SADDLE RIVER BERGEN

08/21/2010

MINISTER

SEAN MCILRAITH

SEAN MCILRAITH

UPPER SADDLE RIVER, NJ 07458

PHILDELPHIA, PA 19104

Deputy Registrar

9/13/2010

CIVIL UNION LICENSE

License No. 2010-1UCU-

07/30/2010	3:50	UPPER SADDLE RIVER
08/20/2010	3:30	09/19/2010 BERGEN

DEPUTY REGISTRAR *Deputy Registrar*

ANNA BELC

KRYSTYN MARIE MCILRAITH

BALTIMORE AVENUE APT D2

BALTIMORE AVENUE APT D2

PHILADELPHIA PHILADELPHIA PA 19104

PHILADELPHIA PHILADELPHIA PA 19104

04/23/1984 26 WARSAW, POLAND

06/27/1987 23 NEW YORK, NY

RYSZARD BELC WARSAW POLAND

GERALD JAMES MCILRAITH BROOKLYN, NY

EWA KRUZA WARSAW POLAND

HELEN BRIDGET DOUGHERTY BROOKLYN, NY

Northwest Bergen Regional Health Commission

Deputy Registrar Issue Date: 10/15/10

This is to certify that the above is correctly copied from a record on file in my office.

Certified copy not valid unless the raised Great Seal of the State of New Jersey or the seal of the issuing municipality or county, is affixed hereon.

REG-42A
JULY 04

Joseph A. Komosinski, State Registrar
Bureau of Vital Statistics

THIS DOCUMENT HAS MULTIPLE SECURITY FEATURES TO DETER FRAUD; VOID IF ALTERED

9. *Wait, you were born in Warsaw?* I ask. *I thought you were born in the mountains, in Krynica.* It is the first thing I notice when I find this civil union. I am writing an essay for which I must riffle through all our things. All the things with my old name, my before-transition name, everything with our old Philadelphia addresses: the one-bedroom where we first lived together, the split-level two-bedroom (*I love that here, when I'm pissed at you, I can just stomp up the stairs,* she said), the little row house we bought when I was seven months pregnant. *No, what?* she says. *Did I write that somewhere?*

10. In order to adopt our children, Anna and I had to provide proof of marriage.

   a. We were married twice, first on August 21, 2010, and then on July 2, 2012.

   b. Our second marriage took place at the Office of the City Clerk in New York City; we always said we would get married when a state we had ties to legalized same-sex marriage, which New York did in July 2011.

     i. But we are the same people who waited nearly three years to adopt Samson, and so we waited over a year.

    ii. When Anna was in her third trimester of pregnancy, we realized we should have as many legal protections as we could get. She was thirty-six weeks pregnant when we got married.

11. Same-sex marriage did not become legal in New Jersey until October 2013, but initially, the Deputy Registrar of Bergen County, New Jersey, accidentally issued us a marriage license.

   a. She called us one morning a few weeks later to report her mistake. *As I was falling asleep last night,* she recounted, *I realized something. The drawer where I keep the civil union licenses is on the one side, and the marriage licenses are on the other side, and, well, I reached in the wrong drawer.*

I see, Anna said.

I am going to need you to send that back, she said.

I don't think so, Anna said.

Well, then you need to destroy it, at least, she said.

I will, Anna said, but we had it framed and hung it in our bathroom, above our college diplomas.

12. We were, the clerk later explained, her first civil union.

M-2012-2

THE CITY OF NEW YORK
OFFICE OF THE CITY CLERK
MARRIAGE LICENSE BUREAU

License Number
S-2012-1510

Certificate of Marriage Registration[13]

This Is To Certify That ANNA BELC

residing at   Philadelphia, PA 19104, United States

born on   04/23/1984   at   Krynica, Poland

and   KRYSTYN MARIE MCILRAITH   New Surname: BELC

residing at   Philadelphia, PA 19104, United States

born on   09/27/1987   at   New York City New York, United States.

Were Married

on   07/02/2012   at   The Office of the City Clerk
      By   141 WORTH STREET
                               NEW YORK, NY 10013
                               United States

as shown by the duly registered license and certificate of marriage of said persons on file in this office.

CERTIFIED THIS DATE AT THE CITY CLERK'S OFFICE

Manhattan   July   02,   12
N.Y.   20

Michael McSweeney
City Clerk of the City of New York

CET-F

M0038687

13. Our New Jersey wedding was a real wedding, with a white dress and a seersucker suit and a cupcake tower and toasts and a portable toilet reported widely by our guests to be quite luxurious. We were married in my parents' big suburban backyard with all our friends present. I was twenty-three, and it was a wild party. In New York, two years later, my best friend from high school met us at City Hall during her lunch break. It was a steamy Monday. We sweated through our shorts and T-shirts as we waited in line at the Social Security office, where I planned to change my name; my civil union hadn't been enough, and I'd been using Belc unofficially for two years. A guard, seeing how pregnant and sweaty Anna was, let her cut a line that snaked around and around a marble office. All I had to do was show them the paper and it was done. Official. Then we went to Shake Shack, had burgers and fries and milkshakes, and took the bus back home.

IN THE COURT OF COMMON PLEAS OF PHILADELPHIA COUNTY
FAMILY COURT DIVISION
ADOPTION BRANCH

IN RE: : _____ TERM, 2016
:
ADOPTION OF: SANSOM RYAN BELC : NO.

CONSENT OF BIRTH FATHER

I, _____ am an adult, having been born on _____

I am single, and I am the biological father of Sansom Ryan Belc, who was born

August 30, 2013, at The Birth Center, in Bryn Mawr, Pennsylvania

The natural mother of the child is Krystyn Marie Belc (McIlraith).[14]

      I hereby voluntarily and unconditionally consent to the adoption of the above

named child.

      I understand that by signing this consent I indicate my intent to permanently give

up all rights to this child.

      I understand said child will be placed for adoption.

      I understand I may revoke this consent to permanently give up all rights to this

child by placing the revocation in writing and serving it upon the agency or adult to

whom the child was relinquished.

      If I am the birth father of the child, I understand that this consent to an adoption is

irrevocable unless I revoke it within 30 days after executing it by delivering a written

revocation to Court of Common Pleas, Family Division, Adoption Branch, 1501 Arch

Street, Philadelphia, Pennsylvania 19102.

      I have read and understand the above and I am signing it as a free and voluntary

act.

                                            _____

14. Around the time our attorneys started sending documents for Samson's adoption back and forth with me and Anna, I started testosterone therapy. I had never embraced or used the term *mother*, but now having to see it on every form, phrased that way—*the natural mother of the child*—made me cringe. It made me rage. My relationship with Samson could be natural without my having to stand up in court and say I was a mother. A human who smells like the inside of the body once he is out: natural. Split open, stitched back: natural. Nothing has ever felt so permanent as ripping open like I did. I stayed in bed, hid from everyone. It was natural. Far from mirrors and other people I spent hours and days and weeks with Samson sleeping curled up on my chest. He fit perfectly on me, belly to belly. I didn't look in the mirror; I could have been anyone. Samson would grip my shirt in his hands and not let go when I tried to separate from him. When he was with Anna he cried and cried. But I rarely got up, rarely let him go. When I was hungry, I let Anna make me peanut butter and jelly, even though, for all her skills, she never spreads the peanut butter quite to the edges of the bread like I like.

AFFIDAVIT OF CONCEPTION

COMMONWEALTH OF PENNSYLVANIA :
                                   SS
COUNTY OF   :

I, KRYSTYN MARIE BELC (McIlraith), attempted to get pregnant in October of

2012. The sperm donor was

I became pregnant on the first attempt but I had a miscarriage at five (5) weeks.

In December, I inseminated on December 11th, 13th and 14th, using needleless [15]

syringes and the sperm of   in my home.

On December 23, 2012, I took a positive pregnancy test.

On December 24, 2012, I had my first bloodwork at the office of

to confirm the pregnancy.

On January 14, 2013, I had an ultrasound at the office of   , which

confirmed the gestational age (6 weeks, 5 days), at which time measurements were all

normal and a heartbeat was seen.

I gave birth to Samson Ryan Belc on August 30, 2013, at [16]

The facts set forth herein are true and correct to the best of my knowledge,

information and belief. I understand that this verification and the facts herein alleged

are subject to the penalties provided by 18 Pa.C.S. Section 4904 (unsworn falsification

to authorities). [17]

15. Inseminating on Tuesday, Thursday, and Friday, I thought, gave me the best chance of success. I spent hours on "trying to conceive" message boards learning about sperm and eggs: how long they could persist, in what conditions. And besides, although most of the books and websites I'd read suggested giving the sperm-haver a day off between attempts, my best shot, in my estimation, came on Thursday, so I considered Friday a what-the-hell kind of last chance.

16. According to a 2016 article in *Obstetric Medicine*, transgender men choose midwifery care at an astronomical rate compared to the general population (46 percent versus 8.2 percent). The author partially attributes this to a desire among transgender people to remain outside hospital settings. Samson was born in America's longest-operating freestanding birth center. It is staffed entirely by nurses and midwives. Other considerations for me, in addition to a desire to remain outside a hospital setting, included a smaller number of providers in the room during delivery—a maximum of two—and

longer prenatal appointments with a focus on my well-being, not just the baby's.

17. In my experience, many queer people are outraged about second parent adoptions, feeling that it is an offensive step, erasing the parentage from birth of nongestational parents. For me, the one always being erased was the boys' donor, a friend whose intimate bond with our family had to be minimized as much as possible in this process. These repeated renunciations bothered me as much as Anna's and my having to adopt our own children.

First Judicial District of Pennsylvania
Court of Common Pleas
Family Division
Adoption Branch
1501 Arch Street, 11th Floor
Philadelphia, PA 19102
(215) 686-4259

Margaret T. Murphy
ADMINISTRATIVE JUDGE
FAMILY DIVISION

Mario S. D'Adamo
DEPUTY COURT ADMINISTRATO!

Walter J. Olszewski
SUPERVISING JUDGE
FAMILY DIVISION

Katherine T. Grasela
CHIEF OF COURT OPERATION!

NOTICE

In re: Samson Ryan Belc   :CP-51-AP -0000503-2016
Sullivan Isaiah Belc   :CP-51-AP -0000504-2016

June 6, 2016

The Petition to Confirm Consent to adoption and Petition for Adoption regarding the above captioned ca
listed for hearing on **July 20, 2016 at 9:00am** in Courtroom "**5E**", Philadelphia Family Court, 1501 A
Street **5th Floor**, Philadelphia, Pennsylvania 19102. After review of your Petition for Adoption, the Cour
determined that pursuant to 23 Pa.C.S. §2101 et al, you will need to submit the following documentatior
days prior to at the scheduled Adoption Hearing to *Prothonotary*, **11th floor, 1501 Arch Street, Philadelp
PA 19102. If not filed timely, administrative action will be considered.**

1. Original Petition to Confirm Consent **re: Samson** to be filed ASAP
2. Original marriage certificate **re: petitioners**
3. Original proof of citizenship **re: Anna** [18]
4. All clearances re: any other adults who reside in home (if applicable) [19]
5. Completed Adoption Decree(s) 3 copies for each adoptee.
6. Please provide the form from the State of Pennsylvania to amend the Birth Certificate completec

[64]

18. Anna became a United States citizen in 2001, soon after the passage of the Child Citizenship Act of 2000. Beginning February 27, 2001, immigrant children born on or after February 28, 1983, automatically became United States citizens if at least one of their parents was an American citizen by birth or naturalization and if they resided permanently in the United States. Anna was about to turn seventeen when this law was passed.

19. Keep in mind that Samson had been living in this home his entire life.

5.   The facts as to Krystyn Marie Belc (McIlraith), female petitioner, are as follows: [20]

    A.   Date and place of birth:

         June 27, 1987, Manhattan, New York

    B.   Racial background and religious affiliation:

         Caucasian, Catholic

    c.   Occupation:

         Teacher [21]

    D.   Relationship to Adoptee by blood or marriage:

         birth mother [22]

20. The facts as to Krystyn Marie Belc (McIlraith): these were liminal months. For the first time, in the early months on testosterone, I was aware when checking the F box on forms that every day I looked less like what someone would expect, seeing that box. My voice cracked. My shoulders bulged. I hoped the judge, if he made me speak at all, would ask as few questions as possible.

21. The hearing, scheduled for July 20, 2016, would take place over a

month after my last day as a School District of Philadelphia employee. I taught fourth graders, sixth graders. They were goofy, sweet. They asked me what was wrong with my voice. I told them I was moving to Michigan, showed them the Upper Peninsula on a map.

    a. My union benefits covered legal fees associated with the second parent adoption; I only paid court fees, hundreds of dollars instead of thousands. We had the same attorney we'd used for Sean's adoption, the one who had written our wills, drafted power of attorney documents for us. We were going to take whatever protection we could get.

22. There are the things one gains by transitioning and the things one loses. There is the new body, the confidence, there is the title *Dad*, the power granted to men. And there is what one loses: the assumption of connection. Of course, sperm is a connection, biological fatherhood is a connection, but it is not the same. The assumption of gestation, of birth, of true creation, that falls away. In the courthouse, I thought, I might experience my last public performance as a birth parent.

IN THE COURT OF COMMON PLEAS OF PHILADELPHIA COUNTY, PENNSYLVANIA
ORPHAN'S COURT DIVISION 23

IN RE: Adoption of   :

    SAMSON RYAN BELC   :

               NOTICE REQUIRED BY ACT 101 OF 2010
               23 Pa. C.S. §§2731-2742

Date: 5/9/16

TO: KRYSTYN MARIE BELC (McILRAITH)

This is to inform you of an important option that may be available to you under Pennsylvania
law. Act 101 of 2010 allows for an enforceable voluntary agreement for continuing contact or
communication following an adoption between an adoptive parent, a child, a birth parent, and/or
a birth relative of the child, if all parties agree and the voluntary agreement is approved by the
court. The agreement must be signed and approved by the court to be legally binding.

A birth relative is defined only as a parent, grandparent, stepparent, sibling, uncle or aunt of the
child's birth family, whether the relationship is by blood, marriage or adoption.

The voluntary agreement may allow you to have continuing contact or communication,
including, but not limited to:

        • Letters and/or emails;
        • Photos and/or videos;
        • Telephone calls and/or text messages; or
        • Supervised or unsupervised visits.

If you are interested in learning more about this option for a voluntary agreement, contact me at
(215) 656-3653 or your attorney, if you have one.

23. I stared at these documents many times over years before I noticed
this. Everything else embedded in the endless packets of legal pa-
perwork was from the First Judicial District Court of Pennsylvania, Court of Common Pleas, Family Division, Adoption Branch.

But this one notice is from Orphans' Court, which, according to the Philadelphia Courts website, *serves to protect the personal and property rights of all persons and entities who are otherwise incapable of managing their own affairs.*

a. *The name "Orphans" in the name of the Court,* the website continues, *is derived from the general definition of "orphan" as one lacking protection, not the common association of a child deprived by the death of his or her parents.*

b. And yet I still keep coming back to it. ORPHAN'S COURT DIVISION

c. Orphans' Court mediates contact among a child, their adoptive parent, and their birth parent.

d. In Samson's case, his adoptive parent and birth parent are married.

e. No formal agreement exists between Samson's donor and our family.

f. We text or e-mail him every few months.

g. Every adult involved agrees it should be more often, but life gets in the way.

h. I see him over the summer a few weeks before Samson turns five. I am in town for the Trans Wellness Conference, and he is there, too. The conference is so crowded at lunchtime that we have to catch a seat on the floor, along the conference center's walls. I eat falafel I walked over half a mile to get, even though I am in the middle of America's sixth largest city, my home, our home, Philadelphia. My children's sperm donor never seems to change, never ages; to me he is always in his early twenties, always a grungy nursing student riding an old black mountain bike around West Philadelphia. But he is a doctor now, married with kids. We both own homes. We are both thirty-one. He asks how my children are, and I give him the basics. He and I are not close, never have been. But whenever we can we try to see each other. Regardless of the trajectory of our lives we are linked forever. We made a person together. Without him Samson would not be Samson. Would not exist. Every time I see him I fight back the urge to say thank you in response to every single thing he says.

   i. I have always been self-conscious about the awkward way I go in for hugs, and I psych myself up for an extra-good one before I say bye.

  ii. There is no way to thank the person who made your children possible.

24. *This one makes me really sad to look at,* Anna says when I unearth these documents over two years after they were drafted.

Why? I ask.

I don't know, she says. *It just does.*

Commonwealth of Pennsylvania

First Judicial District of Pennsylvania
In the Court of Common Pleas
Philadelphia County
Family Division

IN RE ADOPTION OF   :   CP-51-AP-0000503-2016
SAMSON RYAN BELC   :

CERTIFICATE OF ADOPTION

AND NOW, to wit, this 20th day of July, 2016, upon consideration of the Petition of **Anna Belc and Krystyn Marie Belc, nee McIlraith**, for the adoption of **SAMSON RYAN BELC**, a child, and after hearing held thereon by the Court on July 20, 2016, at which time the said minor was present, together with Petitioners, the Court finds that the statements made in the Petition are true, and that the welfare of the child proposed to be adopted will be promoted by such adoption.[26]

All requirements of the Acts of Assembly have been fulfilled and complied with.

It is **ORDERED AND DECREED** that the said adoptee shall have all the legal rights of a child and heir of the said Petitioners.

It is further **DECREED** that the said child shall hereafter be known by the name of **SAMSON RYAN BELC.**[27]

BY THE COURT:

_____
WALTER J. OLSZEWSKI
SUPERVISING JUDGE

In Testimony Whereof, I have hereunto set my hand and affixed the seal of said Court this 20th day of July, 2016.

Eric Feder
Deputy Court Administrator
Director, Office of Judicial Records

By: _____
      Jennifer E. Haughton

25. In the waiting room at family court we sat in plastic chairs and let the boys drive their little metal cars along our legs. They kicked the backs of the chairs in front of them no matter the faces we made at them. We tried to ration their snacks; we had no idea how long it would take. All around other parents did the same; we were all waiting, hoping we'd go home with the children we were trying to comfort. Samson was almost three. Sometimes, before the adoption, I'd say something to him—*Samson, don't use your shirt as a napkin*; *Samson, remember to point your penis in the bowl before you go*—and I'd remember that legally, he was still all mine. The responsibility overwhelmed me. My name on his birth certificate. Anna, a legal stranger. Samson asked why we forgot to bring his costume to the court. I asked *Costume for what?* and he said *For the Redoption.*

    a. re-: again

    b. optio(n): choosing

26. *welfare*: the state of doing well especially in respect to good fortune, happiness, well-being, or prosperity. *child welfare*: social work cen-

tered upon the welfare of children (as upon improvement in health and home conditions) and upon vocational training.

    a. In 2018, Catholic Charities of Buffalo suspended their child welfare services. The agency's CEO said, of prospective LGBTQ parents: *We will serve them for counseling if they're seeking help, but we're not placing a child with them.*

    b. In summer 2020, the Supreme Court will hear *Fulton v. City of Philadelphia*, a case in which Catholic Social Services of Philadelphia asserts that the city is wrongfully excluding them from operating as a foster care agency because they will not allow LGBTQ families to serve as foster parents.

       i. CSS asserts: *CSS sincerely believes that the home study certification endorses the relationships in the home, and therefore it cannot provide home studies or endorsements for unmarried heterosexual couples or same-sex couples.*

    c. What does it mean to promote the welfare of a child in a world that still thinks being in a family like yours is a nonoptimal way to grow up?

27. When we came home that afternoon everything was the same. That day and every day after. At night we sat with Samson, whichever one of us was home, and held his tiny hand when he fell asleep in our bed. When Anna was home, one of us would carry him gingerly to his own room, where he slept in a tiny toddler bed crammed in the corner. When she was at work overnight in the hospital Samson and I would sleep together the way we did the night he was born, curled into each other in the middle of the bed. In the morning we made him cinnamon toast and yogurt with a drizzle of honey and some sliced fruit. We were always tired then

because he always woke up so early. His favorite dinners were meats off the bone—drumsticks, ribs—and he always made a tremendous mess when he ate. When we weren't looking he'd put down his fork and cram food into his mouth with his fists. His favorite color was pink. His favorite things to do were spin, and jump, and flail. He watched TV upside down, his head buried in the couch cushion. He was the same Samson we brought to the courthouse, who was now our son, both of ours'.

Mother/Parent's Name before first marriage: **KRYSTYN MARIE MCILRAITH**

Father/Parent's Name: **ANNA BELC**

Wild Life

When your friends at work become pregnant you come home and tell me everything. The boys are still half in their pajamas and they are all running around the house yelling and scattering their toys as widely as they can. It is eight in the morning and I am emptying the dishwasher and washing berries in a little colander and I am cutting the kids' pancakes and trying to find Samson's lunch box. It is under the couch. My eyes are closed at the breakfast table waiting for coffee to hit me. *Nobody bother your dad before his first cup of coffee*, you say. You are passing out plates and forks like playing cards. You want to talk about your pregnant friends. When they are due and what their partners are like and where they plan to give birth and whether they are sick and what I never say is that I hate these conversations so much. At my CrossFit gym there is another pregnant woman and every other woman wants to talk to her about their births. I make sure not to stand too close because I don't want to seem interested in their birth stories. Trying to look like I am not listening only makes it worse. This is when I see flashes of the bathroom where

I had Samson, of his slimy new head. He came out so sleepy he had to be roused to cry. He was saving energy, we said once we knew him. You told me you learned in nursing school that some women with dementia remember the day they gave birth with great clarity even as everything around them crumbles. It has defined my life, too. When I am around a pregnant person I feel an emptiness where Samson used to be. A professor I respect deeply tells me she is pregnant and I know it's irrational, I know it isn't fair, but the surprise on her face when I tell her about Samson hurts me. She doesn't seem repulsed, just surprised. Who would think. In that moment I know I can never have my past and present at the same time. I hate having to explain how Samson and I are related. I don't want my life, his life, to be a surprise. Most of the time, I don't have to explain. No one asks. Because who would think.

There are things I miss. Before Michigan, before testosterone, sometimes people in Philadelphia would look at me and
Samson and know he was mine, think I made him, and they
would call him beautiful. No one says that anymore; now they
say *You're such a good dad* because now they think I am a man
and no one thinks men can do anything related to children,
least of all make one.

Sometimes I mourn that Samson cannot make his own child, the
way I did. He can be connected with other people by genes but he
can never have what I have with him, with just one other person.
On a screen, my back crinkling white paper my legs lying limp
and restless my belly lubed up a wand pressed into me. *BOY*, the
machine said. In that moment, I was relieved. It seemed an easier
life, the life he would have, this boyhood. Now I know better, or
at least I know different. What I did was beautiful. Sometimes I
miss women, how they loved and accepted me before I took too

many steps out of their world. I miss my mother even though she likes me more now, likes this me who has a beard and broad shoulders and who smiles, smiles all the time. But she used to think we were the same.

I am not sure how much, in those months Samson lived in me, I belonged to me and how much I belonged to him. When I was pregnant I made so many decisions to protect him. When a co-worker put her hands on my shoulders to pull me away from fist-fighting students, she admonished me—*You're pregnant, Belc*. In those moments I had forgotten I was no longer by myself, never would be again. I look at him, five and a half years later, so many years past our physical connectedness, and feel like it's possible he made away with a piece of me. How could someone who looks so much like me have taken nothing with him on his way out? Is it wrong to blame him for some of my loneliness? Did our other children take from you? Samson has left his marks on me, too—these widened hips, these spent breasts, and beyond that, his cells living on inside me. In 1996, a geneticist at Tufts University discovered male fetal cells in a woman twenty-seven years after she had given birth to her son. These cells have been detected as early as seven weeks into pregnancy and have been found inside the brains of deceased mothers. These microchimeric cells, in the first few years, seem to migrate around the human body causing both damage and healing. In wounds they make repairs to their makers. In tumors they have been found trying to rip their creators apart. We have opened ourselves up to them this way. Parts of our children live on inside us, in our very blood, long after they are on the outside.

Samson is curious about how often I look at old pictures. Of us, of you. He isn't old enough to look back. I am obsessed with the photograph of you at Sean's age. You're missing two teeth like he is. Your nose is freckled like his. You're standing in front of a body of water, a lake, I think. You grew up in a housing complex in Warsaw; were you on vacation? You smile big. You talk about a happy childhood. In the picture in which he looks the most like you, Sean is frowning. He is a serious child. He likes books about science. He likes everything to be noted on his calendar. When Sean is having a hard time we talk about your stubbornness, those days you wake up in a bad mood and refuse to let anything make you happy. How you are alike. When he argues with me, about putting his underwear in the hamper, about putting his books back on the shelf, I feel like I'm arguing with you. Having children made you more serious. When Sean smiles, I feel I have cracked a code.

Samson wakes up excited nearly every day. When I started writing about Samson, about how he and I are connected, I often wrote about jealousy. He was a toddler then. My body was still soft from him. He wore Sean's old clothes, jeans and T-shirts with dinosaurs and baseballs. I wore him on my back everywhere we went. He talked a little, mostly about snacks. The border between his body and mine was porous for years: nine months of pregnancy, two years of breastfeeding. I was angry that I would have to stand by and watch someone who looks exactly like me get the childhood I feel I should have had. That I had created, nourished this boyhood. In the last few years, though, things have changed. I got on hormones. Samson is still wild and he laughs more than anyone I know but that doesn't mean his life is easy. He asks when we can meet other families like ours and I say, honestly, that I do not know. *Samson*, I ask him. *Would it be easier if our family had another kid made by me?* He thinks for a long time. *I don't know,* he finally says.

And then there is ZZ. He is still in diapers. Our first two children are thirteen months apart. ZZ came later, after we had practiced a bit. We know now that we can do all the setup we want, but we cannot make their childhoods what we want them to be. When his brothers ask if he is a boy or a girl or both or neither ZZ says, *I am a baby.* In this family there is always a chance to redefine how you see yourself. We catch ourselves comparing him to Sean, to Samson. Unlike our other children, who were conceived at home in our bedroom in West Philadelphia, ZZ was conceived in a doctor's office. I was not there. ZZ is our only child who has always known me as his dad. We are growing up together in a way the other boys and I did not. He was five months old the day I started testosterone. The night ZZ was born, Samson stopped being at the center of our family life, the way the newest person always is.

If I've lost a part of what I had with my mother, with your mother even, I know it is not possible that I still have all of what you fell in love with. You came to my parents' house that first winter break when they went away on vacation and asked me to watch my brothers and sisters. You always wanted a big family, you said. I told my mother I was bringing a friend. That week you watched me coach my little brother's eighth-grade basketball team, drive kids to school in my mother's imposing Chevy Suburban, sit at the kitchen table supervising homework. I cooked family dinners in my mother's kitchen and you were my family for the first time. Was it then that you decided? Sometimes I worry you miss me even though I am right here. How much of that is normal and how much of it isn't? I admit that I am needy. I worry about us. Does everyone feel this way? I have to ask myself that question about so many things. When Samson turned two I weaned him and decided to take testosterone, to move forward. In the pharmacy I called you to tell you I had changed my mind; I could not start. *Only you can decide this one,* you said. There was no guide for the after. When you go to Target you always remember to get me a bottle of Diet Coke from the cold case by the register even though those bottles are overpriced and will probably kill me and every year you wriggle my favorite bourbon into my stocking and when you can, on the rare nights we have off together, you rub my feet while we watch crime TV. But I know you love the self I walked away from, the piece Samson took with him on the way out. Without him I never could have believed in myself enough to say yes. Yes to hormones, yes to finding out how to live. There was barely any time, a year or two in the beginning, when you loved me thinking I was a woman, but for so many years everyone around us still thought I was. The world was so against us, we thought then, and now the walls have collapsed because look at me. Who would think. When I take our children into the men's room people look at Samson, not me, because he loves to wear pink. Things are simple for me now. Safe. I am a dad and you are a mom. The body I had, the body that made Samson, has faded into the past. Samson says that when other children made fun of him for saying his dad made him, his teacher was right there and said nothing. Expecting anyone knows what to say is where he went wrong. We never used to have to go out of our way to make gay friends and I am sorry I did this to us. I never feel paranoid that you will leave me for someone else because she is a woman, but I do worry you miss the part of me other people never think to imagine.

People ask about your births and they mean all three.

You were so beautiful pregnant, in a way that made sense.

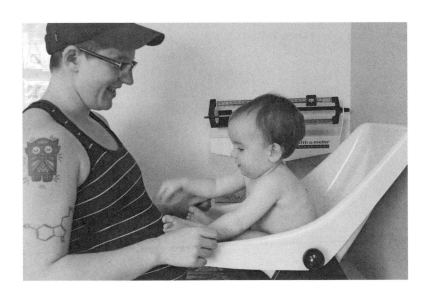

The reason that stories about fetal microchimerism focus on sons' cells found inside mothers' bodies is that the two can be more easily distinguished from each other, due to chromosomal differences between those assigned male and female at birth.

Imagine, you sometimes say, *if we had a daughter. If you had a daughter.* We are both quiet then, thinking of our mothers. What do our cells say about who we are, anyway.

Maybe we already do, I say.

You and Samson often clash the way you and I clash. He needs too openly, plays too wildly. You and Sean and ZZ sit on the couch reading and there is Samson, perched in the windowsill. There is something about him, about me, that cannot be calmed, cannot be stopped.

I worry that when he is thirty-one, like I am, he will feel distant from pictures of his infancy, his toddlerhood, his entire childhood, these years that have defined my life.

Because our children are close in age, many of my memories of their youngest days run together. My hands rattling on the stroller handle, trying to keep them all steady on the moving subway. All those backpacks with crumpled clean clothes and little bags of crushed pretzels at the bottom. The purple backpack that got stolen at the playground in Fishtown. It had our first nice camera inside. So many early mornings, such early mornings I knew every coffee shop in Philadelphia that opened at six. We walked around the neighborhood waiting for you to come home from night shift. Two in the stroller, one on my back. I remember trying to make us all dinner with a toddler strapped to me. How I learned not to make rice after our kids flung handfuls of it all over the room. We have so many pictures of those years. But it was loud, and we were not sleeping, and I was in between versions of myself, and things were not clear. Before we had children it always astounded me that my mother could not remember many of the events I considered central to our childhoods. She dated everything by pregnancy. The six of them. But now I understand. My clearest memories of our family begin in Michigan because the kids started getting older and I was not so tired. We took them out for pizza to celebrate the end of my first semester in graduate school. It was cold, like it always is here. In the restaurant, basketball played on the television in each corner of the room and I looked over to see if Samson was watching but he wasn't. He was only watching me. Often I have felt the most alive playing sports. I just want one child to like basketball but in the end, we control so little. Samson sat so close to me we could have been zipped into the same sweatshirt and I kept inching away only to find him glued to me seconds later. You sat doing puzzles side by side with Sean, enough room for a whole other person between you. My lap and Samson's felt as if they were fusing together. He cries to me on FaceTime whenever I leave town. *I need you here*, he says.

I tell him I am writing about him. He wants to know why.

I can't write about myself without writing about you, is that okay?

It's sort of good and sort of not good, he says.

It is Mother's Day and I want to find a picture of my mother. You worked last night and are sleeping through this day as you do so many other days. I click through photos on my computer. Samson is looking over my shoulder at pictures of me as a child. His eyes flicker with recognition. *It's good that your mom is the type of mom who let you wear dresses, even though you were a boy,* he says. He likes when we have things in common. He sees himself in pictures of me as a child. Our round faces, our flat noses, blue eyes, dresses. And yet we possess powerful, almost dark, masculine energy. Dirty knees, tousled blond hair. I tell him, *No, remember? When I was that age, she thought I was a girl.* He had forgotten. We have had this conversation so many times. *She made me wear dresses,* I say. *She thought that was the right thing to do.* Sean and ZZ are listening from the doorway. There is something much more complicated between me and Samson than between them and their mother; even they know that. Samson has been raised knowing we want him to talk about his gender and he wants to know when I talked to my mother about mine. *I was already an adult*, I say vaguely. He puts his hands on my face so that I have to look straight at him. *So what*, he says, *you were like, sixty? Forty-five?* His junior kindergarten teacher says he has not yet developed much number sense. He is so little and he has never known me to be unsure about myself. There is no way to tell our child that I pretended to be somebody I wasn't until he came along. For everyone else's comfort. My parents reminded us how hard they worked, how much we owed them, and now that I am a parent I see what they mean. I wonder if they think they owe me anything, if they think I shaped who they are. My mother had six babies but I was the first. Samson has forever changed my body and my understanding of who I am and he has continued to push me. When we are shopping for the new school year he says that all-black sneakers will make him the fastest kid on earth, that dresses are just like long comfortable shirts. He is wearing a Philadelphia Phillies T-shirt and a rainbow skirt. He is wearing sparkly flats and a suit of armor. It is hard to let him be him. So much energy going in so many directions. Everything is a competition. He is always down to wrestle. Other children love him and I live in fear that they will turn on him. I cannot separate my understanding of his life from the one I've had, but I have to try. His freedom is something I never could have imagined and it is terrifying to me.

He is not always happy. Who could be? But I fear the turn I took, whenever I took it, away from open smiles from dancing from openhearted love of life. Everyone tells me I look happy now because they know what I was like before. Sometimes when Samson cries I worry he won't be able to stop, that we will live suddenly in a twisted fairy tale in which he is the ever-crying boy. That it will be my fault. What did I leave in him? One night I come home from work and you tell me he has been crying for an hour because your mother is dead. Dishes are piled in the sink and the other kids are watching television because you've been consoling him. It's been a year since she died. His brothers never mention her. And then he is sobbing because I, too, will die one day. Will I die with some of him inside me? Samson was made inside me, from parts of me, and in many ways the person I am now is made from him, too. He has permanently altered my composition. I can tell you are relieved I'm home because you think I can somehow stop him from crying. Most nights are not like this. So often he is unafraid: he is perched in the windowsill pretending to be a peregrine falcon he is singing in the checkout line in Target he is trying to sneak brownie batter out of the bowl in our kitchen and I try to give him space to be happy. Do I love life more now because our children are in it or because he left happiness behind in me?

He wants to know how old I was when I told my mother I was not a girl.

What I did not say before is that there was a pause, a pause so long that as time accumulated I saw him realize he was living through the first time I didn't know what to say to him. Now he has to know me as someone who struggles. I have done such a good job hiding it, before this. Samson's other questions have easy answers. *What is the difference between an insect and an arachnid? What is your favorite restaurant in Philadelphia? Why do you devein shrimp?*

Is he disappointed in me when I don't say *five* or *ten* or *in high school*? Or am I the only one who is disappointed in the answer I have to offer?

In the campus gym I lift weights and watch young men play basketball. I don't work out a lot here because the bathroom is in a locker room, down a long, cinder-block corridor, past communal showers. I am still afraid of a place like that. You are at LEGO Club at the public library with our boys. Chatting, I'm sure, because you make friends easily. There is a policy that one must wear appropriate attire in this gym, except when one participates in shirts versus skins basketball. I watch ten bodies moving and I long so painfully to have had what they have, and yet. When we are all home again you are brushing Samson's hair after his bath and he asks what hair is and you say every part of us is made of cells. *What is a cell*, he says, and you say it is a building block. It has been well over five years and I still stare at his body in awe that he came out of me. You have learned how to say the things about your births that avoid talking about Samson. *With Sean, I pushed for over three hours. With ZZ, things were so quick, so smooth.* Samson fades into the background and you hope he will go unnoticed. I would rather have my own birth than be at one of yours any day. When Sean and ZZ were born I was so tired of seeing you in pain I could barely be happy. I am so much more comfortable with my own pain. When I must disclose that one of them is not mine I say, simply, *He is not my genetic relative.*

After the pediatrician calls me Samson's mother you say you will come with me to Target to buy cat litter and a couple of sticks of butter. You feel bad. I can tell. In the car you run your hands through my hair and say, *It's just so thick.* You say it sexy like. Sometimes you think sex can fix anything. In the back seat, our boys whine for lollipops and complain because it's snowing again. *This is Marquette, Michigan,* I say. Your fingers are long. Your nails are sharp. You pull my hair so hard it hurts. You never want to hurt me, but you do. When the pediatrician said, while looking at me, that most boys get as tall as their moms around twelve we both looked down and pretended she was talking about you. Samson stood in front of her. Samson with his thin, muscular legs and wide chest. Samson, with my face. Her stethoscope placed over his wildly beating heart. So alive, this child I made. Nobody had mistaken me for a mother in years, before the doctor. *You have a beard, for God's sake,* you say in the car on the way to get cat litter and butter. When I looked back up at the doctor, after she called me Samson's mother, she looked at me like she did not know what I was.

In moments like that I pretend to be someone else. A downhill skier. A news anchor. A grocer. A ticket taker on the train. I could stand in the quiet car while people held out their tickets; nobody ever looks up at the ticket taker, and everyone says thank you in the same satisfying tone. There I'd be, holding my hole punch, tiny white punched-out paper circles fluttering to the train floor. I'd give a warm smile, having all the power but wanting people to know everything was okay. The doctor said that Samson is too skinny, but he is like me: too full of not knowing what to do with his body to stay still for very long. He was born in Philadelphia, a city with hundreds of parks and recreation centers, places to burn all that energy off. He has always been like this, so thin; you joked that I made skim milk. You and your jokes—you're the one who joked about my height; you said, when the doctor said Samson was in the eighty-fifth percentile, you said, *Wow, I wonder how old he'll be when he's taller than you.* You're the reason the doctor called me Samson's mom. In the bottle, my milk always looked blue when held up to the light. I remember that, the whine and squeeze of the pump, the blue milk, barely a wisp of fat on top, sitting in our fridge in Philadelphia.

In the back seat our kids fight over bouncy balls they got from the free bin in the doctor's office. Strapped in like they are there is only so much damage they can do. She called me she. She called me his mom. A thousand-mile move, away from everyone who knew me before. Away from everyone who saw me carry him. After years, now, of testosterone, still this word: *Mom*. I can never get away. On the way to Target you pull my hair. You say, *You are so lucky to have this hair*, and this is what every woman who ever cut it completely off has said to me as it all falls to the floor. On testosterone, my hair keeps getting thicker, coarser. After I say nothing for a long time, you say that it must have been his birth certificate; once someone sees Samson's birth certificate, you say, they can never unsee it. It must have been in his medical file, the one we transferred, when we moved here, to a small town where it is always snowing. Yeah, I say. The birth certificate says *Mother*. Then my name. The doctor was never seeing me; she saw a mother. We used to love taking our kids to the pediatrician; their doctor in Philadelphia knew us, ended every visit with, *Keep up the good work!* The doors at this Target in Upper Michigan whoosh open with the same sound you can hear anywhere in America. A sound not unlike a train door. Warm air washes over the five of us: you, me, and the three children we took turns making. Rows of items wait the same here as they do everywhere, so many ways to make us feel better. Lightweight cat litter has changed our lives. With four sticks of butter I can make dozens of cookies. White chocolate macadamia. Brown butter oatmeal. I'll rest the dough in the fridge so they come out absolutely perfect. You want to make me, your children's dad, feel better, so you buy me a hot coffee, load the kids all into a single cart, and insist that you steer.

Just as fetal cells can be detected in their gestational parents long after birth, we transmit our cells into our children. Our cells can persist and multiply in them for decades, too.

Chimera: an organism containing two distinct sets of DNA.

In addition to through pregnancy and birth, cell transfer can occur during breastfeeding: *maternal cells can infiltrate the progeny via the digestive tract.*

While pregnant I was concerned that my child would inherit what I consider my worst traits, especially my anxiety.

And yet I continued to infiltrate his body with my own cells for two years after his birth.

I think all the time about when I was at Jiu-Jitsu camp and you nursed him because he could not go to sleep without me.

Do you ever think about it?

The problem with reading about the science of pregnancy is that I cannot help being angry at the words *mother* and *maternal*.

Maternal-fetal medicine describes the medical care provided to those in the relationship between one woman and one or more fetuses of unspecified gender.

Instead of *mother*, I say *gestational parent*, but the phrase often confuses people.

Gestational implies only the bodily act, while *maternal* nods to the relationship that follows.

In Greek mythology the Chimera is a lion with a snake for a tail and a goat's head protruding from the middle of her back.

In architecture the word can be used to describe any fantastic or mythical creature used for decorative purposes.

In architecture this is also called a *grotesque*.

Sightings of the deep-sea chimaera, or ghost shark, are rare; the pointy-nose chimaera was first caught on video in 2016.

Looking back, perhaps I should have used the word *uncommon* when talking to Samson about our relationship, instead of *rare*.

Rare imbues a specialness that perhaps Samson has blown up.

I'm rare, he says proudly.

Everyone came from someone, I say.

I admit the ghost shark is a terrifying creature, scarier to me than the mythical Chimera.

The males have retractable sex organs on their heads; the females are believed to have a pouch in which they can store sperm for the future.

Our sperm remains in storage at a bank with the understanding that you may or may not use it and I may or may not use it.

In online support groups I learn that many doctors still tell their transmasculine patients that they need to have a hysterectomy within five years of beginning testosterone therapy, despite little evidence to support this recommendation.

I think about having another baby all the time.

It's not something I often talk about.

When I watch the video of the fish swimming slowly near the ocean floor I feel I am seeing something I should not be seeing, something that should remain hidden.

They literally look like a fish put together by a committee, the director of a shark research center says.

Their faces look stitched together, monstrous.

Is this how people react to seeing pictures of me pregnant?

It's hard to talk with you about who should have our next child, if we have a next child, without feeling like it's a selfish thing to do, making another person whose history, even their body, will forever be entangled with yours.

When I am told I should include pictures of my adult self in my writing, I resist: Isn't that just giving people what they want to see?

The secretary calls soon after we enroll our boys in the local elementary school: *I just have a few questions about your children's birth certificates.*

I have tried a number of different condensed speeches to explain our family in situations like this, when someone is just looking for a simple understanding of who is what to whom, but they always leave everyone in the room feeling uncomfortable.

I like pictures of me pregnant.

Samson's difference from other children follows him around wherever he goes.

I had my doctor write the letter I needed to change my birth certificate, but I never sent it.

Infiltrate: Samson and I are invaders of each other's lives.

Chimera can, finally, refer to a dream or illusion.

How will you feel, you ask, *if he lies and says I made him?*

Everyone in this town recommends the same barber. So I go. We sit on hard plastic chairs, me and four other men. Our beat-up canvas jackets hang on a single coat rack, our cracked winter hands hang between our spread knees, and our eyes all look up at the barber, then back down at our boots. I have fifteen crumpled dollars in my pocket, twelve for the cut and three for tip. This barber, he knows how to talk to men. The men in the chair talk about sports and the military and places they've seen. I think of my barber back home, about paying thirty-five bucks for the cut and that's without tip. I had a public school teacher's salary then, and the city hospital paid you so much, it seems now. I remember the women barbers and how their hands felt in my hair, right, okay, before I found my guy, who is from California and has a sweet, goofy smile. Waiting for my turn to get shorn by this strange man in this strange northern town I think about how everyone back home knew what I was, how that felt then like they knew who I was. How safe I felt there, even looking the way I did. Cuts there took a half hour and I looked exactly how I wanted to look, after.

A fresh, queer cut. I lived somewhere made just for people like me. It is my turn and the barber knows right away I'm not from around here. *Philadelphia*, he says, *I hope that doesn't mean you're an Eagles fan.* I know that I would fit in better here if I learned about football, if I knew how tools worked, if I knew how to dress a deer, but I don't want to fit in. I thought maybe I did, but now I'm not so sure. After the cut, which takes what feels like sixty tense seconds, I take a selfie. I look like I'm seven, and too clean, and like my mom took me for this cut because I'm going for my First Holy Communion. But I laugh because I am twenty-nine and this is the only boyhood I get, these first few months of this remote Michigan town, these first few months of testosterone. Every day my brief boyhood is ending. *I'm on my way home*, I text you, and send the picture of my new haircut, my only haircut in this shop where I do and do not fit in with the row of men waiting in plastic chairs along the wall. *Well, it's something*, you write.

After that, every few weeks you shave my head in the bathtub. I sit naked on the wooden stool and you stand behind me, cutting so close to my head I look bald in certain light. The moment after one of your haircuts is the closest I come to religion. In our damp bathroom church I step out of the tub covered in discarded hair and trim my beard in the sink mirror before showering. Samson has been growing out his hair for over a year. For months his bangs have fallen in his eyes and he wears pins, clips, ties, headbands, and sweatbands but still wild blond pokes through and through. Samson says he will never have a beard but also says he likes mine. He rubs his hands along my face and calls me beautiful because that is the word I always use for him. His name feels fuller in my mouth now that I worry one day he won't want it. I tell you it makes me anxious to think about how different he is from most boys, from our other boys, and you say *Well, that's on you.* It is my job to be okay with what I made. Samson is sweet and soft in a way I'm terrified of crushing. In his little white drawers, dresses stack on leggings stack on jeans. There are bracelets and LEGO creations scattered on his windowsill. You wonder if Sean would have needed his ankle braces, if he would need speech therapy, had anyone else made him. Sean looks just like your mother. He is skeptical of me just like she was. But what good is the wondering, we know. We know it does not help our children who are alive, so alive, in front of us right now. They are us and they are their donor, but mostly they are themselves.

When I shaved my head for the first time everyone was shocked but I did not care. You said you were surprised how perfectly round my skull was. It was the first time anyone ever said the word *per-fect* about my body. Your long fingers on my head felt new and wonderful. You held my hand as we walked across campus, heads turning. The air so cold so good rushing all over my scalp. What did we know, then? Samson says other children do not believe in dads who make babies. When he says this my stomach turns like it did when he was old enough to eat something other than my milk because that meant we were separating. We are separating. Thread by thread I am letting him fall away from me. There are no stories of his life that could begin without me but many that could end that way. I do not like to write about Samson as he is now because I cannot make him a character like I've made you into one here. You can handle it. I can only handle writing about the Samson who used to smear berries all over his face. You stuffed them lovingly into a little mesh feeder and taught him to wrap his hands around food that wasn't me. His eyes so blue, like mine, his face smudged all over with red and purple sweet. Samson says he doesn't want to be the only child on this Earth made by his dad even though I've assured him he isn't, showed him pictures of dads and children I've only met on the Internet. They don't always seem real to me either. Samson is older now, holds dark berries gently in his fingers before placing them on his tongue, sacred like. The Samson who needs me constantly is as gone as the me who made him. I miss the way his head felt when he used to let me shave it. So round and prickly, so much like mine. My heart burns when I look at old pictures of him. I gave him this wild life.

ACKNOWLEDGMENTS

I would not know how to think or write about family without the mothers who shaped my worldview and this book: Helen McIlraith, Ewa Belc, Mary Dougherty, and Joan McIlraith.

Growing up in a big family fractures every story in a way that I find disorderly and wonderful. Thank you, Gerry, Mike, Sean, Ryan, Kathleen, and Kelsey McIlraith for leaning into the creative chaos that is our big family and for accepting my own slippery version of my life.

I am so grateful for the gifts of time and teaching and friendship I found in Michigan's Upper Peninsula in the writing program at Northern Michigan University. Endless thank you to the faculty and to my peers who read so many early yearnings that became this book. I have been lucky to have amazing teachers, especially Rachel May. Thank you, Monica McFawn, for years of solid writing advice and for urging me to have fun. Thank you, Jennifer A.

Howard, for being a generous mentor and friend. Thank you to my writing school buddies, especially Sara Ryan, for being the person one is told one may find in a writing program, and to Alex Lehto-Clark, for snowy late nights in my kitchen drinking coffee and beer and making trans art. Finally, thanks, Emily Wegemer, for managing the wonderful Marquette coffee shop where this book finally came together, for lattes and friendship.

Thank you to the readers and editors at the publications who saw and boosted my work before it was in book form. Thank you to the Sustainable Arts Foundation for pulling my little essays out of the stack and giving me both the belief my work was worth childcare time and the money to get some. Thank you to my internet writing friends, especially Tiswit. Shout out to my agent, Ashley Lopez, who has shown deep confidence in me and this project since it was just emerging. And thanks to everyone at Counterpoint, especially to Jenny Alton and Jordan Koluch, for making my pile of papers into a beautiful physical object.

Thank you every fierce trans writer who came before me and gave me stories to read and chew on while I considered my own. You inspire me, and you push me.

Sean Silas, Samson Ryan, and Sullivan Isaiah, thanks for helping me grow up and stay young, all at the same time.

Anna Belc, I write almost always to you for a reason.

Several of the essays in this book appeared in slightly different form in the chapbook *In Transit* (the Cupboard Pamphlet), as well as in the following magazines: *Granta, Black Warrior Review, Tin House Flash Fidelity, Sonora Review, Redivider, Grist Online, Split Lip Magazine, Jellyfish Review, Pidgeonholes, Sonora Online, The Adroit Journal, Pigeon Pages, Breadcumbs Magazine,* and *Best of the Net 2018.*

REFERENCES

THE MACHINE

Kane, D., W. Grassi, R. Sturrock, and P. V. Balint. "A brief history of musculoskeletal ultrasound: 'From bats and ships to babies and hips.'" *Rheumatology* 43, no. 7 (July 2004): 931–933. doi.org/10.1093/rheumatology/keh004.

Lemay, Helen Rodnite. *Women's Secrets: A Translation of Pseudo-Albertus Magnus De Secretis Mulierum with Commentaries.* New York: State University of New York Press, 1992.

Nicolson, Malcolm, and John E. E. Fleming. *Imaging and Imagining the Fetus: The Development of Obstetric Ultrasound.* Baltimore: Johns Hopkins University Press, 2013.

FIRST SEEN IN PRINT

Centers for Disease Control. *A Journalist's Guide to Shaken Baby Syndrome: A Preventable Tragedy.* U.S. Department of Health & Human Services.

Densley, James, and Jillian Peterson. "The Violence Project Data Are of Mass Shootings in the United States, 1966–2019." The Violence Project: Mass Shooting Data & Research, 2019.

BREASTS: A HISTORY

Blume, Judy. *Are You There God? It's Me, Margaret.* New York: Yearling, 1970.

Blume, Judy. "!@#$% Happens!" *Judy's Blog.* judyblumeblog.blogspot.com/2012/09/happens.html.

Lorde, Audre. *The Cancer Journals: Special Edition.* San Francisco: Aunt Lute Books, 2006.

Mock, Janet. *Redefining Realness.* New York: Atria Books, 2014.

Nelson, Maggie. *The Argonauts.* Minneapolis: Graywolf Press, 2015.

Petizmeier, Sarah, et al. "Health Impact of Chest Binding among Transgender Adults: A Community-Engaged, Cross-Sectional Study." *Culture, Health & Sexuality* 19, no. 1 (2017), 64–75.

Prose, Francine, et al. *Master Breasts.* New York: Aperture, 1998.

Stryker, Susan. *Transgender History.* Berkeley: Seal Press, 2008.

Vogel, Paula. *The Mammary Plays: Two Plays.* New York: Theatre Communications Group, 1997.

Williams, Florence. *Breasts: A Natural and Unnatural History.* New York: Norton, 1994.

Yalom, Marilyn. *A History of the Breast.* New York: Ballantine Books, 1997.

HOW TO PHOTOGRAPH YOUR NEWBORN

Birnholz, J. C., and B. R. Benacerraf. "The Development of Human Fetal Hearing." *Science* 222, no. 4623 (November 1983): 516–518.

IN THE COURT OF COMMON PLEAS

Drury, Tracey. "Catholic Charities to Phase Out Adoption to Avoid the Conflict of Serving Gay Couples." *Buffalo Business First*, August 23, 2018.

Liptak, Adan. "Supreme Court to Hear Case on Gay Rights and Foster Care." *The New York Times*, February 24, 2020.

Obedin-Maleker, J., and H. Makadon. "Transgender Men and Pregnancy." *Obstetric Medicine* 9, no. 1 (2016).

WILD LIFE

Learn, Joshua Rapp. "Mysterious Ghost Sharks' Sex Habits Revealed." *National Geographic*, June 15, 2017. www.national geographic.com.au/animals/mysterious-ghost-sharks-sex -habits-revealed.aspx.

Shute, Nancy. "Beyond Birth: A Child's Cells May Help or Harm the Mother Long after Delivery." *Scientific American*, April 30, 2010.

KRYS MALCOLM BELC's work has appeared in *Granta*, *Black Warrior Review*, *The Rumpus*, and elsewhere, and has been supported by the Sustainable Arts Foundation. Belc lives in Philadelphia with his partner and their three young children. Find out more at krysmalcolmbelc.com.